PRACTICING PRIVACY LITERACY
IN ACADEMIC LIBRARIES

Theories, Methods, and Cases

edited by
Sarah Hartman-Caverly and
Alexandria Chisholm

Association of College and Research Libraries
A division of the American Library Association

Chicago, Illinois 2023

The paper used in this publication meets the minimum requirements of American National Standard for Information Sciences–Permanence of Paper for Printed Library Materials, ANSI Z39.48-1992. ∞

Library of Congress Control Number: 2023944962

Copyright ©2023 by the Association of College and Research Libraries.

All rights reserved except those which may be granted by Sections 107 and 108 of the Copyright Revision Act of 1976.

Printed in the United States of America.

27 26 25 24 23   5 4 3 2 1

CONTENTS

VII   DEDICATION

IX   PREFACE
Alexandria Chisholm

XI   ACKNOWLEDGMENTS

XII   INTRODUCTION
Alexandria Chisholm

PART I. WHAT IS PRIVACY LITERACY?

3   CHAPTER 1. Privacy as Respect for Persons: Reimagining Privacy Literacy with the Six Private I's Privacy Conceptual Framework
Sarah Hartman-Caverly and Alexandria Chisholm

25   CHAPTER 2. Data Is Not a Mirror: A Privacy-Digital Wellness Model as Preservation of the Incomputable Self
Alexandria Chisholm

49   CHAPTER 3. Developing a Privacy Research Lab: Activities and Impact of Prilab
Mary Francis and Dustin Steinhagen

PART II. PROTECTING PRIVACY

65   CHAPTER 4. Protecting Patron Privacy in Access Services: Looking at the Laws
Jamie Marie Aschenbach

85   **CHAPTER 5.** Putting Privacy into Practice: Embedding a Privacy Review into Digital Library Workflows
Virginia Dressler

103   **CHAPTER 6.** Libraries, Privacy, and Surveillance Capitalism: The Looming Trouble with Academia and Invasive Information Technologies
Andrew Weiss

PART III. EDUCATING ABOUT PRIVACY

125   **CHAPTER 7.** The Promise of Theory-Informed Pedagogy: Building a Privacy Literacy Program
Alexandria Chisholm and Sarah Hartman-Caverly

151   **CHAPTER 8.** Preparing the Next Generation of Privacy Leaders?: The Intersection of Business Ethics and Privacy Education
Emily Mross

173   **CHAPTER 9.** Our Students Are Online Consumers: Using Privacy Literacy to Challenge Price Discrimination
Joshua Becker

187   **CHAPTER 10.** Privacy Literacy and Engineering
Paul McMonigle and Lori Lysiak

203   **CHAPTER 11.** Teaching Privacy Using Learner-Centered Practices in a Credit-Bearing Context
Scott W. H. Young and Sara Mannheimer

227   **CHAPTER 12.** Amplifying Student Voices: Developing a Privacy Literacy Conversation
Melissa N. Mallon and Andrew Wesolek

PART IV. ADVOCATING FOR PRIVACY

249   **CHAPTER 13.** Understanding Student Perspectives on Learning Analytics to Enable Privacy Advocacy and Policy Design
Michael R. Perry, Andrew D. Asher, Kristin A. Briney, Mariana Regalado, Abigail Goben, Maura A. Smale, Dorothea Salo, and Kyle M. L. Jones

265 **CHAPTER 14.** Building a Culture of Privacy through Collaborative Policy Development
Margaret Heller

283 **CHAPTER 15.** Privacy Pedagogy: Aligning Privacy Advocacy with Course Design Standards
Lindsey Wharton, Liz Dunne, and Adam Beauchamp

301 **CHAPTER 16.** What Successful Students Know: Promoting Privacy Literacy and Positive Digital Citizenship through Credit-Bearing Courses and Co-Curricular Partnerships
Theresa McDevitt, Crystal Machado, Melissa Calderon, Jaqueline McGinty, Jennifer McCroskey, and Ann Sesti

329 **CHAPTER 17.** Lateral Privacy Literacy: Peer-led Professional Privacy Literacy Learning Experiences
Sarah Hartman-Caverly

359 **CONCLUSION.** Privacy Work is Library Work
Sarah Hartman-Caverly

363 **ABOUT THE AUTHORS**

DEDICATION

For Lucy and Henry, and all your future tenses.
– SHC

For my parents, who instilled in me the profound importance of privacy, and my husband who taught me to only see challenges and opportunities. – AC

For our students. You inspire us to advocate for libraries that empower you to cultivate and celebrate your **identities,**
explore new **ideas**,
safeguard your bodily and contextual **integrity**,
pursue meaningful **intimacies**,
freely collaborate and **interact**, and
voluntarily **isolate** in solitude.

You deserve a world that respects your privacy. Our hope is that we can help you create it.
– SHC and AC

PREFACE

Alexandria Chisholm

Truthfully, this book began in January 2018 when Sarah and I first started working together. Within that first month, we connected about our shared interest in privacy—Sarah's interest stemmed from government surveillance and threats to intellectual freedom, and mine from corporate surveillance and behavioral manipulation. She was the theory-wonk, and I was the pedagogical geek. Together, we quickly started trading ideas that snowballed well beyond our original plan for a single workshop. Within the next two years, we had a successful four-part series along with several publications and presentations under our belt. In short, a rewarding teaching-research collaboration was born.

During this journey, we have been privileged to teach (and learn from) hundreds of perceptive and insightful undergraduate students. It quickly became evident through those interactions that the popular adage "privacy is dead" was *entirely* false. Students—while perhaps not fully understanding the complexity of our current information ecosystem or surveillance capitalist practices—care *deeply* about their privacy and the rights it safeguards. What they lack is a way to articulate their concerns and guidance on how to act in the face of the overwhelming digital resignation that plagues us all.

Beyond students, we've also had the opportunity to train and connect with passionate, talented library workers across the country. What we discovered was a general discontent with the current trajectory of professional privacy ethics and a palpable apprehension of the technological expertise required of engaging in privacy literacy work.

It was this confluence of factors—students' entreaty for privacy literacy and librarians' anxiety over professional self-efficacy—that inspired this book. A way to support your desire to advance privacy literacy and create privacy advocates and educators for our students.

As a teaching team, we've always operated under a philosophy of "privacy is about respect for persons, not about protecting data." We hope this book can help evolve privacy practices at your institution to re-center the *individuals* behind the data and the *ethics* behind the work—and to make privacy literacy a bit less daunting.

ACKNOWLEDGMENTS

We are indebted to the work of scholars, journalists, activists, and artists who have led the way in privacy and critical surveillance studies. Our work is significantly shaped by contributions from Veronica Barassi, Ruha Benjamin, Julie E. Cohen, Oscar Gandy, Chris Gilliard, Ben Grosser, Thilo Hagendorff, Mireille Hildebrandt, Helen Nissenbaum, Cathy O'Neil, Neil Richards, Tijmen Schep, Daniel Solove, Edward Snowden, Sherry Turkle, Alan Westin, and Shoshana Zuboff.

Thank you for sharing your ideas with the world.

INTRODUCTION

Alexandria Chisholm

Privacy is a core value of librarianship.[1] With rapid technological change and seemingly continuous threats to institutional funding, academic libraries have had to reinvent themselves, reassert their value, and reevaluate their role within academia.[2] Though the last two decades have seen renewed commitments to protecting patron privacy,[3] conflicting priorities stemming from institutional assessment and learning analytics have muddied privacy practices in academic libraries.[4]

Furthermore, emerging technology adoption is seductive under the persistent pressure to justify our relevance. Over the years, many ethical critiques of library practices have emerged from the enthusiastic adoption of social media,[5] their handling of database vendor contracts,[6] and academic libraries' complicity and participation in learning analytics practices of their home institutions.[7] Privacy concerns continue to develop as libraries explore and integrate smart voice assistants[8] and other artificial intelligence and machine learning applications.[9]

To be clear, these technologies are not inherently *bad*. The concern lies in the minimal consideration of how widespread adoption and implementation of these tools and practices will impact patron privacy—and even less discussion of *how* to address privacy concerns.

This book is intended to fill a gap in the library literature and join recent publications such as *The Rise of AI: Implications and Applications of Artificial Intelligence in Academic Libraries*[10] and *Managing Data for Patron Privacy: Comprehensive Strategies for Libraries*[11] in exploring emerging technology adoption and data collection practices in libraries along with the subsequent privacy implications. *Practicing Privacy Literacy in Academic Libraries* provides evidence-based, theory-informed, practical models for incorporating privacy literacy into academic librarianship and serves as a handbook for professionals who seek to incorporate privacy literacy into library instruction and other areas of academic library practice.

Mirroring Article VII of the Library Bill of Rights, which calls for libraries to "advocate for, educate about, and protect people's privacy," this book is organized into four parts.[12] The first section, What is Privacy Literacy?, establishes background and context with three chapters—two explicating privacy theory and closing with a case study of applied privacy theory.

In Chapter 1, Privacy as Respect for Persons: Reimagining Privacy Literacy with the Six Private I's Framework, authors Sarah Hartman-Caverly and Alexandria Chisholm elucidate the complexity of privacy theory through their original privacy conceptual model, offering a new, sustainable approach to privacy literacy by centering individuals over technology.

In Chapter 2, Data is not a Mirror: A Privacy-Digital Wellness Model as Preservation of the Incomputable Self, author Alexandria Chisholm illuminates the tangled connection among privacy, digital wellness, and identity, positing a new model to disambiguate digitally rendered reflections from identity and individual well-being.

In Chapter 3, Developing a Privacy Research Lab: Activities and Impact of PriLab, authors Mary Francis and Dustin Steinhagen present a case study of privacy literacy in practice through a privacy-focused research lab made up of faculty, students, and librarians at Dakota State University.

The second section, Protecting Privacy, dives into patron privacy. The first two chapters focus on practical privacy protections in Access Services and archives/digital libraries, ending with a chapter examining academic libraries' complicity in student data collection.

In Chapter 4, Protecting Patron Privacy in Access Services: Looking at the Laws, author Jamie Marie Aschenbach explores the major US federal laws that pertain to access services and patron privacy and provides guidance for librarians to improve practices at their institutions.

In Chapter 5, Putting Privacy into Practice: Embedding a Privacy Review into Digital Library Workflows, author Virginia Dressler discusses how to outline and integrate a privacy review into existing digital libraries workflows, which is critical to creating ethically sound and equitable digital collections.

In Chapter 6, Libraries, Privacy, and Surveillance Capitalism: The Looming Trouble with Academia and Invasive Information Technologies, author Andrew Weiss uses surveillance capitalism as a framework to examine the role academic libraries play in the practice of student data collection.

The third section, Educating About Privacy, offers a variety of case studies on educating our communities about privacy literacy from workshop series and disciplinary contexts to credit-bearing instruction and fellowships.

In Chapter 7, The Promise of Theory-Informed Pedagogy: Building a Privacy Literacy Program, authors Alexandria Chisholm and Sarah Hartman-Caverly detail their theory-informed approach to teaching a successful, sustainable privacy literacy program with extensive pedagogical and theoretical considerations.

In Chapter 8, Preparing the Next Generation of Privacy Leaders? The Intersection of Business Ethics and Privacy Education, author Emily Mross explores consumer privacy, perceptions of privacy in business ethics education, and the library's role in the business curriculum, with a specific case study of undergraduate business ethics education at Penn State University.

In Chapter 9, Our Students Are Online Consumers: Using Privacy Literacy to Challenge Price Discrimination, author Joshua Becker offers a case study of a course-integrated price discrimination lesson that utilizes VPNs and other privacy-protecting technologies.

In Chapter 10, Privacy Literacy and Engineering, authors Paul McMonigle and Lori Lysiak investigate the role of academic librarians in the privacy literacy education of engineering students.

In Chapter 11, Teaching Privacy Using Learner-Centered Practices in a Credit-Bearing Context, authors Scott W. H. Young and Sara Mannheimer deliver a case study of a semester-long, credit-bearing privacy literacy course at Montana State University.

In Chapter 12, Amplifying Student Voices: Developing a Privacy Literacy Conversation, authors Melissa N. Mallon and Andrew Wesolek reflect on their experience developing and delivering a privacy literacy fellowship at Vanderbilt University.

The fourth and final section, Advocating for Privacy, addresses how we continue to grow momentum and advance privacy literacy practices beyond the walls of the academic library and across campus.

In Chapter 13, Understanding Student Perspectives on Learning Analytics to Enable Privacy Advocacy and Policy Design, authors Michael R. Perry, Andrew D. Asher, Kristin A. Briney, Mariana Regalado, Abigail Goben, Maura A. Smale, Dorothea Salo, and Kyle M. L. Jones recount their Data Doubles collaboration, sharing the structure and design of their research instruments to support library workers in replicating and adapting their learning analytics investigation for privacy advocacy initiatives at their local institutions.

In Chapter 14, Building a Culture of Privacy through Collaborative Policy Development, author Margaret Heller offers a case study following the privacy process from policy creation to implementation at Loyola University Chicago.

In Chapter 15, Privacy Pedagogy: Aligning Privacy Advocacy with Course Design Standards, authors Lindsey Wharton, Liz Dunne, and Adam Beauchamp present a case study of privacy-centered course design practices at Florida State University.

In Chapter 16, What Successful Students Know: Promoting Privacy Literacy and Positive Digital Citizenship through Credit-Bearing Courses and Co-Curricular Partnerships, authors Theresa McDevitt, Crystal Machado, Melissa Calderon, Jaqueline McGinty, Jennifer McCroskey, and Ann Sesti deliver case studies from Indiana University of Pennsylvania of how cross-campus digital citizenship initiatives can be implemented and supported by academic library workers.

Finally, in Chapter 17, Lateral Privacy Literacy: Peer-Led Professional Privacy Literacy Learning Experiences, author Sarah Hartman-Caverly examines content and learning design considerations for privacy literacy learning experiences offered by, and for, library workers.

The goal of this book is to document academic library privacy literacy initiatives in their time of emergence, advance applications of privacy literacy as an expanding literacy[13] in the field of academic librarianship, and contribute to the professional discussion about core library values and how they are reflected in current practice.

Privacy issues touch upon every individual's life, span all disciplines, and intersect with some of the world's most pressing issues, yet there is a dearth of support in higher education for this needed literacy. With growing social justice issues related to algorithmic bias and the disparate impact of surveillance, it is more important than ever for librarians to assume leadership in advocating for and educating about privacy. Academic library workers have an ethical obligation grounded in our core values to fill this vacuum within academia. Hopefully, the ensuing chapters broaden your understanding of privacy literacy and inspire creativity and action.

NOTES

1. "Core Values of Librarianship," Advocacy, Legislation & Issues, American Library Association, last modified January 2019, https://www.ala.org/advocacy/advocacy/intfreedom/corevalues.
2. Megan Oakleaf, *The Value of Academic Libraries: A Comprehensive Research Review and Report* (Association of College & Research Libraries, 2010), https://www.ala.org/acrl/sites/ala.org.acrl/files/content/issues/value/val_report.pdf; Kyle M. L. Jones, Kristin A. Briney, Abigail Goben, Dorothea Salo, Andrew Asher, and Michael R. Perry, "A Comprehensive Primer to Library Learning Analytics

Practices, Initiatives, and Privacy Issues," *College & Research Libraries* 81, no. 3 (2020): 570–91, https://doi.org/10.5860/crl.81.3.570.
3. Alison Macrina, "Library Freedom Project," accessed September 2, 2022, https://libraryfreedom.org/; "More Than a Week – 'Choose Privacy' is Now an Everyday Choice," American Library Association, last modified June 19, 2018, https://www.ala.org/news/member-news/2018/06/more-week-choose-privacy-now-everyday-choice.
4. Kyle M. L. Jones and Dorothea Salo, "Learning Analytics and the Academic Library: Professional Ethics Commitments at a Crossroads," *College & Research Libraries* 70, no. 3 (2018): 304–23, https://doi.org/10.5860/crl.79.3.304.
5. Jeff Lilburn, "Commercial Social Media and the Erosion of the Commons: Implications for Academic Libraries," *portal: Libraries and the Academy* 12, no. 2 (2012), https://doi.org/10.1353/pla.2012.0013.
6. Dorothea Salo and Stephen Kharfen, "Ain't Nobody's Business If I Do (Read Serials)," *The Serials Librarian* 70 (2016), https://doi.org/10.1080/0361526X.2016.1141629.
7. Sarah Hartman-Caverly, "Our 'Special Obligation': Library Assessment, Learning Analytics, and Intellectual Freedom," in *Academic Libraries and the Academy: Strategies and Approaches to Demonstrate Your Value, Impact, and Return on Investment*, eds. Marwin Britto and Kirsten Kinsley (Chicago: Association of College & Research Libraries, 2018), 47–73; Sarah Prindle and Amber Loos, "Information Ethics and Academic Libraries: Data Privacy in the Era of Big Data," *Journal of Information Ethics* 26, no. 2 (2017): 22–33.
8. Miriam E. Sweeney and Emma Davis, "Alexa, Are You Listening? An Exploration of Smart Voice Assistant Use and Privacy in Libraries," *Information Technology and Libraries* 39, no. 4 (2021), https://doi.org/10.6017/ital.v39i4.12363; Marie L. Radford, "Reference Next," in *Envisioning the Future of Reference: Trends, Reflections and Innovations*, eds. Diane Zabel and Lauren Reiter (Santa Barbara: Libraries Unlimited, 2020), 52–53.
9. Amanda Wheatley and Sandy Hervieux, "Artificial Intelligence in Academic Libraries: An Environmental Scan," *Information Services & Use* 39, no. 4 (2019): 347–56, https://doi.org/10.3233/ISU-190065.
10. Sandy Hervieux and Amanda Wheatley, *The Rise of AI: Implications and Applications of Artificial Intelligence in Academic Libraries* (Chicago: Association of College & Research Libraries, 2022).
11. Kristin Briney and Becky Yoose, *Managing Data for Patron Privacy: Comprehensive Strategies for Libraries* (Chicago: American Library Association, 2022).
12. "Library Bill of Rights," Advocacy, Legislation & Issues, American Library Association, last modified January 29, 2019, https://www.ala.org/advocacy/intfreedom/librarybill/.
13. Ginny Boehme, Alex D. McAllister, Thomas R. Caswell, Kyle Denlinger, Michael Flierl, Anita R. Hall, Cindy Li, Brian D. Quigley, Minglu Wang, and Andrew Wesolek, "Expanding Literacies," in *ACRL 2021 Environmental Scan* (Chicago: Association of College & Research Libraries, 2021), 17–18.

BIBLIOGRAPHY

American Library Association. "Core Values of Librarianship." Advocacy, Legislation & Issues. Last modified January 2019. https://www.ala.org/advocacy/advocacy/intfreedom/corevalues.
———. "Library Bill of Rights." Advocacy, Legislation & Issues. Last modified January 29, 2019. https://www.ala.org/advocacy/intfreedom/librarybill/.
———. "More Than a Week – 'Choose Privacy' is Now an Everyday Choice." Last modified June 19, 2018. https://www.ala.org/news/member-news/2018/06/more-week-choose-privacy-now-everyday-choice.
Boehme, Ginny, Alex D. McAllister, Thomas R. Caswell, Kyle Denlinger, Michael Flierl, Anita R. Hall, Cindy Li, Brian D. Quigley, Minglu Wang, and Andrew Wesolek. "Expanding Literacies." In *ACRL 2021 Environmental Scan*, 17–18. Chicago: Association of College & Research Libraries, 2021.
Briney, Kristin, and Becky Yoose. *Managing Data for Patron Privacy: Comprehensive Strategies for Libraries*. Chicago: American Library Association, 2022.

Hartman-Caverly, Sarah. "Our 'Special Obligation': Library Assessment, Learning Analytics, and Intellectual Freedom." In *Academic Libraries and the Academy: Strategies and Approaches to Demonstrate Your Value, Impact, and Return on Investment*, edited by Marwin Britto and Kirsten Kinsley, 47–73. Chicago: Association of College & Research Libraries, 2018.

Hervieux, Sandy, and Amanda Wheatley. *The Rise of AI: Implications and Applications of Artificial Intelligence in Academic Libraries*. Chicago: Association of College & Research Libraries, 2022.

Jones, Kyle L. M., Kristin A. Briney, Abigail Goben, Dorothea Salo, Andrew Asher, and Michael R. Perry. "A Comprehensive Primer to Library Learning Analytics Practices, Initiatives, and Privacy Issues." *College & Research Libraries* 81, no. 3 (2020): 570–91. https://doi.org/10.5860/crl.81.3.570.

Jones, Kyle M. L., and Dorothea Salo. "Learning Analytics and the Academic Library: Professional Ethics Commitments at a Crossroads." *College & Research Libraries* 70, no. 3 (2018): 304–23. https://doi.org/10.5860/crl.79.3.304.

Lilburn, Jeff. "Commercial Social Media and the Erosion of the Commons: Implications for Academic Libraries." *portal: Libraries and the Academy* 12, no. 2 (2012). https://doi.org/10.1353/pla.2012.0013.

Macrina, Alison. "Library Freedom Project." Accessed September 2, 2022. https://libraryfreedom.org/.

Oakleaf, Megan. *The Value of Academic Libraries: A Comprehensive Research Review and Report*. Chicago: Association of College & Research Libraries, 2010. https://www.ala.org/acrl/sites/ala.org.acrl/files/content/issues/value/val_report.pdf.

Prindle, Sarah, and Amber Loos. "Information Ethics and Academic Libraries: Data Privacy in the Era of Big Data." *Journal of Information Ethics* 26, no. 2 (2017): 22–33.

Radford, Marie L. "Reference Next." In *Envisioning the Future of Reference: Trends, Reflections and Innovations*, edited by Diane Zabel and Lauren Reiter, 52–53. Santa Barbara: Libraries Unlimited, 2020.

Salo, Dorothea, and Stephen Kharfen. "Ain't Nobody's Business If I Do (Read Serials)." *The Serials Librarian* 70 (2016). https://doi.org/10.1080/0361526X.2016.1141629.

Sweeney, Miriam E., and Emma Davis. "Alexa, Are You Listening? An Exploration of Smart Voice Assistant Use and Privacy in Libraries." *Information Technology and Libraries* 39, no. 4 (2021). https://doi.org/10.6017/ital.v39i4.12363.

Wheatley, Amanda, and Sandy Hervieux. "Artificial Intelligence in Academic Libraries: An Environmental Scan." *Information Services & Use* 39, no. 4 (2019): 347–56. https://doi.org/10.3233/ISU-190065.

PART I
What is Privacy Literacy

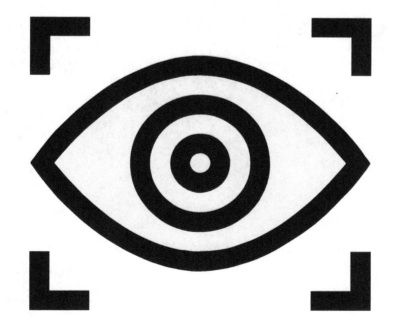

CHAPTER 1

PRIVACY AS RESPECT FOR PERSONS:

Reimagining Privacy Literacy with the Six Private I's Privacy Conceptual Framework

Sarah Hartman-Caverly and Alexandria Chisholm

INTRODUCTION

The cavalier data capture that underpins what Shoshanna Zuboff termed surveillance capitalism[1] is constant and ubiquitous. A 2019 Pew Research Center survey finds more than 90 percent of respondents believing that some or all of their online activity is tracked by corporations and nearly 70 percent believing that companies track their offline behavior as well. Most respondents distrust companies to handle their personal data ethically and worry that the risks of corporate surveillance outweigh the benefits. But if surveillance is everywhere, then so is the possibility for privacy. The same Pew survey found that a majority of respondents follow privacy news and expressed interest in both government regulations restricting corporate data use and better tools to enable individuals to manage their personal data.[2]

Yong Jin Park claims that a four-pronged approach to privacy is necessary in order to avoid an encroaching future of inescapably totalitarian digital surveillance: privacy by design, privacy by market, privacy by law, and privacy by norm.[3] Privacy by design addresses the capability of digital technologies to capture and transmit behavioral surplus, Zuboff's term for the data generated by technology-mediated activities.[4] Privacy by market implies that companies will respond to consumer demand for increased privacy, though Park admits that profit motives are a driving force of surveillance capitalism.[5] Privacy by law refers to government regulations that limit corporate data capture and use, yet Park observes that "even the 2018 [European Union General Data Protection Regulation], which purports to give citizens the power to access Facebook's databases and delete any transactional records it holds, cannot *instruct* citizens about the importance of privacy and how to exercise data control while participating in digital lives."[6] This leaves privacy by norm, an underlying culture of valuing privacy, which animates privacy as a way of being in the world that becomes encoded in concomitant design, law, and market practices.

But privacy is just one norm among many, including the necessity of digital participation, the human need for connection, the allure of personalization, and the comfort of convenience. Julie E. Cohen observes that "privacy must be chosen, and it is deeply intertwined with other societal commitments that also represent normative choices."[7] Cohen advocates for a reimagining of privacy theory that contributes to "sufficiently private and privacy-valuing subjects"[8]—people who will thread the social fabric with pro-privacy choices and uncompromising demand for privacy, such that privacy is again regarded as a norm among norms. One approach that Cohen recommends for inspiring such privacy-valuing subjects is privacy education,[9] but Thilo Hagendorff argues current approaches to privacy literacy (PL) aren't up to the task. Hagendorff faults PL efforts for focusing too narrowly on technological solutions while burdening users with the responsibility to protect personal privacy in a social and technical reality that disincentivizes—if not outright disallows—privacy-preserving choices.[10] One thing on which Park, Cohen, and Hagendorff agree is a need for new approaches to PL—one in which people, not data or systems, are the central consideration of privacy.

This chapter proposes the Six Private I's Privacy Conceptual Framework as a tool for enriching PL practices with theory that is grounded in privacy norms (figure 1.1). The purpose of Six Private I's is to facilitate consideration of privacy with a primary focus on the benefits of privacy in the human experience. The title "Six Private I's" refers to privacy's role in personal *identity*, *intellect*ual activities, contextual and bodily *integrity*, *intimacy*, social *interaction*, and voluntary withdrawal into seclusion (or *isolation*). The model depicts these concentric zones of information agency distinguished by boundaries of access and disclosure that each person negotiates in order to sustain a sense of self and to participate in a broad range of relationships.[11] Six Private I's is both informed by seemingly universal principles of privacy in the human experience and yet open enough to accommodate a range of phenomenologies, value systems, and choices related to privacy and disclosure. Six Private I's visualizes the benefits of privacy, contributing to a conceptual vocabulary that PL practitioners can use to inform learning design, programming, and advocacy efforts in the service of renewing privacy norms.

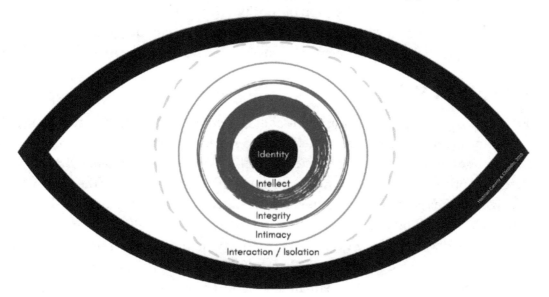

FIGURE 1.1

Six Private I's Privacy Conceptual Framework. Note: An onion model depicting concentric zones of information agency—identity, intellect, integrity, intimacy, and interaction/isolation—characterized by increasing information access and disclosure. CC BY-SA the authors.

SIX PRIVATE I'S PRIVACY CONCEPTUAL FRAMEWORK

The restoration of privacy norms requires new ways to think and talk about privacy—a new conceptual framework for privacy. Six Private I's Privacy Conceptual Framework (figure 1.1) models privacy as, in Cohen's words, "an environmental condition and a related entitlement (or set of entitlements) relating to that condition."[12] The environmental condition is the ability to determine access to the self by others—to regulate information flows across personal, social, spatial, and technological boundaries. The set of entitlements comprises personhood (*identity*), intellectual freedom (*intellect*), contextual and bodily *integrity*, intimate relationships (*intimacy*), free association (*interaction*), and voluntary withdrawal into solitude (*isolation*). The concentric arrangement of these entitlements, separated by metaphysical and physical boundaries that increase in dynamism and permeability from the inside-out, conveys what Cohen described as the "dynamic maintenance of breathing room" that is achieved by regulating information flows across these borders.[13] The following exploration of the Six Private I's onion model provides a close theory-informed examination of each frame of the model, juxtaposing the benefits of privacy with examples of harms when privacy is impaired.

IDENTITY

Privacy is necessary for cultivating individual identity as a product of autonomy, self-determination, individualism, social interaction, and personal growth.[14] In their foundational law review article, Samuel D. Warren and Louis D. Brandeis described privacy as "part of the more general right to the immunity of the person—the right to one's personality."[15] Cohen later credited privacy with protecting "environmental serendipity" and "a robust sense of agency," conditions that Charles Fried claimed were necessary to exercising "freedom to define ourselves" because they guard those experiences "at the heart of our notion of ourselves as persons among persons."[16] Jeffrey H. Reiman asserted that privacy is an informational "social ritual" and precondition of personhood "necessary to the creation of *selves* out of human beings," and Stanley I. Benn grounded privacy in a view of individuals as self-aware, conscious, autonomous agents.[17] As identity is dynamic, privacy across the lifespan is essential, giving individuals "freedom to escape, reject, and modify such identities."[18]

Data Doubles, Panoptic Sort, and the Right to be Forgotten

Describing privacy as a "dignity-related good," Cohen observes that "a comprehensive collection of data about an individual is vastly more than the sum of its parts."[19] This computational holism refers to the data double, an algorithmic construct based on analysis and modeling of an individual's personal data footprint and to which the living individual is continuously compared, held accountable, and fine-tuned.[20] For example, Arielle Pardes reported for *Wired* that many companies are turning to artificial intelligence to sort and rank job applicants, test their soft skills, and evaluate their personalities for organizational fit, leading applicants to distort their self-presentation in order to match the model hire.[21] It is this data double that subjects individuals to surveillance capitalism and the panoptic sort, the unprecedented capability of both public- and private-sector entities to monitor and influence individuals in their daily lives.[22] Once hired, an employee may be subject to ongoing workplace surveillance and "smart AI coaching," a constant stream of nudges designed to optimize productivity.[23] Personal data capture renders individual identities fixed and observable and interferes with self-making by subjecting individuals to a two-way information flow that collects and analyzes personal data and outputs nudges and other psychobehavioral stimuli.[24]

Discussing the three broad categories of personal data—consciously given, automatically monitored (metadata), and modeled (the data double)—Jacquelyn Burkell advocates for a "'right to be forgotten'" in light of a persistent data double which "threatens freedom, autonomy, and even identity, limiting our capacity to define ourselves and live the lives we choose to live."[25] While elements of personal identity can be consciously formed and performed, the raw material of personality is at some level innate and pre-cognitive.[26] Thus, the first informational border crossing in Six Private I's is from the most internal, even subconscious self of identity into the actively cognitive domain of the mind: intellect.

INTELLECT

Intellectual privacy ensures autonomy in the process of idea and belief formation through information exploration and intellectual experimentation. Neil Richards defines intellectual privacy as "protection from surveillance or interference when we are engaged in the processes of generating ideas," adding that it "guards our ability to make up our minds freely."[27] Privacy also constitutes "a private sphere of moral valuation," free from social validation and within which individuals determine inner meaning.[28] Intellectual privacy provides environmental conditions for creativity, innovation, and entrepreneurship.[29]

Learning, and the very act of changing one's mind, rely on conditions of intellectual privacy.[30] Under conditions of diminished privacy, learning is impacted by narrowing "the acceptable spectrum of belief and behavior."[31] Intellectual privacy is needed to exercise intellectual freedom "so that paths to truth and discovery can be pursued even in directions that offend dominant opinion."[32] US case law recognizes that expressive freedoms are buttressed by intellectual privacy.[33] Scott Skinner-Thompson takes this one step further, advocating that the exercise of privacy is itself an expressive act deserving of First Amendment protection in the US.[34]

Impaired intellectual privacy disrupts the regulation of information flows. Information inputs can be altered by the panoptic sort, which impacts individuals' access to "the flow of information about their environment."[35] Individuals experience distress at having their mental processes surveilled or influenced, causing decisional interference comprised of "small nudges away from thinking, reading, or talking about novel or dangerous ideas."[36] Warren and Brandeis suggested that loss of privacy would engender intellectual and social impacts, including distraction, impeded critical thinking, inhibited empathy, and apathy,[37] seemingly anticipating sentiment manipulation,[38] dark patterns,[39] and the polarizing effects of networked interactions more than a century ago.[40]

Chilling Effect

The extended cognition capabilities of information technology thus present an intellectual freedom paradox: as technology makes information more accessible, it also makes monitoring and influencing the use of information more powerful.[41] Chilling effect doctrine recognizes that the mere potential for surveillance, in addition to fear of social sanction or official punishment, not only deters individuals from exercising rights of free expression but also distorts information-seeking and thinking.[42] Brandeis extolled privacy as a necessary environmental condition for First Amendment-protected activities in his dissenting opinion in *Olmstead v. United States*, which was later cited in the *Katz v. United States* decision overturning *Olmstead*.[43] In contemporary times, the expansion of public-private partnerships in surveillance activities under programs like the National Strategy for Countering Domestic Terrorism exerts new social, political, and technological chilling effects on intellectual privacy and free expression.[44] Hildebrandt further suggests we are at risk of "cognitive automation," internalizing thought processes that mimic algorithmic reasoning.[45]

Intellectual privacy protects the activities of the mind and is a necessary condition for expressive and associational acts at outer zones of privacy. The next informational border crossing comprises integrity in information flows between the self and other, including both contextual and bodily integrity.

INTEGRITY

Privacy protects the individual's "right to be let alone" and freedom from unwarranted outside interference.[46] This freedom from undue external influence evokes privacy as "resistance to being used against one's will."[47] Privacy therefore protects the integrity of personal identity and intellect, as well as of the body and of relationships with others.

Contextual Integrity

Helen Nissenbaum defined the phrase "contextual integrity" to describe norms of information flows between self and other.[48] Contextual integrity comprises two informational norms: appropriateness and distribution. Appropriateness refers to the right people knowing the right things at the right time. Distribution refers to the flow of information across the self-other boundary, and further on to third parties downstream. Nissenbaum asserts that "there are no arenas of life not governed by norms of information flow, no information or spheres of life for which 'anything goes.'"[49] Alan Westin observed that this contextual integrity is preserved through limited, partial, and protected communications.[50] As an environmental condition of privacy, contextual integrity supports self-determination, enabling individuals to perform myriad social roles and to participate in a broad range of distinct relationships and associations.[51]

Loss of contextual integrity constitutes context collapse and occurs when personal information flows violate accepted norms of appropriateness or distribution.[52] Context collapse not only impacts the individual subject but relational well-being and social role performance as well.[53] For example, the sale of deidentified user data from the Grindr dating app, which primarily serves the LGBTQ community, enabled analysts to "infer things like romantic encounters between specific users based on their device's proximity to one another" and surmise user identities "based on their patterns, habits and routines" through location tracking, resulting in users being targeted based on their sexuality and outed without their consent.[54] Data brokers for real-time ad exchanges distribute personal data through spidering networks of third parties, potentially reaching thousands of entities, including US government agencies. The pervasive automation of personal data collection, coupled with the properties of web data, are favorable environmental conditions for context collapse.[55]

Bodily Integrity

Westin observed that privacy "arises in the biological and social processes of all life," describing territoriality and flight distance as universal privacy mechanisms found throughout the animal kingdom.[56] Furthermore, he cataloged aspects of sensory privacy, including touch, smell, sound, or "visual intrusion."[57] In their formative work, Warren and Brandeis asserted that the metaphysical right to privacy is an expansion of the physical right to be secure in one's body and private property.[58] Iris Marion Young renews this mind-body linkage, proposing a return from the mainly cognitive and mental constructs of contemporary privacy discourse to more spatial and material bases of the concept by theorizing "personal space" embodied by the "home." According to her, "The home is an arrangement of things in this space, according to the life habits of those who dwell in it."[59] Young also noted the symbiotic relationship of the body and physical space in the creation of personal space; an individual adapts their body to the space, but the space is also a reflection of the habits and activities of the individual's body. Furthermore, personal space supports an individual's ability to have bodily integrity as well as to engage in activities unobserved.[60]

While contextual and bodily integrity can be considered separately, they also share linkages. In the US, legal recognition of the right to privacy and bodily integrity in reproductive choice-making was established in the once precedential *Griswold v. Connecticut* and *Roe v. Wade* decisions.[61] The June 2022 *Dobbs v. Jackson Women's Health Organization* decision overrules *Roe*'s recognition that a "heightened protection of individual privacy" includes abortion access.[62] In addition to abdicating abortion access laws to the states, the legal change led to widespread concerns about context collapse due to the capability of period tracking apps to divulge data that would enable law enforcement to infer when a user was seeking an abortion.[63] The *Dobbs* decision further calls into question Supreme Court cases on the privacy rights protecting contraception use, same-sex intimate relationships, and same-sex marriage, demonstrating the connections between bodily integrity and intimacy.[64]

INTIMACY

The establishment of intimacy requires the ability and willingness to relinquish personal privacy to, and with, another.[65] Such self-disclosure necessitates a prior state of self-concealment.[66] Thus, Fried recognized privacy as necessary for "respect, love, friendship, and trust."[67] Responding to Fried, Reiman extended the role of privacy in intimacy as being central to establishing a shared sense of caring for the other—"a reciprocal desire to share present and future intense and important experiences together, not merely to swap information."[68] Ferdinand David Schoeman asserted that intimate self-disclosure is a means by which members of intimate associations "envalue personal experiences which are intrinsically or objectively valueless."[69] Kenneth L. Karst described "intimate associations" as social entities and sites of "joint decisionmaking" that warrant considerations for privacy protection beyond those afforded to members individually.[70]

Artificial Intimacy

Reflecting on the role of technology in human relationships, evolutionary biologist Rob Brooks observes that "the processes that build friendship and love can be emulated by algorithmic processes too."[71] Artificial intimacy is characterized by artificial intelligence applications designed to mimic social interactions, enticing human users to make contact, disclose information, deepen engagement, and even fall in love.[72] Dating app companies purposely deploy chatbots to onboard new users, nudge their app activity, and upsell them to paid accounts, insidiously taking advantage of users whose desire for intimacy makes them particularly vulnerable—all while collecting and capitalizing on their data.[73] As social technology use increased during the COVID-19 pandemic, concomitant public health measures like social distancing and masking exacerbated what psychology professor Michelle Drouin calls an "intimacy famine."[74]

Intimacy implies a particular closeness, depth, and duration of association—it describes many, but certainly not all, of one's social interactions and concomitant information flows. Beyond the bounds of intimacy lies the most peripheral zone of privacy, the general environs of social interaction from which individuals withdraw into isolation.

INTERACTION AND ISOLATION

Human beings are both individual and relational in their identities.[75] Associational privacy must be more than the sum of members' personal privacy interests because organizations themselves fulfill unique social roles, including as contexts for intra- and intergroup negotiation, as engines of economic freedom and market competition, as checks on state power, and as sites of cultural activity.[76] As with intimate associations, the privacy of individual members participating in an interaction is insufficient to protect the privacy interests of the association as a whole. This relational autonomy is established by differentially regulating information flows between members and across the member-nonmember boundary.[77] Lack of privacy for social interactions distorts these social relationships and other forms of free association.[78]

Complementing the freedom of association is the freedom to voluntarily withdraw into seclusion—to be alone and in isolation from others. The privacy of solitude provides individuals a reprieve from social roles, expectations, obligations, and stimuli.[79] Warren and Brandeis recognized this at the turn of the twentieth century; even then, the "intensity and complexity of life" made the ability to "retreat from the world" for "solitude and privacy ...more essential to the individual."[80] The privacy tort of "intrusion upon seclusion" enshrines the common law right to privacy in voluntary isolation and provides freedom from unwarranted mental distress stemming from surveillance and interference.[81] By the turn of the twenty-first century, Anita L. Allen and Iris Marion Young echo this assertion, defining privacy as a repose necessary to fulfilling social obligations and recognizing personal space and the home as "material support for identity" enabling individuals a place to withdraw from society.[82]

Sacred Privacy

Faith communities exemplify the benefit of privacy to both interaction in free association and to isolation in voluntary seclusion. Saudi Arabia, home to the holy Muslim cities of Mecca and Medina, was largely closed to tourists until reforms that began in 2019. Non-Muslims were prohibited from entering Mecca, the destination of the *hajj* pilgrimage. The city now welcomes tourists of all faiths, although non-Muslims still refrain from entering the Great Mosque where millions of pilgrims ritually circle the Kaaba shrine in any given year. The prohibition on access to the mosque by non-Muslims provides associational privacy to pilgrims, thereby preserving the ritual sacredness of the place where Muslims fulfill one of the Five Pillars of Islam.[83]

By comparison, solitary retreat is a pillar of Buddhism. Buddhism scholar Reginald A. Ray explains that

> retreat combines solitude and the practice of meditation, where you begin to actually explore your own mind.... Something happens on solitary retreat that cannot happen in a group situation and certainly doesn't happen during individual practice at home. We see for ourselves that within each human being is the Buddha-nature.[84]

Ray goes on to describe how solitary retreat enables practitioners to cultivate compassion for others and dwell in the present: "Far from being an antisocial practice, retreat practice frees you to love people in a uniquely powerful way."[85] Sacred privacy is one example of the benefit from social privacy that preserves the freedom of association as well as from solitary privacy that protects the individual who withdraws from society into seclusion.

Six Private I's Privacy Conceptual Framework depicts the benefits of privacy in the human experience as six concentric zones of informational agency. *Identity* comprises the individual sense of self and the exercise of agency and autonomy in self-making. This self-making can be impaired by an information environment shaped by the panoptic sort and animated by nudges that herd and tune the target individual based on the algorithmic construct of their data double. *Intellect* describes activities of the mind. The freedom to think, inquire, believe, express, and explore ideas flourishes under conditions of intellectual privacy, while the loss of privacy can engender a chilling effect. Contextual *integrity* ensures that personal information is accessible to appropriate others through acceptable means of distribution, allowing individuals to participate in a diverse range of social roles and relationships, while bodily *integrity* preserves the sanctity and security of the body and home through spatial privacy and the right to be left alone. *Intimacy* describes the closest relationships between life partners and confidants, which rely on a shared sense of privacy that is cultivated through mutual self-disclosure. Intimacy is increasingly mimicked by technologies that satiate the human need for attention and care while simultaneously exploiting these vulnerabilities to monetize data captured at ever deeper levels of self. *Interaction* refers to the social privacy that protects freedom of association for a wide range of groups, from commercial entities to faith communities; *isolation* describes the reprieve that comes from voluntary withdrawal into solitude. Six Private I's provides a person-centered framework that regards people, rather than data or technology, as the central consideration of privacy.

PEELING BACK THE LAYERS: DESIGN CHOICES IN THE SIX PRIVATE I'S

The design of Six Private I's reflects a specific ethical orientation to privacy norms: that people, rather than data, are the subject of privacy. The regulation and exchange of information about persons are central to privacy theory.[86] The authors posit that "privacy is a value system before it is a technology,"[87] and that "privacy is about respect for persons, not just protection for data."[88] Complementing existing frameworks which depict algorithmic and data harms,[89] Six Private I's focuses instead on the benefits of privacy in the human condition, depicting dimensions of the human experience rather than attributes of data or technology. These dimensions are arranged concentrically to convey that moving from the center of the model (identity) toward the periphery of the model (interaction/isolation) represents moving from a state of low information access and disclosure to a state of high information access and disclosure (or, in the case of isolation, intentional avoidance of high information access and disclosure). Furthermore, these dimensions also progress from the metaphysical concepts of identity, intellectual activity, and contextual integrity to the embodied states of bodily integrity, intimacy, and social interaction/isolation.

Privacy is also theorized as an activity of self-other boundary management.[90] Drawing on Cohen's formulation of privacy as boundary maintenance,[91] we depict the boundaries between these dimensions as increasingly permeable from the inside out: nearly impenetrable at the inner level of identity and highly fluid at the outer layer of social interaction, as represented by the thickness and saturation of the lines that separate the layers of the onion model visualization. The content and arrangement of Six Private I's align closely with Altman and Taylor's social penetration theory, which describes increasing access to concealed and core elements of the self over the lifespan of social relationships.[92] Comprising the public persona, the intimate personality, and the private self, the social penetration theory onion model maps personal information access along a continuum of relationship intensity, from low-intensity public interactions to high-intensity intimate relationships.[93] Six Private I's extends social penetration theory by surfacing intellect, contextual integrity, and bodily integrity as benefits of privacy alongside the private identity, intimate relationships, and the public persona of interaction and isolation.

Altman derived privacy regulation theory from social penetration theory and defined privacy as the process of regulating one's accessibility and openness to others.[94] Altman's privacy regulation theory is consistent with Cohen's claims that privacy is the "fundamentally dynamic" process of maintaining and regulating informational boundaries to preserve "breathing room" for individuals to engage simultaneously in autonomous and socially constructed self-creation.[95] Privacy regulation theory also reflects Westin's zones of privacy: personal, intimate, social, and threat.[96] These dynamics are visualized in the Six Private I's Privacy Conceptual Framework (figure 1.1), which depicts concentric zones of informational agency distinguished by boundaries marking access and information flows. Altogether, Six Private I's provides an interpretive approach to the social phenomenon of privacy by depicting the relationships between identity, intellectual activities, contextual and bodily integrity, intimacy, interaction and isolation as a product of personal information access and disclosure.

SIX PRIVATE I'S AND PRIVACY BY NORM

The introduction of computing into daily life activities has nudged the social order in the direction of surveillance and disclosure, altering social norms, system design affordances, and human behavior to facilitate surveillance and data capture.[97] In a social order of surveillance capitalism, behavioral surplus is algorithmically processed into one's data double, a construct that informs a feedback loop that nudges one's thoughts, beliefs, values, choices, and behaviors—fundamental aspects of the human experience.[98] Such unprecedented ability to monitor and interfere with others amplifies the harms of surveillance, whether interpersonal, corporate, or governmental. Surveillance exerts disparate impacts, exacerbating existing social, political, and economic power imbalances—yet loss of privacy ultimately impacts every individual, regardless of demography.[99] Ubiquitous surveillance undermines personhood itself, "because it deliberately deceives a person about [their] world, thwarting, for reasons that *cannot* be [their] reasons, [their] attempts to make a rational choice."[100]

Cohen, Hagendorff, and Park call for new approaches to privacy education as a strategy for reviving privacy norms.[101] Librarians are uniquely positioned to contribute to this PL work, as they are simultaneously professionals with a grounding in information ethics and educators with a broad reach in the education, industry, and community sectors.[102] ACRL recognizes PL as an expanding literacy, and librarians are developing approaches to PL instruction that teach "privacy literacy as a thought process."[103] Such emerging teaching and learning contexts require new teaching materials and learning objects.

This chapter presents a privacy conceptual framework, Six Private I's (figure 1.1), and outlines the underpinning privacy theory. The Six Private I's framework informs an approach to PL understood as "a suite of knowledge, behaviors, and critical dispositions regarding the information constructs of selfhood, expressive activities, and relationships"[104] rather than a prescription for personal information hygiene and privacy-protecting technologies. Six Private I's intentionally centers people as the subject of privacy rather than data or technology. The framework can be used in learning activities, such as to guide the identification of privacy considerations in a case study or as a visual supplement to a lecture or textual explanation of privacy concepts. (For more on the use of Six Private I's in PL learning activities, see the chapters Data Is Not a Mirror: A Privacy-Digital Wellness Model as Preservation of the Incomputable Self and The Promise of Theory-Informed Pedagogy: Building a Privacy Literacy Program.) It can also be used as a communication design aid, to craft learning experiences or stakeholder communications about privacy topics that surface the many nuanced contributions of privacy to people's lives. (For more on the use of Six Private I's in PL communication design, see the chapter, Lateral Privacy Literacy: Peer-Led Professional Privacy Literacy Learning Experiences.)

Information ethics involves consideration of "what must we not do" given the design and capabilities of emerging information forms and technologies and for recognition that "people are entitled to their secrets."[105] In order to preserve contextual integrity while making use of information, it is necessary to consider whether such information use "harms subjects; interferes with their self-determination; or amplifies undesirable inequalities in status, power, and wealth."[106] By elucidating information flows across the boundaries of identity, intellect, contextual and bodily integrity, intimacy, interaction and isolation, Six Private I's Privacy Conceptual Framework recenters the person as the primary consideration of privacy and restores privacy to its status as a norm among norms.

ACKNOWLEDGMENTS

Thank you to open reviewers Andrew Weiss and EB for your deep engagement with the chapter draft. Your thoughtful comments helped us craft the final manuscript!

NOTES

1. Shoshana Zuboff, *The Age of Surveillance Capitalism: The Fight For A Human Future At The New Frontier Of Power* (New York: Public Affairs, 2019).
2. Brooke Auxier, Lee Rainie, Monica Anderson, Andrew Perrin, Madhu Kumar, and Erica Turner, "Americans and Privacy: Concerned, Confused, and Feeling a Lack of Control Over Their Personal Information," Pew Research Center, last modified November 15, 2019, https://www.pewresearch.org/internet/2019/11/15/americans-and-privacy-concerned-confused-and-feeling-lack-of-control-over-their-personal-information/.
3. Yong Jin Park, *The Future of Digital Surveillance: Why Digital Monitoring Will Never Lose Its Appeal in a World of Algorithm-Driven AI* (Ann Arbor: University of Michigan, 2021), 109.
4. Zuboff, *The Age of Surveillance Capitalism*, 80.
5. Park, *The Future of Digital Surveillance*, 37–38.
6. Ibid., 110 (emphasis added).
7. Julie E. Cohen, "Turning Privacy Inside Out," *Theoretical Inquiries into Law* 20, no. 1 (2019): 5, https://doi.org/10.1515/til-2019-0002.
8. Cohen, "Turning Privacy Inside Out," 3.
9. Ibid., 26.
10. Thilo Hagendorff, "Privacy Literacy and Its Problems," *Journal of Information Ethics* 27, no. 2 (2018): 130.
11. Sarah Hartman-Caverly and Alexandria Chisholm, "Privacy Literacy Instruction Practices in Academic Libraries: Past, Present, and Possibilities," *IFLA Journal* 46, no. 4 (2020): 307, https://doi.org/10.1177/0340035220956804.
12. Cohen, "Turning Privacy Inside Out," 20.
13. Ibid.
14. Julie E. Cohen, "Examined Lives: Informational Privacy And The Subject As Object," *Stanford Law Review* 52, no. 5 (2000): 1400, 1408, 1425, https://doi.org/10.2307/1229517; Julie E. Cohen, "What Privacy Is For," *Harvard Law Review* 126, no.7 (2013): 1911, https://harvardlawreview.org/2013/05/what-privacy-is-for/; Edward J. Bloustein, "Privacy as an Aspect of Human Dignity: An Answer to Dean Prosser," in *Philosophical Dimensions of Privacy: An Anthology*, ed. Ferdinand David Schoeman (Cambridge: Cambridge University Press, 1984), 163.
15. Samuel D. Warren and Louis D. Brandeis, "The Right to Privacy," *Harvard Law Review* 4, no. 5 (1890): 207, https://doi.org/10.2307/1321160.

16. Cohen, "What Privacy Is For," 1; Charles Fried, "Privacy," *Yale Law Journal* 77 (1968): 478, 485, https://digitalcommons.law.yale.edu/ylj/vol77/iss3/3.
17. Jeffrey H. Reiman, "Privacy, Intimacy, and Personhood," *Philosophy & Public Affairs* 6, no. 1 (1976): 39, https://www.jstor.org/stable/2265060 (emphasis in original); Stanley I. Benn, "Privacy, Freedom, and Respect for Persons," in *Philosophical Dimensions of Privacy: An Anthology*, ed. Ferdinand D. Schoeman (Cambridge: Cambridge University Press, 1984), 228, https://doi.org/10.1017/CBO9780511625138.009.
18. Anita L. Allen, "Coercing Privacy," *William and Mary Law Review* 40, no. 3 (1999): 754, https://scholarship.law.wm.edu/wmlr/vol40/iss3/3; see also Cohen, "Turning Privacy Inside Out," 12–13.
19. Cohen, "Examined Lives," 1398.
20. Cohen, "What Privacy Is For," 1917; Mireille Hildebrandt, "Privacy as Protection of the Incomputable Self: From Agnostic to Agonistic Machine Learning," *Theoretical Inquiries in Law* 20, no. 1 (2019): 85, 92, https://doi.org/10.1515/til-2019-0004; Daniel J. Solove, *Understanding Privacy* (Cambridge: Harvard University Press, 2008), 119; Zuboff, *The Age of Surveillance Capitalism*, 94.
21. Arielle Pardes, "How Job Applicants Try to Hack Resume-Reading Software," *Wired* (February 16, 2022), https://www.wired.com/story/job-applicants-hack-resume-reading-software/.
22. Oscar Gandy, *The Panoptic Sort: A Political Economy of Personal Information* (Boulder: Westview, 1993), 1; Shoshana Zuboff, "Big Other: Surveillance Capitalism and the Prospects of an Information Civilization," *Journal of Information Technology* 30, no. 1 (2015): 75, http://doi.org/10.1057/jit.2015.5; Zuboff, *The Age of Surveillance Capitalism*, 94.
23. Jorge Amar, Shreya Majumder, Zachary Surek, and Nicolai von Bismarck, "How AI Driven Nudges Can Transform an Operation's Performance," McKinsey & Company, February 11, 2022, https://www.mckinsey.com/business-functions/operations/our-insights/how-ai-driven-nudges-can-transform-an-operations-performance.
24. Cohen, "Turning Privacy Inside Out," 12–13; Richard A. Wasserstrom, "Privacy: Some Arguments And Assumptions," in *Philosophical Dimensions Of Privacy: An Anthology*, ed. Ferdinand David Schoeman (Cambridge: Cambridge University Press, 1984), 327, https://doi.org/10.1017/CBO9780511625138.015.
25. Jacquelyn Burkell, "The Future Of Privacy Lies In Forgetting The Past," *European Data Protection Law Review* 3, no. 4 (2017): 436, http://doi.org/10.21552/edpl/2017/4/4.
26. Krzysztof J. Gorgolewski, Dan Lurie, Sebastian Urchs, Judy A. Kipping, R. Cameron Craddock, Michael P. Milham, Daniel S. Marguilies, and Jonathan Smallwood, "A Correspondence Between Individual Differences in the Brain's Intrinsic Functional Architecture and the Content and Form of Self-Generated Thoughts," *PloS One* 9, no. 5 (2014), Article e97176: 12, https://doi.org/10.1371/journal.pone.0097176; Shigeyuki Ikeda, Hikaru Takeuchi, Yasuyuki Taki, Rui Nouchi, Ryoichi Yokoyama, Yuka Kotozaki, Seishu Nakagawa, Atsushi Sekiguchi, Kunio Iizuka, Yuki Yamamoto, Sugiko Hanawa, Tsuyoshi Araki, Carlos M. Miyauchi, Kohei Sakaki, Takayuki Nozawa, Susumu Yokota, Daniele Magistro, and Ryuta Kawashima, "A Comprehensive Analysis of the Correlations Between Resting-State Oscillations in Multiple-Frequency Bands and Big Five Traits," *Frontiers in Human Neuroscience* 11, Article 321 (2017): 7, https://doi.org/10.3389/fnhum.2017.00321; Chandra Sripada, Mike Angstadt, Saige Rutherford, Daniel Kessler, Yura Kim, Mike Yee, and Elizaveta Levina, "Basic Units of Inter-Individual Variation in Resting State Connectomes," *Scientific Reports* 9, no. 1 (2019): 8–9, https://doi.org/10.1038/s41598-018-38406-5.
27. Neil Richards, *Intellectual Privacy: Rethinking Civil Liberties In The Digital Age* (Oxford: Oxford University Press, 2015), 5, 95.
28. Ferdinand David Schoemann, "Privacy and Intimate Information," in *Philosophical Dimensions of Privacy: An Anthology*, ed. Ferdinand David Schoeman (Cambridge: Cambridge University Press, 1984), 413; see also Benn, "Privacy, Freedom, and Respect for Persons," 242.
29. Cohen, "Examined Lives," 1427.

30. Cohen, "Examined Lives," 1424; Barrington Moore, Jr., *Privacy: Studies in Social and Cultural History* (Armonk: M. E. Sharpe, 1984), 76; Alan F. Westin, *Privacy and Freedom* (New York: Atheneum, 1967), 24, 36–37.
31. Cohen, "Examined Lives," 1426.
32. Westin, *Privacy and Freedom*, 24.
33. Richards, *Intellectual Privacy*, 10.
34. Scott Skinner-Thompson, *Privacy at the Margins* (Cambridge: Cambridge University Press, 2021).
35. Gandy, *The Panoptic Sort*, 89; see also Burkell, "The Future of Privacy Lies," 437.
36. Richards, *Intellectual Privacy*, 162; see also Solove, *Understanding Privacy*, 166; Wasserstrom, "Privacy," 322.
37. Warren and Brandeis, "The Right to Privacy," 196.
38. Paul Lewis, "'Our Minds Can Be Hijacked': The Tech Insiders Who Fear a Smartphone Dystopia," *The Guardian* (October 6, 2017), https://www.theguardian.com/technology/2017/oct/05/smartphone-addiction-silicon-valley-dystopia.
39. Christina Animashaun, "Dark Patterns, the Tricks Websites Use to Make You Say Yes, Explained," Vox, April 1, 2021, https://www.vox.com/recode/22351108/dark-patterns-ui-web-design-privacy.
40. Thomas B. Edsall, "We're Staring at Our Phones, Full of Rage for 'the Other Side,'" *New York Times* (June 15, 2022), https://www.nytimes.com/2022/06/15/opinion/social-media-polarization-democracy.html.
41. Julie E. Cohen, "A Right To Read Anonymously: A Closer Look at 'Copyright Management' in Cyberspace," *Connecticut Law Review* 28 (1996): 1, https://scholarship.law.georgetown.edu/facpub/814/; Richards, *Intellectual Privacy*, 128.
42. Benn, "Privacy, Freedom, and Respect for Persons," 230; Cohen, "A Right to Read Anonymously," 38, 68; Frederick Schauer, "Fear, Risk and The First Amendment: Unraveling The Chilling Effect," *Boston University Law Review* 58 (1978): 689, 697, https://scholarship.law.wm.edu/facpubs/879; Wasserstrom, "Privacy," 324.
43. Olmstead v. United States, 277 U.S. 438, Supreme Court of the United States (1928), https://www.law.cornell.edu/supremecourt/text/277/438; Katz v. United States, 389 U.S. 347, Supreme Court of the United States (1967), https://www.law.cornell.edu/supremecourt/text/389/347; Richards, *Intellectual Privacy*, 7, 141.
44. "National Strategy for Countering Domestic Terrorism," Executive Office of the President National Security Council, last modified June 2021, https://www.whitehouse.gov/wp-content/uploads/2021/06/National-Strategy-for-Countering-Domestic-Terrorism.pdf; Hina Shamsi and Hugh Handeyside, "Biden's Domestic Terrorism Strategy Entrenches Bias and Harmful Law Enforcement Power," ACLU, last modified July 9, 2021, https://www.aclu.org/news/national-security/bidens-domestic-terrorism-strategy-entrenches-bias-and-harmful-law-enforcement-power.
45. Hildebrandt, "Privacy as Protection of the Incomputable Self," 10.
46. Justice Tomas M. Cooley as quoted in Warren and Brandeis, "The Right to Privacy," 195.
47. Garret Keizer, *Privacy* (New York: Picador, 2012), 20.
48. Helen Nissenbaum, "Privacy as Contextual Integrity," *Washington Law Review* 79 (2004): 136–38, https://digitalcommons.law.uw.edu/wlr/vol79/iss1/10.
49. Nissenbaum, "Privacy as Contextual Integrity," 137.
50. Westin, *Privacy and Freedom*, 37.
51. Cohen, "Examined Lives," 1426–27; James Rachels, "Why Privacy is Important," *Philosophy & Public Affairs* 4, no. 4 (1975): 330, http://www.jstor.org/stable/2265077; Schoemann, "Privacy and Intimate Information," 408.
52. danah michele boyd, *Taken Out of Context: American Teen Sociality in Networked Publics* (Berkeley: University of California Berkeley, 2008), 34, https://www.danah.org/papers/TakenOutOfContext.pdf.
53. Schoeman, "Privacy and Intimate Information," 408.

54. Byron Tau and Georgia Wells, "Grindr User Data Was Sold Through Ad Networks," *Wall Street Journal* (May 2, 2022), https://www.wsj.com/articles/grindr-user-data-has-been-for-sale-for-years-11651492800.
55. boyd, *Taken Out of Context*, 26, 34; Cohen, "A Right to Read Anonymously," 76.
56. Westin, *Privacy and Freedom*, 11.
57. Ibid., 9.
58. Warren and Brandeis, "The Right to Privacy," 193–94.
59. Iris Marion Young, "A Room of One's Own: Old Age, Extended Care, and Privacy," in *On Female Body Experience: "Throwing Like a Girl" and Other Essays* (Oxford: Oxford University Press, 2005), 156.
60. Young, "A Room of One's Own," 170.
61. Griswold v. Connecticut, 381 U.S. 479, Supreme Court of the United States (1965), https://www.law.cornell.edu/supremecourt/text/381/479; Roe v. Wade, 410 U.S. 113, Supreme Court of the United States (1973), https://www.law.cornell.edu/supremecourt/text/410/113.
62. Amy Gajda, "How *Dobbs* Threatens to Torpedo Privacy Rights in the US," *Wired* (June 29, 2022), https://www.wired.com/story/scotus-dobbs-roe-privacy-abortion/.
63. Steph Black, "How Period-Tracking Apps Track More Than Your Period," *Rewire News Group*, June 24, 2022, https://rewirenewsgroup.com/article/2022/06/24/how-period-tracking-apps-track-more-than-your-period/; Joseph Cox, "Data Broker is Selling Location Data of People Who Visit Abortion Clinics," *Motherboard*, Vice, May 3, 2022, https://www.vice.com/en/article/m7vzjb/location-data-abortion-clinics-safegraph-planned-parenthood; Gennie Gebhart and Daly Barnett, "Should You Really Delete Your Period Tracking App?," Electronic Frontier Foundation, last modified June 30, 2022, https://www.eff.org/deeplinks/2022/06/should-you-really-delete-your-period-tracking-app.
64. "Editorial: Congress Must Protect Rights to Contraception and Same-sex Relationships," *Los Angeles Times* (June 28, 2022), https://www.latimes.com/opinion/story/2022-06-28/editorial-congress-should-protect-rights-to-contraception-and-same-sex-relationships.
65. Fried, "Privacy," 211.
66. Keizer, *Privacy*, 37; Allen, "Coercing Privacy," 739.
67. Fried, "Privacy," 477.
68. Reiman, "Privacy, Intimacy, and Personhood," 33.
69. Schoemann, "Privacy and Intimate Information," 406.
70. Kenneth L. Karst, "The Freedom of Intimate Association," *The Yale Law Journal* 89, no. 4 (1980): 661, https://doi.org/10.2307/795978.
71. Rob Brooks, "Artificial Intimacy: Where Gossip, Relationships and Social Media Intersect," *The Guardian* (June 5, 2021), https://www.theguardian.com/society/2021/jun/05/artificial-intimacy-where-gossip-relationships-and-social-media-intersect.
72. Rob Brooks, "The Age of Artificial Intimacy is Already Upon Us," *Psychology Today* (September 8, 2021), https://www.psychologytoday.com/intl/blog/artificial-intimacy/202109/the-age-artificial-intimacy-is-already-upon-us.
73. Taylor Mooney, "That Data Profile You're Swiping On May Not Actually Be Human," CBS News, November 10, 2019, https://www.cbsnews.com/news/dating-apps-bots-and-fake-profiles-online-cbsn-documentary/.
74. Amy Barrett, "Intimacy Famine: Are Smartphones Really Making Us Less Lonely?," *Science Focus*, BBC, March 12, 2022, https://www.sciencefocus.com/the-human-body/intimacy-famine/.
75. Hildebrandt, "Privacy as Protection of the Incomputable Self," 86.
76. Cohen, "Turning Privacy Inside Out," 23; Westin, *Privacy and Freedom*, 23, 43–44.
77. Rachels, "Why Privacy Is Important," 328, 330.
78. Wasserstrom, "Privacy," 329.
79. Westin, *Privacy and Freedom*, 9, 33, 35.
80. Warren and Brandeis, "The Right to Privacy," 196.

81. William L. Prosser, "Privacy," in *Philosophical Dimensions of Privacy: An Anthology*, ed. Ferdinand David Schoeman (Cambridge: Cambridge University Press, 1984), 109; Warren and Brandeis, "The Right to Privacy," 196.
82. Young, "A Room of One's Own," 178; see also Allen, "Coercing Privacy," 739.
83. Heba Hashem, "Tourists Flock to Saudi Arabia as the Country Opens to Foreign Visitors," Salaam Gateway, March 9, 2022, https://salaamgateway.com/story/tourists-flock-to-saudi-arabia-as-the-country-opens-to-foreign-visitors.
84. Ted Rose, "The Power of Solitude," *Tricycle* (Spring 2005), https://tricycle.org/magazine/power-solitude/.
85. Rose, "The Power of Solitude."
86. Fried, "Privacy," 482; Warren and Brandeis, "The Right to Privacy," 194, 211; Westin, *Privacy and Freedom*, 7.
87. Hartman-Caverly and Chisholm, "Privacy Literacy Instruction Practices in Academic Libraries," 317.
88. Sarah Hartman-Caverly and Alexandria Chisholm, "Transforming Privacy Literacy Instruction: From Surveillance Theory to Teaching Practice," *LOEX Conference Proceedings 2021*, 1, https://commons.emich.edu/loexconf2021/8/.
89. Jacob Leon Kröger, Milagros Miceli, and Florian Müller, "How Data Can Be Used Against People: A Classification of Personal Data Misuses," SSRN, last modified December 30, 2021, https://dx.doi.org/10.2139/ssrn.3887097; Rebecca Kelly Slaughter, Janice Kopec, and Mohamad Batal, "Algorithms and Economic Justice: A Taxonomy of Harms and a Path Forward for the Federal Trade Commission," last modified August 2021, https://yjolt.org/sites/default/files/23_yale_j.l._tech._special_issue_1.pdf.
90. Moore, *Privacy*, 9.
91. Cohen, "What Privacy is For," 2.
92. Irwin Altman and Dalmas A. Taylor, *Social Penetration: The Development of Interpersonal Relationships* (New York: Holt, Rinehart and Winston, 1973): 17, 136.
93. Altman and Taylor, *Social Penetration*, 19.
94. Irwin Altman, *The Environment And Social Behavior: Privacy, Personal Space, Territory, Crowding* (Monterey: Brooks/Cole, 1975), 46.
95. Cohen, "What Privacy is For," 2.
96. Westin, *Privacy and Freedom*, 9.
97. Hildebrandt, "Privacy as Protection of the Incomputable Self," 91, 94.
98. Zuboff, *The Age of Surveillance Capitalism*, 94.
99. Nina Gerber, Nina, Paul Gerber, and Melanie Volkamer, "Explaining The Privacy Paradox: A Systematic Review Of Literature Investigating Privacy Attitude And Behavior," *Computers & Security* 77 (2018): 255, https://doi.org/10.1016/j.cose.2018.04.002; Solove, *Understanding Privacy*, 79, 132, 134.
100. Benn, "Privacy, Freedom, and Respect For Persons," 230 (emphasis in original; gendered language revised).
101. Cohen, "Turning Privacy Inside Out," 26; Hagendorff, "Privacy Literacy and Its Problems"; Park, *The Future of Digital Surveillance*, 109–110.
102. Richards, *Intellectual Privacy*, 177; Christina L. Wissinger, "Privacy Literacy: From Theory to Practice," *Communications in Information Literacy* 11, no. 2 (2017): 382, https://doi.org/10.15760/comminfolit.2017.11.2.9.
103. Association of College & Research Libraries, "2021 Environmental Scan," last modified April 2021, https://www.ala.org/acrl/sites/ala.org.acrl/files/content/publications/whitepapers/EnvironmentalScan2021.pdf; Wissing, "Privacy Literacy," 386; Dana Rotman, "Are You Looking At Me? Social Media And Privacy Literacy," last modified February 8, 2009, 2, https://www.ideals.illinois.edu/handle/2142/15339.
104. Hartman-Caverly and Chisholm, "Privacy Literacy Instruction Practices in Academic Libraries," 306.
105. Richards, *Intellectual Privacy*, 3; Nissenbaum, "Privacy as Contextual Integrity," 128.

106. Nissenbaum, "Privacy as Contextual Integrity," 154–55; see also Daniel J. Solove, "The Myth Of The Privacy Paradox" [pre-print], *George Washington Law Review* 89 (2020): 49–50, http://dx.doi.org/10.2139/ssrn.3536265.

BIBLIOGRAPHY

Allen, Anita L. "Coercing Privacy." *William and Mary Law Review* 40, no. 3 (1999): 723–57. https://scholarship.law.wm.edu/wmlr/vol40/iss3/3.

Association of College & Research Libraries. "2021 Environmental Scan." Last modified April 2021. https://www.ala.org/acrl/sites/ala.org.acrl/files/content/publications/whitepapers/EnvironmentalScan2021.pdf.

Altman, Irwin. *The Environment and Social Behavior: Privacy, Personal Space, Territory, Crowding*. Monterey: Brooks/Cole, 1975.

Altman, Irwin, and Dalmas A. Taylor. *Social Penetration: The Development of Interpersonal Relationships*. New York: Holt, Rinehart and Winston, 1973.

Amar, Jorge, Shreya Majumder, Zachary Surek, and Nicolai von Bismarck. "How AI Driven Nudges Can Transform an Operation's Performance." McKinsey & Company. February 11, 2022. https://www.mckinsey.com/business-functions/operations/our-insights/how-ai-driven-nudges-can-transform-an-operations-performance.

Animashaun, Christina. "Dark Patterns, the Tricks Websites Use to Make You Say Yes, Explained." Vox. April 1, 2021. https://www.vox.com/recode/22351108/dark-patterns-ui-web-design-privacy.

Auxier, Brooke, Lee Rainie, Monica Anderson, Andrew Perrin, Madhu Kumar, and Erica Turner. "Americans and Privacy: Concerned, Confused, and Feeling a Lack of Control Over Their Personal Information." Pew Research Center. Last modified November 15, 2019. https://www.pewresearch.org/internet/2019/11/15/americans-and-privacy-concerned-confused-and-feeling-lack-of-control-over-their-personal-information/.

Barrett, Amy. "Intimacy Famine: Are Smartphones Really Making Us Less Lonely?" *Science Focus*. BBC. March 12, 2022. https://www.sciencefocus.com/the-human-body/intimacy-famine/.

Benn, Stanley I. "Privacy, Freedom, and Respect for Persons." In *Philosophical Dimensions of Privacy: An Anthology*, edited by Ferdinand David Schoeman, 223–44. Cambridge: Cambridge University Press, 1984. https://doi.org/10.1017/CBO9780511625138.009.

Black, Steph. "How Period-Tracking Apps Track More Than Your Period." *Rewire News Group*. June 24, 2022. https://rewirenewsgroup.com/article/2022/06/24/how-period-tracking-apps-track-more-than-your-period/.

Bloustein, Edward. J. "Privacy as an Aspect of Human Dignity: An Answer to Dean Prosser." In *Philosophical Dimensions of Privacy: An Anthology*, edited by Ferdinand David Schoeman, 156–202. Cambridge: Cambridge University Press, 1984.

boyd, danah michele. *Taken Out of Context: American Teen Sociality in Networked Publics*. Berkeley: University of California Berkeley, 2008. https://www.danah.org/papers/TakenOutOfContext.pdf.

Brooks, Rob. "Artificial Intimacy: Where Gossip, Relationships and Social Media Intersect." *The Guardian* (June 5, 2021). https://www.theguardian.com/society/2021/jun/05/artificial-intimacy-where-gossip-relationships-and-social-media-intersect.

———. "The Age of Artificial Intimacy is Already Upon Us." *Psychology Today* (September 8, 2021). https://www.psychologytoday.com/intl/blog/artificial-intimacy/202109/the-age-artificial-intimacy-is-already-upon-us.

Burkell, Jacquelyn. "The Future of Privacy Lies in Forgetting the Past." *European Data Protection Law Review* 3, no. 4 (2017): 435–37. http://doi.org/10.21552/edpl/2017/4/4.

Cohen, Julie E. "A Right to Read Anonymously: A Closer Look at 'Copyright Management' in Cyberspace." *Connecticut Law Review* 28 (1996): 1–77. https://scholarship.law.georgetown.edu/facpub/814/.

———. "Examined Lives: Informational Privacy and the Subject as Object." *Stanford Law Review* 52, no. 5 (2000): 1373–438. https://doi.org/10.2307/1229517.

———. "Turning Privacy Inside Out." *Theoretical Inquiries into Law* 20, no. 1 (2019): 1–31. https://doi.org/10.1515/til-2019-0002.

———. "What Privacy Is For." *Harvard Law Review* 126, no.7 (2013): 1904–33. https://harvardlawreview.org/2013/05/what-privacy-is-for/.

Cox, Joseph. "Data Broker is Selling Location Data of People Who Visit Abortion Clinics." *Motherboard*. Vice. May 3, 2022. https://www.vice.com/en/article/m7vzjb/location-data-abortion-clinics-safegraph-planned-parenthood.

Edsall, Thomas B. "'We're Staring at Our Phones, Full of Rage for 'the Other Side.'" *New York Times* (June 15, 2022). https://www.nytimes.com/2022/06/15/opinion/social-media-polarization-democracy.html.

Executive Office of the President National Security Council. "National Strategy for Countering Domestic Terrorism." Last modified June 2021. https://www.whitehouse.gov/wp-content/uploads/2021/06/National-Strategy-for-Countering-Domestic-Terrorism.pdf.

Fried, Charles. "Privacy." *Yale Law Journal* 77 (1968): 475–93. https://digitalcommons.law.yale.edu/ylj/vol77/iss3/3.

Gajda, Amy. "How *Dobbs* Threatens to Torpedo Privacy Rights in the US." *Wired* (June 29, 2022). https://www.wired.com/story/scotus-dobbs-roe-privacy-abortion/.

Gandy, Oscar. H. *The Panoptic Sort: A Political Economy of Personal Information*. Boulder: Westview, 1993.

Gebhart, Gennie, and Daly Barnett. "Should You Really Delete Your Period Tracking App?" Electronic Frontier Foundation. Last modified June 30, 2022. https://www.eff.org/deeplinks/2022/06/should-you-really-delete-your-period-tracking-app.

Gerber, Nina, Paul Gerber, and Melanie Volkamer. "Explaining The Privacy Paradox: A Systematic Review of Literature Investigating Privacy Attitude and Behavior." *Computers & Security* 77 (2018): 226–61. https://doi.org/10.1016/j.cose.2018.04.002.

Gorgolewski, Krzysztof J., Dan Lurie, Sebastian Urchs, Judy A. Kipping, R. Cameron Craddock, Michael P. Milham, Daniel S. Marguilies, and Jonathan Smallwood. "A Correspondence Between Individual Differences in the Brain's Intrinsic Functional Architecture and the Content and Form of Self-Generated Thoughts." *PloS One* 9, no. 5 (2014), Article e97176: 1–16. https://doi.org/10.1371/journal.pone.0097176.

Griswold v. Connecticut. 381 U.S. 479. Supreme Court of the United States. 1965. https://www.law.cornell.edu/supremecourt/text/381/479.

Hagendorff, Thilo. "Privacy Literacy and its Problems." *Journal of Information Ethics* 27, no. 2 (Fall 2018): 127–45.

Hartman-Caverly, Sarah, and Alexandria Chisholm. "Privacy Literacy Instruction Practices in Academic Libraries: Past, Present, and Possibilities." *IFLA Journal* 46, no. 4 (2020): 305–27. https://doi.org/10.1177/0340035220956804.

———. "Transforming Privacy Literacy Instruction: From Surveillance Theory to Teaching Practice." *LOEX Conference Proceedings 2021*. https://commons.emich.edu/loexconf2021/8/.

Hashem, Heba. "Tourists Flock to Saudi Arabia as the Country Opens to Foreign Visitors." *Salaam Gateway*. March 9, 2022. https://salaamgateway.com/story/tourists-flock-to-saudi-arabia-as-the-country-opens-to-foreign-visitors.

Hildebrandt, Mireille. "Privacy as Protection of the Incomputable Self: From Agnostic to Agonistic Machine Learning." *Theoretical Inquiries in Law* 20, no. 1 (2019): 83–121. https://doi.org/10.1515/til-2019-0004.

Ikeda, Shigeyuki, Hikaru Takeuchi, Yasuyuki Taki, Rui Nouchi, Ryoichi Yokoyama, Yuka Kotozaki, Seishu Nakagawa, Atsushi Sekiguchi, Kunio Iizuka, Yuki Yamamoto, Sugiko Hanawa, Tsuyoshi Araki, Carlos M. Miyauchi, Kohei Sakaki, Takayuki Nozawa, Susumu Yokota, Daniele Magistro, and Ryuta Kawashima. "A Comprehensive Analysis of the Correlations Between Resting-State Oscillations in

Multiple-Frequency Bands and Big Five Traits." *Frontiers in Human Neuroscience* 11, Article 321 (2017): 1–11. https://doi.org/10.3389/fnhum.2017.00321.

Karst, Kenneth L. "The Freedom of Intimate Association." *The Yale Law Journal* 89, no. 4 (1980): 624–92. https://doi.org/10.2307/795978.

Katz v. United States. 389 U.S. 347. Supreme Court of the United States. 1967. https://www.law.cornell.edu/supremecourt/text/389/347.

Keizer, Garret. *Privacy*. New York: Picador, 2012.

Kröger, Jacon Leon, Milagros Miceli, and Florian Müller. "How Data Can Be Used Against People: A Classification of Personal Data Misuses." SSRN. Last modified December 30, 2021. https://dx.doi.org/10.2139/ssrn.3887097.

Lewis, Paul. "'Our Minds Can Be Hijacked': The Tech Insiders Who Fear a Smartphone Dystopia." *The Guardian* (October 6, 2017). https://www.theguardian.com/technology/2017/oct/05/smartphone-addiction-silicon-valley-dystopia.

Los Angeles Times Editorial Board. "Editorial: Congress Must Protect Rights to Contraception and Same-sex Relationships." *Los Angeles Times* (June 28, 2022). https://www.latimes.com/opinion/story/2022-06-28/editorial-congress-should-protect-rights-to-contraception-and-same-sex-relationships.

Mooney, Taylor. "That Data Profile You're Swiping on May Not Actually Be Human." CBS News. November 10, 2019. https://www.cbsnews.com/news/dating-apps-bots-and-fake-profiles-online-cbsn-documentary/.

Moore, Barrington, Jr. *Privacy: Studies in Social and Cultural History*. Armonk: M. E. Sharpe, 1984.

Nissenbaum, Helen. "Privacy as Contextual Integrity." *Washington Law Review* 79 (2004): 119–57. https://digitalcommons.law.uw.edu/wlr/vol79/iss1/10.

Olmstead v. United States. 277 U.S. 438. Supreme Court of the United States. 1928. https://www.law.cornell.edu/supremecourt/text/277/438.

Pardes, Arielle. "How Job Applicants Try to Hack Resume-Reading Software." *Wired* (February 16, 2022). https://www.wired.com/story/job-applicants-hack-resume-reading-software/.

Park, Yong Jin. *The Future of Digital Surveillance: Why Digital Monitoring Will Never Lose Its Appeal in a World of Algorithm-Driven AI*. Ann Arbor: University of Michigan, 2021.

Prosser, William L. "Privacy." In *Philosophical Dimensions of Privacy: An Anthology*, edited by Ferdinand David Schoeman, 104–55. Cambridge: Cambridge University Press, 1984.

Rachels, James. "Why Privacy is Important." *Philosophy & Public Affairs* 4, no. 4 (1975): 323–33. http://www.jstor.org/stable/2265077.

Reiman, Jeffrey H. "Privacy, Intimacy, and Personhood." *Philosophy & Public Affairs* 6, no. 1 (1976): 26–44. https://www.jstor.org/stable/2265060.

Richards, Neil. *Intellectual Privacy: Rethinking Civil Liberties in the Digital Age*. Oxford: Oxford University Press, 2015.

Roe v. Wade. 410 U.S. 113. Supreme Court of the United States. 1973. https://www.law.cornell.edu/supremecourt/text/410/113.

Rose, Ted. "The Power of Solitude." *Tricycle* (Spring 2005). https://tricycle.org/magazine/power-solitude/.

Rotman, Dana. "Are You Looking at Me? Social Media and Privacy Literacy." Last modified February 8, 2009. https://www.ideals.illinois.edu/handle/2142/15339.

Schauer, Frederick. "Fear, Risk and The First Amendment: Unraveling the Chilling Effect." *Boston University Law Review* 58 (1978): 685–732. https://scholarship.law.wm.edu/facpubs/879

Schoeman, Ferdinand David. "Privacy and Intimate Information." In *Philosophical Dimensions of Privacy: An Anthology*, edited by Ferdinand David Schoeman, 403–18. Cambridge: Cambridge University Press, 1984.

Shamsi, Hina, and Hugh Handeyside. "Biden's Domestic Terrorism Strategy Entrenches Bias and Harmful Law Enforcement Power." ACLU. Last modified July 9, 2021. https://www.aclu.org/news/national-security/bidens-domestic-terrorism-strategy-entrenches-bias-and-harmful-law-enforcement-power.

Skinner-Thompson, Scott. *Privacy at the Margins*. Cambridge: Cambridge University Press, 2021.

Slaughter, Rebecca Kelly, Janice Kopec, and Mohamad Batal. "Algorithms and Economic Justice: A Taxonomy of Harms and a Path Forward for the Federal Trade Commission." Last modified August 2021. https://yjolt.org/sites/default/files/23_yale_j.l._tech._special_issue_1.pdf.

Solove, Daniel J. *Understanding Privacy*. Cambridge: Harvard University Press, 2008.

———. "The Myth of the Privacy Paradox" [Pre-print]. *George Washington Law Review* 89 (2020): 1–42. http://dx.doi.org/10.2139/ssrn.3536265.

Sripada, Chandra, Mike Angstadt, Saige Rutherford, Daniel Kessler, Yura Kim, Mike Yee, and Elizaveta Levina. "Basic Units of Inter-Individual Variation in Resting State Connectomes." *Scientific Reports* 9, no. 1 (2019): 1–12. https://doi.org/10.1038/s41598-018-38406-5.

Tau, Byron, and Georgia Wells. "Grndr Data Was Sold Through Ad Networks." *Wall Street Journal* (May 2, 2022). https://www.wsj.com/articles/grindr-user-data-has-been-for-sale-for-years-11651492800.

Warren, Samuel D., and Louis D. Brandeis. "The Right to Privacy." *Harvard Law Review* 4, no. 5 (1890): 193–220. https://doi.org/10.2307/1321160.

Wasserstrom, Richard A. "Privacy: Some Arguments and Assumptions." In *Philosophical Dimensions of Privacy: An Anthology*, edited by Ferdinand David Schoeman, 317–32. Cambridge: Cambridge University Press, 1984. https://doi.org/10.1017/CBO9780511625138.015.

Westin, Alan F. *Privacy and Freedom*. New York: Atheneum, 1967.

Wissinger, Christina L. "Privacy Literacy: From Theory to Practice." *Communications in Information Literacy* 11, no. 2 (2017): 378–89. https://doi.org/10.15760/comminfolit.2017.11.2.9.

Young, Iris Marion. "A Room of One's Own: Old Age, Extended Care, and Privacy." In *On Female Body Experience: "Throwing Like a Girl" and Other Essays*. Oxford: Oxford University Press, 2005.

Zuboff, Shoshana. "Big Other: Surveillance Capitalism and the Prospects of an Information Civilization." *Journal of Information Technology* 30, no. 1 (2015): 75–89. http://doi.org/10.1057/jit.2015.5.

———. *The Age of Surveillance Capitalism: The Fight for a Human Future at the New Frontier of Power*. New York: Public Affairs, 2019.

CHAPTER 2

DATA IS NOT A MIRROR:
A Privacy-Digital Wellness Model as Preservation of the Incomputable Self

Alexandria Chisholm

OUR EVER-EVOLVING RELATIONSHIP WITH TECHNOLOGY

As I sit to work on this chapter, I am struck by how my writing process has been curtailed, impeded, and muddied by many of the topics and issues it will cover. Eternally distracted by email alerts, inexplicably realizing that I've been scrolling through Twitter for nearly an hour and taunted by the approximately 120 browser tabs full of things I'll *definitely read later*. As a mid-'80s baby, I cannot escape the controversial moniker of "Millennial"—labeled "digital natives," my generation has been dissected and overexamined since childhood, only to grow up being derided for capitalism's many failings throughout our burgeoning adulthood. Beyond all the trite scrutiny, it's noteworthy that we've had a front-row seat to the world's rapidly transforming technological landscape and, by extension, privacy culture.

There are distinct memories that I cannot help but view as formative in both my personal and professional life. My generation has come of age experiencing the widespread integration of home computers, the internet, mobile connectivity,

25

and social media in real time. We straddled the line of analog and digital, living these major transitions during our formative years. As an innately privacy-centric individual, I have watched with great trepidation as technology has slowly seeped into every nook and cranny of the human experience. From the launch of Facebook's newsfeed—at the time, deemed creepy and stalkerish by all—to the pervasive adoption of smartphones and our subsequent inability to hold a sustained face-to-face conversation. Looking back, it's alarming to recognize our own easy enchantment with the surveillance architectures that serve as the bedrock of so many of our modern dilemmas, from filter bubbles and misinformation to fragmented attention. But don't worry, I'm sure someone will develop an app or browser extension to solve that. After all, technological harms beget technological solutions.

These widespread transformations have acutely shifted our relationships—not just to technology but also to each other, society at large, our environment, and even ourselves—having a major impact on our overall well-being. Recent history has seen sweeping technological growth. In just two decades, internet usage increased from around only half of US adults to 93 percent.[1] During that same timeframe, mobile phone ownership has risen from 62 to 97 percent; furthermore, in just ten years—from 2011 to 2021—smartphone adoption increased from 35 to 85 percent.[2] In 2005, only 5 percent of Americans participated in social media; by 2011, membership had grown to half; in 2021, 72 percent use at least one social media platform.[3] With widespread user adoption, intimacy has been critically transformed by these technologically mediated communication systems;[4] outdoor recreation has dropped while screen time now exceeds active leisure time;[5] and our reliance on technology to mediate our information flows and real-world experiences continues to expand daily.[6]

Now a pervasive technology, mobile devices dominate our daily life. On average, we interact with our phones over 2,600 times per day, and about three in ten US adults report that they are "almost constantly" online.[7] This has serious implications when considering recent findings that high levels of internet use can impact cognitive brain functions such as causing divided attention, difficulty maintaining sustained concentration, as well as memory and recall—a condition labeled by researchers as the "online brain."[8]

Socializing online is now the most common way that young adults interact with their peers, with many citing increased anxiety in face-to-face interactions.[9] In multiple studies, students reported that media, particularly their cell phones, have become literal extensions of their persons, providing emotional comfort, vital social connection, and access to the "real world."[10] Separation from mobile devices is often cited as anxiety-inducing and isolating, many even experiencing "phantom vibrations."[11] Furthermore, technology affords individuals a sense of instancy—the ability to process emotions and thoughts in real time, leading to the perception that "feelings are not fully experienced until they are communicated."[12]

Alarming details are constantly unearthed about social media's impact. These platforms have cultivated an environment of parasociality—a one-sided psychological relationship with media personalities in place of genuine intimacy—going so far as to dull and diminish our interactions with real-life friends and family.[13] YouTube and TikTok are suspected to be contributing factors in the increasing number of mass psychogenic illnesses, even spawning a new term: mass social media-induced illness.[14] And recent revelations from the Facebook Files illustrate precisely how little Big Tech companies like Meta care about the well-being of their users in the face of corporate growth and earnings.[15]

Increasingly, technology is both a window and mirror—directing our interactions with others and shaping how we view ourselves. As Mirielle Hildebrandt states, "we look back upon our self via the gaze of others,"[16] and when factoring technology into the equation, this gaze becomes datafied, extending our self-worth to algorithmically rendered reflections.

WELLNESS IN FLUX

It does not take extensive reflection on technology's rapid transformation of modern life to recognize how it intersects with individual well-being. Nearly everyone can cite ways in which technology is influencing their wellness, for better or worse. The mobile connectivity paradox defined as "the experience of being caught between autonomy and a loss of control" perfectly embodies this tension.[17] What better expresses our relationship to modern technology than the tug of war between empowerment and dependency?

Wellness is a holistic concept that touches on all facets of the human experience. The National Wellness Institute defines it as "an active process through which people become aware of, and make choices toward, a more successful existence."[18] Popularly depicted in the form of a wellness wheel, various dimensions of wellness are often identified to create a model demonstrating the integrated and dynamic nature of these characteristics that contribute to a balanced, healthy, and fulfilling life. For the purposes of this discussion, I will outline the following dimensions of wellness: *spiritual and emotional*, including self-esteem, life purpose, values and beliefs, stress level, reflection, and self-awareness; *intellectual*, in regard to education, learning, curiosity, and creative pursuits; *physical*, referring to diet, fitness, sleep, relaxation, and environment; *financial and professional*, in regards to budgeting, income, work-life balance, purpose, and fulfillment; *social*, concerning relationships, including the time committed to and the quality and intimacy of those relations, communication, and systems of support; and finally, *fun and recreational*, referring to leisure time, hobbies, and outlets for passions.

The pervasiveness of mobile technologies hides its role in shaping society. Ubiquitous connectivity has restructured everyday life, leading to context collapses as our relationships and social roles become disconnected from time and space, blurring lines, and leaving no distinction between the private, public, and professional.[19] Tech giants are covetous in their protection of proprietary algorithms, illustrating the information asymmetries upholding their power over individual users who are largely unaware of the processes continuously shaping their worldview.[20] My collaborator Sarah Hartman-Caverly and I stress that amid the vast and sweeping integration of technology within all spaces of society, it is imperative that we reformulate our understanding of wellness with special consideration to ubiquitous mobile connectivity.[21]

As defined by Mariek Vanden Abeele,

> Digital wellbeing is a subjective individual experience of optimal balance between the benefits and drawbacks obtained from mobile connectivity.... People achieve digital wellbeing when experiencing maximal controlled pleasure and functional support, together with minimal loss of control and functional impairment.[22]

Vanden Abeele's dynamic systems approach acknowledges that wellness is an experiential state that can change over time, varies from person to person, and critiques over-simplistic methods of digital wellness that do not consider how persons, devices, and contexts interact. Person-specific factors consider each user and their distinct qualities, such as personality traits and mood; device-specific factors acknowledge system design features including attention engineering, persuasive design, and inherent portability and availability; finally, context-specific factors refer to the context collapse—when many social roles coexist in a single environment[23]—due to ubiquitous connectivity.[24]

Digital wellness involves the *intentional use* of technology in maintaining *awareness* of and *exercising choices* toward one's optimal, balanced existence. Just as it is beneficial to our well-being to explore and acknowledge our individual identity—contributing greatly to Vanden Abeele's person-specific factors—it is also vital for us to investigate and identify device- and context-specific factors of digital wellness. These factors are less visible to the end-user but contribute no less greatly to our overall well-being, as illustrated by her dynamic systems approach. For individuals to effectively integrate technology into their lives and routines, they must not only have a thorough knowledge of the available choices but also a clear picture of all relevant factors, whether overt or concealed.

ALGORITHMICALLY RENDERED REFLECTIONS

In the pursuit of a whole, fulfilling life, humans constantly seek ways to become healthier, happier, and more productive. As Sherry Turkle observed, "Overwhelmed by the pace that technology makes possible, we think about how new, more efficient technologies might help dig us out."[25] It is in this overwhelmed information state that our desire to grow and improve often manifests in a datafication of wellness.

According to anthropologist Veronica Barassi, "One of the big changes brought by surveillance capitalism is the introduction of the cultural belief that data offers us a deeper form of knowledge," inspiring individuals to record and hoard data on their mundane daily activities in the name of productivity, efficiency, and wellness.[26] Many popular apps and technologies are created in support of individual well-being; everything from traditional notions of wellness—such as fitness, dieting, and mental health—to apps that support financial, social, recreational, and intellectual well-being. The hope is that with enough data, we can discover an objective, unbiased reflection of our lives, habits, and fundamental self.

But what can we learn from tracking our daily behaviors? To what extent can we really quantify ourselves or the human experience? Is data, as many espouse, truly a mirror of our authentic selves? Hildebrandt theorizes an "incomputable self" essential to human existence which resists quantification, arguing that we must "*protect what counts but cannot be counted.*"[27] Ergo, we must ask, what is the cost of technologically mediated self-knowledge?

As explicated by Hartman-Caverly and me, these self-tracking activities *can* and *do* have positive impacts on individuals; however, the quantified self—defined as "self-knowledge through numbers"—is only scratching the surface of the surveillance architectures at play and highlights what Shoshanna Zuboff calls "the problem of the two texts."[28] The public-facing text—services marketed by platforms, especially social connection and self-expression—and the shadow text—the extraction and exploitation of behavioral surplus data, deliberately hidden from the user—of these technologies reveal vastly different intentions, creating a direct need for the integration of privacy literacy into digital wellness.

WHAT'S PRIVACY GOT TO DO WITH IT?

Privacy is notoriously difficult to define. As central to the human experience, it seems a contradiction that most individuals—who could not live a fully actualized life without privacy—cannot describe its meaning. I favor the straightforward definition offered by Garret Keizer, who asserts that privacy is a "resistance to being used against one's will."[29] That human impulse to resist interference and manipulation varies in its expression from culture to culture yet maintains its essence across contexts, so much so that it is included in the United Nations' Universal Declaration of Human Rights.[30]

While there is a desire to distill this cultural universal into a succinct characterization, in reality, it is highly nuanced. The Six Private I's Privacy Conceptual Model provides a framework with which to discuss the varying dimensions that span from our most exposed and vulnerable surface—that of interaction and isolation—to our most protected and unknowable foundation—individual identity.[31] At its core, privacy protects our ability to have a sense of individual *identity*, including our innermost thoughts, morals, and personality. This is followed by our capacity to form independent thoughts and beliefs, explore our curiosities, and embark on creative endeavors with our *intellect*. The next sphere, *integrity*, refers to both *bodily integrity*—our right to literally be left alone and to enjoy spatial privacy—and *contextual integrity*, which is when the right people know the right things about us at the right time. Bordering that is *intimacy*, which refers to the shared privacy or confidentiality that is necessary to have intimate relationships with loved ones and close friends. And finally, at its outermost sphere, privacy protects our *interaction* and *isolation*—our right to freedom of association and ability to voluntarily withdraw into solitude.

These privacy dimensions have obvious parallels to facets of individual well-being, as outlined in figure 2.1. Direct comparisons can be made, though the relationships are not finite or isolated as they do not account for the interrelated, complex nature of these systems. The Six Private I's Privacy Conceptual Model depicts the increasingly impervious nature of each concentric zone of agency while, in contrast, the wellness wheel characterizes dimensions of wellness as actively connected and interdependent. While the dynamics of each model differ, the relationship between privacy and wellness is symbiotic and can be used to develop a new model of digital wellness that thoroughly considers the increasingly

Data is Not a Mirror   31

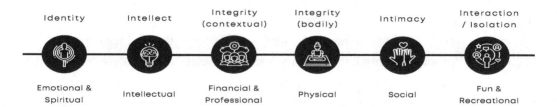

FIGURE 2.1

Depicts direct parallels of privacy dimensions outlined in the Six Private I's Privacy Conceptual Model to various wellness dimensions. CC BY-SA the author

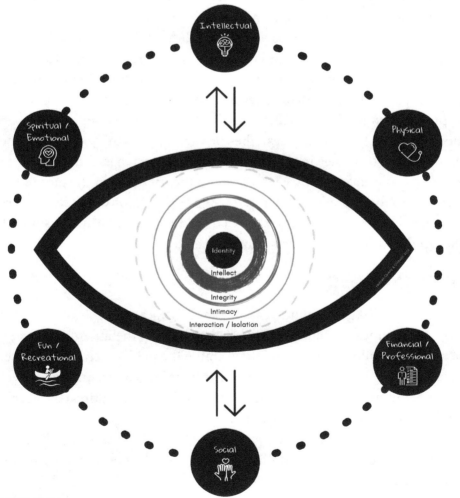

FIGURE 2.2

The Privacy-Digital Wellness Model illustrates the reciprocal relationship between the spheres of privacy as outlined in the Six Private I's Privacy Conceptual Framework and various wellness dimensions. CC BY-SA the author

permeable boundaries of privacy in the context of individual well-being, as illustrated in figure 2.2. The deeper the zone of privacy, the greater the potential for harm or benefit to individual well-being.

Violations of privacy often have cascading effects on individual well-being, with each zone of privacy having its own unique impact based on the infringement. For example, a bodily integrity violation, such as revenge porn, could have a major impact on mental health, intimate relationships, and professional aspirations.[32] In contrast, activities in the service of each wellness dimension can lead to privacy violations within a specific sphere. For instance, use of a dating app in the service of social and emotional well-being could lead to targeted advertising or a data breach that could inadvertently expose an individual's sexuality or gender designation, upsetting their contextual integrity and identity.[33]

I argue that the strength of each wellness dimension is directly correlated to the *autonomy* and *control* an individual exerts over related spheres of privacy. Under this presumption, *loss of control* over aspects of privacy has undeniably negative impacts on associated dimensions of well-being. This loss of control is often precipitated by the surveillance architectures inherent to our increasingly connected world. Julie Cohen describes privacy as "breathing room for socially situated subjects to engage in processes of boundary management through which they define and redefine themselves."[34] As boundaries blur in the face of ubiquitous connectivity, it is evident that the reciprocal relationship between privacy and wellness is exacerbated and amplified by the hidden harms of surveillance capitalism that threaten boundary management.

HIDDEN HARMS

The intersection of digital wellness and privacy becomes most glaring in the tension between the wellness benefits afforded to the user and the inherent obligation to corporate profitability. If we choose to examine the public-facing text, we see the ideal, net positive of these technologies. The benefits are vast and seductive with promises to automate, gamify, and improve our daily lives, ultimately assisting in goal achievement and self-actualization.

Most digital wellness approaches suggest that simple awareness of technology dependencies leads to user control; however, research shows that disconnecting from social media does not produce long-term, sustainable behavioral changes and is merely a Band-Aid on wellness concerns.[35] These practices are largely focused on individuals seeking equilibrium and control within the established system—a system built upon information asymmetries that force systemic coercion of digital participation and present no meaningful alternatives.[36] As critiqued by Hartman-Caverly and me, while digital minimalism practices can be helpful and are often the best that we can do in the face of digital resignation, they only address *individual responsibility* and do not adequately challenge *systemic issues* and subsequent privacy implications.[37]

To tackle systemic issues, digital wellness approaches require examination of the shadow text, which illuminates the commercial interests and potential pitfalls of adoption. The privacy theater in which Big Tech participates—such as offering built-in tools to assist in reducing the influence of technology while continually implementing techniques to intentionally manipulate us into increased engagement for profit—set us up to be the antagonist in our own story, distorting the digital reflection through which we view ourselves. We cannot overlook the potential hidden harms in our quest for individual well-being because our seemingly innocuous digital participation can come back to haunt us, due to datafication—"the transformation of social action into online quantified data, thus allowing for real-time tracking and predictive analysis"[38]—and what danah boyd labels the properties of networked publics—wherein the web data we produce is persistent, replicable, scalable, and searchable.[39] Digital wellness must account for these data harms in order to address and combat privacy violations that could indelibly damage our well-being. We are running a marathon with potential life-long impact, not a short-distance sprint. Screen time monitoring and digital detoxes are not the panaceas to our problems.

MIRROR, MIRROR ON THE WALL, CAN BIG DATA TELL US ANYTHING AT ALL? DATAISM AND THE ATTENTION ECONOMY

Mobile health is estimated to be a $100–$300 billion market by 2026, accompanied by wearable technology's projected valuation of $118 billion by 2028.[40] Why is our health data so incredibly profitable? While *our* goals may be to improve personal well-being, wellness-supporting technologies primarily exist to collect and process our sensitive biometric data through what Zuboff labels the extraction/prediction imperative.[41] Our data is lucrative because it enables Big Tech to study, predict, and nudge our behaviors toward profitable ends.

Akin to, and perhaps borne from, these capitalist data collection practices is a new, accepted paradigm within academia and society, known as dataism—"a belief in the objectivity of quantification and in the potential of tracking all kinds of human behavior and sociality through online data."[42] The idea is that if behavioral data is collected surreptitiously and outside of an individual's knowledge, then that behavior is unsullied by surveillance-induced self-censorship and thus represents pure human behavior.[43] The assumption that big data is an authentic reflection of humanity serves as justification for surveillance capitalism's invasive data collection. However, dataism does not account for the fact that platform ecosystems are built upon systemic manipulation to monetize user attention.[44]

When applied to the current information ecosystem existing under surveillance capitalism, attention is *essential* to datafication. Surveillance architectures are designed to not only monitor our behavior but also to manipulate it at scale. To discuss and understand concepts relating to attention engineering, it is first important to understand the attention economy that undergirds surveillance capitalism, where our attention is a finite resource.[45] As hypothesized by social scientist Herbert Simon, "[I]n an information-rich world, the wealth of information means a dearth of something else: a scarcity of whatever it is that information consumes. What information consumes is rather obvious: it consumes the attention of its recipients."[46] It is the deficit of time that generates value, stirring Big Tech's motivation to greedily capture as much user attention as possible.

We often characterize the process behind behavioral data capture as surveillance, the act of observing and recording user activity on-platform. A more apt label would be captology, an *active manipulation* of user behavior to *perpetuate* data capture. These traps, as labeled by Nick Seaver, are alterations of an online environment to encourage profitable behaviors in the user.[47] It is within these traps, where "to a large extent *we are* the environment that is being reconfigured"[48] that we discover the crux of technology's influence on privacy and wellness, the antithesis of our privacy definition, the "resistance to being used against one's will."[49]

Attention engineering is a series of methods with which surveillance capitalists shape our behaviors by keeping us engaged with their products and services through captivation metrics, which gauge "the ability of a system to capture user attention, or 'engagement.'"[50] User activity logs containing our behavioral surplus data are taken and interpreted through a psychological lens with the sole purpose of manipulating behavior to conform to desired outcomes—in most cases, this means keeping users on-platform for lengthier, sustained periods of time. Platforms achieve this through recommendation engines or algorithmic personalization, which mathematically predict personal preferences through captivation metrics created from our data exhaust.[51] "Algorithmic recommendation has settled deep into the infrastructure of online cultural life, where it has become practically unavoidable."[52] Much like ubiquitous technology hides its power in shaping social norms, personalization's success is due to its pervasiveness, with its influence disguised by its banality. Personalization is tediously commonplace, with nearly all information consumed through algorithmic intervention.

Two highly recognizable persuasive design features are infinite scroll and autoplay. Both are forms of intermittent conditioning, a technique borrowed from the gambling industry, meant to lull users into a state of immersion, time and space distortion, and self-forgetting to increase engagement.[53] Just think of YouTube's watch next, Amazon's product recommendations, or TikTok's "For You" feed—personalization has become entrenched in our online experiences and shapes how we encounter everything from potential purchases to news and entertainment to our relationships and *selves*. As we get lost in the hypnotic scroll and boundless feeds of information designed *just for us*, we are ironically and metaphorically "feeding" the algorithmic beast with increased behavioral metrics, proliferating our own chronic captivation and influencing our self-image and well-being.

These engagement traps lead us to the next form of attention engineering, choice architecture, which consist of system design features used to subtly condition and reward user activity.[54] These include push notifications and engagement metrics—think likes, shares, retweets, and other ways we interact with social media content. Calculated design choices are made as to which quantifications are made visible to the user and which remain hidden, based on what will increase engagement.[55]

Largely living our lives in highly commodified digital spaces, it feels as though all our actions, including our innermost thoughts, have become commodities. In this environment, we view our social capital through the lens of quantification—where success is measured by social media metrics.[56] This has led to what Benjamin Grosser calls the "metricated social self" where individuals express their agency through engagement metrics—our likes and retweets essentially represent our tastes, beliefs, and opinions.[57] In reverse, without engagement and high metrics on our content, the algorithm renders us virtually invisible on-platform. For many, this impacts well-being, identity, and self-worth. This algorithmic power essentially "results in a reversal of the Panopticon, where the threat of constant visibility is changed into a threat of constant invisibility."[58] What a clever way to seduce us into unwittingly giving up our data and privacy—by playing upon our insecurities and threatening our right to be known.

The metricated social self, a perception that benefits Big Tech's data-hungry practices, is in direct conflict with Hildebrandt's "incomputable self."[59] Big Tech would like us to buy into the ideologies of dataism—that data is a mirror with which we can view our true selves—because it is to their benefit. Yet, acceptance of this belief puts our privacy, identity, and well-being at risk. As Hildebrandt asserts,

> …the self develops in relation to the world it inhabits. Overdependence on computational decision-systems may result in a shrinking of the inner self, as we learn to internalize the logic of computational feedback to better adapt to our new environment. The elasticity, ex-centricity and ecological nature of the inner mind are what makes us human, but thereby also vulnerable to being hacked by an environment that is conducive to cognitive automation.[60]

Though we are susceptible to persuasion, we need not yield our identity and actions to algorithmic powers. We can yet choose autonomy and agency, privacy, and well-being.

WELLNESS IMPLICATIONS OF DATA CAPTURE

If digital wellness is the *intentional use* of technology in *maintaining awareness* of, and *exercising choices* toward, one's optimal existence, then what are the consequences of these hidden harms? How do these manipulative practices, concealed within surveillance capitalists' shadow text, impede our ability to actively work toward a more successful, optimal existence?

For one, time and attention are truly finite resources that cannot be restored. When we lose ourselves to mindless scrolling and experience fragmented attention we can suffer from diminished relationships, hobbies, and intellectual endeavors—in short, we lose the capacity for fun, fulfilling lives without ample time and attention to dedicate to those ventures that *matter*. This is not to say that wasting time with fun, mindless activities is wrong, but rather that the *loss of control* built into these apps and technologies by design diminishes our agency while also violating our privacy. The attention economy encourages optimizing everything we do toward efficiency. "[W]hen a market value is assigned to every utterance, we're acquiescing to the premise that no other sort of value matters as much."[61] The context collapse wrought by ubiquitous mobile connectivity has broken down the walls personal and professional, leading us to assign value to time in ways that do not allow us the space for leisure and reflection.

The immersive, personalized online experience rendered from excessive personal data collection has also created filter bubbles—"the intellectual isolation that can occur when websites make use of algorithms to selectively assume the information a user would want to see, and then give information to the user according to this assumption"[62]—shaping individuals' exaggerated worldviews and perspectives. These echo chambers greatly contribute to the increasing divisiveness we are experiencing within society. While "fake news" and misinformation are certainly major societal concerns, the unchecked algorithmic intervention through which we progressively encounter our world is the underlying, latent threat. Entrenched in content that entertains and enrages, never challenging ourselves to empathize or think critically, we simply float in a state of intellectual isolation. We have become comfortably numb in our personalized ouroboros of self-righteousness.

As demonstrated by countless studies and articles, the consequences of invasive data collection can be vast and far-reaching. While awareness of surveillance capitalism among the public is on the rise, the mechanisms and extent of algorithmic influence are still obscured. Even if cognizance continues to increase, algorithms are still black boxes, treated as precious trade secrets outside of the public's knowledge or oversight. This algorithmic opacity is problematic when decision-making can cause real-life harm.[63]

Consciously given and automatically monitored data is collected about us every day in both online and "real-world" environments. Beyond merely assembling vast amounts of data about groups and individuals, these data are applied to machine learning algorithms to create predictions about us through use of modeled data.[64] What most believe is harmlessly utilized for targeted advertising, is also being deployed to organize individual, autonomous human beings into convenient categories. Our innermost thoughts, intellectual inquiries, relationships, and recreational diversions—made possible by the spheres of privacy outlined in the Six Private I's—are being exposed to corporate entities and reduced to flattened representations for the ease of increased automation. We are stripped of our uniqueness to render stereotypes of convenience. The confidence with which machine learning systems are deployed leads to over-deterministic assumptions about us due to the choice architecture environments that make inferences about us, our desires, how we want to spend our time, and more.[65] Manipulation is built into the framework, so how can the subsequent data provide a clear, untainted reflection of an individual?

As we come to rely more and more on the ever-present apps and mobile technologies in our lives, an unconscionable amount of personal data is continuously generated. For many, the scale and scope of such data make predictive analytics a foregone solution to societal issues. Despite their seeming objectivity, algorithms embody ideological systems within their code and as a result further reproduce society's existing inequities in what Ruha Benjamin calls the "New Jim Code."[66] These algorithmic decision-making systems threaten the financial, professional, and personal wellness of individuals, particularly those within marginalized groups creating disparate impacts.[67] Predictive analytics using data to reduce individuals' decisions and lived experiences into dehumanized categories removes agency, context, and nuance. Increasingly, individuals are denied critical social services and economic mobility opportunities such as housing, unemployment, food stamps, job interviews, and more due to algorithmic decision-making systems that operate with little to no oversight or accountability.[68]

In many cases, these surveillance capitalist practices do more than impede our ability to work toward a more successful, optimal existence—they actively *work against* our capacity to self-determine our futures. As pervasive data collection is progressively normalized and ceaselessly introduced into all spheres of society, generations of citizens are being raised with their entire lifespan—from *before* birth—monitored and recorded.[69] We cannot know the impact of such inescapable surveillance, but Barassi hypothesizes that children are losing their right to self-construct and self-define in public with futures characterized by data-inferred narratives completely out of their control.[70] Our right to the future tense—"the right to act free of the influence of illegitimate forces that operate outside our awareness to influence, modify, and condition our behavior"—is being threatened.[71] Whether accurate or not, digital profiling is becoming the foregone decision-making model within our society, consequences reverberating amid facets of privacy and well-being.

REJECTING OUR MANIPULATED REFLECTIONS

More time spent on the platform leads to more activity logged and increased data capture, contributing to heightened personalized experiences, creating algorithmic feedback loops that perpetuate the cycle of engagement. To Big Tech, the accuracy of the user profile, or capturing the essence of an individual, is far less valuable than their desired outcome: engagement. If we are captivated and thus trapped, they have succeeded in their intent, whether improving our lives or not. Facilitating individual well-being and self-improvement is *not* their goal, even if it may be ours. And our intent amounts to little when power clearly leans heavily on the side of corporations. By recognizing the connection between privacy and personal well-being, we can explore opportunities for both conscious consideration of these subtle persuasive design choices and their effects on our attention, along with advocacy and government oversight of personal data capture and algorithmic decision-making systems.

The Privacy-Digital Wellness Model is one way to make links between privacy and personal well-being unambiguous. The model serves as both a tool to proactively preserve the strength of wellness dimensions and as a framework to analyze the wellness implications of data harm—both real and potential. First, it operates as a cost-benefit analysis of wellness-supporting technology integration against potential data harms. As we explore and introduce new wellness-supporting technologies into our routine, we should assess data collection practices and algorithmic influences to preemptively set privacy boundaries. Will the new Apple Watch period and ovulation tracking feature assist women in their birth control and family planning? Very possibly! Or could that data—whether by data breach or brokerage—be used to control women's bodily autonomy and right to choose? It may not seem *likely*, but it *is possible*, especially given the privacy aftershocks in a post-Roe America.[72] Everyone's decision will look different when weighing wellness benefits against privacy risks, but the model will make hidden harms explicit. Reciprocally, the model functions as a framework to identify and examine the impact of privacy violations upon facets of well-being. How do our algorithmically rendered reflections reverberate through our lives upsetting the balance of our overall wellness and self-image? As we lose autonomy and control over our private spaces—both physical and intangible—the strength of our wellness is diminished with cascading impacts, based on the depth of the privacy sphere. The Privacy-Digital Wellness Model serves as a tool to map these snowballing effects and articulate resulting harm.

As we have seen, we are increasingly self-constructing in online spaces.[73] In the act of self-construction, we are manipulated into the quantification of our thoughts and behaviors, then thrown into feedback loops—through our newsfeeds and other algorithmic personalization features—that reinforce engagement through persuasive design, whether it brings out our best selves or not. During this process, we leave behind data exhaust that leads to behavioral profiling—flattened representations of who we are based on commercial interests. In our quest for health, wellness, and self-improvement, we are exploited, secretly contributing to our shrinking agency and autonomy by accepting the inevitability of the surveillance architectures hidden within everyday technologies.

These practices raise huge questions regarding individual identity, choice, and consent. While we *think* we are digital citizens who are participating in online public spaces to develop our identity, share our thoughts, and make social connections, we are more akin to what Veronica Barassi calls "datafied citizens" who are defined by the narratives created through our digital exhaust.[74] Can cookie-cutter profiles really embody human complexity? After all, "a representation is not the same as what is represented."[75] When we are force-fed content based on our *manipulated* behaviors, how can we mature beyond our past or current selves?

Digital wellness requires time and space to discover who we are outside of algorithmic forces. Time, and by extension attention, is the one truly finite resource in our lives. We can never rewind life or get back the hours spent illuminated by the soft glow of our smartphones while we remain vacantly unaware of the world surrounding us. Collectively, we need to ask ourselves who we want to be and how we want to relate to each other as humans. Is this the future we want to embrace? Do we want our thoughts, hobbies, intellectual inquiries, errant thoughts, relationships, and identities to be monetized and manipulated for commercial interests? Beyond that, do we want our stolen moments of highly personal, decontextualized details to *define* us and influence or determine our future opportunities? Standing on the precipice of a future that would have us blindly accept the tradeoff of ubiquitous surveillance for the convenience of "smart" technologies and algorithmic personalization, we must ask ourselves if we are ready to cede control of our agency. Is the shallow pool of luxury surveillance how we would like to characterize wellness? The fusion of digital wellness and privacy literacy offers us a model to address the issues of agency, self-determination, and our "right to the future tense."[76]

Hildebrandt states that "our self is born from the *friction caused by* and the *resistance against* the way others address and define us."[77] Let us resist our assigned algorithmic categories and choose to define ourselves. Let us choose the individual well-being that privacy affords us through the incomputable self.

ACKNOWLEDGMENTS

Much appreciation to Andrew Wesolek for his kind and insightful chapter review. And a special thank you to my privacy partner in crime, Sarah, for pushing me to be a better librarian and scholar since the day we met—this, my first solo publication, would never have happened without your support.

NOTES

1. "Internet/Broadband Fact Sheet," Pew Research Center, April 7, 2021, https://www.pewresearch.org/internet/fact-sheet/internet-broadband/.
2. "Mobile Fact Sheet," Pew Research Center, April 7, 2021, https://www.pewresearch.org/internet/fact-sheet/mobile/.
3. "Social Media Fact Sheet," Pew Research Center, April 7, 2021, https://www.pewresearch.org/internet/fact-sheet/social-media/.

4. Sherry Turkle, *Alone Together: Why We Expect More from Technology and Less from Each Other* (New York: Basic Books, 2011).
5. John Meyer, "Survey finds "alarming" drop in outdoor recreation, especially among kids," *The Denver Post* (January 20, 2020), https://theknow-old.denverpost.com/2020/01/29/us-kids-outdoor-recreation-down/232438/; Eleanor Krause and Isabel V. Sawhill, "How free time became screen time," Brookings, September 13, 2016, https://www.brookings.edu/blog/social-mobility-memos/2016/09/13/how-free-time-became-screen-time/.
6. "Data Never Sleeps 9.0," DOMO, 2022, https://www.domo.com/learn/infographic/data-never-sleeps-9.
7. Michael Winnick, "Putting a Finger on Our Phone Obsession," *dscout*, June 16, 2016, https://blog.dscout.com/mobile-touches; Andrew Perrin and Sara Atske, "About Three-in-Ten U.S. Adults Say They Are 'Almost Constantly' Online," Pew Research Center, March 26, 2021, https://www.pewresearch.org/fact-tank/2021/03/26/about-three-in-ten-u-s-adults-say-they-are-almost-constantly-online/.
8. Joseph Firth, John Torous, Brendon Stubbs, Josh A. Firth, Genevieve Z. Steiner, Lee Smith, Mario Alvarez-Jimenez, et al., "The 'Online Brain': How the Internet May Be Changing Our Cognition," *World Psychiatry* 18, 2 (2019): 119–29, https://doi.org/10.1002/wps.20617.
9. Monica Anderson and Jingjing Jiang, "Teens, Friendships and Online Groups," Pew Research Center, November 28, 2018, https://www.pewresearch.org/internet/2018/11/28/teens-friendships-and-online-groups/; Turkle, *Alone Together*.
10. Jessica Roberts and Michael Koliska, "The Effects of Ambient Media: What Unplugging Reveals About Being Plugged In," *First Monday* 19, 8 (2014), https://doi.org/10.5210/fm.v19i8.5220; Susan D. Moeller, "Going 24 Hours without Media," The world UNPLUGGED, 2019, https://worldunplugged.wordpress.com/.
11. Roberts and Koliska, "The Effects of Ambient Media."
12. Turkle, *Alone Together*, 175.
13. Brendan Mackie, "Why Can't We Be Friends," *Real Life Magazine* (July 1, 2021), https://reallifemag.com/why-cant-we-be-friends/.
14. Grace Brown, "They Saw a YouTube Video. Then They Got Tourette's," *Wired* (January 9, 2021), https://www.wired.co.uk/article/tourettes-youtube-jan-zimmermann; Julie Jargon, "Teen Girls Are Developing Tics. Doctors Say TikTok Could Be a Factor," *Wall Street Journal* (October 9, 2021), https://www.wsj.com/articles/teen-girls-are-developing-tics-doctors-say-tiktok-could-be-a-factor-11634389201.
15. Georgia Wells, Jeff Horwitz, and Deepa Seetharaman, "Facebook Knows Instagram Is Toxic for Many Teen Girls, Company Documents Show," *The Wall Street Journal* (September 14, 2021), https://www.wsj.com/articles/facebook-knows-instagram-is-toxic-for-teen-girls-company-documents-show-11631620739.
16. Mirielle Hildebrandt, "Privacy as Protection of the Incomputable Self: From Agnostic to Agonistic Machine Learning," *Theoretical Inquiries in Law* 20, no. 1 (2019): 89, https://doi.org/10.1515/til-2019-0004.
17. Mariek Vanden Abeele, "Digital Wellbeing as a Dynamic Construct," *Communication Theory* (2020): 3, https://doi.org/10.1093/ct/qtaa024.
18. "The Six Dimensions of Wellness," National Wellness Institute, 2020, https://nationalwellness.org/resources/six-dimensions-of-wellness/.
19. Mariek Vanden Abeele, Ralf De Wolf, and Rich Ling, "Mobile Media and Social Space: How Anytime, Anyplace Connectivity Structures Everyday Life," *Media and Communication* 6, no. 2 (2018): 5–8, https://doi.org/10.17645/mac.v6i2.1399.
20. Geoffrey Lightfoot and Tomasz Piotr Wisniewski, "Information Asymmetry and Power in a Surveillance Society," *Information and Organization* 24, (2014): 214–35, https://doi.org/10.1016/j.infoandorg.2014.09.001.

21. Alexandria Chisholm and Sarah Hartman-Caverly, "Privacy Literacy: From Doomscrolling to Digital Wellness," *portal: Libraries and the Academy* 22, no. 1 (2022), https://doi.org/10.1353/pla.2022.0009.
22. Vanden Abeele, "Digital Wellbeing," 6–7.
23. danah boyd, "Taken Out of Context: American Teen Sociality in Networked Publics" (PhD diss., University of California Berkeley, 2008).
24. Vanden Abeele, "Digital Wellbeing," 8–13.
25. Turkle, *Alone Together*, 280.
26. Veronica Barassi, *Child Data Citizen: How Tech Companies Are Profiling Us from before Birth* (Cambridge, MA: MIT Press, 2020), 40.
27. Hildebrandt, "Privacy as Protection of the Incomputable Self," 96.
28. Sarah Hartman-Caverly and Alexandria Chisholm, "Wellness Beyond Measure: Privacy Dimensions of Digital Wellness," Vanderbilt University, March 25, 2021, https://doi.org/10.26207/2em6-0r88; "Quantified Self," accessed December 4, 2021, https://quantifiedself.com/; Shoshanna Zuboff, *The Age of Surveillance Capitalism: The Fight for a Human Future at the New Frontier of Power* (New York: Public Affairs, 2019), 185.
29. Garret Keizer, *Privacy* (New York: Picador, 2012), 20.
30. Irwin Altman, "Privacy Regulation: Culturally Universal or Culturally Specific," *Journal of Social Issues* 33, no. 3 (1977): 66–84, https://doi.org/10.1111/j.1540-4560.1977.tb01883.x; "Universal Declaration of Human Rights," United Nations, accessed November 20, 2021, https://www.un.org/en/about-us/universal-declaration-of-human-rights.
31. Sarah Hartman-Caverly and Alexandria Chisholm, "Privacy Literacy Instruction Practices in Academic Libraries: Past, Present, and Possibilities," *IFLA Journal* 46, no. 4 (2020): 306–07, https://doi.org/10.1177/0340035220956804; Sarah Hartman-Cavelry and Alexandria Chisholm, "Privacy as Respect for Persons," in *Practicing Privacy Literacy in Academic Libraries*, eds. Sarah Hartman-Caverly and Alexandria Chisholm (Chicago: ACRL, 2023).
32. Mudasir Kamal and William J. Newman, "Revenge Pornography: Mental Health Implications and Related Legislation," *Journal of the American Academy of Psychiatry and the Law* 44, no. 3 (2016): 359–67.
33. Joseph Cox, "The Inevitable Weaponization of App Data is Here," Vice, July 21, 2021, https://www.vice.com/en/article/pkbxp8/grindr-location-data-priest-weaponization-app.
34. Julie Cohen, "Turning Privacy Inside Out," *Theoretical Inquiries into Law* 20, no. 1 (2019): 12–13, https://doi.org/10.1515/til-2019-0002.
35. Nancy K. Baym, Kelly B. Wagman, and Christopher J. Persaud, "Mindfully Scrolling: Rethinking Facebook After Time Deactivated," *Social Media + Society* 6, no. 2 (2020): 1, https://doi.org/10.1177/2056305120919105.
36. Barassi, *Child Data Citizen*, 34.
37. Chisholm and Hartman-Caverly, "Doomscrolling to Digital Wellness."
38. Jose van Dijck, "Datafication, Dataism and Dataveillance: Big Data Between Scientific Paradigm and Ideology," *Surveillance & Society* 12, no. 2 (2014): 198.
39. boyd, "Out of Context," 27.
40. "mHealth Apps Market Size to Reach USD 101,550 Million by 2026 at CAGR 18.4% | Valuates Reports," CISION PR Newswire, March 15, 2021, https://www.prnewswire.com/news-releases/mhealth-apps-market-size-to-reach-usd-101-550-million-by-2026-at-cagr-18-4--valuates-reports-301247312.html; "Wearable Technology Market Size, Share & Trends Analysis Report By Product," Grand View Research, October 2021, https://www.grandviewresearch.com/industry-analysis/wearable-technology-market.
41. Zuboff, *The Age of Surveillance Capitalism*, 87–92.
42. van Dijck, "Datafication," 201.
43. Angela Xiao Wu and Harsh Taneja, "Platform Enclosure of Human Behavior and its Measurement: Using Behavioral Trace Data Against Platform Episteme," *new media & society* 23, no. 9 (2021), https://doi.org/10.1177/1461444820933547.

44. Wu and Taneja, "Platform Enclosure," 2654.
45. Herbert A. Simon, "Designing Organizations for an Information-Rich World," in *Computers, Communications, and the Public Interest*, ed. Martin Greenberger (Baltimore, MD: Johns Hopkins University Press, 1971), 40.
46. Simon, "Designing Organizations," 40.
47. Nick Seaver, "Captivating Algorithms: Recommender Systems as Traps," *Journal of Material Culture* 24, no. 4 (2019): 421–36, https://doi.org/10.1177/1359183518820366.
48. Hildebrandt, "Privacy as Protection of the Incomputable Self," 105.
49. Keizer, *Privacy*, 20.
50. Seaver, "Captivating Algorithms," 429.
51. Michael Schrage, *Recommendation Engines* (Cambridge, MA: MIT Press, 2020), 2.
52. Seaver, "Captivating Algorithms," 431.
53. Christian Montag, Bernd Lachmann, Marc Herrlich, and Katharina Zweig, "Addictive Features of Social Media/Messenger Platforms and Freemium Games against the Background of Psychological and Economic Theories," *International Journal of Environmental Research and Public Health* 16, no. 14 (2019): 5, https://doi.org/10.3390/ijerph16142612.
54. Richard H. Thaler, Cass R. Sunstein, and John P. Balz, "Choice Architecture," SSRN (2010), https://papers.ssrn.com/sol3/papers.cfm?abstract_id=1583509.
55. Benjamin Grosser, "What Do Metrics Want? How Quantification Prescribes Social Interaction on Facebook," *Computational Culture*, no. 4 (2014): 7–9, http://computationalculture.net/what-do-metrics-want/.
56. Grosser, "What Do Metrics Want?," 5.
57. Ibid., 9–12.
58. Ibid., 14.
59. Hildebrandt, "Incomputable Self".
60. Ibid., 105.
61. Kaitlyn Tiffany, "You Can't Escape the Attention Economy," *The Atlantic* (June 14, 2021), https://www.theatlantic.com/technology/archive/2021/06/how-memes-become-money/619189/.
62. "Filter Bubble," Techopedia, last modified May 17, 2018, https://www.techopedia.com/definition/28556/filter-bubble.
63. Hildebrandt, "Incomputable Self," 99.
64. Chris Ip, "Who Controls Your Data?," Engadget, September 4, 2018, https://www.engadget.com/2018-09-04-who-controls-your-data.html.
65. Hildebrandt, "Incomputable Self," 86.
66. Ruha Benjamin, *Race After Technology* (Cambridge: Polity, 2019).
67. Cathy O'Neil, *Weapons of Math Destruction* (New York: Broadway Books, 2016); Salon Barocas and Andrew D. Selbst, "Big Data's Disparate Impact," *California Law Review* 104, (2016), http://dx.doi.org/10.2139/ssrn.2477899.
68. Karen Hao, "The Coming War on the Hidden Algorithms that Trap People in Poverty," *MIT Technology Review* (December 4, 2020), https://www.technologyreview.com/2020/12/04/1013068/algorithms-create-a-poverty-trap-lawyers-fight-back/; Lauren Kirchner, "When Zombie Data Costs You a Home," The Markup, October 6, 2020, https://themarkup.org/locked-out/2020/10/06/zombie-criminal-records-housing-background-checks.
69. Barassi, *Child Data Citizen*.
70. Ibid., 133–50.
71. Zuboff, *Surveillance Capitalism*, 194.
72. Nicole Wetsman, "Apple adds souped-up period and ovulation tracking to Apple Watch Series 8," The Verge, September 7, 2022, https://www.theverge.com/2022/9/7/23341259/apple-watch-series-8-ovulation-period-tracking-temperature-sensor; Nicole Wetsman, "Cycle-tracking apps

stand behind their privacy policies as Roe teeters," The Verge, May 6, 2022, https://www.theverge.com/2022/5/6/23060000/period-apps-privacy-abortion-roe-supreme-court.
73. Turkle, *Alone Together*; Barassi, *Child Data Citizen*.
74. Barassi, *Child Data Citizen*, 10–13.
75. Hildebrandt, "Incomputable Self," 90.
76. Zuboff, *Surveillance Capitalism*, 328–47.
77. Hildebrandt, "Incomputable Self," 89.

BIBLIOGRAPHY

Altman, Irwin. "Privacy Regulation: Culturally Universal or Culturally Specific." *Journal of Social Issues* 33, no. 3 (1977): 66–84. https://doi.org/10.1111/j.1540-4560.1977.tb01883.x.

Anderson, Monica, and Jingjing Jiang. "Teens, Friendships and Online Groups." Pew Research Center. November 28, 2018. https://www.pewresearch.org/internet/2018/11/28/teens-friendships-and-online-groups/.

Barassi, Veronica. *Child Data Citizen: How Tech Companies Are Profiling Us from Before Birth*. Cambridge, MA: The MIT Press, 2020.

Barocas, Salon, and Andrew D. Selbst. "Big Data's Disparate Impact." *California Law Review* 104 (2016): 671–732. http://dx.doi.org/10.2139/ssrn.2477899.

Baym, Nancy K., Kelly B. Wagman, and Christopher J. Persaud. "Mindfully Scrolling: Rethinking Facebook After Time Deactivated." *Social Media + Society* 6, no. 2 (2020): 1–10, https://doi.org/10.1177/2056305120919105.

Benjamin, Ruha. *Race After Technology*. Cambridge: Polity, 2019.

boyd, danah. "Taken Out of Context: American Teen Sociality in Networked Publics." PhD diss., University of California Berkeley, 2008.

Brown, Grace. "They Saw a YouTube Video. Then They Got Tourette's." *Wired* (January 9, 2021). https://www.wired.co.uk/article/tourettes-youtube-jan-zimmermann.

Chisholm, Alexandria, and Sarah Hartman-Caverly. "Privacy Literacy: From Doomscrolling to Digital Wellness." *portal: Libraries and the Academy* 22, no. 1 (2022). https://doi.org/10.1353/pla.2022.0009.

CISION PR Newswire. "mHealth Apps Market Size to Reach USD 101,550 Million by 2026 at CAGR 18.4%." Valuates Reports. March 15, 2021. https://www.prnewswire.com/news-releases/mhealth-apps-market-size-to-reach-usd-101-550-million-by-2026-at-cagr-18-4--valuates-reports-301247312.html.

Cohen, Julie. "Turning Privacy Inside Out." *Theoretical Inquiries into Law* 20, no. 1 (2019): 12–13. https://doi.org/10.1515/til-2019-0002.

Cox, Joseph. "The Inevitable Weaponization of App Data is Here." Vice, July 21, 2021. https://www.vice.com/en/article/pkbxp8/grindr-location-data-priest-weaponization-app.

DOMO. "Data Never Sleeps 8.0." Accessed November 10, 2021. https://www.domo.com/learn/infographic/data-never-sleeps-8

Firth, Joseph, John Torous, Brendon Stubbs, Josh A. Firth, Genevieve Z. Steiner, Lee Smith, Mario Alvarez-Jimenez, et al., "The 'Online Brain': How the Internet May Be Changing Our Cognition." *World Psychiatry* 18, 2 (2019): 119–29. https://doi.org/10.1002/wps.20617.

Fogg, B. J., Gregory Cuellar, and David Danielson. "Motivating, Influencing, and Persuading Users." In *The Human-Computer Interaction Handbook*, edited by Andrew Sears and Julie A. Jacko. New York: Lawrence Erlbaum, 2008.

Grand View Research. "Wearable Technology Market Size, Share & Trends Analysis Report By Product." October 2021. https://www.grandviewresearch.com/industry-analysis/wearable-technology-market.

Grosser, Benjamin. "What Do Metrics Want? How Quantification Prescribes Social Interaction on Facebook." *Computational Culture*, no. 4 (2014). http://computationalculture.net/what-do-metrics-want/.

Hartman-Caverly, Sarah, and Alexandria Chisholm. "Privacy as Respect for Persons: Reimagining Privacy Literacy with the Six Private I's Framework." In *Practicing Privacy Literacy in Academic Libraries*, edited by Sarah Hartman-Caverly and Alexandria Chisholm. Chicago: ACRL, 2023.
———. "Privacy Literacy Instruction Practices in Academic Libraries: Past, Present, and Possibilities." *IFLA Journal* 46, no. 4 (2020): 305–27. https://doi.org/10.1177/0340035220956804.
———. "Wellness Beyond Measure: Privacy Dimensions of Digital Wellness." Vanderbilt University. March 26, 2021. https://doi.org/10.26207/2em6-0r88.
Hao, Karen. "The Coming War on the Hidden Algorithms that Trap People in Poverty." *MIT Technology Review* (December 4, 2020). https://www.technologyreview.com/2020/12/04/1013068/algorithms-create-a-poverty-trap-lawyers-fight-back/.
Hildebrandt, Mireille. "Privacy as the Protection of the Incomputable Self: From Agnostic to Agonistic Machine Learning." *Theoretical Inquiries in Law* 20, no. 1 (2019): 83–121. https://doi.org/10.1515/til-2019-0004.
Ip, Chris. "Who Controls Your Data?" Engadget. September 4, 2018. https://www.engadget.com/2018-09-04-who-controls-your-data.html.
Jargon, Julie. "Teen Girls Are Developing Tics. Doctors Say TikTok Could Be a Factor." *Wall Street Journal* (October 9, 2021). https://www.wsj.com/articles/teen-girls-are-developing-tics-doctors-say-tiktok-could-be-a-factor-11634389201.
Kamal, Mudasir, and William J. Newman. "Revenge Pornography: Mental Health Implications and Related Legislation." *Journal of the American Academy of Psychiatry and the Law* 44, no. 3 (2016): 359–67.
Keizer, Garret. *Privacy*. New York: Picador, 2012.
Kirchner, Lauren. "When Zombie Data Costs You a Home." The Markup. October 6, 2020. https://themarkup.org/locked-out/2020/10/06/zombie-criminal-records-housing-background-checks.
Krause, Eleanor, and Isabel V. Sawhill. "How free time became screen time." Brookings. September 13, 2016. https://www.brookings.edu/blog/social-mobility-memos/2016/09/13/how-free-time-became-screen-time/.
Lightfoot, Geoffrey, and Tomasz Piotr Wisniewski. "Information Asymmetry and Power in a Surveillance Society." *Information and Organization* 24, (2014): 214–35. https://doi.org/10.1016/j.infoandorg.2014.09.001.
Mackie, Brendan. "Why Can't We Be Friends." *Real Life Magazine* (July 1, 2021). https://reallifemag.com/why-cant-we-be-friends/.
McCarthy, Justin. "One in Five U.S. Adults Use Health Apps, Wearable Trackers." Gallup. December 11, 2019. https://news.gallup.com/poll/269096/one-five-adults-health-apps-wearable-trackers.aspx.
Meyer, John. "Survey finds "alarming" drop in outdoor recreation, especially among kids." *The Denver Post* (January 20, 2020). https://theknow-old.denverpost.com/2020/01/29/us-kids-outdoor-recreation-down/232438/.
Moeller, Susan D. "Going 24 Hours without Media." The World UNPLUGGED. 2019. https://worldunplugged.wordpress.com/.
Montag, Christian, Bernd Lachmann, Marc Herrlich, and Katharina Zweig. "Addictive Features of Social Media/Messenger Platforms and Freemium Games against the Background of Psychological and Economic Theories." *International Journal of Environmental Research and Public Health* 16, no. 14 (2019): 1–16. https://doi.org/10.3390/ijerph16142612.
National Wellness Institute. "The Six Dimensions of Wellness." Accessed March 9, 2021. https://nationalwellness.org/resources/six-dimensions-of-wellness/.
Odell, Jenny. *How to Do Nothing: Resisting the Attention Economy*. Brooklyn: Melville House, 2019.
O'Neil, Cathy. *Weapons of Math Destruction*. New York: Broadway Books, 2016.
Perrin, Andrew, and Sara Atske. "About three-in-ten U.S. adults say they are 'almost constantly' online." Pew Research Center. March 26, 2021. https://www.pewresearch.org/fact-tank/2021/03/26/about-three-in-ten-u-s-adults-say-they-are-almost-constantly-online/.

Pew Research Center. "Internet/Broadband Fact Sheet." April 7, 2021. https://www.pewresearch.org/internet/fact-sheet/internet-broadband/.

———. "Mobile Fact Sheet." April 7, 2021. https://www.pewresearch.org/internet/fact-sheet/mobile/.

———. "Social Media Fact Sheet." April 7, 2021. https://www.pewresearch.org/internet/fact-sheet/social-media/.

Quantified Self. "Quantified Self: Self Knowledge Through Numbers." Accessed December 4, 2021. https://quantifiedself.com/.

Roberts, Jessica, and Michael Koliska. "The Effects of Ambient Media: What Unplugging Reveals About Being Plugged In." *First Monday* 19, 8 (2014). https://doi.org/10.5210/fm.v19i8.5220.

Schrage, Michael. *Recommendation Engines*. Cambridge, MA: MIT Press, 2020.

Seaver, Nick. "Captivating Algorithms: Recommender Systems as Traps." *Journal of Material Culture* 24, no. 4 (2019): 421–36. https://doi.org/10.1177/1359183518820366.

Simon, Herbert A. "Designing Organizations for an Information-Rich World." In *Computers, Communications, and the Public Interest*, edited by Martin Greenberger. Baltimore, MD: Johns Hopkins University Press, 1971.

Statistia. "Number of mobile app downloads worldwide from 2016 to 2020." Last modified January 2021. https://www.statista.com/statistics/271644/worldwide-free-and-paid-mobile-app-store-downloads/.

———. "Percentage of the global population that used a mobile app or fitness tracking device to track their health as of 2016, by age." Last modified 2017. https://www.statista.com/statistics/742448/global-fitness-tracking-and-technology-by-age/.

Techopedia. "Filter Bubble." Last modified May 17, 2018. https://www.techopedia.com/definition/28556/filter-bubble.

Thaler, Richard H., Cass R. Sunstein, and John P. Balz. "Choice Architecture." SSRN (2010). https://papers.ssrn.com/sol3/papers.cfm?abstract_id=1583509.

Tiffany, Kaitlyn. "You Can't Escape the Attention Economy." *The Atlantic* (June 14, 2021). https://www.theatlantic.com/technology/archive/2021/06/how-memes-become-money/619189/.

Turkle, Sherry. *Alone Together: Why We Expect More from Technology and Less from Each Other*. New York: Basic Books, 2011.

United Nations. "Universal Declaration of Human Rights." Accessed November 20, 2021. https://www.un.org/en/about-us/universal-declaration-of-human-rights.

Vanden Abeele, Mariek M. P. "Digital Wellbeing as a Dynamic Construct." *Communication Theory* (2020): 1–24. https://doi.org/10.1093/ct/qtaa024.

Vanden Abeele, Mariek, Ralf De Wolf, and Rich Ling. "Mobile Media and Social Space: How Anytime, Anyplace Connectivity Structures Everyday Life." *Media and Communication* 6, no. 2 (2018): 5–14. https://doi.org/10.17645/mac.v6i2.1399.

van Dijck, Jose. "Datafication, Dataism and Dataveillance: Big Data Between Scientific Paradigm and Ideology." *Surveillance & Society* 12, no. 2 (2014): 197–208.

Vivrekar, Devangi. "Persuasive Design Techniques in the Attention Economy: User Awareness, Theory, and Ethics." Master's thesis, Stanford University, 2018.

Wells, Georgia, Jeff Horwitz, and Deepa Seetharaman. "Facebook Knows Instagram Is Toxic for Many Teen Girls, Company Documents Show." *The Wall Street Journal* (September 14, 2021). https://www.wsj.com/articles/facebook-knows-instagram-is-toxic-for-teen-girls-company-documents-show-11631620739.

Wetsman, Nicole. "Apple adds souped-up period and ovulation tracking to Apple Watch Series 8." The Verge. September 7, 2022. https://www.theverge.com/2022/9/7/23341259/apple-watch-series-8-ovulation-period-tracking-temperature-sensor.

———. "Cycle-tracking apps stand behind their privacy policies as Roe teeters." The Verge. May 6, 2022. https://www.theverge.com/2022/5/6/23060000/period-apps-privacy-abortion-roe-supreme-court.

Winnick, Michael. "Putting a Finger on Our Phone Obsession." *dscout*. June 16, 2016. https://blog.dscout.com/mobile-touches.

Wu, Angela Xiao, and Harsh Taneja. "Platform Enclosure of Human Behavior and its Measurement: Using Behavioral Trace Data Against Platform Episteme." *new media & society* 23, no. 9 (2021): 2650–67. https://doi.org/10.1177/1461444820933547.

Zuboff, Shoshanna. *The Age of Surveillance Capitalism: The Fight for a Human Future at the New Frontier of Power*. New York: Public Affairs, 2019.

CHAPTER 3

DEVELOPING A PRIVACY RESEARCH LAB:
Activities and Impact of PriLab

Mary Francis and Dustin Steinhagen

This chapter provides details on a privacy-focused research lab (PriLab), which is made up of faculty, students, and a librarian at Dakota State University in Madison, South Dakota. PriLab has taken a multi-pronged approach to the promotion and development of privacy. First, the group conducts, presents, and publishes privacy research. From budding scholars to experienced academics, this group explores all aspects of the research process. Secondly, the group has focused on developing privacy courses as well as reviewing the privacy curriculum offered across institutions of higher education. Finally, PriLab approaches privacy as interdisciplinary. It considers various aspects of data privacy, ranging from the psychological underpinning of social engineering to the technical details of performing privacy audits.

NEED FOR PRIVACY EDUCATION

Privacy concerns increasingly hit the news when a breach occurs at a large company. These situations arise with the increasing use of Big Data analytics. Big Data entails a large volume of data, a variety of data formats, rapid collection of data, and a complex interpretation of data.[1] This commercialization of personal data is at odds with privacy rights. Pence notes that not only must there be an increase in education on the use of Big Data but there must also be an increase in education on how Big Data impacts privacy. He goes on to say that this education should be put into the general curriculum "since all students need to understand how Big Data will affect their lives."[2]

Privacy as a field of study is found within yet also beyond a focus on security. There has long been a call for individuals with privacy expertise. In 2010, Shapiro noted that companies needed individuals with specific skills and expertise in privacy to take part in the design of new systems and products in order to implement privacy from the beginning rather than dealing with it when an issue arises.[3] This call for privacy-related jobs has come to pass with the International Association of Privacy Professionals (IAPP) noting that the demand for privacy-related positions is very high with the largest segment in mid-level positions, such as program managers and directors, privacy analysts, and product managers who are responsible for building, maintaining, or maturing privacy programs.[4]

The increase in the need for privacy jobs comes from all types of companies. Beyond dealing with privacy at a specific company, there has also been an increase in the privacy industry with the number of privacy vendors more than quintupling from forty-four to 259 between 2017 and 2019.[5] The increased demand has come from several factors, such as the increased use of data analytics, a recognition of privacy concerns, and the passing of various data privacy laws.

In Steinhagen et al.'s inventory of privacy programs in higher education, privacy was split into three major subdisciplines: legal/compliance, management, and technology.[6] Examples of privacy work roles can be found in Farber.[7] Legal and compliance roles include privacy attorneys and data protection officers (DPOs); privacy managers could include chief privacy officers (CPOs) as well as privacy product managers; and technical privacy roles include privacy engineers and designers of novel privacy-enhancing technologies.

As there is a growing increase in the number of privacy-related jobs, there will be increased demand for courses and programs focused on privacy. In considering this growing demand for privacy education, a research project was conducted by PriLab that inventoried the current state of formal privacy education at institutions of higher education. The inventory included information on 115 privacy programs and 333 privacy courses offered at 99 institutions around the world. The data collected reveal several aspects of the current state of privacy education. At all levels of analysis, legal and compliance topics dominate the privacy education landscape, with management and technical offerings scarce or nonexistent (see figures 3.1, 3.2, and 3.3). Interdisciplinary courses and programs are more common than management and technical offerings but are far less common than legal and compliance offerings at each level of analysis. These factors combined indicate that

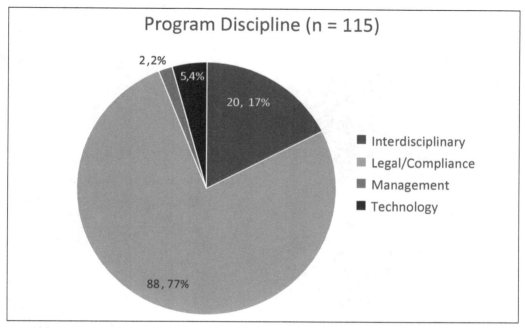

FIGURE 3.1
Distribution of privacy programs by discipline.

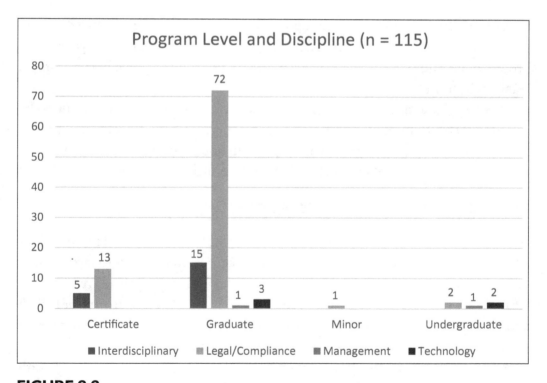

FIGURE 3.2
Distribution of privacy programs by discipline and level.

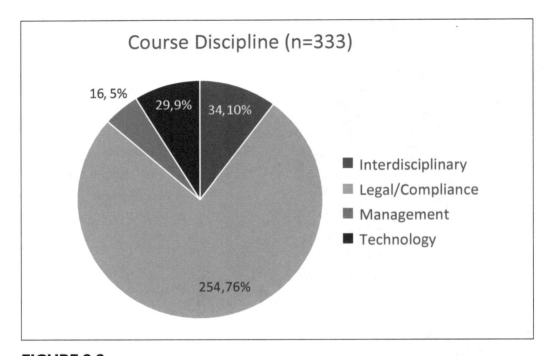

FIGURE 3.3
Distribution of privacy courses by discipline.

the current state of privacy education is narrowly focused on graduate education and legal and compliance topics, despite the current demand for non-legal privacy professionals and the fact that privacy is an interdisciplinary issue beyond simple legal application.[8]

It is likely that additional privacy courses and programs will continue to be added to institutions of higher education. This increase not only requires libraries to support the new programs but also opens up opportunities for new collaborations due to the inherent connection between libraries and privacy.

DEVELOPMENT OF A PRIVACY LAB

As can be seen, there is a need for individuals with privacy knowledge and skills and a growing push to provide education in that area. In an effort to tap into that emerging area as well as address personal interest in privacy, a privacy research lab (PriLab) was established at Dakota State University (DSU). The growth of PriLab and the range of projects stemming from the members only further highlight how privacy and privacy education will continue to expand.

DSU is a public institution. It has a headcount of approximately 3,000 with approximately 2,000 FTE. DSU has a technology focus with a mission statement noting "DSU provides learning that integrates technology and innovation to develop graduates ready to contribute to local, national, and global prosperity."[9] While technology is a component of all the majors on campus from education to the arts and sciences, The Beacom College of Computer and Cyber Sciences comprises the majority of the university's focus. This college claims over one-third of the student body within twelve degree programs and additional certificate and minor programs.

This focus on technology and computer sciences provides a foundation for individuals interested in privacy, especially data privacy, which pervades much of the content found within courses looking at network and software security. However, while many consider privacy as just one aspect of technology security, there are those who recognize that security is actually a component of privacy. This is because, without the need for privacy, there is no need to develop security measures. Some of those individuals who understood the importance of privacy developed a research group set up to consider privacy and what it means both personally and within larger systems.

In January 2019, the first members of PriLab met with a librarian to request assistance related to conducting a literature review. The group was originally comprised of one faculty member and two graduate students who shared an interest in privacy. This first project focused on researching the various definitions of privacy in order to work toward a common understanding of the idea. While assisting on this project, the librarian started to attend the weekly meetings of the group.

During the first year, the weekly meetings provided numerous just-in-time opportunities to provide research-related insights and instruction. Some of the topics that were addressed include the selection of appropriate research databases, search techniques, interlibrary loan service, and citation management software. As the literature review came together, the librarian began assisting with the writing of the paper, sharing details on how to write a scholarly work and how to structure a paper for publication. Finally, the paper was ready for publication and instruction was offered on how to find an academic publisher. The acceptance of the paper at a conference finally led to discussion on preparing a talk and presenting at a conference.[10] Throughout this time, the librarian became an active member and contributor to the PriLab group. For additional discussion on librarians' activities in a research lab, see Carroll, Eskridge, and Chang who provide a study looking at the integration of a librarian into a research lab.[11]

Since the first year of PriLab, the group has continued to grow and produce academic work. Membership is driven in a couple of ways. First, the faculty member and graduate students, in their role as graduate assistants teaching courses, find and ask students to join after they show an interest in privacy. This often occurs if a student selects to research some aspect of privacy for a class project or paper. Secondly, members of the group may bring in one of their classmates to the meetings. Finally, some students have selected some aspect of privacy for their dissertations and through committee member selection and word of mouth find their way to PriLab.

During the 2020–2021 school year, the weekly meetings were moved to Zoom to accommodate COVID concerns as well as the inclusion of distance students. Even with the loosening of COVID restrictions, the meetings continue to be held online, which allows for additional members to be involved. About a dozen individuals attend the weekly meetings and actively work on various projects.

Currently, PriLab operates with no funding. Research labs at DSU do not receive institutional funding. Different grants have been considered as possible ways to get funding to hire graduate assistants to work on specific projects. The group continues to meet simply as a way to expand the scholarly and academic accomplishments of the members. In considering the number of members within the group, it is important to think about how many people can meet at one time and still feel like part of a productive group. With a dozen members, individuals can still share their ideas, but there are times when everyone is not able to provide in-depth discussion. As the lab continues to grow membership, it is likely that smaller groups will meet separately based on specific projects or specific areas of focus.

IMPACT OF PRIVACY SCHOLARSHIP ON PRILAB

Privacy is an interesting area to study for multiple reasons. First, it is a topic that impacts everyone's daily life as they decide or do not decide what personal information they share. It also lacks a clear definition, which allows for open debate and discussion on its merits and structure in different contexts. It also can be viewed as an abstract philosophical idea and a concrete action with consequences. This variety means that there is a breadth of research that has been done on privacy.

Some of the most influential writings in the development of PriLab have come from some of the current leading privacy scholars: Solove, Nissenbaum, and Cavoukian. Solove is a law professor who studies privacy and has written mass-market books on the connection between privacy and information technology. In particular, his work on privacy harms has inspired the lab to not only think about the abstract impact of privacy but also how privacy violations can impact the individual.[12] Nissenbaum developed the theory of contextual integrity, which notes how when thinking about privacy, it is critical to put it within context, with some circumstances and situations requiring more robust privacy.[13] Cavoukian created an approach to systems engineering, called Privacy by Design (PbD),[14] that puts privacy at the forefront. Both Nissenbaum and Cavoukian's ideas are important as PriLab considers how privacy can and should be applied in the integration of privacy within a data system.

Not only are there various overall conceptions of privacy, but various disciplines approach privacy with different lenses. Pavlou notes how the law literature considers privacy as a right or entitlement, social psychology literature considers privacy as a state of limited access or isolation, and information systems literature views privacy as control over information.[15] Smith, Dinev, and Xu reviewed a number of articles across disciplines and developed two broad categories in which to place the definitions. Value-based definitions view privacy as a human right integral to that society's moral system. Cognate-based definitions refer to an individual's mind, perceptions, and cognition rather than a strict moral value.[16] These disciplinary approaches have all been applied in the research conducted by PriLab. In the research looking at international and state data laws, the focus has been on the rights of the consumer in relation to how businesses use their data. The research that is being done looking at how to implement privacy within industry focuses on who has control and access to the data.

Beyond the academic research that has been done on privacy, the members of PriLab have also been impacted by and use a number of international and national laws and standards. The European Union's General Data Protection Regulation (GDPR), the California Consumer Privacy Act (CCPA), other state laws, and standards such as ISO/IEC 27701 have all influenced not only how privacy is considered but also why it must be addressed.

PRILAB ACTIVITIES

Privacy is an interesting concept for a research lab in that it has a multitude of meanings and focuses across numerous disciplines. This allows faculty and students from different fields to come together and address the topic from different areas while building on each other's knowledge. The PriLab group has students studying cyber defense and cyber operations, which focuses on the technical application of security, and students studying cyber leadership and intelligence, which focuses on political culture, leadership, and digital forensics. This mixture has resulted in projects that focus on the technical aspects of implementing privacy within systems as well as theoretical considerations of what privacy entails.

Research

The research output of the members of PriLab has varied. There have been traditional academic publications including presentations at conferences and journal articles.[17] Some of the early scholarly work of PriLab focused on trying to understand more of the foundational aspects of privacy and what it means within different contexts—for example, looking at privacy principles and how they are addressed in international law and codes of ethics. From this foundation, the current scholarship being conducted by the group is looking at privacy within specific areas. One project currently underway is looking at privacy in relation to self-driving vehicles.

As the group continues to develop, there have also been advances in ways to address privacy within industry. There has been progress and continued study into the development of privacy tools and services that could be implemented and commercialized for industries as they deal with new data privacy regulations. These projects are aided when doctoral students look at resources that would benefit them within their assorted businesses and then bring that research to PriLab and their dissertations.

There have also been nonacademic presentations with a series of talks held with a local community group. This group is comprised of older individuals who get together monthly to hear about various topics as a form of lifelong learning. Three sessions were delivered over three years, covering the topics of personal privacy, defense against social engineering scams, and defense against brainwashing. The presenters were impressed with the depth of questions asked by attendees, highlighting that a concern with online personal information crosses a range of individuals. This type of community outreach has slowed with increased scholarly projects; however, it will likely be integrated into a possible student club as discussed below.

LibGuide

One of the first contributions of the library for PriLab was the development of a LibGuide.[18] It was important for the students to have a basic understanding of what privacy means. To that end, links and citations to the major authors and seminal works on privacy were included. However, since privacy has different meanings within various contexts, it was also important to include some articles that provide views of privacy within different disciplines.

Since PriLab does not restrict its privacy research to a singular topic, a range of different disciplines were selected as having a connection to privacy, including computer science, education, governmental/state standards, governmental/

international, health/medicine, historic/cultural views of privacy, human subject research/IRB, journalism, law enforcement, legal, librarianship, math, philosophy, psychology, and sociology. For each of these areas, a search was conducted to find highly cited articles addressing privacy. While the LibGuide does not try to provide a comprehensive bibliography on privacy literature, it does offer students an annotated selection of articles on the topic.

One of the goals of PriLab is to advance the privacy education of students through research and formal education. To that end, the guide also provides links to some freely available courses that address privacy and some privacy-related majors and programs from universities across the United States. This review of educational programs also assists during the curriculum development that is occurring on campus.

The LibGuide is also meant to serve as a resource for selected frequently asked questions within the group. The most pressing of these is where to submit the products of the research that is being conducted. To help the research submission process, the guide also contains a listing of conferences, journals, and professional organizations related to privacy. This provides a range of options for students looking to share their research. Many of these titles have either a computer science or legal focus.

The LibGuide is shared with all new members as a resource for readings and journals. Students also suggest and share resources that are added to the site. In looking at the usage statistics for the site, it has continued to have consistent page views since its creation.

Textbook

A major PriLab undertaking is an upcoming textbook on data privacy management led by Kevin Streff, coauthored by Lisa McKee, and edited by Dustin Steinhagen. The textbook will provide a comprehensive overview of privacy management as well as the core background knowledge privacy professionals should have, making it especially suitable for use in introductory privacy, privacy management, security, and business management courses. Most notably, the textbook presents a comprehensive risk-based methodology for managing privacy within organizations, covering all aspects of the data privacy management program from privacy risk assessment to privacy auditing, and everything in between, which is not found in any current textbook on the subject matter. At the time of writing, the full first draft is nearly complete, and a publisher is being finalized. The plan is to monetize the project in order to fill a perceived gap in the privacy management textbook market.

The textbook will contain fourteen chapters, starting with a detailed introductory overview of the world of privacy, data privacy, and data privacy management in chapter 1. The book's contents cover a range of topics from privacy law and regulation to privacy auditing to data privacy programs. The concluding chapter contains various short vignettes of emerging concepts, issues, and technologies with profound implications for the data privacy field; these topics will include neurotechnology, artificial intelligence, privacy engineering, and deep fakes, among many more. The first thirteen chapters all have accompanying quiz questions, discussion questions, hands-on exercises, and case studies to aid privacy educators with planning their curriculum and assessing their students' learning. As these types of end-of-chapter exercises are virtually non-existent in contemporary options for data privacy management texts, our textbook will be filling a major void by providing the first privacy management textbook with these offerings. The textbook content includes

- Chapter 1 – Overview of Data Privacy
    - Covers introductory privacy concepts, including the scholarly definitions of privacy, identity, the OECD privacy principles, the history of privacy, and why privacy is valued in society.
- Chapter 2 – Privacy Harms
    - Provides a deep dive of Solove's taxonomy of sixteen privacy harms as well as alternative taxonomies for privacy harms.
- Chapter 3 – Privacy Law & Regulations
    - Outlines the major privacy laws and regulations around the world.
- Chapter 4 – Data Privacy Program
    - Illustrates, at a high level, the complete data privacy management program developed by Kevin Streff.
- Chapter 5 – Privacy Assessments
    - Explains methodologies for conducting privacy risk assessments.
- Chapter 6 – Privacy Risk Management
    - Expands on methodologies and frameworks for managing privacy risk.
- Chapter 7 – Privacy Vendor Management
    - Explains approaches for managing privacy risk when doing business with third-party contractors.
- Chapter 8 – Privacy Education Training and Awareness
    - Covers privacy workforce development topics, including privacy education opportunities, privacy certifications and training, and how to spread privacy awareness within an organization.

- Chapter 9 – Physical and Environment Controls
  - Discusses physical countermeasures for protecting privacy and security.
- Chapter 10 – Privacy Response Programs
  - Explains methodologies for effectively remediating privacy incidents, such as breaches of personal data.
- Chapter 11 – Privacy Policy
  - Discusses how to write and implement effective privacy policies, which are the critical documents put in place by management to ensure that privacy risk is being managed appropriately within the organization.
- Chapter 12 – Privacy Auditing
  - Explains methodologies for testing and verifying privacy controls.
- Chapter 13 – Privacy Metrics
  - Illustrates how to utilize privacy metrics to gain insight and make incremental improvements to the maturity of an organization's privacy program.
- Chapter 14 – Emerging Concepts in Data Privacy
  - Provides diverse vignettes of emerging concepts and issues in the data privacy field that hold profound significance for the future of the field, including brain-hacking concerns, psychometrics, and differential privacy, among other topics.

PriLab is being utilized as a forum to recruit privacy researchers to assist with writing and editing the textbook. This assistance has taken many forms, from PriLab members volunteering to help write whole topics sections within chapters to contributing individual case studies or emerging concept pieces for chapter 14 to engaging in internal peer editing and review of the chapter drafts. The fact that PriLab attracts researchers with a diversity of professional backgrounds, ambitions, and research interests made it especially suitable as a source of contributors for this upcoming privacy management textbook. For instance, one PriLab member with a background in cybersecurity curriculum development is assisting with aligning the quiz questions with the learning objectives. In total, approximately eight PriLab members have become involved with writing this textbook.

Future Student Club

One of the possible future activities of PriLab is the development of a student club. As a research lab, the group focuses on the research, writing, and publishing of academic work. To that end, many of the student members are either master's or doctoral students. However, privacy is a topic that appeals to a wide range of individuals. The student club would be open to all students and would focus more on personal privacy concerns and sharing current news about privacy. Topics such as data breaches and facial recognition software development would provide discussions with both an ethical and technical aspect. The expectation is that a faculty member would serve as club advisor with club officers coming from a mix of undergraduate and graduate students. This group could hold sessions and workshops for others taking about privacy literacy and resources that are available to help maintain privacy while online. Such an organization would raise the awareness of privacy across campus and thus feed into membership of PriLab where research will be conducted.

CONCLUSION

The work of PriLab highlights the fact that privacy is not a one-dimensional topic owned by a specific group or discipline. Rather, for the impact of privacy to be fully understood, it must be considered from a multitude of angles with different individuals each providing their own insights. While each member of PriLab has their own connection to privacy, the group dynamics allow individuals to work together and explore the junction of new ideas. This collaboration has promoted privacy well beyond what could have been done singularly.

The interest and work of PriLab have also helped in the approval of a graduate-level Data Privacy certificate program at DSU. The certificate was approved in 2022 with the plan to expand the program into a stackable master's degree and possible doctorate. There will likely be a symbiotic growth between the degree program and PriLab membership. This growth in formalized education also harkens back to the need for individuals with knowledge and skills in privacy as discussed in the beginning of the chapter.

Overall, interest in privacy provides another academic offshoot for librarians to provide support. Not only have librarians traditionally considered privacy and confidentiality a critical component of their work, but they have also established systems and policies that address that concern. When talking to others who are designing new systems, it is easy for librarians to say, "Within our system, we do this to protect individual privacy and this is the impact on our system."

As companies and schools look to gather more data on individuals, it is important to have voices also highlighting the importance of privacy. By simply being able to articulate why privacy is important, librarians will be an important component in the future design and implementation of privacy. Engaging with faculty and students either in the classroom, in a research group, or in conversation allows librarians to enhance support of privacy literacy.

NOTES

1. Harry Pence, "Will Big Data Mean the End of Privacy," *Journal of Educational Technology Systems* 44, no. 2 (2015): 53–267.
2. Pence, "Will Big Data," 265.
3. Stuart Shaprio, "Privacy by Design: Moving from Art to Practice," *Communications of the AMC* 53, no. 6 (2010): 26–28.
4. Jennifer Bryant, "Privacy Job Market at 'Full-Tilt Hiring Boogie,'" *International Association of Privacy Professionals* (October 6, 2021), https://iapp.org/news/a/privacy-job-market-at-full-tilt-hiring-boogie/.
5. D. Ingram, "Can privacy be big business? A wave of startups thinks so," NBC Universal, February 3, 2020, https://www.nbcnews.com/tech/security/can-privacy-be-big-business-wave-startups-thinks-so-n1128626.
6. Dustin Steinhagen, Chase Lucas, Mary Francis, Mark Lawrence, and Kevin Streff, "In Inventory of Privacy Curricula Offerings in Higher Education," *Information Systems Education Journal* 19, no. 3 (2021): 21–30.
7. D. J. Farber, "The Advent of Privacy Engineering," BigID, August 10, 2018, https://bigid.com/blog/the-advent-of-privacy-engineering/.
8. Dustin Steinhagen, Chase Lucas, Mary Francis, Mark Lawrence, and Kevin Streff, "In Inventory of Privacy Curricula Offerings in Higher Education," *Information Systems Education Journal* 19, no. 3 (2021): 21–30.
9. "Mission, Vision, & Values," Dakota State University, accessed September 15, 2021, https://dsu.edu/about-dsu/mission-vision-values.html.
10. Quentin Covert, Dustin Steinhagen, Mary Francis, and Kevin Streff, "Towards a Triad for Data Privacy," *Hawaii International Conference on System Sciences* 53 (2020).
11. Alexander Carroll, Honora Eskridge, and Bertha Chang, "Lab-Integrated Librarians: A Model for Research Engagement," *College & Research Libraries* 81, no. 1 (2020): 8–26.
12. Daniel Solove, "Conceptualizing Privacy," *California Law Review* 90, no. 4 (2002); Daniel Solove, "A Taxonomy of Privacy," *University of Pennsylvania Law Review* 154, no. 3 (2006); Daniel Solove, "'I've Got Nothing to Hide' and Other Misunderstandings of Privacy," *San Diego Law Review* 44 (2008).
13. Hellen Nissenbaum, "Privacy as Contextual Integrity," *Washington Law Review* 79 (2004): 101–39; Hellen Nissenbaum, "Contextual Approach to Privacy Online," *Dædalus* 140, no. 4 (2011): 32–48.
14. Ann Cavoukian, *Privacy by Design: From Rhetoric to Reality* (Information and Privacy Commissioner of Ontario, 2012).
15. Paul A. Pavlou, "State of the Information Privacy Literature: Where Are We Now and Where Should We Go?," *MIS Quarterly* 35, no. 4 (2011).
16. H. Jeff Smith, Tamara Dinev, and Heng Xu, "Information Privacy Research: An Interdisciplinary Review," *MIS Quarterly* 35, no. 4 (2011).
17. Steinhagen, Lucas, Francis, Lawrence, and Streff, "In Inventory of Privacy Curricula"; Dustin Steinhagen, Houssain Kettani, "An Inventory of Existing Neuroprivacy Controls," *Proceedings of the 4th International Conference on Information Systems and Data Mining* (2020), 77–83; Mary Francis, "The Treatment of Privacy in Professional Codes of Ethics: An International Survey," *Library Quarterly* 91, no. 3 (2021): 304–21; Mary Francis, Quentin Covert, Dustin Steinhagen, and Kevin Streff, "An Inventory of International Privacy Principles: A 14 Country Analysis," *Hawaii International Conference on System Sciences* 53 (2020); Quentin Covert, Dustin Steinhagen, Mary Francis, and Kevin Streff, "Towards a Triad for Data Privacy," *Hawaii International Conference on System Sciences* 53 (2020); Patrick Gallo and Houssain Kettani, "On Privacy Issues with Google Street View," *CLEAR Conference*

(2019); Quentin Covert and Kevin Streff, "Data Privacy Simulator," *CLEAR Conference* (2019); Dustin Steinhagen, "DSU's Introductory Data Privacy Course," *CLEAR Conference* (2019).
18. "Privacy," Karl E. Mundt Library, accessed September 15, 2021, https://library.dsu.edu/privacy.

BIBLIOGRAPHY

Bryant, Jennifer. "Privacy Job Market at 'Full-Tilt Hiring Boogie.'" *International Association of Privacy Professionals*. October 6, 2021. https://iapp.org/news/a/privacy-job-market-at-full-tilt-hiring-boogie/.

Cavoukian, Ann. *Privacy by Design: From Rhetoric to Reality*. Information and Privacy Commissioner of Ontario. 2012.

Carroll, Alexander, Honora Eskridge, and Bertha Chang. "Lab-Integrated Librarians: A Model for Research Engagement." *College & Research Libraries* 81, no. 1 (2020): 8–26.

Covert, Quentin, Dustin Steinhagen, Mary Francis, and Kevin Streff. "Towards a Triad for Data Privacy." *Hawaii International Conference on System Sciences* 53 (2020).

Covert, Quentin, and Kevin Streff. "Data Privacy Simulator." *CLEAR Conference* (2019).

Dakota State University. "Mission, Vision, & Values." Accessed September 15, 2021. https://dsu.edu/about-dsu/mission-vision-values.html.

Farber, D. J. "The Advent of Privacy Engineering." BigID. August 10, 2018. https://bigid.com/blog/the-advent-of-privacy-engineering/

Francis, Mary. "The Treatment of Privacy in Professional Codes of Ethics: An International Survey." *Library Quarterly* 91, no. 3 (2021): 304–21.

Francis, Mary, Quentin Covert, Dustin Steinhagen, and Kevin Streff. "An Inventory of International Privacy Principles: A 14 Country Analysis." *Hawaii International Conference on System Sciences* 53 (2020).

Gallo, Patrick, and Houssain Kettani. "On Privacy Issues with Google Street View." *CLEAR Conference* (2019).

Ingram, D. "Can privacy be big business? A wave of startups thinks so." NBC Universal. February 3, 2020. https://www.nbcnews.com/tech/security/can-privacy-be-big-business-wave-startups-thinks-so-n1128626.

Karl E. Mundt Library. "Privacy." Accessed September 15, 2021. https://library.dsu.edu/privacy.

Nissenbaum, Hellen. "Contextual Approach to Privacy Online." *Dædalus* 140, no. 4 (2011): 32–48.

———. "Privacy as Contextual Integrity." *Washington Law Review* 79 (2004): 101–39.

Pavlou, Paul A. "State of the Information Privacy Literature: Where Are We Now and Where Should We Go?" *MIS Quarterly* 35, no 4 (2011): 977–88.

Pence, Harry. "Will Big Data Mean the End of Privacy." *Journal of Educational Technology Systems* 44, no. 2 (2015): 53–267.

Shaprio, Stuart. "Privacy by Design: Moving from Art to Practice." *Communications of the AMC* 53, no. 6 (2010): 26–28.

Smith, H. J., T. Dinev, and H. Xu. "Information Privacy Research: An Interdisciplinary Review." *MIS Quarterly* 35, no. 4 (2011): 989–1015.

Solove, Daniel. "A Taxonomy of Privacy." *University of Pennsylvania Law Review* 154, no. 3 (2006): 477–560.

———. "Conceptualizing Privacy." *California Law Review* 90, no. 4 (2002): 1087–1155. https://doi.org/10.2307/3481326.

———. "'I've Got Nothing to Hide' and Other Misunderstandings of Privacy." *San Diego Law Review* 44 (2008): 745–72.

Steinhagen, Dustin. "DSU's Introductory Data Privacy Course." *CLEAR Conference* (2019).

Steinhagen, Dustin, and Houssain Kettani. "An Inventory of Existing Neuroprivacy Controls." *Proceedings of the 4th International Conference on Information Systems and Data Mining* (2020), 77–83.

Steinhagen, Dustin, Chase Lucas, Mary Francis, Mark Lawrence, and Kevin Mark. "In Inventory of Privacy Curricula Offerings in Higher Education." *Information Systems Education Journal* 19, no. 3 (2021): 21–30.

PART II
Protecting Privacy

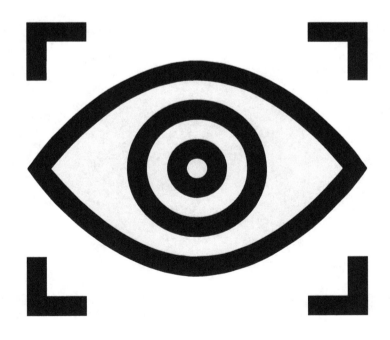

CHAPTER 4

PROTECTING PATRON PRIVACY IN ACCESS SERVICES:
Looking at the Laws

Jamie Marie Aschenbach

INTRODUCTION

This chapter explores the privacy that patrons at post-secondary academic libraries can expect in their interactions. Access Services is the touchpoint, sometimes the only touchpoint, of academic students to the library. As the Access Services staff and faculty have unfettered permissions to view and change patron accounts in the integrated library system (ILS), there is a chance of infringing on patron privacy. This chapter will start with an introduction to Access Services and librarians and privacy. It will then discover the major American federal laws that cover patron privacy as it pertains to Access Services in the library. Then, the chapter will discuss techniques librarians can implement to safeguard patron privacy.

ACCESS SERVICES IN GENERAL

Access Services generally includes circulation of materials, reserve materials and processes, interlibrary loan, and stacks maintenance. Access Services is responsible for patron records maintenance in the integrated library system (ILS). This includes personally identifiable information such as mailing address, phone number, email, and student identification number.

Access Services staff and faculty must walk the fine line between customer service and privacy. The personally identifiable information (PII) is needed to maintain records of what materials are checked out to whom in order to maintain a robust collection. However, without strong rules against sharing this information, Access Services could run afoul of federal laws and regulations, and professional codes of conduct.

LIBRARIANS AND PRIVACY

Librarians have a long practice of protecting patron privacy. It is part of librarians' profession to protect the "anonymous reading" conducted by their patrons.[1] Patron privacy and a patron's right to intellectual freedom are so ingrained that it appears in our code of ethics.[2] The third principle of the American Library Association (ALA) Code of Ethics states, "We protect each library patron's right to privacy and confidentiality with respect to information sought or received and resources consulted, borrowed, acquired or transmitted."[3] The Library Bill of Rights from the ALA addresses the patron's right to information and the "free access to ideas" while explicitly stating "all people …possess a right to privacy and confidentiality in their library use."[4]

The ALA's Policy concerning Confidentiality of Personally Identifiable Information about Library Users states clearly that the right to privacy is found in the United States Constitution.[5] The free and open use of library materials and this exchange of ideas is at the core of our profession. In the Privacy Toolkit, ALA has put together resources for librarians to study and put into action.[6] The toolkit states, "Privacy is essential to the exercise of free speech, free thought, and free association. Lack of privacy and confidentiality chills people's choices, thereby suppressing access to ideas."[7] This basis of patron privacy allows patrons to not be concerned with their choice in reading or research to be found out by others. Access Services employees must be held to a high standard to protect patrons' free choices in information-gathering behavior.

The National Education Association, which defines an educator to include "education support professionals" such as librarians, also strongly states a commitment to student and professional privacy in its Code of Ethics of the Education Profession.[8] Under Principle I: Commitment to the Student, paragraph 8 states the educator "[s]hall not disclose information about students obtained in the course of professional service unless disclosure serves a compelling professional purpose or is required by law."[9] In Principle II: Commitment to the Profession, the National Education Association states in Paragraph 6, the educator "[s]hall not disclose information about colleagues obtained in the course of professional service unless disclosure serves a compelling professional purpose or is required by law."[10]

This commitment to privacy in the profession is evident through the actions of librarians. For example, in Vermont in 2008, librarians were instrumental in getting a state law passed that protects patron library records privacy.[11] This state law codified the ALA Code of Ethics to protect patrons from having their circulation records and computer usage records from being disclosed.[12] To get this passed through the Vermont legislature took the Vermont Libraries Association two years of working with the Vermont School Library Association and the legislators to have hearings and write the legislation.[13]

This strong privacy view, however, conflicts with certain aspects of federal law, even when the federal law is regarding privacy.

AMERICAN FEDERAL LAWS REGARDING PRIVACY AND RELEASE OF ACADEMIC LIBRARY PATRON RECORDS

There are several federal laws that seem to protect academic library patron privacy, yet there are exceptions and other laws that seem to allow those records to be requested on a whim. This section will cover the three major federal laws that impact academic library patron privacy: the Family Educational Rights and Privacy Act (FERPA),[14] the USA PATRIOT Act,[15] and the Freedom of Information Act (FOIA).[16] While there are other federal laws that impact libraries and institutions of higher learning, they have minimal effect on PII and will not be covered in this section.

Family Educational Rights and Privacy Act (FERPA)

FERPA was passed in 1974 and has been amended several times since then.[17] FERPA's intention is to protect student information unless the student poses a risk of harm to self or others.[18] A student is defined as a person who is or has attended an institution, whether K-12 or higher education, and about whom the institution maintains educational records.[19]

Academic library records could be covered by FERPA based on the language of the statute defining "education records" as "those records, files, documents, and other materials which – (i) contain information directly related to a student; and

(ii) are maintained by an educational agency or institution or by a person acting for such agency or institution."[20] The regulations clarify records to mean "any information recorded in any way."[21]

Libraries record information to protect their collections by tracking which patrons have which materials on loan at any given time generally using an Integrated Library System (ILS). The ILS also usually contains a patron's personal identification of some type such as phone number, email address, physical address, and student ID number. In such instances, academic library records meet the standard of education records.

The FERPA regulations further define covered institutions to include "each of its components (such as a department within a university)."[22] Academic libraries are such a department within their respective universities.

Educational records can be released and used by education officials for a legitimate educational interest.[23] In the instance of library records, the librarians and library staff can use the ILS to identify who has which materials.

FERPA mandates that federal sums can be withheld if a university is not in compliance,[24] essentially making FERPA a contractual agreement for funding from the federal government more than an enforcement mechanism.[25] While FERPA does not allow for a private cause of action for disclosing information,[26] there is also no protection from FOIA or state open record laws for state schools.[27] Disclosure of student records under FERPA is not prohibited; it simply imposes a penalty for doing so.[28] Courts have held that state schools must disclose student information under state open records laws that would otherwise be protected by FERPA.[29]

Subpoenas for student records can be requested "in the context of terrorism-related investigations" under the USA PATRIOT Act amendment to FERPA.[30] This is why an amendment was made so as to not shoehorn these requests in under the health and safety exception. These two major exceptions account for the majority of disclosures.

USA PATRIOT Act

A general overview of how the USA PATRIOT Act was passed and how it has impacted academic libraries is beyond the scope of this chapter.[31] The USA PATRIOT Act provides a way for the federal government to seek National Security Letters with little or no evidence to recover information about anyone.[32] Under the USA PATRIOT Act, the federal government has been given unprecedented power to obtain information about its citizens and inhabitants. As one writer stated, "It is not just the fact of abuse, but the potential for abuse that is so troubling about the powers that the government has been given."[33]

Through the expanded use of pen register orders under Section 216 of the USA PATRIOT Act, "the government is capable of watching what patrons are reading online, while they are reading it."[34] Pen registers were created when they were used for looking for phone numbers dialed.[35] Now they can be used to see what computer programs and web pages are being accessed in real time.[36] Pen register orders can't be used to read the message, but the types of programs used collect this information anyway and it is to be stripped from the information (web address) that can be used.[37]

Section 213 of the USA PATRIOT Act allows National Security Letters to go out as a way to sneak a peek at the records on a patron in order to get a Foreign Intelligence Surveillance Act (FISA) warrant.[38] National Security Letters under the USA PATRIOT Act can be used to obtain library records circumventing FERPA and requiring the library to not notify the patron.[39] Librarians across the country have been posting signs in libraries telling patrons that the USA PATRIOT Act "prohibits library workers from informing you if federal agents have obtained records about you."[40] These actions acknowledge the federal laws that protect—and don't protect—patron library privacy.[41] Some library directors have taken to informing the library board that the FBI hasn't been there that month, leaving it unsaid that if the statement isn't made, then the FBI has been there.[42]

The USA PATRIOT Act allows National Security Letters to be served by FBI agents on anyone regardless of whether they were under criminal investigation or not.[43] The numbers show the expanded use of National Security Letters.[44] In 2000, "8,500 [National Security Letters] were issued; by contrast, between 2003 and 2005 the FBI issued more than 143,000 [National Security Letters], only one of which led to a conviction in a terrorism case."[45] It is estimated that there were "roughly 30,000 National Security Letters" issued in 2005 alone.[46]

Since the passing of the USA PATRIOT Act, librarians did not publicly identify any uses of the act against libraries,[47] and in 2003, then Attorney General John Ashcroft stated that Section 215 had never been used to obtain library records.[48] But a case out of Connecticut turned Ashcroft's statement on its head.

The Connecticut Four

Until 2005, there was no jurisprudence on how or if a Section 215 warrant, a National Security Letter, could be served on a library for a patron's records.[49] In 2005, two FBI agents served library director George Christian, known as John Doe in the court filings, with a National Security Letter for information about who used the computers at a branch library.[50] This put all the library's computer patrons at risk of suspicion for terrorist-related acts without any of the patrons knowing or having a way to find out that this was happening.[51] The National Security Letter had a lifetime gag order.[52]

Mr. Christian called another library director and the executive committee of the library consortium, and they all met with the consortium's attorney.[53] As they all read the National Security Letter, they were all bound by the gag order.[54]

In April of 2006, the FBI withdrew the National Security Letter request and the gag order.[55] That is when Mr. Christian spoke out.[56] As the case was not litigated on the issues, there is currently no case law on the application of National Security Letters served on libraries.[57]

As there is no case law or legislative guidance on National Security Letters, academic libraries can be served National Securities Letters and have a gag order placed on them. It is important to make sure that the library director or dean is served and not the Access Services staff. The director or dean has the authority to reply to the National Security Letter and has established networks to the provost, president, and legal counsel for assistance in complying with the letter. Access Services personnel may be asked to help gather the information at the request of the director or dean but should not accept service of the letter.

Freedom of Information Act (FOIA) Laws and State Sunshine Laws

The FOIA and state sunshine laws were created to have government transparency but can often be at odds with FERPA. FOIA is especially important to state universities and colleges as they are funded generally through federal money.

In *United States v. Miami University*, the Sixth Circuit Court of Appeals held that educational records are protected from disclosing personally identifying information to third parties under state sunshine laws.[58] In *Miami University*, The *Chronicle of Higher Education* requested student disciplinary actions for a specific time frame.[59] The Ohio Supreme Court held that university student disciplinary records were not educational records under FERPA and that the records must be disclosed with personally identifiable information pursuant to the state's sunshine laws.[60] After complying with the Court's decision, Miami University released the requested records to the *Chronicle*.[61] The Department of Education (DOE), upon learning of this disclosure, brought action in Federal Court.[62] DOE requested a finding of whether disciplinary records were educational records under FERPA and, if so, sought an injunction prohibiting the release of the records under

FERPA.[63] The court held education records are protected from disclosure to third parties under FOIA but that the outcome of disciplinary procedures are not.[64] Under this reasoning, library records would be protected unless they result in a disciplinary procedural outcome.

In *Chicago Tribune Company v. University of Illinois Board of Trustees*, the Federal District Court of Northern Illinois, nine years after the decision in *Miami University*, held that FERPA does not prohibit the release of educational records, it merely prevents "the disclosure of portions of the records requested."[65] In *Chicago Tribune*, the paper sought information regarding preferential treatment in admissions, including the parents' names and addresses and the university personnel who were contacted regarding admissions.[66] The university denied the request pursuant to FERPA.[67] The court held the disclosure should be made as FERPA merely represents a contract clause that does not prohibit disclosure under Illinois sunshine laws.[68] Under this reasoning, the court would likely hold academic library records could be disclosed under Illinois sunshine laws as FERPA is only a contract clause that does not prohibit disclosure of the records.

Both cases show the importance of knowing the state's sunshine laws.

There are some additional state privacy laws that have to be consulted in each jurisdiction regarding what is defined as a state library.[69] Some state laws protect only public libraries, which can be broadly defined to include any library receiving state or federal funds.[70] Coverage of state laws may focus on the information or on the privacy of the patron.[71] Exceptions to disclose to third parties can include law enforcement warrants, consent of the patron, or library administrative needs.[72]

There are four aspects of state privacy laws: (1) the institution type, (2) the targeted record or information, (3) the action, and (4) the exceptions.[73] How they may be applied differently in the courts is by explicit inclusion or exclusion by omission.[74] Some states' privacy laws only protect certain institutions. For example, in Connecticut, libraries "maintained by schools and institutions of higher education" are excluded from protection and records can be disclosed.[75] Ohio covers academic libraries and protects a patron's personally identifiable information by not allowing disclosure of this information.[76] Illinois does not allow for the circulation records of patrons to be released, holding the actions of patrons in libraries to be protected.[77] Exceptions are made in all three states for court orders.[78]

There are state library confidentially statutes in forty-eight states,[79] and the American Libraries Association maintains a complete list on its website.[80]

FERPA provides guidance to schools in that if they cannot comply with FERPA due to state sunshine laws, there "is a requirement that the school report the potential conflict to the [Family Policy Compliance Office]."[81] But even the Family

Policy Compliance Office "is on record as stating that FERPA does not preempt conflicting state law."[82] Even when there is a conflict in state laws and FERPA, courts have held "FERPA does not preempt state laws requiring disclosure," meaning the school has to follow state law, not FERPA.[83]

KEEPING UP WITH LEGAL CHANGES

Part of what an Access Services Librarian needs to do is stay apprised of changes in the law. For state privacy law, ALA maintains a website that should be checked often.[84]

For federal law, search for changes using the GovInfo website.[85] Using a legal database such as Lexis, Westlaw, Bloomberg Law, or HeinOnline, you can update the case law stated here to see where it was cited and see how the updating court deferred or continued the cases' reasoning.

You can also keep apprised of changes to FERPA, as the Department of Education has a website dedicated to privacy.[86] For changes, challenges, and issues regarding the USA PATRIOT Act, ALA has a website that is kept up to date with relevant information to librarians.[87] FOIA changes can be tracked at the FOIA website.[88] State sunshine laws can be tracked at Ballotpedia, which comprehensively tracks state sunshine laws as well as relevant court cases.[89]

WHAT'S AN ACCESS SERVICES LIBRARIAN TO DO?: CREATING PRIVACY POLICIES AND PRACTICES THAT MATTER

While the three main laws affecting patron privacy have been discussed, there are other federal laws that may come into play, such as the Digital Millennium Copyright Act,[90] the Communications Assistance for Law Enforcement Act,[91] and others.[92] An understanding of all relevant and related laws is needed to make informed policy decisions.

There are no hard-and-fast rules regarding protecting the patron's privacy, and each library needs to look at its patrons' needs and the jurisdictional laws that may apply.[93] Drafting a privacy policy requires distinguishing between records that would be protected under FERPA, internet usage that would be discoverable under the USA PATRIOT Act, and activities and communications that would fall under other federal laws.[94]

Best practices would include not disclosing information without a warrant. Even though Bobbie, standing in front of you, wants to know who has the book she's looking for, and you can see Jamal has the book, this information should not be disclosed. If your library has a recall system in place, Bobbie could place a hold on the book, but should never know who had the book before her.

In Access Services, the policy should also embody conduct by circulation staff. Especially important is not sharing PII or any patron records with patrons or others asking about it. Circulation staff should also be cautioned against looking up patron records in the ILS for their own personal use; the personally identifiable information in the patron records should remain confidential and not be available for staff on a whim.

When drafting a privacy policy, librarians can start by looking at the four types of library privacy that librarians protect: (1) circulation records, (2) electronic records, (3) internet activity, and (4) behavior.[95] By looking at these four types of privacy, librarians can begin to draft a meaningful privacy policy.

Privacy in Circulation Records

Circulation records are generally now kept in an ILS. This makes it convenient to access records but also makes it easy for these records to be discoverable by third parties under FOIA requests. Librarians need to evaluate who can access the records and how the records are accessed.[96] Librarians need to consider what records need to be kept versus what records would be nice to keep.[97] In general, material records should only be tied to patron records as long as the patron holds the material and not any longer.

The library's data retention policy should balance the need of the library to retain control and ownership of materials with the patron's privacy and freedom to explore intellectual content.[98] This requires thought and functional knowledge of the ILS. Most of the popular ILSs do not keep checkout data once the material is returned. This should be checked in the library's ILS to ensure patron privacy. The basic rule of thumb is to "keep as little historical information as possible."[99]

Librarians should also assess how circulation statistics are retained.[100] Statistics should be scrubbed of patron data and item records should not identify the patrons.[101] Ideally, the circulation statistics reported, and therefore kept by the ILS, are deidentified with a limited amount of, if any, demographic data.

Email letters sent by the ILS should be tied to the patron record only until the material is returned and the checkout is deleted from the system.[102] Once the material is returned or paid for (such as lost or damaged materials) the letters should be removed from the patron's record. Purchasing a replacement for a lost or damaged book should be done without reference to the specific patron.

With course reserves, professors may ask for who checked out their materials or circulation statistics. Access Services should not provide a list of who checked out the materials, nor should it even be stored in the ILS. Rather, deidentified information such as the number of circulations by date can be provided.

Privacy in Electronic Records

In addition to circulation records, some libraries use the ILS or other programs to log computer usage transactions and reference interactions.[103] Like circulation statistics, these should not identify individual patrons or contain a patron's PII. Data for assessment and reporting should be collected with the patron records deidentified. For example, for annual reports, the number of times an item circulated or the number of circulations are not dependent upon patron identifiable information. For assessment of the collection, there is no need to tie the information back to individual patron records. Most ILSs will deidentify patron information in their reports.

Services from third-party vendors are trickier for librarians to deal with. Both the library and the vendor share the responsibility for the privacy and security of the patron's information.[104] The best way for librarians to ensure that patrons' privacy is covered is through negotiation with third-party vendors to increase patron privacy protection and know the vendors' privacy policies.[105] At the very least, third-party vendors should use anonymization and limit the use of data collection.[106] The vendor should also allow patrons to access their own user data and be able to "scrub" this data from the vendor website or database if they so choose.[107] These records should also be scrubbed from the vendors' records as soon as the anonymized data is used.

Vendor negotiations are the major way to protect patron records. The negotiations not only include the price but also the use of patron data and privacy. There are limitations pursuant to private sector data capture and data brokerage that the big vendors engage in.[108] These large vendors are increasingly selling the data collected on patrons as data brokers, including selling this information to law enforcement.[109] Librarians must try to negotiate on behalf of their patrons to not have their data sold. It is written in the ALA's Code of Ethics that "we protect each library user's right to privacy and confidentially" in both the type of information sought and the resources used.[110] While many vendors collect this type of information about our patrons, it is our ethical duty to negotiate these practices for the privacy of our patrons.

Other records not stored in library systems that can identify patrons include extended networks such as the campus Active Directory.[111] In cases like this, academic librarians should defer to their Information Technology department for their expertise in securing those databases. A partnership between the library and the Information Technology department should be made and address the issue of remote authentication through Active Directory. Remote authentication should be done through a virtual private network (VPN) to mask the patron's IP address from vendors.[112]

Library applications, such as the LibApps suite of programs from Springshare, also need to be scrubbed of identifiable patron information. The fewer records kept that have patron identification the better.

Chat logs and transcripts should be deleted upon satisfactory conclusion of the chat. This may mean that a chat log is kept for a day or two while the chat in question is being researched and replied to. After the chat is completed, it should be deleted or at least deidentified. This includes IP address information as well as information that identifies the patron specifically such as name, email, or student identification numbers.

Study space reservation systems should be deidentified on all public-facing aspects. Only a few librarians should have access to the identity of the patron who has reserved a study space. The logs for the name of the patron reserving the study space should be deidentified daily or weekly, depending upon the reservation policy. It is suggested that the logs be deidentified daily, with a reservation policy that limits the use of study space as time per day not time per week.

Forms present a longer-term issue. Forms for services, such as poster printing, which require attachments, should be deidentified after the service is performed. This may include deleting attachments to the forms. Forms for internal use, such as material holds, should be deidentified after the material is checked out. Upon checkout, the material is tracked through the ILS, and deidentification should occur as described above.

Surveys can provide useful information and should always be deidentified. Demographic information can be useful, but the collection of it should be viewed as discoverable by the public at large. Care should be taken to only collect demographic data that is absolutely necessary to code the results of the survey. For example, if you are asking about year in school, it should be pertinent to the other questions asked. Surveys should never ask for a patron's name, contact information, or school identification number. Surveys should also scrub the IP address after collection is complete.

Privacy in Patron Internet Activity

Public computer management logs should be deleted daily so as to not be discoverable with National Security Letters under the USA PATRIOT Act.[113] The library should make a policy about computer usage and tracking which patrons use the computers. It needs to address what computer privacy protections are granted. When managing a public set of computers, the library needs to address how those computers are assigned.

Patron computers should be set up with privacy protections, such as limiting the use of cookies and enabling the blocking of extensions.[114] Patron computers should also offer Tor browsers for online anonymity when patrons are browsing online.[115] The patron computers should erase all logins, cookies, and extensions when the patron logs off the computer. In most cases, a form of ID is not needed. In academic libraries especially, the patron's active directory account can be used to log in to the patron computers. If patrons log in with their active directory ID, the computers should be set up to automatically scrub the data once the patron logs out. This prevents the next patron from knowing who was logged in before them.

Libraries should use secure communication protocols (HTTPS) on their websites, catalogs, and discovery services.[116] By moving to HTTPS for library websites, the patron is not tracked when exploring the library's online services.[117] This is especially important in an academic setting as students may be assigned to research controversial topics. This research should not be traceable to a patron's personally identifiable information. Also, it allows for chat transactions to remain truly anonymous.

Teaching, and using, strong password strategies such as using a password manager with a strong password and using two-factor authorization should be the norm.[118] This teaches patrons to take charge of their security and privacy online in and out of the library. By using two-factor authentication with a password manager, patrons have greater control of their privacy, and taken together with other methods of protecting privacy, patrons will have the flexibility of saved passwords and logins without privacy issues.

Privacy in Patron Behavior

Patron behavior in the library is the least able to plan for in a policy and should be carried out in practice. If a patron is reading a book in the library, there is really no way for the library to keep others from seeing, and reporting on, what the patron is reading. Informing patrons of their rights and protections while in the library is really all the library can do.

On patron computers, there should be a polarizing screen so that the information being seen by the patron cannot be seen by others unless they are directly behind the patron. This keeps patron searches and information sought private. Depending on the location of the computers, polarizing screens can also prevent glare on the screen from lights and sun.

CREATING A PRIVACY POLICY

Access Services should be included in creating the library's overall privacy policy. The Access Services department is privy to a lot of information, most notably circulation procedures and policies, and has reason to access the personally identifiable information of patrons. A good privacy policy will present the "what" of privacy in the library.[119] The policy should be followed up by procedures that implement the policy.

A good starting point is the ALA's Privacy Field Guides.[120] These informative guides walk a librarian through the language needed to create a policy as well as ask questions to draft the language.[121] Look at other libraries' privacy policies. Use those to guide you in drafting yours. Review the draft with all of the library stakeholders, including librarians, professional staff, and even student workers.[122] This will allow for many voices to be heard and is more likely to be adopted and used by all of the stakeholders since they had a voice in drafting it.

Procedures to implement the privacy policy should be drafted and issued soon after the policy is adopted.[123] The procedures are the on-the-ground implementation of the privacy policy. Issuing the procedures includes training the librarians and staff in implementing the policy. Regular training for the confidentiality of patron identifiable information should be part of the annual workflow for Access Services.

CONCLUSION

At first glance, it may seem that federal law does protect academic library patron privacy, but it is actually up to the library to be proactive in protecting their patrons' privacy. There is some measure of privacy in FERPA, but the USA PATRIOT Act, FOIA, and state sunshine laws can be used to circumvent FERPA. Only by libraries creating specific library policies and implementing specific practices can libraries truly protect the privacy of their patrons. While this chapter focused on academic libraries, all libraries could benefit from the information provided about how the USA PATRIOT Act, FOIA, and state sunshine laws affect them. Since this chapter was limited to American law, patron privacy in another jurisdiction can and will look different. Within each state, the privacy laws will look different and state law should be looked to for guidance.

ACKNOWLEDGMENTS

The author wishes to acknowledge the support of the Access Services team over the past three years which has enabled her to write this chapter. She would also like to acknowledge her husband, Thomas Aschenbach, who freed up the author's time to write from home.

NOTES

1. Anne Klinefelter, "The Role of Librarians in Challenges to the USA Patriot Act," *North Carolina Journal of Law and Technology* 5 (2004): 222.
2. "Code of Ethics of the American Library Association," American Library Association, accessed August 8, 2022, https://www.ala.org/tools/ethics.
3. "Code of Ethics," American Library Association.
4. "Library Bill of Rights," American Library Association, last modified January 29, 2019, http://www.ala.org/advocacy/intfreedom/librarybill.
5. "Policy Concerning Confidentiality of Personally Identifiable Information about Library Users," American Library Association, last modified July 7, 2006, http://www.ala.org/advocacy/intfreedom/statementspols/otherpolicies/policyconcerning.
6. "Privacy Tool Kit," American Library Association, last modified May 29, 2007, http://www.ala.org/advocacy/privacy/toolkit.
7. "Privacy and Confidentiality: Library Core Values," American Library Association, last modified May 29, 2007, https://www.ala.org/advocacy/privacy/values.
8. "Code of Ethics," National Education Association, last modified September 14, 2020, https://www.nea.org/resource-library/code-ethics-educators.
9. "Code of Ethics," National Education Association.
10. Ibid.
11. Trina Magi, "A Privacy Victory in Vermont," *American Libraries* 39, no. 8 (September 2008): 60.
12. Magi, "Privacy Victory," 61.
13. Ibid., 61–62.
14. FERPA, 20 U.S.C. § 1232g (2012 & Supp. IV 2016).
15. USA PATRIOT Act, 115 Stat. 272 (2001).
16. FOIA, 5 U.S.C. §552 (2012 & Supp. IV 2016).
17. FERPA, 20 U.S.C. § 1232g (2012 & Supp. IV 2016).
18. FERPA, 20 U.S.C. § 1232g (2012 & Supp. IV 2016), 34 C.F.R. § 99 (202).
19. FERPA, 34 C.F.R. § 99.3 (2022); Clifford A. Ramirez, *FERPA Clear and Simple: The College Professional's Guide to Compliance* (New York: Jossey-Bass, 2009), 56.
20. FERPA 20 U.S.C. § 1232g(a)(4)(A) (2012 & Supp. IV 2016).
21. FERPA, 34 C.F.R. § 99.3 (2022).
22. FERPA, 34 C.F.R. § 99.1(d) (2022).
23. FERPA, 34 C.F.R. § 99.31(a)(1) (2022); Ramirez, *FERPA Clear and Simple*, 57–59; Eastern Connecticut State University v. Freedom of Information Commission, 17 Conn. L. Reptr. 588 (1996) (holding that the recording of a student disciplinary hearing could be released to a faculty member for a "legitimate educational interest in the student's behavior.").
24. FERPA, 20 U.S.C. § 1232(g)(b) (2012 & Supp. IV 2016); Gretchen McCord, *What You Need to Know About Privacy Law: A Guide for Librarians and Educators* (Santa Barbara, CA: Libraries Unlimited, 2013), 16–17.
25. Chicago Tribune Company v. University of Illinois Board of Trustees, 781 F. Supp. 2d 672 (N.D. Ill. 2011).
26. Lynn M. Daggett, "FERPA in the Twenty-First Century: Failure to Effectively Regulate Privacy for All Students," *Catholic University Law Review* 58 (2008): 64–67.
27. Mathilda McGee-Tubb, "Deciphering the Supremacy of Federal Funding Conditions: Why State Open Records Law Must Yield to FERPA," *Boston College Law Review* 53 (2012), 1064.
28. McGee-Tubb, "Deciphering the Supremacy," 1064.

29. Ibid., 1065.
30. FERPA, 20 U.S.C. § 1232g(j) (2012 & Supp. IV 2016).
31. For well-written overviews of the USA PATRIOT Act, *see generally* Beryl A. Howell, "Seven Weeks: The Making of the USA PATRIOT Act," *George Washington Law Review* 72 (2004): 1145 (providing a legislative history in a readable form); Michael J. Woods, "Counterintelligence and Access to Transactional Records: A Practical History of the USA PATRIOT Act Section 215," *Journal of National Security Law and Policy* 1(2005): 37 (providing an analysis of Section 215); and Susan N. Herman, "The USA PATRIOT Act and the Submajoritarian Fourth Amendment," *Harvard Civil Rights Civil Liberties Law Review* 41 (2006): 67 (showing the impacts on the Fourth Amendment).
32. McCord, *What You Need to Know About Privacy Law*, 24–25; Susan Nevelow Mart, "Protecting the Lady from Toledo: Post-USA PATRIOT Act Electronic Surveillance at the Library," *Law Library Journal* 96 (2004): 450.
33. Susan Nevelow Mart, "Protecting the Lady from Toledo: Post-USA PATRIOT Act Electronic Surveillance at the Library," *Law Library Journal* 96 (2004): 466.
34. Nevelow Mart, "Protecting the Lady," 453.
35. Ibid., 454.
36. Ibid.
37. Ibid., 449–57.
38. Leah Sandwell-Weiss, "A Look at the USA PATRIOT Act Today: Recent Proposed Legislation to affect Anti-Terrorism Efforts, Individual Rights," *American Association of Law Libraries Spectrum* 8, no 9 (July 2004): 10.
39. McCord, *What You Need to Know About Privacy Law*, 24–25.
40. Emily Drabinski, "Repression and Resistance in Higher Education," *Radical Teacher*, No. 85 (Winter 2006): 12.
41. Drabinski, "Repression and Resistance," 13.
42. Ibid., 12.
43. Amy Goodman and David Goodman, "America's Most Dangerous Librarians: Meet the Radical Bookworms Who Fought the Patriot Act – And Won," *Mother Jones* (September/October 2008), https://www.motherjones.com/politics/2008/09/americas-most-dangerous-librarians.
44. Alison Leigh Cowan, "Four Librarians Finally Break Silence in Records Case," *The New York Times* (May 31, 2006): B3, https://www.nytimes.com/2006/05/31/nyregion/31library.html.
45. Goodman and Goodman, "America's Most Dangerous."
46. Cowan, "Four Librarians," B3.
47. Klinefelter, "The Role of Librarians," 219.
48. Klinefelter, "The Role of Librarians," 220; Nevelow Mart, "Protecting the Lady," 464.
49. Nevelow Mart, "Protecting the Lady," 464–73.
50. Doe v. Gonzales, 386 F. Supp. 2d, 66, 70 (D. Conn., 2005); Goodman and Goodman, "America's Most Dangerous."
51. "Librarians Stand Again Against FBI Overreach," *Hartford Courant* (September 28, 2016), http://www.courant.com/opinion/op-ed/hc-op-librarians-stand-up-to-patriot-act-again-20160927-story.html.
52. Goodman and Goodman, "America's Most Dangerous."
53. Goodman and Goodman, "America's Most Dangerous"; Cowan, "Four Librarians," B3.
54. Goodman and Goodman, "America's Most Dangerous."
55. "Librarians Stand," *Hartford Courant*; Goodman and Goodman, "America's Most Dangerous."
56. "Librarians Stand," *Hartford Courant*.
57. Doe v. Gonzales, 449 F.3d 415, 420-21 (2d Circ., 2006).
58. United States v. Miami University, 294 F.3d 797 (6th Cir. 2001).
59. United States v. Miami University, 294 F.3d 797, 804 (6th Cir. 2001).
60. Ibid.

61. Ibid.
62. Ibid.
63. Ibid.
64. United States v. Miami University, 294 F.3d 797, 812-14 (6th Cir. 2001).
65. Chicago Tribune Company v. University of Illinois Board of Trustees, 781 F. Supp. 2d 672, 676 (N.D. Ill. 2011).
66. Chicago Tribune Company v. University of Illinois Board of Trustees, 781 F. Supp. 2d 672, 673-674 (N.D. Ill. 2011).
67. Chicago Tribune Company v. University of Illinois Board of Trustees, 781 F. Supp. 2d 672, 674 (N.D. Ill. 2011).
68. Chicago Tribune Company v. University of Illinois Board of Trustees, 781 F. Supp. 2d 672, 676 (N.D. Ill. 2011).
69. Tomas A. Lipinski, "Legal Issues Involved in the Privacy Rights of Patrons in 'Public' Libraries and Archives," in *Libraries, Museums, and Archives: Legal Issues and Ethical Challenges in the New Information Era*, ed. Tomas A. Lipinski (Lanham, MD: Scarecrow Press, 2002), 96–97.
70. Lipinski, "Legal Issues," 96–97.
71. Ibid., 98–99.
72. Ibid., 100–01.
73. Mary Minow and Tomas A. Lipinski, *The Library's Legal Answer Book* (Chicago: American Library Association, 2003), 174–90.
74. Minow and Lipinski, *The Library's Legal Answer Book*, 174–90. A comparison chart of state library privacy laws can be found at Minow and Lipinski, *The Library's Legal Answer*, 200–10 and G 242–46. See also Kathryn Martin, "Note: The USA Patriot Act's Application to Library Patron Records," *Journal of Legislation* 29 (2013): 289.
75. Confidentiality of Records, Conn. Gen. Stat. §11-25 (2021).
76. Releasing Library Record or Patron Information, Ohio Rev. Code Ann. §149.432 (LexisNexis 2022).
77. Illinois State Freedom of Information Act, 5 Ill. Comp. Stat. 140 (2010).
78. Confidentiality of Records, Conn. Gen. Stat. §11-25 (2021); Illinois State Freedom of Information Act, 5 Ill. Comp. Stat. 140 (2010); Releasing Library Record or Patron Information, Ohio Rev. Code Ann. §149.432 (LexisNexis 2022).
79. Barbara M. Jones, *Protecting Intellectual Freedom in Your Academic Library: Scenarios from the Front Lines* (Chicago: American Library Association, 2009), 162–63.
80. "State Privacy Laws Regarding Library Records," American Library Association, http://www.ala.org/advocacy/privacy/statelaws.
81. Daggett, "FERPA in the Twenty-First Century," 97.
82. Ibid., 99.
83. McGee-Tubb, "Deciphering," 1065.
84. "State Privacy Laws," American Library Association.
85. "GovInfo," U.S. Government Publishing Office, accessed September 6, 2022, https://www.govinfo.gov.
86. "Family Education Rights and Privacy Act (FERPA)," United States Department of Education, August 25, 2021, https://www2.ed.gov/policy/gen/guid/fpco/ferpa/index.html; "Protecting Student Privacy," United States Department of Education, accessed August 10, 2022, https://studentprivacy.ed.gov/.
87. "USA PATRIOT Act," American Library Association, May 29, 2020, https://www.ala.org/advocacy/patriot-act.
88. "Freedom of Information Act Statute," United States Department of Justice, 2016, https://www.foia.gov/foia-statute.html.
89. "State Sunshine Laws," BallotPedia, accessed August 10, 2022, https://ballotpedia.org/State_sunshine_laws.
90. Online Copyright Infringement Liability Limitation Act, 112 Stat. 2860 (1998).

91. Interception of Digital and Other Communications, 47 U.S.C. §§ 1001-10 (2012 & Supp. IV 2016).
92. Lee Ann Torrans, *Law and Libraries: The Public Library* (Santa Barbara, CA: Libraries Unlimited, 2004), 33–34; Jones, *Protecting Intellectual Freedom*, 173–76.
93. Torrans, *Law and Libraries*, 31.
94. Ibid., 34.
95. Ibid., 29.
96. Ibid., 32–33.
97. Ibid.
98. Matt Backstrom, "Use, Security, and Ethics of Data Collection: Data Collection Retention, Use, and Security," in *Protecting Patron Privacy: A LITA Guide*, ed. Bobbi Newman and Bonnie Tijerna (Lanham, MD: Rowan & Littlefield, 2017), 42.
99. Drabinski, "Repression," 13.
100. Jeannette Woodward, *What Every Librarian Should Know About Electronic Privacy* (Santa Barbara, CA: Greenwood Publishing Group, 2007), 123–25.
101. Woodward, *What Every Librarian*, 123–25.
102. Ibid.
103. Jones, *Protecting Intellectual Freedom*, 176–82.
104. Lori Bowen Ayre, "Protecting Patron Privacy: Vendors, Libraries, and Patrons Each Have a Role to Play," *Collaborative Librarianship* 9, no. 1 (2017): 2, https://digitalcommons.du.edu/collaborativelibrarianship/vol9/iss1/2.
105. William Marden, "Third-Party Services in Libraries," in *Protecting Patron Privacy: A LITA Guide*, eds. Bobbi Newman and Bonnie Tijerna (Lanham, MD: Rowan & Littlefield, 2017), 73–79.
106. Bowen Ayre, "Protecting Patron Privacy," 3.
107. Ibid., 304.
108. Sarah Lamdan, "Librarianship at the Crossroads of ICE Surveillance," *In the Library with the Lead Pipe* (November 13, 2019), https://www.inthelibrarywiththeleadpipe.org/2019/ice-surveillance.
109. Lamdan, "Librarianship at the Crossroads."
110. "Code of Ethics," American Library Association.
111. Woodward, *What Every Librarian Should Know*, 128–30.
112. Lamdan, "Librarianship at the Crossroads."
113. Woodward, *What Every Librarian Should Know*, 126.
114. Bowen Ayre, "Protecting Patron Privacy," 1.
115. Alison Macrina, "Protecting Patron Privacy," *Library Journal* (March 30, 2017), https://www.library-journal.com/story/protecting-patron-privacy.
116. Bowen Ayre, "Protecting Patron Privacy," 1; Marshall Breeding, "Protecting Patron Privacy: Libraries Are Failing to Use HTTPS," *American Libraries* 2, no. 1 (2017): 78, https://journals.ala.org/index.php/jifp/article/view/6248; Macrina, "Protecting Patron Privacy."
117. Macrina, "Protecting Patron Privacy."
118. Ibid.
119. Stephen Henson, "Developing and Writing Library Policies and Procedures," Nebraska Library Commission, last modified October 5, 2017, http://nlc.nebraska.gov/directorsguidebook/docs/Henson_Policies%20and%20Procedures.pdf.
120. "Privacy Field Guides," American Library Association, last modified April 25, 2014, https://www.ala.org/advocacy/privacy/fieldguides.
121. For example, "Privacy Policies," American Library Association, last modified April 25, 2014, https://www.ala.org/advocacy/sites/ala.org.advocacy/files/content/privacyconfidentiality/PrivacyPolicies-Privacy-Advocacy-Guides_v2.pdf.
122. Henson, "Developing and Writing."
123. Ibid.

BIBLIOGRAPHY

American Library Association. "Code of Ethics of the American Library Association," https://www.ala.org/tools/ethics.
———. "Library Bill of Rights." Last modified June 30, 2006. http://www.ala.org/advocacy/intfreedom/librarybill.
———. "Policy Concerning Confidentiality of Personally Identifiable Information about Library Users." Last modified July 7, 2006. http://www.ala.org/advocacy/intfreedom/statementspols/otherpolicies/policyconcerning.
———. "Privacy and Confidentiality: Library Core Values." Last modified May 29, 2007. https://www.ala.org/advocacy/privacy/values.
———. "Privacy Field Guides." Last modified April 25, 2014. https://www.ala.org/advocacy/privacy/fieldguides.
———. "Privacy Policies." Last modified April 25, 2014. https://www.ala.org/advocacy/sites/ala.org.advocacy/files/content/privacyconfidentiality/PrivacyPolicies-Privacy-Advocacy-Guides_v2.pdf.
———. "Privacy Tool Kit." Last modified May 29, 2007. http://www.ala.org/advocacy/privacy/toolkit.
———. "State Privacy Laws Regarding Library Records." Last updated May 29, 2017. http://www.ala.org/advocacy/privacy/statelaws.
———. "USA PATRIOT Act." Last updated May 29, 2020. https://www.ala.org/advocacy/patriot-act.
Backstrom, Matt. "Use, Security, and Ethics of Data Collection: Data Collection Retention, Use, and Security." In *Protecting Patron Privacy: A LITA Guide*, edited by Bobbi Newman and Bonnie Tijerna. Lanham, MD: Rowan & Littlefield, 2017.
BallotPedia. "State Sunshine Laws." Accessed August 10, 2022. https://ballotpedia.org/State_sunshine_laws.
Bowen Ayre, Lori. "Protecting Patron Privacy: Vendors, Libraries, and Patrons Each Have a Role to Play." *Collaborative Librarianship* 9, no. 1 (2017). https://digitalcommons.du.edu/collaborativelibrarianship/vol9/iss1/2.
Breeding, Marshall. "Protecting Patron Privacy: Libraries Are Failing to Use HTTPS." *American Libraries* 2, no. 1 (2017). https://journals.ala.org/index.php/jifp/article/view/6248.
Chicago Tribune Company v. University of Illinois Board of Trustees, 781 F. Supp. 2d 672 (N.D. Ill. 2011).
Confidentiality of Records, Conn. Gen. Stat. §11-25 (2021).
Cowan, Alison Leigh. "Four Librarians Finally Break Silence in Records Case." *The New York Times* (May 31, 2006), B3. https://www.nytimes.com/2006/05/31/nyregion/31library.html.
Daggett, Lynn M. "FERPA in the Twenty-First Century: Failure to Effectively Regulate Privacy for All Students." *Catholic University Law Review* 58 (2008).
Doe v. Gonzales, 386 F. Supp. 2d, 66 (D. Conn., 2005).
Doe v. Gonzales, 449 F.3d 415 (2d Circ., 2006).
Drabinski, Emily. "Repression and Resistance in Higher Education." *Radical Teacher*, no. 85 (Winter 2006): 12.
Eastern Connecticut State University v. Freedom of Information Commission, 17 Conn. L. Reptr. 588 (1996).
FERPA, 20 U.S.C. § 1232g (2012 & Supp. IV 2016).
FERPA, 34 C.F.R. § 99 (202).
FOIA, 5 U.S.C. §552 (2012 & Supp. IV 2016).
Goodman, Amy, and David Goodman. "America's Most Dangerous Librarians: Meet the Radical Bookworms Who Fought the Patriot Act – And Won." *Mother Jones* (September/October 2008). https://www.motherjones.com/politics/2008/09/americas-most-dangerous-librarians.
Hartford Courant. "Librarians Stand Again Against FBI Overreach." *Hartford Courant* (September 28, 2016). http://www.courant.com/opinion/op-ed/hc-op-librarians-stand-up-to-patriot-act-again-20160927-story.html.

Henson, Stephen. "Developing and Writing Library Policies and Procedures." Nebraska Library Commission. Last modified October 5, 2017. http://nlc.nebraska.gov/directorsguidebook/docs/Henson_Policies%20and%20Procedures.pdf.

Herman, Susan N. "The USA PATRIOT Act and the Submajoritarian Fourth Amendment." *Harvard Civil Rights Civil Liberties Law Review* 41 (2006).

Howell, Beryl A. "Seven Weeks: The Making of the USA PATRIOT Act." *George Washington Law Review* 72 (2004): 1145.

Illinois State Freedom of Information Act, 5 Ill. Comp. Stat. 140 (2010).

Interception of Digital and Other Communications, 47 U.S.C. §§ 1001-10 (2012 & Supp. IV 2016).

Jones, Barbara M. *Protecting Intellectual Freedom in Your Academic Library: Scenarios from the Front Lines.* Chicago: American Library Association, 2009.

Klinefelter, Anne. "The Role of Librarians in Challenges to the USA Patriot Act." *North Carolina Journal of Law and Technology* 5 (2004): 222.

Lamdan, Sarah. "Librarianship at the Crossroads of ICE Surveillance." *In the Library with the Lead Pipe* (November 13, 2019). https://www.inthelibrarywiththeleadpipe.org/2019/ice-surveillance.

Lipinski, Tomas A. "Legal Issues Involved in the Privacy Rights of Patrons in 'Public' Libraries and Archives." In *Libraries, Museums, and Archives: Legal Issues and Ethical Challenges in the New Information Era*, edited by Tomas A. Lipinski. Lanham, MA: Scarecrow Press, 2002.

Macrina, Alison. "Protecting Patron Privacy." *Library Journal* (March 30, 2017). https://www.libraryjournal.com/story/protecting-patron-privacy.

Magi, Trina. "A Privacy Victory in Vermont." *American Libraries* 39, no. 8 (September 2008).

Marden, William. "Third-Party Services in Libraries." In *Protecting Patron Privacy: A LITA Guide*, edited by Bobbi Newman and Bonnie Tijerna, 73–79. Lanham, MD: Rowan & Littlefield, 2017.

Martin, Kathryn. "Note: The USA Patriot Act's Application to Library Patron Records." *Journal of Legislation* 29 (2013): 289.

McCord, Gretchen. *What You Need to Know About Privacy Law: A Guide for Librarians and Educators* (Santa Barbara, CA: Libraries Unlimited, 2013).

McGee-Tubb, Mathilda. "Deciphering the Supremacy of Federal Funding Conditions: Why State Open Records Law Must Yield to FERPA." *Boston College Law Review* 53 (2012).

Minow, Mary, and Tomas A. Lipinski. *The Library's Legal Answer Book*. Chicago: American Library Association, 2003.

National Education Association. "Code of Ethics." Last modified September 14, 2020. https://www.nea.org/resource-library/code-ethics-educators.

Nevelow Mart, Susan. "Protecting the Lady from Toledo: Post-USA PATRIOT Act Electronic Surveillance at the Library." *Law Library Journal* 96 (2004).

Online Copyright Infringement Liability Limitation Act, 112 Stat. 2860 (1998).

Ramirez, Clifford A. *FERPA Clear and Simple: The College Professional's Guide to Compliance*. New York: Jossey-Bass, 2009.

Releasing Library Record or Patron Information, Ohio Rev. Code Ann. §149.432. LexisNexis 2022.

Sandwell-Weiss, Leah. "A Look at the USA PATRIOT Act Today: Recent Proposed Legislation to affect Anti-Terrorism Efforts, Individual Rights." *American Association of Law Libraries Spectrum* 8, no 9 (July 2004): 10.

Torrans, Lee Ann. *Law and Libraries: The Public Library*. Santa Barbara, CA: Libraries Unlimited, 2004.

United States Department of Education. "Family Education Rights and Privacy Act (FERPA)." August 25, 2021. https://www2.ed.gov/policy/gen/guid/fpco/ferpa/index.html.

———. "Protecting Student Privacy." Accessed August 10, 2022. https://studentprivacy.ed.gov/.

United States Department of Justice. "Freedom of Information Act Statute." Last updated 2016. https://www.foia.gov/foia-statute.html.

United States v. Miami University, 294 F.3d 797 (6th Cir. 2001).

U.S. Government Publishing Office. "GovInfo." Accessed September 6, 2022. https://www.govinfo.gov.

USA PATRIOT Act, 115 Stat. 272 (2001).

Woods, Michael J. "Counterintelligence and Access to Transactional Records: A Practical History of the USA PATRIOT Act Section 215." *Journal of National Security Law and Policy* 1 (2005).

Woodward, Jeannette. *What Every Librarian Should Know About Electronic Privacy*. Santa Barbara, CA: Greenwood Publishing Group, 2007.

CHAPTER 5

PUTTING PRIVACY INTO PRACTICE:
Embedding a Privacy Review into Digital Library Workflows

Virginia Dressler

INTRODUCTION

Digital librarians and digital archivists often encounter aspects of privacy throughout digitization projects, though only recently have more specific practical guidelines and parameters for this kind of work been discussed for practitioners to apply locally. This chapter addresses how to outline and integrate a privacy review into existing digital library workflows. Additionally, creating a *culture* and *awareness* of privacy is crucial in the effort to incorporate privacy review into practice by committing to consistently address privacy in digital library production workflows as a regular process.

The chapter offers some working definitions of private data and information and provides suggestions to integrate a privacy review into existing digital content production workflows, much like how practitioners will regularly use certain guidelines for digitization benchmarks (such as the Federal Agencies Digital Guidelines Initiative or the National Archives' "Technical Guidelines for Digitizing Archival Materials for Electronic Access"). A framework of personally identifiable information (PII) and other types of private information are summarized using national specifications (United States). Additionally, selected federal laws and statutes such as Family Educational Rights and Privacy Act (FERPA) and the Health Insurance Portability and Accountability Act of 1996 (HIPAA) are included to provide guidance around protected private information included under such codes, which may be of use for some institutions and collections. However, many circumstances may require more discussion and discernment to assess private and sensitive information.

Suggestions for talking points for internal working groups are outlined for institutions of varying sizes to begin to define and create documentation for privacy reviews and how to have conversations around defining private information locally. Ideas about how to incorporate the privacy review within an existing production workflow are shared and, lastly, a review of existing resources is included. It is paramount as gatekeepers to creating and publishing digital collections that we work toward more ethical and sound practices.

The importance of adding a privacy review to a digital library or digital archive production is critical in creating more ethically sound and equitable digital collections. While the added measure of a privacy review is time-consuming and laborious, it is also paramount in the role of the practitioner to be a conscientious and ethical gatekeeper, taking responsibility for the information openly disseminated through institutional platforms. The review process can be implemented into a digital project in a similar vein to a copyright review and, as such, be seen as something essential and important.

Privacy is an elusive term—oftentimes, it is hard to pinpoint and define as individuals each bring their own definitions and expectations around the concept, making any application of a static definition of privacy a cumbersome and impossible task. This aspect is important to start as it greatly impacts any kind of work around privacy review and protections. Some types of private information may have some guiding principles here in the United States with protection from FERPA and HIPAA, which may provide some direction depending on the nature of your collection and institution. However, many areas of privacy fall outside of legal parameters. "Determining what is sensitive or embarrassing information (rather than legally protected information) is often a personal judgment, further complicating the process."[1]

PRIVATE DATA: WORKING DEFINITIONS AND CONSIDERATIONS

First, a note to distinguish the difference between private and sensitive information. Private information is personal information that can identify an individual and is to be protected from unauthorized use by another, whereas sensitive information involves potentially embarrassing information that an individual may want to keep private.[2] This is important to note since there are different ways to review content for either type of information, once your institution has agreed upon a working definition of private and sensitive information. Danielson notes that privacy is "the ability to control personal data—how it circulates in society, in archives, in publications and on the Internet."[3] Sensitive information may fall into more ethical areas that are grayer to discern (and therefore use a different tool to review and assess on a case-by-case basis).

One resource that is helpful in guiding internal discussion around identifying private information is *Guide to Protecting the Confidentiality of Personally Identifiable Information (PII): Recommendations of the National Institute of Standards and Technology (NIST)*, published in 2010. The approach outlined in this publication is described as a risk-based approach and stresses the importance of tailoring an outline and application protecting PII for each institution. Further, "Organizations should minimize the use, collection, and retention of PII to what is strictly necessary to accomplish their business purpose and mission."[4] The guide also provides some great examples of the types of information that should be protected, such as any personal identification number, addresses, financial information, date/place of birth, etc. But perhaps more thought-provoking are the areas that are a little more difficult to easily identify or define, such as "information about an individual that is linked or linkable to one of the above (e.g., race, religion, weight, activities, geographical indicators, employment information)."[5] The guide also pushes for each institution to define its own policies and procedures for handling private information as well as recommendations to de-identify (or redact) PII when possible. And finally, a recommendation to consult with general counsel or privacy officers once this documentation is ready for review.

Another important document to assist with creating a tailored privacy review at an institution would be a privacy impact assessment (PIA). This approach has been outlined by Strauß in the following framework:[6]

1. Identify pieces of information/data, and how is it processed.
2. Is there third-party involvement?
3. What is the life cycle of the information?
4. What information is collected, and how is it being used and processed?
5. What are the risks and likelihood of risk?
6. Recommendation for existing or new controls to protect against risk.
7. Documentation of risk resolution and residual risks (retaining a PIA report).

Answering the questions above will help guide some of the conversations around PII and also help with decision-making around retention. Additionally, some institutions may want to complete a privacy audit as part of this work. The American Library Association (ALA) provides some great resources to get started with privacy audits and checklists.[7] It is important to consider a privacy review in both digitized and born-digital projects.

LEGAL GUIDANCE

While the United States can be viewed as lagging in overarching data privacy laws compared to the European Union and other countries, one can look to some guidance from a few federal laws. One exception to this statement would be the more recent laws for California residents in the California Consumer Privacy Act (CCPA) and New York residents in the New York Privacy Act (NYPA), though it has been speculated that more states will soon follow suit. The Family Educational Rights and Privacy Act (FERPA) and Health Insurance Portability and Accountability Act (HIPAA) provide two federal legal frameworks for the specification of personally identifiable information and private data, which are helpful resources for practitioners to guide privacy protections in certain types of documents.

Family Educational Rights and Privacy Act (FERPA)

FERPA is a federal law that protects the privacy of student education records.[8] FERPA requires consent from a student before disclosing education records and certain types of personal information from education records, and the protection of FERPA extends to the lifetime of the student (or, in the case of a minor, the lifetime of the parent or guardian). What does or does not constitute a student record is an interesting next question in this process. Neiger states, "FERPA applies much more broadly to all records directly related to a student that are maintained by the institution, including non-academic disciplinary records, financial aid records, documents related to NCAA investigations, general correspondence from students, and even a student's employment file"; Neiger notes there is often confusion around what constitutes a student education record. Further, "The plain meaning of the statutory language reveals that Congress intended for the definition of 'education records' to be broad in scope."[9] Education records are defined as being (1) directly related to a student and (2) maintained by an educational agency or institution or by a party acting for the agency or institution.[10] Again, this is an area to talk about locally at an institution and come to agreements as to what documents are included in FERPA protection.

The protection of FERPA is geared towards PII, which includes (*but is not limited to*)
- the student's name;
- the name of the student's parent or other family members;
- the address of the student or student's family;
- a personal identifier, such as the student's social security number, student number, or biometric record;
- other indirect identifiers, such as the student's date of birth, place of birth, or mother's maiden name;
- other information that, alone or in combination, is linked or linkable to a specific student that would allow a reasonable person in the school community who does not have personal knowledge of the relevant circumstances to identify the student; or
- information requested by a person who the educational …institution reasonably believes knows the identity of the student to whom the education record relates.[11]

The list does, however, conflict with the disclosure of "directory information," an allowable exception in FERPA with prior notice to the student or parent/guardian and an option for the student/parent/guardian to opt out of such disclosure.

Under FERPA, directory information includes

> the student's name; address; telephone listing; electronic mail address; photograph; date and place of birth; major field of study; grade level; enrollment status (e.g., undergraduate or graduate, full-time or part-time); dates of attendance; participation in officially recognized activities and sports; weight and height of members of athletic teams; degrees, honors and awards received; and the most recent educational agency or institution attended.[12]

FERPA provides some guidance for certain types of records, though has a few areas that can lead to some confusion for practitioners needing more straightforward information around redaction and protected information. One last interesting side note is that FERPA does not provide any private right of enforcement—the Department of Education can enforce FERPA, but the student, parent, or guardian cannot.

Health Insurance Portability and Accountability Act of 1996 (HIPAA)

The HIPAA privacy rule (issued in 2000, updated in 2002 and 2013) and protections apply specifically to medical records, outlining the use and sharing of an individual's health information. The rule allows the use of information for medical treatment and payment for health care, but "all other uses and disclosures of personal health information, including scholarly and historical research uses, require individual written authorization or strict compliance with HIPAA's 'safe harbor' provisions."[13] The protected health information (PHI) is individually identifiable health information that is transmitted or maintained in any medium (electronic, oral, or paper), excluding certain educational and employment records and excluding information on those individuals who have been deceased for longer than fifty years.[14] Repositories that are considered a "covered entity," "hybrid entity," or "business associate" of a covered entity must adhere to the Privacy Rule;[15] however, there is less guidance for repositories that fall outside of these organizations but contain collections with medical records or information. Under protected entities, information such as names, dates of birth, medical records, diagnosis, and images of patients cannot be made public.

PHI can include

- names
- postal address information
- telephone numbers
- fax numbers
- electronic mail addresses
- Social Security numbers
- medical record numbers
- health plan beneficiary numbers
- account numbers
- certificate/license numbers
- vehicle identifiers and serial numbers, including license plate numbers
- device identifiers and serial numbers
- Web Universal Resource Locators (URLs)
- Internet protocol (IP) address numbers
- biometric identifiers, including finger and voice prints
- full-face photographic images and any comparable images[16]

And similar to the scenario of what may constitute a medical record, this point can be contentious as well. Letocha[17] advises consultation with legal counsel to make these determinations and how institutional policy may apply locally. A medical record is information held by a hospital medical records office (or other providers) used to make healthcare decisions about the individual patient.

One tactic used by Duke University Medical Center Archive is to redact PHI information from any inlets of discovery[18] before dissemination or publication. It is important to set definitions of protected pieces of information locally.

To compare the differences in PII between FERPA and HIPAA, the Center for Disease Control and Protection (CDC) has provided some guidance on what types of information and under what circumstances protections apply,[19] as seen in table 5.1. The table was adapted to include types of information not protected.

TABLE 5.1

Overview of FERPA and HIPAA Personally identifiable information and private data coverage and protections.

	WHO MUST COMPLY	TYPE(S) OF INFORMATION PROTECTED	TYPE(S) OF INFORMATION NOT PROTECTED
FERPA	Any public or private school: • Elementary • Secondary • Post-secondary Any state or local education agency Any of the above must receive funds under an applicable program of the US Department of Education.	Student Education Record. Records that contain information directly related to a student and which are maintained by an educational agency or institution or by a party acting for the agency or institution. Note: the definition of what constitutes as an educational record varies from institution to institution, and generally only applies to the lifetime of the student.	Directory information, such as name, address, telephone listing, date and place of birth, participation in officially recognized activities and sports, and dates of attendance.
HIPAA	Every healthcare provider who electronically transmits health information in connection with certain transactions. • Health plans • Healthcare clearinghouses Business associates that act on behalf of a covered entity, including claims processing, data analysis, utilization review, and billing.	Protected Health Information: Individually identifiable health information that is transmitted or maintained in any form or medium (electronic, oral, or paper) by a covered entity or its business associates, excluding certain educational and employment records.	De-identified health information, which has been completed by the following options: (1) formal determination by a qualified statistician or (2) the removal of specified identifiers of the individual and of the individual's relatives, household members, and employers is required, and is adequate only if the covered entity has no actual knowledge that the remaining information could be used to identify the individual. Certain disclosures permissable by covered entities for pre-defined use.

PRIVACY IN DIGITAL COLLECTIONS
Privacy and Access

A number of resources were reviewed, though very few offer clear directives for the practitioner around addressing privacy in digital project management. Consistency is important throughout any kind of review, which is difficult when little or no guidance is available for this type of work. "Institutions without guidelines for selection require archivists to make personal decisions about the appropriateness of digitizing individual items,"[20] and this creates problems for consistently addressing privacy issues. Ultimately, a privacy review and considerations are not a "one size fits all" approach, even at times within the same collection.[21]

Other disciplines and fields like medicine have also struggled with the decision between privacy and access in digital content, particularly in regard to sensitive health information. Gariépy-Saper and Decarie[22] discuss the advantages of the move of electronic health records from more secured local access to cloud-based services. "We consider health information to be a universal need,"[23] and highlight the benefits of reducing the barriers to access information in many cases while also cautioning against the potential risks.

LeClere addresses "how archivists negotiate their competing interests of providing open access to archives against maintaining individual privacy."[24] The author adds some tactics that have already been used to address privacy issues in digital archives; in the selection and curation before digitization, requesting permissions from donor or content owner, redacting private and/or sensitive information, public disclaimers, and posting take-down policies for online content.[25] LeClere interviewed archivists about digitization work, specifically looking at how the individual related to privacy questions during a project.

Crossen-White highlights the disclosure of personal information via digital archives with potential harm, such as information from the Booth's Poverty Map of London that discloses names and a variety of personal information in the associated notebooks or searches in *The Times* digital archive for early twentieth-century drug-taking activity. And while the subjects in the digital archives may be deceased, there was still a concern for the privacy of the subjects' descendants. "However, the emergence of 'citizen historians', lacking any formal research training, means that the [digital] archives are being accessed by a growing number of users who will have given little thought to ethical concerns that could arise from the results of their searches."[26] The author also outlines a situation in 2014 when the Irish government shut down a website that provided personal information on living persons and found a potential for digital archives to cause harm. Lastly,

"Digital archives can rapidly reveal a long forgotten incident with the potential to create harm and possibly not even to the principal individual connected to the content."[27] Crossen-White notes that when topics are especially sensitive (violent assault, intimidation, etc.), more care should be taken to address privacy issues.

Chenier addresses ethical aspects of information contained in transcripts and audio from the Archives of Lesbian Oral Testimony (ALOT), where privacy concerns were not only from the interviewee but also individuals named in the transcripts. Chenier wonders, "Even if narrators are fully out, what about the people they name in their interviews?"[28] Chenier notes privacy protection for narrators in projects such as the Library of Congress Slave Narratives from the Federal Writers' Project, the United States Holocaust Museum Memory Project, and the Veterans Oral History Project. The author also discusses the context of consent, where an individual may be comfortable with permissions for more closed access and not with a fully disclosed version, and scenarios where an individual may also change their mind over time about access. The author highlights an approach from the British Library to reconfirm consent before posting digital material online.[29]

Privacy Models for Digital Collections

Chenier[30] shares the dissemination policy for the ALOT digital archive, which includes options for an interviewee to select open or restricted access, a donor-driven approach to the degree of anonymization in a digital item, and a method for participants to retract consent at any time. When participants (or family members) cannot be located for permission, an edited clip will be presented.

While Goldman and Pyatt addressed privacy in born-digital content, they outlined a process at Duke University Archives when an audit was conducted to reveal potentially sensitive digital material contained in digital files, which acted "as a catalyst to elevate the security of their born-digital records."[31] And addressing social media archives, Velte reports that many institutions implement an embargo period before public access is allowable. Additionally, Velte discusses the idea of a model of moderated access for web and electronic archives.[32]

The 2013 CLIR report *Born Digital: Guidance for Donors, Dealers, and Archival Repositories* advises, "When staff, time, or technology constraints do not allow for review of sensitive email messages or other files, discuss restrictions on researcher access for a defined period of time."[33] Similarly, Zastrow discusses an approach with letters contained in the Japanese American Veterans collection that were presented in a subset, with approval from the donor for a selection of letters that were not deemed to contain sensitive or personal information. The author also discusses archiving emails from congressional offices in their capacity as an archivist in Congress and states, "I appeal to [the congressmen's] sense of history and the integrity and transparency of the record."[34] Similarly, LeClere discusses an approach where two institutions sought permission before digitization projects,[35] building a framework of consent into workflows.

Addressing Privacy Locally

No matter the size of the institution, an initial discussion around private information and tactics to protect PII is important. Depending on which state your institution is in, there may be some additional state laws to help guide this conversation. As well, the type of institution will also provide some insights. If the collection includes educational records and is maintained by an educational institution, there are FERPA guidelines to apply; likewise, if the collection contains medical information, HIPAA may be applied as guidance, even if the institution is not a covered entity.

Discussions around privacy are often hard without examples to refer to, much like the "I know it when I see it" ideology from the 1964 *Jacobellis v. Ohio* case[36] on identifying pornography. Having specific examples to discuss with an internal working group will help illustrate privacy issues when possible. Individuals relate to privacy in different ways, in how we think about privacy in our own application and world. "While in practice, the implication of privacy varies from person to person. For example, someone considers salary to be sensitive information while someone doesn't; someone cares much about privacy while someone cares less."[37]

Putting Practice into Production

The Responsible Access workflows were published in 2020 by the University of California Berkeley Library, a set of four adaptable workflows that include privacy, copyright, ethics, and contracts. These documents can be tailored to the institution and state needs, providing a mechanism to guide the processes and provide a better way to ensure consistency. In the template, for example, specific definitions of PII and classifications at UC Berkeley are directly linked from the workflows that include specific state protections.[38]

One section to highlight from figure 5.1 is the privacy torts, which include intrusion upon seclusion, public disclosure of private facts, painting someone in a false light, and appropriation of name, voice, and likeness.

Putting Privacy into Practice   95

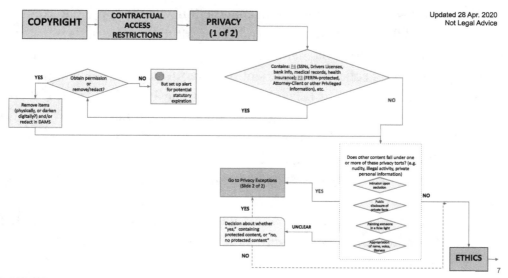

FIGURE 5.1

Privacy workflow. Berkeley Library (University of California), Responsible Access Workflows. CC-BY-NC 4.0, used with permission.

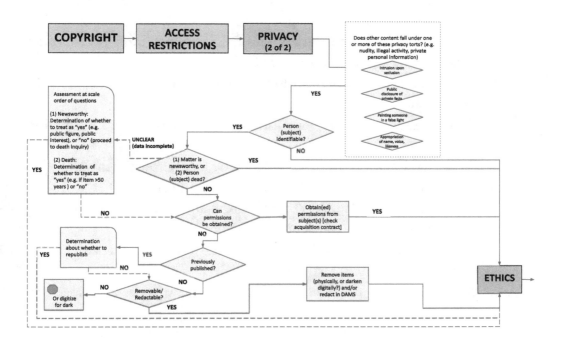

FIGURE 5.2

Privacy Workflow Part II. Berkeley Library (University of California), Responsible Access Workflows. CC-BY-NC 4.0, used with permission.

The privacy workflow can be used in conjunction with the copyright, contracts, and ethics workflows from Berkeley, and the institution can decide what order makes the most sense to implement into production. For example, if the digitization project entails a collection representing an underrepresented community, a decision to place an ethics or privacy review first may be a good tactic if there is concern about potential harm in disclosing information. One decision tree used for HIPAA-related decisions was provided in Letocha's "Changes to the Privacy Rule of HIPAA" and determining the likelihood of HIPAA protections.[39]

And in *Framing Privacy in Digital Collections with Ethical Decision Making*,[40] the following framework was provided:

A. Questions to be posed to the original item or collection (digital or analog):
1. What was the original **context** of the information/collection?
2. What was the original **purpose** of the information/collection?
3. Who was the original **audience** of the information/collection?
    Do the answers from Section A inform and impact the public levels of access or restriction to the information?
    Are there alternate paths to enable some level of access through redaction or other restrictions?

B. Questions to be posed to the notion of the original content creator (if known), or directly toward the information itself:
1. Who retains **control** of the information (or perhaps more importantly, who should)?
2. Does **consent** need to be attained before disseminating information broadly?
3. What level of **awareness** has been made to any constituents as to the planned publication and distribution of the information?
    Do the answers from Section B inform and impact decisions on levels of access or restriction to the information?
    Are there alternate paths to enable some level of access through redaction or other restrictions?

Additionally, figure 5.3 provides a one-page overview of privacy aspects to consider and start conversations around implementing a process internally by reviewing and identifying potentially private information.

Much like the Responsible Access Workflows, the Dressler-Kearns checklist can be adapted to the needs of the individual institution. The checklist can also provide a point of documentation for institutions to retain to record decisions around privacy. The checklist can also serve to provide a reference and talking points for working groups to address particularly privacy concerns and issues.

> **DRESSLER-KEARNS ANALOG TO DIGITAL PRIVACY CHECKLIST AND ACTION DECIDER**
>
> Assess the content and take into consideration all legal and moral guidelines under which your organization is bound, such as copyright, state laws, federal (such as FERPA and HIPAA), in-house policy, and donor agreements.
>
> Does your organization hold distribution rights or copyrights to the analog document? If this answer is no, do not publish digitized materials, though Title 17 of the US Code permits archives to make preservation copies of archival copyrighted materials.
>
> Before disseminating content, conduct a privacy review. In some cases, your institution may elect to redact private information or decide not to publish content.
>
> Does the analog document disclose personal information that your organization would not share with an onsite researcher?
> Such as:
> - Social security number
> - Address
> - Personal names
> - Some institutions may allow the disclosure of directory information such as personal names, so long as no other identifying information also present
> - Medical records
> - Refer to HIPAA privacy rules for more information around protecting medical information
> - Student records (grade information that can include letter grades, pass/fail, satisfactory/unsatisfactory, withdrawn, etc.)
> - Financial records
> - Religious records
> - Other unique identifiers (Driver's license numbers, student identification numbers, etc.)
>
> Does the analog document hold information that might be considered
> - Embarrassing
> - Personally damaging
> - Erroneous
>
> Has a person or publisher connected to the content in the analog document contacted the institution with a take-down request?
>
> Frontline archivists' determined course of action:
> - Upload or leave the content unedited.
> - Upload or leave the content up with redaction or restricted access.
> - Take it down, embargo content or do not publish
>
> If frontline archivists cannot make one of these selections, submit this report and checklist to the supervisor who will consult, if necessary, with the organization's legal counsel.

FIGURE 5.3

Dressler-Kearns analog to Digital Privacy Checklist and Action Decider.[41]

CONCLUSION

One can work with legal counsel as well as library administrators to determine the types of information to be protected (depending on the institution and state laws) and adapt the Berkeley workflows and the Digital Privacy Checklist to create a document for an internal privacy review. Any level of privacy review will indeed require additional resources of time and labor; however, protecting disclosure of private information is an important part of creating more ethically sound and responsible digital collections and archives. Additional resources for staff professional development have also been included in Appendix A.

Implementing a privacy review process can be incorporated into the digital production workflow process, whether reviewing physical or born-digital materials for private information as an initial step or during a post-production review. The additional labor to complete privacy assessment and reviews will need to be addressed at the onset of digital project proposals, and additional hours (and potentially creating new positions to address privacy specifically) be dedicated to ensuring these processes are implemented. It is crucial to address privacy and acknowledge the process involved with a privacy review, and this will also be a critical piece of running ethical digital initiatives.

ACKNOWLEDGMENTS

A special thanks to Doug Kubinski from the Office of General Counsel at Cleveland State University, who was incredibly helpful in navigating the nuances of FERPA and sharing his expert knowledge. Also, thank you to my employer, Kent State University Libraries, for research leave to complete this work.

APPENDIX A
STAFF PROFESSIONAL DEVELOPMENT RESOURCES FOR PRIVACY REVIEWS

- American Library Association Privacy Field Guides (https://www.ala.org/advocacy/privacy/fieldguides). Designed for academic, public, and school libraries of all types.
    - How to Talk about Privacy
    - Privacy Audits
    - Privacy Policies
- A Roadmap for Achieving Privacy in the Age of Analytics. Geared toward web privacy and analytics but with some excellent resources on privacy, including
    - Values-based assessment toolkit
    - Privacy Leadership Training
    - Privacy Certification System
- Digital Library Federation's Privacy and Ethics in Technology (PET) working group (https://wiki.diglib.org/Privacy_and_Ethics_in_Technology)
- Prioritizing Privacy – Data Ethics Training for Library Professionals (https://prioritizingprivacy.org/)
- Privacy and Confidentiality steering committee, American Archivists (https://www2.archivists.org/groups/privacy-and-confidentiality-section)
    - Privacy and Confidentiality bibliography (https://privacyandconfidentiality.wordpress.com/bibliography/)
- "Responsible Access Workflows," University of California (Berkeley Library)

NOTES

1. Ellen LeClere, "Breaking rules for good? How archivists manage privacy in large-scale digitisation projects," *Archives and Manuscripts* 34 (2018): 293.
2. LeClere, "Breaking rules for good?," 291.
3. Ibid., 184.
4. Erika McCallister, Tim France, and Karen Scarfone, "Guide to Protecting the Confidentiality of Personally Identifiable Information (PII): Recommendations of the National Institute of Standards and Technology," *NIST Special Publication* (2010): 2.
5. McCallister, France, and Scarfone, "Guide to Protecting the Confidentiality," 3.
6. Stefan Strauß, "Privacy analysis- privacy impact assessment," in *The Ethics of Technology, Methods and Approaches*, ed. S.O. Hansson (London: Rowman & Littlefield, 2017), 146–47.
7. "How to Talk about Privacy," "Privacy Policies," "Privacy Audits," and other titles in the Privacy Field Guides series, American Library Association, "Privacy Field Guides" (2021), https://www.ala.org/advocacy/privacy/fieldguides.

8. 20 U.S.C. § 1232g; 34 CFR Part 99.
9. Belanger v. Nashua, N.H., Sch. Dist., 856 F. Supp. 40, 48 (D.N.H. 1994).
10. 34 C.F.R. § 99.3.
11. Ibid.
12. 34 C.F.R. § 99.31(a)(11) and 99.3.
13. Menzi L. Behrnd-Klodt, "Appendix 4: The Brave New World of 21st-Century Medical Records Privacy in the U.S. and Canada, Contrasted with the European Data Privacy Model," in *Privacy and Confidentiality Perspectives: Archivists & Archival Records*, eds. Menzi L. Behrnd-Klodt and Peter J. Walsh (Chicago: Society of American Archivists, 2005), 286.
14. Phoebe Evans Letocha, "Changes to the Privacy Rule of HIPAA," Privacy and Confidentiality Roundtable, 2013, 4.
15. More information on the types of entities can be found on the U.S. Department of Health & Human Services webpage, https://www.hhs.gov/hipaa/index.html.
16. 45 C.F.R. § 164.514(e)(2).
17. Letocha, "Changes to the Privacy Rule," 6.
18. "What Does that Archival Restriction Really Mean? Demystifying HIPAA, Part 4," Duke University Medical Center Archives, https://archives.mc.duke.edu/blog/what-does-archival-restriction-really-mean-demystifying-hipaa-part-4.
19. Health Information & Privacy: FERPA and HIPAA, 2022.
20. LeClere, "Breaking rules for good?," 298.
21. LeClere, "Breaking rules for good?," 291; Ashlyn Velte, "Ethical Challenges and Current Practices in Activist Social Media Archives," *The American Archivist* 81, no. 1 (2018): 115.
22. Katherine Gariépy-Saper and Nicholas Decarie, "Privacy of electronic health records: A review of the literature," *Journal of the Canadian Health Libraries Association / Journal De l'Association Des bibliothèques De La Santé Du Canada* 42, no. 1 (2021).
23. Gariépy-Saper and Decarie, "Privacy of electronic health records," 75.
24. LeClere, "Breaking rules for good?," 290.
25. Ibid., 292.
26. Holly Crossen-White, "Using digital archives in historical research: What are the ethical concerns for a 'forgotten' individual?," *Research Ethics* 11, no. 2 (2015): 110.
27. Crossen-White, "Using digital archives," 115.
28. Elise Chenier, "Privacy Anxieties: Ethics versus Activism in Archiving Lesbian Oral History Online," *Radical History Review*, no. 122 (2015): 134.
29. Chenier, "Privacy Anxieties," 136.
30. Ibid.
31. Ben Goldman and Timothy D. Pyatt, "Security Without Obscurity: Managing Personally Identifiable Information in Born-Digital Archives," *Library and Archival Security* 26, no. 1-2 (2013): 38.
32. Velte, "Ethical Challenges and Current Practices," 123.
33. Gabriela Redwine, Megan Barnard, Kate Donovan, Erika Farr, Michael Forstrom, Will Hansen, Jeremy Leighton John, Nancy Kuhl, Seth Shaw, and Susan Thomas, "Born Digital: Guidance for Donors, Dealers, and Archival Repositories," Washington DC: Council on Library and Information Resources, 2013: 10.
34. Jan Zastrow, "Digital Acquisitions and Donor Relations: Assets, Apprehensions, and Anxieties," *Computers in Libraries* 36, no. 5 (2016): 18.
35. LeClere, "Breaking rules for good?," 299.
36. Jacobellis v. Ohio, 378 U.S. 184 (1964).
37. Lei Xu, Jiang Chunxiao, Yi Qian, and Yong Ren, "The Conflict Between Big Data and Individual Privacy," in *Data Privacy Games*, eds. Lei Xu, Chunxiao Jiang, Yi Qian, and Yong Ren (Cham: Springer International Publishing, 2018), 16.

38. Examples: Data Classification Standards and directives on the level of protection mandated for certain identified types of PII from the Berkeley Information Security Office, https://security.berkeley.edu/data-classification-standard#levels.
39. Letocha, "Changes to the Privacy Rule," 9.
40. Virginia Dressler, *Framing Privacy in Digital Collections with Ethical Decision Making* (San Rafael, CA: Morgan & Claypool, 2018), 73.
41. Dressler-Kearns analog to Digital Privacy Checklist and Action Decider, from "Probing archivists' perceptions and practices in privacy," *The Journal of Archives and Records* (2022).

BIBLIOGRAPHY

American Library Association. "Privacy Field Guides" (2021). https://www.ala.org/advocacy/privacy/fieldguides.

Anderson-Zorn, April, and Dallas Long. "Digitize Your Yearbooks: Creating Digital Access While Considering Student Privacy and Other Legal Issues." *Journal of Contemporary Archival Studies* 8 (2021). https://elischolar.library.yale.edu/jcas/vol8/iss1/14/.

Behrnd-Klodt, Menzi L. "Appendix 4: The Brave New World of 21st-Century Medical Records Privacy in the U.S. and Canada, Contrasted with the European Data Privacy Model." In *Privacy and Confidentiality Perspectives: Archivists & Archival Records*, edited by Menzi L. Behrnd-Klodt and Peter J. Walsh. Chicago: Society of American Archivists, 2005.

Berkeley Information Security Office. "Data Classification Standards." *University of California*. Last modified July 1, 2022. https://security.berkeley.edu/data-classification-standard#levels.

Center for Disease Control and Protection (CDC). "Health Information & Privacy: FERPA and HIPAA." 2022. https://www.cdc.gov/phlp/publications/topic/healthinformationprivacy.html.

Chenier, Elise. "Privacy Anxieties: Ethics versus Activism in Archiving Lesbian Oral History Online." *Radical History Review* 122 (2015): 129–41. https://doi.org/10.1215/01636545-2849576.

Crossen-White, Holly. "Using digital archives in historical research: What are the ethical concerns for a 'forgotten' individual?" *Research Ethics* 11, no. 2 (2015): 108–19.

Danielson, Elena S. *The Ethical Archivist*. Chicago: Society of American Archivists, 2010.

Dressler, Virginia. *Framing Privacy in Digital Collections with Ethical Decision Making*. San Rafael, CA: Morgan & Claypool, 2018.

Dressler-Kearns analog to Digital Privacy Checklist and Action Decider. "Probing archivists' perceptions and practices in privacy." *The Journal of Archives and Records* (2022). https://doi.org/10.1080/23257962.2022.2073207.

Duke University Medical Center Archives. "What Does that Archival Restriction Really Mean? Demystifying HIPAA, Part 4." https://archives.mc.duke.edu/blog/what-does-archival-restriction-really-mean-demystifying-hipaa-part-4.

Gariépy-Saper, Katherine, and Nicholas Decarie. "Privacy of electronic health records: A review of the literature." *Journal of the Canadian Health Libraries Association / Journal De l'Association Des bibliothèques De La Santé Du Canada* 42, no. 1 (2021): 74–84. https://doi.org/10.29173/jchla29496.

Goldman, Ben, and Timothy D. Pyatt. "Security Without Obscurity: Managing Personally Identifiable Information in Born-Digital Archives." *Library and Archival Security* 26, no. 1-2 (2013): 37–55. https://doi.org/10.1080/01960075.2014.913966.

LeClere, Ellen. "Breaking rules for good? How archivists manage privacy in large-scale digitisation projects." *Archives and Manuscripts* 34 (2018): 289–3008. https://www.tandfonline.com/doi/full/10.1080/01576895.2018.1547653.

Letocha, Phoebe Evans. "Changes to the Privacy Rule of HIPAA." Presentation, Privacy and Confidentiality Roundtable, Society of American Archivists. New Orleans, LA, August 14, 2013). http://iis-exhibits.library.ucla.edu/alhhs/HIPAA_SAA_handout_Letocha_2013.pdf.

McCallister, Erika, Tim France, and Karen Scarfone. *Guide to Protecting the Confidentiality of Personally Identifiable Information (PII): Recommendations of the National Institute of Standards and Technology.* NIST Special Publication (2010).

McDonald, Steven J. "Fundamentals of Fundamental FERPA." 2019 Lawyers New to Higher Education Workshop, National Association of College and University Attorneys (2019).

Neiger, Jan Alan. "FERPA vs. Public Records Laws." *National Association of College and University Attorneys* 14, no. 5 (2016).

Redwine, Gabriela, Megan Barnard, Kate Donovan, Erika Farr, Michael Forstrom, Will Hansen, Jeremy Leighton John, Nancy Kuhl, Seth Shaw, and Susan Thomas. *Born Digital: Guidance for Donors, Dealers, and Archival Repositories.* Washington DC: Council on Library and Information Resources, 2013.

Strauß, Stefan. "Privacy analysis- privacy impact assessment." In *The Ethics of Technology, Methods and Approaches*, edited by S.O. Hansson, 143–56. London: Rowman & Littlefield, 2017.

University of California, Berkeley Library. "Responsible Access Workflows" (2020). https://docs.google.com/presentation/d/1V66PGpIq9xqXxdvngpD3rkAMoIw2hIyVVDS4Iv4VFOM/edit#slide=id.g7ffa9d7047_0_2.

U.S. Department of Health & Human Services. "Summary of the HIPAA Privacy Rule." Accessed August 15, 2022. https://www.hhs.gov/hipaa/for-professionals/privacy/laws-regulations/index.html.

Velte, Ashlyn. "Ethical Challenges and Current Practices in Activist Social Media Archives." *The American Archivist* 81, no. 1 (2018): 112–34.

Xu, Lei, Chunxiao Jiang, Yi Qian, and Yong Ren. "The Conflict Between Big Data and Individual Privacy." In *Data Privacy Games*, edited by Lei Xu, Chunxiao Jiang, Yi Qian, and Yong Ren, 1–43. Cham: Springer International Publishing, 2018. https://doi.org/10.1007/978-3-319-77965-2_1.

Young, Scott W. H., Sara Mannheimer, Jason A. Clark, and Lisa Janicke Hinchliffe. "A Roadmap for Achieving Privacy in the Age of Analytics A White Paper from a National Forum on Web Privacy and Web Analytics." 2019. https://doi.org/10.15788/20190416.15445.

Zastrow, Jan. "Digital Acquisitions and Donor Relations: Assets, Apprehensions, and Anxieties." *Computers in Libraries* 36, no. 5 (2016): 26–28.

CHAPTER 6

LIBRARIES, PRIVACY, AND SURVEILLANCE CAPITALISM:

The Looming Trouble with Academia and Invasive Information Technologies

Andrew Weiss

INTRODUCTION: PEAK PRIVACY AND THE GROWTH OF THE INFORMATION ECONOMY

The contemporary academic library is a hybrid of physical and digital worlds, a place used as much for the literal space it sets aside for its users as for the cyberspace it provides them. Despite the emphasis on digital information resources and the recent shift to more open collaborative study spaces, libraries nevertheless maintain their historical reputations as contemplative spaces that offer the experience of private personal inquiry with the quiet atmosphere required for study and reflection. Regardless of what they use a library for, patrons still expect a private experience, unhindered from prying eyes when they use physical facilities or information resources. But what happens when the privacy and seclusion of a library's physical space collide with the two-way mirror hyper-connectivity of digital space? What happens when one's physical flesh-and-bone life merges with a digital realm designed as much for control and the nudging of behaviors as the free exchange of information? What happens when the reputation of the library, built over centuries as the physical embodiment of the depth, breadth, and future potential of human knowledge, encounters the aims and motives of the digital economy?

This chapter seeks to examine the implications of such scenarios, especially as digital technology encroaches on the physical world, putting personal privacy at risk. Setting aside the obvious dangers of hacking sensitive personal data for a moment, the psychological implications for this lost sense of privacy are immense. Anything, no matter how innocent—like a child's teddy bear or The Elf on a Shelf—that can be connected to the internet has the capability to surveil us without our consent. Innocuous, but invasive. We begin to lose trust, then, in the large online institutions just as they are now getting even larger and more powerful. Surveillance technology itself has advanced in recent years, moving from analog recording devices to digital video and audio, capable of recording an ongoing and nearly unlimited volume of nearly everything you write, speak, and even communicate non-verbally to others.

Libraries have done much to combat both invasive technology and its supporting apparatus of policies over the years. The profession's initial pushback to the post-9/11 PATRIOT Act in the early-2000s is a clear example of how the field's reputation could grow through public resistance to invasive state-sponsored surveillance. But the game has also changed. Certainly, few could foresee the swift corporate takeover of the internet since 2000 after the dot-com bubble burst—especially from companies that either did not exist at the time (e.g., Facebook) or were still so unproven that they didn't warrant outsized attention (e.g., Google and Amazon). Neither could anyone foresee the degree to which "big data," and information itself, would become the ubiquitous commodity that simultaneously aids and controls users—making *cyber*space appropriate.[1]

Not limited to the world of commercial enterprise, privacy issues are growing in academia in two main areas as well. First, student data tracking is being employed more often by universities for assessing student academic achievement. Second, third-party products and vendors are capable of harvesting and marketing student information, including things like BioButton, a health-monitoring wearable device from BioIntelliSense,[2] and Respondus[3] or Proctorio,[4] two remote proctoring platforms used widely in higher education.

This chapter examines the role that academic libraries play—wittingly and unwittingly—in the practice of gathering patron information during the use of common library vendor products. While the erosion of student privacy may be an acceptable tradeoff for some in higher education, librarians should attempt to alleviate the tensions among students who are uncomfortable with behavioral monitoring. It is essential that librarians learn to balance the need for and right to privacy with the push to foster student success through data tracking and monitoring. Librarians must also be strong privacy advocates and find ways to protect their users' privacy at all costs; otherwise, libraries risk losing the trust of their constituents. Some strategies toward these goals will be examined.

DOES OPENNESS EQUAL MODERNISM?

Where does this urge to know about student behavior come from? One theory is that from the Renaissance period onward, the open pursuit of knowledge and the erosion of taboos and so-called "forbidden" knowledge, has become synonymous with a kind of general modernity where the world has reoriented its perspective from one of adhering to past tradition to one advocating future innovation. As Roger Shattuck writes in *Forbidden Knowledge: From Prometheus to Pornography*, "open knowledge appears to stand for modernity itself."[5] In his expansive look at how people deal with difficult truths or behaviors, Shattuck finds that we still have ideas of knowledge that should not be shared, but these concerns are often disregarded and seen as antithetical to "modern" thinking. In fact, the idea has become so entrenched and axiomatic that to suggest either knowledge or technology be restricted is to court controversy and risk being seen as a censor or a Luddite.[6]

Surely, the benefits of open knowledge have been primarily good. The results include the sharing of life-saving procedures, a better understanding of individual and societal-wide behaviors and pathologies, a faster sharing of ideas that counteract negative stereotypes, and a greater awareness of self-destructive superstitions. The shift toward the open pursuit of knowledge at all costs has its greatest example in the open access movement. The reasoning is that open access to knowledge represents humanism at its best: the sharing of life-improving scientific discovery and new knowledge, openly available for the benefit of all. However, there are times when the nuances of open knowledge are disregarded or downplayed, relegating issues to well-worn, misunderstood exceptions to the general assumption that open knowledge is good knowledge.

There are still issues with the widespread release of information that is *truly* dangerous in an existential sense—for example, the manufacturing of nuclear weapons, the unleashing of dangerous weaponized viruses, or the release of compromising information that can endanger people. Such threats logically need to be kept under tight legal controls. There are also ideas and concepts, perhaps less existentially dangerous than nuclear weapons, that are nevertheless considered taboo in many cultures. Certain ideas that are taboo come to be avoided by people within those cultures. To spread this information within that culture may cause consternation or dismay among members.

UNEQUAL POWER AND THE INDIVIDUAL

Despite these exceptions, there is nevertheless a conflation of open knowledge with personal information. The current issues found with the generation of personal data on a widespread scale (considered part of the five Vs of big data—velocity, volume, value, variety, and veracity) exacerbate this problem.[7] Information technology has the capacity to record so much about a person's behavior that it can pinpoint identities and erode one's privacy at much faster speeds and far more extensively and accurately than in the past. It is at this point that we must address the power imbalance that arises from this.

The overreach of openness in our personal lives may be the defining feature of our current world. In one good example of how openness is encroaching on privacy, as well as eroding our consent for the sharing of information about ourselves, we look no further than "Lenna," the first digital image put on the internet. The image, scanned by computer scientists in the early 1970s, has proliferated online despite the lack of consent of the original photographer, the magazine it appeared in (*Playboy*), or the subject herself, Lenna Forsén. It amounts to the perpetual loss of agency at the heart of online life, bending the legal tenets of personal privacy built up in the analog and paper-based world.[8] The lesson is that the data keeps replicating, in a perpetual loop, unable to be deleted completely, beyond the control of not only the first digitizer, the original photographer and publisher but also the subject herself.

Yet, similar to Lenna and her undying image, we are not much further removed from a completely surveilled and documented student body forced to cope with a similar lack of power to control or counteract its seemingly perpetual effects. According to Katherine Magnan in her report "The Surveilled Student," students are increasingly monitored across campuses all over the United States, especially with regard to remote learning anti-cheating software.[9] Fifty-four percent of institutions currently use this type of monitoring software and 23 percent have intentions to adopt it, conceivably reaching nearly 80 percent of all institutions in higher education. Other types of monitoring include 23 percent of colleges and universities that use active video surveillance of students, 39 percent that use passive video surveillance, and 23 percent that monitor software on students' computers.[10]

While the nominal reason for the surveillance has been stated as aiding in student success, ensuring their safety, or preventing cheating, often the result "is really about power and control, and universities …looking for certainty in very uncertain times."[11] It is suggested that universities are looking for a technological solution to a problem where one doesn't yet exist, forcing surveillance technologies on their students, ultimately creating more long-term problems for them than solving the short-term ones at hand. Indeed, the software itself may be subject to hacking, leaving many students vulnerable to bad actors. Education, according to Microsoft Security Intelligence data, is the area that is "most threatened by malware."[12] In the mind of one educational tracking critic, "Online-proctoring software itself …is essentially 'malware' to begin with."[13] Yet, higher education persists in paying for these services.

A THEORY OF SURVEILLANCE CAPITALISM

If Google, Facebook, and other companies seem to be different, it is perhaps because they are. IT companies like Google or Facebook do not function on the same social contract as past corporations. Instead, these companies exist at "hyperscale," far beyond anything seen before, signaling a new model of capitalism. But what does this hyperscale entail, exactly? Shoshanna Zuboff's work on surveillance capitalism provides library and information science with an important framework to examine the influence IT companies have on the wider society.[14] Through this lens, we can start to see the ways in which libraries contribute—mostly unwittingly—to the development and persistence of the surveillance state.

Zuboff examines the conceptual underpinnings of capitalism itself and the impact that digital technologies and data tracking can have on our economics and social structures, especially in terms of "a new logic of accumulation."[15] Where capitalism normally accumulates wealth through reciprocal relationships that depend on individuals as both a source of employees and as customers, IT companies can distance themselves from such "structural reciprocities."[16] More simply, companies extract data and information about people and their behaviors (including both their employees and their customers) while minimizing the social responsibility of their actions and policies. This allows them to avoid oversight from government regulations or organizations.

The implication of losing more traditional socially conscientious relationships between companies and societies should not be ignored. Corporate accountability in the United States has been waning for decades as companies move offshore or become multinational and multi-jurisdictional. Hyper-scaling has further eroded the social fabric of all countries at an unprecedented pace, burdening already-asymmetrical power relationships with even more inequalities. If we view surveillance capitalism and its major exemplar companies both as an outgrowth of the military-industrial complex and as a new type of powerful and unassailable corporate entity operating at hyperscale, we begin to see the incredibly large-scale pathological trends in future organizations and the eventual move toward a pervasive surveillance-capitalist dystopia. In much the same way, certain industries now create *hyperobjects*, which, as Timothy Morton argues, exist beyond the capacity of a single person to fully grasp their power and reach. As a result, they have the capability of influencing us without our being able to see their full shape, scope, and scale. This is much like the internet: we see the surface of a mirror but are unable to realize the totality of what's operating behind that mirror. Certain multinational information technology companies exist at such a massive scale that it becomes impossible for a single person to physically experience them in their totality. In other words, as Morton writes, "We can't point to them directly."[17]

LIBRARIES AND SURVEILLANCE CAPITALISM

Since libraries exist outside the cutthroat world of the billion- and trillion-dollar IT titans, it is easy to downplay their part in this and to assume that librarians have little to do with these wider machinations and "real-world" problems. It's easy to believe, as well, that libraries have a minimal impact in the world of surveillance capitalism, beyond the library profession's general advocacy for patron privacy. But this severely downplays the role that libraries currently play in the information economy and the clear relationship that libraries have had with companies that deal in surveillance and data tracking. In the early 2000s, during the height of the book digitization efforts of Google, libraries were partners in the mass digitization of nearly 20 to 30 million print books.[18] Mass digitization projects that started in the mid-1990s and early-2000s, such as UMI's theses and dissertations, gave libraries a clear path to contributing works of great cultural value to the online environment. These digitization projects have undoubtedly provided libraries with beneficial services, especially with Google Books offshoots like HathiTrust or the fiercely independent and sometimes bleeding-edge Internet Archive.

Digitization of content itself is generally perceived on the surface as benign, providing clear benefits to library users. However, one of the more damning revelations has been how academic libraries play active roles in supporting the *economics* of surveillance through such digital collections. This situation, unfortunately, speaks to the diversification of the companies that control most of the database content that libraries purchase or subscribe to. Academic publishing worldwide is a $19 billion industry, rivaling the music and film industries in terms of overall sales. By itself, publishing conglomerate Clarivate's estimated revenue for 2022 is $2.875B to $2.935B,[19] while well-known market share leader Elsevier's profit margins approach 40 percent of their nearly $10 billion-dollar yearly revenues.[20] Academic publishing is, in fact, lucrative to the point of absurdity given how much of the labor-intensive aspects (especially the research itself, peer-review, quality control, and editing) are covered by public funds, supported by non-profit educational institutions, or provided freely (or with token payment) by researchers and scholars themselves. Even the costs associated with printing are minimal now that journals are disseminated almost exclusively online.[21] Nevertheless, these companies no longer focus merely on journal publishing and database development. Many have pivoted to the tracking and collection of user data, which appears to be where the largest potential for profits currently exists. They have pivoted so far that, according to Ulrich Herb, publisher Elsevier (now called RELX) can be said to no longer be primarily in the business of distributing and selling scientific publications but is instead in the business of "information analytics."[22]

Of course, cost-cutting and adapting to meet market demand are at the heart of capitalism itself. Well-known library vendor UMI (University Microfilms) first began as a producer of information products on microfilm, later transferred to digital content, and is now part of the multinational corporation, Clarivate, which also dabbles in digital data brokering—their "real-world data product." How a company such as UMI moved from information products produced on microfilm to a major component of a large data broker's portfolio may represent the history of capitalism in the information age writ large. As Clarivate's website describes it, "[o]ur real world data product includes more than 300 million longitudinal covered lives, 2 million healthcare providers and 98% of payers in the United States, with visibility into 100 million electronic health records (EHR)."[23] That last figure is nearly one in three people living in the United States. Chances are that many of these people will be users of our libraries, whether student, faculty, staff, or community members.

But there's no way for us to know if the information is being used properly. Indeed, indications are that aggregated user data is being used for whatever strikes a client's fancy. Clarivate's advertising copy for their data brokerage services asks, "What real world data are you missing?" and suggests that their clients "Get in touch to discuss your data needs."[24] Here, corporate clients are asked to consider what data they might need for their targeted users. It is clear that the selling of data to business is a primary revenue stream for this and other companies of its ilk—a far cry from theses and dissertations processed onto microfilm.

While the selling of data might not seem especially bad in the context of anonymized medical records for use in scientific or medical research, we don't know what else this data is used for. Occasionally, the information and data gathered about general information behavior comes from libraries, but if it is crossed and matched with the medical records of those users, murky ethical dilemmas arise, especially "in relation to identity articulation, collective privacy, data bias, raced and gendered discrimination, and socioeconomic inequality."[25] We don't know, for instance, who Clarivate's clients are and what their plans are for the data about its users. Systemic and cultural biases built into algorithms are well-documented by Noble in her book *Algorithms of Oppression*.[26] Yet without proper transparency and oversight, it is possible that the aggregated data generated by library vendors and the tools developed by them to sift through it perpetuate similar inequalities and prejudices.

Overdrive, one of the most used vendors in libraries, provides us with yet another example of how companies meddle with user confidentiality and privacy. According to Hilburn, this primary e-resource vendor provides users with a technology that flags and then scores titles to determine whether something might be deemed objectionable by the patron.[27] While it may be useful on the surface, the company is also "looking to be the final arbiter of what content is appropriate and what the emotional tenor of a book is on behalf of millions of diverse patrons. The line between library mission and vendor profit suddenly [appears] stark."[28]

However, as Lamdan cogently notes in her review of corporate information surveillance, "Librarianship at the Crossroads of ICE Surveillance," the issue is not *solely* that the companies are engaged in the brokering of data or creating a kind of "pre-cognitive" service that can anticipate and shape our wants and needs through better algorithms. The real problem for libraries and higher education in general is that *we allow them to get away with it*.[29] Librarians routinely fail to push back hard enough to keep the companies honest in their dealings. Librarians need to step up to help mitigate these problems that stem, in part, from the vendors they choose to support. Library action may be limited due to a lack of knowledge about the problem, the inability to truly negotiate good terms with vendors, or the calculation that the vendor's services outweigh potential downsides.

THE POTENTIAL DAMAGE TO LIBRARIES AND THEIR USERS

Failure to push back hard enough could diminish the trust people have in libraries, altering their perceptions of them as general public goods so that they are seen more as politicized spaces rather than shared common spaces. Indeed, they may come to be perceived as untrustworthy on one side of the political spectrum, while the other side of the spectrum may see them in need of vigilant protection of their "purity." The risks of both politicized attitudes are apparent for they both fail to appreciate the need for all perspectives to be represented. Librarians, in turn, will be seen as complicit in creating a lack of trust.

History demonstrates what happens when libraries lose the trust of their constituents, especially when seen as the tools of a repressive regime. Rebecca Knuth's examination of the destruction of libraries, *Libricide*, is full of examples of how libraries become targets for new regimes as well as for attacking armies.[30] Sometimes libraries are convenient targets for political aggression, but other times they become part of the social control apparatus and central to the monitoring of information and how it is disseminated. A library need not be attacked from the outside to be ruined. Sometimes that happens from within. Soviet libraries, for example, heavily censored and revised their collections based on the prevailing politics of the day, an ongoing decades-long reaction to perceived external and internal threats by its leadership that severely compromised the trust of users.[31] Clearly, with the yearly attempts to censor books in libraries across the United States, these issues persist.

Libraries in a free society need to push back against the threat to control information by continuing to assert their core ethical values. One would like to think in a Post-*Roe v. Wade* United States that library patrons would still be able to learn about reproductive health without being tracked or having their searches blocked or redirected. Seeking out such information should be unfettered, but this is by no means guaranteed. We cannot take for granted the ability to seek information without the fear of reprisal. This impacts our very being, forcing us to realize that "privacy is central …to human dignity and central to democracy."[32] The stark reminder of how easily a sense of freedom can be broken plays out in people's information-seeking behavior, including when using libraries. Many women may now perceive negative consequences when seeking out information about abortion in some regions of the United States, which may negatively impact their well-being. Chatman's theory of information poverty is especially illuminating here. She suggests that the decision to risk exposure of a personal problem is often *not* taken due to a perception that negative consequences outweigh the benefits. In other words, people—women especially—have to weigh the risks of seeking out certain information. If the risk seems too high, many will cease looking, which can ultimately devolve into "a maladaptive closed loop," where a necessary action (like going to a doctor) is not taken and one's life gets worse.[33]

But this is a far wider problem than a regional interstate issue. If patrons feel their searches are being monitored and that law enforcement could potentially spy on their inquiries—even within the library—the dampening effect on patron information-seeking behavior will likely increase. Research has shown that just being cognizant of the *possibility* of being observed while seeking certain subjects alters user information behavior. Jonathon Penney finds that people are far less willing to look up topics they think are controversial when they have been made aware of the NSA's PRISM surveillance program.[34] Other studies find similar dampening effects on user information behavior. Marthews and Tucker find that "cross-nationally, users were less likely to search using terms that they believed might get them in trouble with the US government."[35] They ultimately warn of government surveillance's potential "chilling effects" on the overall search behavior of internet users.[36]

Ignoring or downplaying the issue of surveillance will not only impact students' trust in libraries in general but may also narrow research topics that might be seen as too controversial in an overly politicized and polarized society. Considering that the stakes are much higher for certain segments of the population, it is imperative to review how much and how far-reaching the surveillance of library patrons may be by certain information technology companies.

BIG DATA, BIG BROTHER: DATA BROKERS AND THE PROBLEMS OF MASSIVE SCALE AND MASSIVE SCOPE

Much has been made so far of the large well-known multinational corporations such as Google, Apple, and Facebook as well as RELX and other prominent academic publishers, but the information broker is, unfortunately, not confined to just these well-known companies. There are at least 120 data brokers operating in the US, probably more, but they often work in the shadows with little oversight. Although they tend to operate behind the scenes, their impact on our lives is arguably just as powerful as higher-profile companies.

To combat the problems libraries are facing, we need to know who the data brokers are and how much we are supporting them with our database subscriptions. While this author has no illusions about how difficult it would be to drop subscriptions from many of the prominent publishers—especially if accreditation is on the line for universities—it is necessary to be as transparent as possible about where our money is going and whom it is supporting. If we do not know the wider impact of our financial support on society at large, we cannot make the necessary decisions to keep or drop certain resources. We must be able to make ethical decisions based on reasonable calculations of how our actions might overall impact us all positively or negatively.

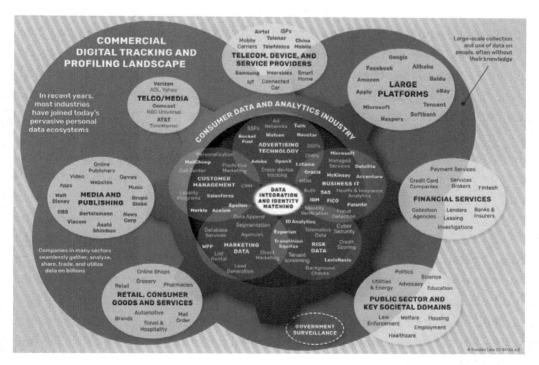

FIGURE 6.1

Visualization of the commercial digital tracking and profiling landscape of data brokers. (Source: Wolfie; Cracked Labs) © Cracked Labs, CC BY-SA 4.0.[37]

As seen in figure 6.1, Austrian independent research institute Cracked Labs visualizes the complexity of the data tracking and profiling landscape of the online world.[38] The illustration maps the full range of online surveillance and tracking organizations from media and publishing, telecoms, IT platforms, finance, public sector, and retail. Each of the brokers listed in the illustration focuses on the specific types of data they collect, ranging from customer management, advertising technologies, business IT, to risk data, and finally marketing data. Many of these companies also overlap in the types of data they collect, making it extremely difficult to determine specifically what is collected and for what purpose.

The largest data broker in the United States is Acxiom, seen covering both "customer management" and "marketing data" segments in the illustration. Acxiom claims to have files on 10 percent of the world's population—nearly 1 billion people, with 23,000 computer servers processing more than 50 trillion data transactions each year.[39] It keeps an average of 1,500 data points on more than 200 million Americans, 62 percent of the country's population. Likely, most of you reading this book have a digital trail they are tracking. Their "Digital Dossiers" comprise a combination of online and offline data, which reveals information about our life choices, class, spending, and where we live. As brokers, though, they don't necessarily work with the data itself. Instead, they sell it to their clients, packaging the content in such a way as to maximize profit, while tantalizing them with richer and richer "leads" for selling. The more granular the information, the better the portrait of the potential customer base a sales team might reach. Customers for Acxiom include credit card companies, banks, insurance companies, brokerage firms, telecommunications companies, retailers, automakers, and pharmaceutical companies—half, it seems, of "the largest one-hundred corporations" in the US.[40]

The problem with Acxiom's online user surveillance becomes even worse when confronted with the realization that the company has worked with the FBI, the Pentagon, and the US Department of Homeland Security. Most egregiously, the company employed former military personnel on its board of directors, paying one to work "as a lobbyist, primarily in relation to the Department of Defense and Homeland Security ...[and] helping set up the technological systems for total surveillance of the U.S. and global population."[41] Acxiom later worked with the airline JetBlue to use public and private traveler records in a purported defense against terrorist attacks.

Of course, we shouldn't just pick on Acxiom. The notorious *Cambridge Analytica* once held psychological profiles of *220 million US citizens* based on 5,000 separate data sets. There are many other data brokers of varying sizes, each operating within their own spheres of influence, that similarly deal in the buying and selling of personal information. Such data brokers in the United States include Experian, a credit score company; Epsilon, a "global marketing company" that turns "data into personalized customer experiences—driving growth for some of the most well-known brands worldwide";[42] CoreLogic, provider of "consumer, financial and property data;" Datalogix, yet another consumer data collection company; inome, which owns the background check service "Intelius," and Recorded Future, which focuses on "real-time threat intelligence."[43] Additionally, RELX was reported to have provided data to ICE.[44] In 2005, Choicepoint, formerly a data aggregator and later a part of LexisNexis Risk Solutions (another RELX subsidiary), "sold significant amounts of personal information on 145,000 consumers to a group of identity thieves in California, resulting in at least 700 known cases of fraud and identity theft."[45]

In the end, the problem with data brokers and their role in perpetuating surveillance capitalism is that the scale and scope of the data being brokered across such varied disciplines and industries is far beyond most individuals' comprehension; the data is being used far beyond stated, nominal intentions, and it often feels we are powerless to stop it. We are indeed living in a world that is dominated by hyperscales and hyperobjects (whether it be massive digital libraries, online databases, Zottabytes of information, plastic pollution, nuclear power, and so on), central to the complex systems we have co-created with billions of other people, operating beyond the comprehension of any one individual. Additionally, as companies expand and consolidate, it can be quite easy to remain unaware that the products offered to libraries are also part and parcel to the very companies that track and broker data. Sometimes, in the case of LexisNexis Risk Solutions, the companies do not even bother to hide those links, brazenly assuming librarians and scholars working for universities and other knowledge organizations are fine with the situation.

MITIGATING THE PROBLEMS: SOLUTIONS AND FIRST STEPS

This chapter has endeavored to examine how libraries are intertwined with the growing and pervasive problems of surveillance as it is implemented in information products. The main issue is the third-party data collecting, aggregating, and brokering of user data carried out via the very systems we subscribe to for patrons. The stakes from the misuse of user data are sufficiently high to make the threat of surveillance *essential* to identify. If libraries become seen as another part of a state-sponsored surveillance apparatus, or an exploitative for-profit data mining endeavor, their modern reputations as open and generally inclusive organizations serving the public good will assuredly suffer. Librarians need to find ways to promote and advocate for user privacy and confidentiality while being aware of unethical corporate practices and insist upon using products *that do not encroach upon the privacy of their users*.

It will be a very fine line to toe indeed to keep user needs and protections in balance. Supporting data protection laws such as the European Union's General Data Protection Regulation (GDPR) and California's Consumer Privacy Act, and Vermont General Assembly, H.764, Act 171, is a small first start. Although

Vermont became the first state to attempt regulation of data brokers, the law doesn't provide much information to consumers about the brokers themselves.[46] We don't know, for example, whose data is collected in a broker's database or who they sell it to. We can't access our own data in their databases or directly appeal to these brokers to opt out of data collection. And so, we are left in the dark and unable to determine definitively just who these data brokers are. What are the implications of their actions on human privacy, free societies, and democratic institutions themselves?

But advocacy for ever stronger stances against the biggest players in the surveillance capitalist world is going to be essential. To do this, we must counteract the canard of digital data "pragmatism" that many proponents of surveillance capitalism blindly promote, and which, in the wrong hands, becomes twisted to become a kind of menacing digital data cynicism. Indeed, the notion of pragmatism, if that's really what it is, has nothing to do with the situation we are in. A consumer's choice to control their data—which means that they have the power to *choose* personally beneficial outcomes for themselves and on their own terms—often winds up *not being a choice at all*, given hard-to-read boilerplate language user agreements or, worse, the one-way-mirror of silent observation that many websites employ. Librarians need to better understand not only the stakes involved and the scope of the problem but also how to speak of user agency in terms of privacy and confidentiality.

LIBRARY-CENTRIC PRIVACY RESOLUTIONS: ALA AND BEYOND

One approach has been to develop pragmatic ways to deal on a larger scale with the problems of breaches of privacy. The American Library Association, for example, adopted the "resolution against misusing data surveillance" as a first step toward drawing attention to the issues of privacy in libraries. The resolution involves several important stances, including standing "firmly against behavioral data surveillance of library use and users."[47] It further urges librarians not to allow their organizations to exchange user data with vendors for financial gain; the resolution also provides some guidelines on acting ethically to ensure that services are not denied, that privacy settings are strictest by default, and that librarians become educated about privacy and confidentiality rights. Most importantly, the resolution suggests that libraries make sure that the vendors they deal with are in actual compliance with privacy regulations.[48]

But this is easier said than done. Making sure library vendors stay honest without significant oversight or recourse from the library side may be an impossible task. As seen above, there are numerous vendors and many of them are part of larger entities, as in the case of RELX, where one subset of vendors deals with libraries (e.g., LexisNexis, Scopus, and Science Direct), while another subset (Choicepoint, Accuity, Cirium) deals primarily with data brokering. The best we may be able to do is merely keep vigilant and broadcast the connections between vendors and data brokering in order to preserve some amount of transparency, however toothless that may be.

Certainly, a good step for all libraries would be to begin adopting similar resolutions that are visible to patrons, and even some that require acknowledgment of reading so that patrons are aware of library policies and intentions. Ultimately, as Dave Shumaker argues, we cannot be neutral bystanders in the war on information. For him, the ALA's library bill of rights and similar guidelines are "are even less relevant than they used to be."[49] Instead, he argues, we need to move out of our generally politically neutral stance and must "promote the positive basis for our judgments [through] information literacy."[50] In other words, we must get back to core principles of information use that benefit the user primarily.

Another approach is to begin advising patrons directly about the importance of privacy and the strategies that can be taken to protect oneself. The Electronic Frontier Foundation (EFF), for example, has created the *Surveillance Self-Defense: Tips, Tools and How-tos for Safer Online Communications*.[51] Their guides provide clear actions that users can take to deal with potential privacy pitfalls. Their use of "security scenarios" might be adopted by libraries to help with user-specific contexts and examples to show exact steps and precautions to take to avoid privacy breaches. Like the management of data and the confidential provision of information that has been done by libraries for generations, privacy might become an important information management domain for librarians. Following in the footsteps of EFF, libraries might become strong advocates for and advisors of privacy for all library patrons. This is a truly promising direction libraries might take to improve the lives of their patrons and would serve to help distance libraries from the rapacious data gathering of the vendors they hire.

Finally, librarians *at the very least* might consider drafting comments on the value of patron privacy in their mission, vision, and values statements along with incorporating steps toward ensuring and enshrining user privacy within their libraries' strategic plans. These minor assertions on the value of privacy can develop into something more robust in the future. Modest as this is, a commitment to privacy has to start somewhere.

FINAL THOUGHTS

What do we ultimately envision for the future of library privacy? Do we acquiesce? Do we resist? Currently, we engage in a little of both: remaining advocates for the privacy of our patrons, yet willing to financially support the very vendors that compile information about them. We sincerely appear to respect the user's privacy in searching for information and what they choose to seek out, yet we also support a system that routinely surveils nearly anyone that operates within it. We are essentially drowning in a firehose of our own data, now used with the specific purpose of flooding our own selves to make profits for someone else. We are exploited and exploiter all wrapped in one without recourse to avoid exploitation, and we appear to get less and less in return for the money we spend.

In some ways, too, we are moving into a new era beyond the values and conundrums posed by modernism and postmodernism, which we might consider enlightenment and its deconstruction built upon an abundance of petro-technologies. Library futures are moving beyond this toward the age of massive self-sustaining information systems that function far more like Morton's *hyperobject*, a proverbial iceberg mostly invisible and existing beyond one person's full comprehension. What we need to help us is a renewed social contract that holds privacy as an essential and important right. We also need to develop updated scenarios for patrons to help them navigate the complex information world, something that librarians have been doing for generations. Librarians could have no better goal than advocating for the free and unfettered use of information without fear of political or social reprisals reasonably balanced with the needs of individuals and their right to privacy.

ACKNOWLEDGMENTS

The author would like to acknowledge Sarah Hartman-Caverly, Alexandria Chisolm, Sara Mannheimer, and Andrew Wesolek for their useful advice and commentary in helping this chapter take shape.

NOTES

1. Omri Ben Shahar, "Privacy is the New Money, Thanks to Big Data," *Forbes* (April 1, 2016), https://www.forbes.com/sites/omribenshahar/2016/04/01/privacy-is-the-new-money-thanks-to-big-data/?sh=307f2b263fa2.
2. "BioIntelliSense," BioIntelliSense, last updated 2022, https://biointellisense.com/.
3. "Respondus Monitor," Respondus, last updated 2022, https://web.respondus.com/he/monitor/.
4. "Securing the integrity of online assessments," Proctorio, last updated 2022, https://proctorio.com/.

5. Roger Shattuck, *Forbidden Knowledge: From Prometheus to Pornography* (New York: St. Martin's Press, 1996), 167.
6. Shattuck, *Forbidden Knowledge*.
7. Andrew Weiss, *Big Data Shocks: An Introduction to Big Data for Librarians and Information Professionals* (Blue Ridge Summit: Rowman & Littlefield, 2018), 26.
8. Jennifer Ding with Jan Diehm and Michelle McGhee, "Can Data Die? Tracking the Lenna Image," The Pudding, October 2021, https://pudding.cool/2021/10/lenna/.
9. Katherine Mangan, "The Surveilled Student," *The Chronicle of Higher Education* (February 15, 2021), https://www.chronicle.com/article/the-surveilled-student?utm_source=Iterable&utm_medium=email&utm_campaign=campaign_3492351_nl_Academe-Today_date_20220107&cid=at&source=ams&sourceid=.
10. Katherine Mangan, "The Surveilled Student."
11. Ibid.
12. Taylor Swaak, "A Vulnerability in Proctoring Software Should Worry Colleges, Experts Say," *The Chronicle of Higher Education* (January 6, 2022), https://www.chronicle.com/article/a-vulnerability-in-proctoring-software-should-worry-colleges-experts-say.
13. Swaak, "A Vulnerability in Proctoring Software."
14. Shoshana Zuboff, *The Age of Surveillance Capitalism: the Fight for a Human Future at the New Frontier of Power* (New York: PublicAffairs, 2019).
15. Shoshana Zuboff, "Big Other: Surveillance Capitalism and the Prospects of an Information Civilization," *Journal of Information Technology* 30, no. 1 (March 1, 2015): 75, doi. 10.1057/jit.2015.5.
16. Zuboff, "Big Other," 80.
17. Timothy Morton, *Hyperobjects: Philosophy and Ecology after the End of the World* (Minneapolis: University of Minnesota Press, 2013), 12.
18. Andrew Weiss, *Using Massive Digital Libraries* (Chicago: ALA TechSource, 2014).
19. "Clarivate Successfully Completes Acquisition of ProQuest," Clarivate, December 1, 2021, https://clarivate.com/news/clarivate-successfully-completes-acquisition-of-proquest/?utm_campaign=EM_Global_CA_ThumbBt_Customer_Announcement_XBU_Global_2021_EN&utm_medium=email&utm_source=Eloqua&elqTrackId=82fd75ad29514e7c96e010fd966d16a7&elq=8b8dc4fd9ebf49bbb944d74867b04d23&elqaid=18764&elqat=1&elqCampaignId=8085.
20. Martin Hagve, "The money behind academic publishing," *Tidsskrift Den norske legeforening*, August 17, 2020, https://tidsskriftet.no/en/2020/08/kronikk/money-behind-academic-publishing.
21. Hagve, "The money behind academic publishing."
22. Ulrich Herb, "Steering science through Output Indicators & Data Capitalism," *Proceedings of the 23rd Congress of the European Society of Veterinary and Comparative Nutrition*, Turin, Italy, 2019, https://digitalcommons.unl.edu/scholcom/125/.
23. "Real World Data," Clarivate, last updated 2022, https://clarivate.com/products/real-world-data/.
24. "Real World Data," Clarivate.
25. Tanya Kant, "A history of the data tracked user," *The MIT Press Reader* (October 8, 2021), https://thereader.mitpress.mit.edu/a-history-of-the-data-tracked-user/?utm_source=pocket-newtab.
26. Safiya Umoja Noble, *Algorithms of Oppression: How Search Engines Reinforce Racism* (New York: New York University Press, 2018).
27. Jessica Hilburn, "Big Data Clashes With Patron Privacy: OverDrive's Digipalooza 2021," *Information Today* (August 10, 2021), http://newsbreaks.infotoday.com/NewsBreaks/Big-Data-Clashes-With-Patron-Privacy-OverDrives-Digipalooza--148369.asp.
28. Hilburn, "Big Data Clashes."
29. Sarah Lamdan, "Librarianship at the crossroads of ICE surveillance," *In the Library with the Lead Pipe* (November 13, 2019), https://www.inthelibrarywiththeleadpipe.org/2019/ice-surveillance/.
30. Rebecca Knuth, *Libricide: The Regime-Sponsored Destruction of Books and Libraries in the Twentieth Century* (Westport, CT: Praeger, 2003).

31. Robert A. Rogers, "Censorship and Libraries in the Soviet Union," *Journal of Library History, Philosophy, and Comparative Librarianship* 8, no. 1 (1973): 22–29.
32. Natasha Singer and Brian X. Chen, "In a Post-Roe World, the Future of Digital Privacy Looks Even Grimmer," *The New York Times* (July 13, 2022), https://www.nytimes.com/2022/07/13/technology/personaltech/abortion-privacy-roe-surveillance.html.
33. Beth St. Jean, Ursula Gorham, and Elizabeth Bonsignore, *Understanding Human Information Behavior: When, How, and Why People Interact with Information* (Lanham, MD: Rowman & Littlefield, 2021), 197.
34. Jonathon Penney, "Chilling Effects: Online Surveillance and Wikipedia Use," *Berkeley Technology Law Journal* 31, no. 1 (2016): 117, https://ssrn.com/abstract=2769645.
35. Alex Marthews and Catherine E. Tucker, "Government Surveillance and Internet Search Behavior," *SSRN Electronic Journal* (2014), doi: 10.2139/ssrn.2412564.
36. Marthews and Tucker, "Government Surveillance."
37. Christl Wolfie, "Corporate Surveillance in everyday life: How companies collect, combine, analyze, trade, and use personal data on billions." Cracked Labs, 2017, last updated 2022, https://crackedlabs.org/en/corporate-surveillance/infographics.
38. Wolfie, "Corporate Surveillance in everyday life."
39. John Bellamy Foster and Robert W. McChesney, "Surveillance Capitalism: Monopoly Finance Capital, the Military-industrial Complex, and the Digital Age," *Monthly Review* (July 1, 2014), https://monthlyreview.org/2014/07/01/surveillance-capitalism/.
40. Foster and McChesney, "Surveillance Capitalism."
41. Ibid.
42. "The industry's most advanced data-driven marketing," Epsilon, last updated 2022. https://us.epsilon.com.
43. Steven Melendez and Alex Pasternack, "The data brokers quietly buying and selling your personal information," *Fast Company* (March 2, 2019), https://www.fastcompany.com/ 90310803/here-are-the-data-brokers-quietly-buying-and-selling-your-personal-information.
44. Lamdan, "Librarianship at the crossroads."
45. "FAQ on ChoicePoint: The ChoicePoint ID Theft Case: What it Means," American Civil Liberties Union (ACLU), last updated 2022, https://www.aclu.org/other/faq-choicepoint.
46. Vermont General Assembly, H.764, Act 171, https://legislature.vermont.gov/bill/status/2018/H.764.
47. "Resolution on the Misuse of Behavioral Data Surveillance in Libraries," Advocacy, Legislation and Issues, American Library Association, last updated 2022, https://www.ala.org/advocacy/intfreedom/datasurveillanceresolution.
48. "Resolution on the Misuse," Advocacy.
49. Dave Shumaker, "Librarians Can't Be Neutral in the War on Information," *Information Today, Inc.* (April 12, 2022), http://newsbreaks.infotoday.com/NewsBreaks/Librarians-Cant-Be-Neutral-in-the-War-on-Information-152307.asp.
50. Shumaker, "Librarians Can't Be Neutral."
51. "Surveillance Self-Defense: Tips, Tools and How-tos for Safer Online Communications," Electronic Frontier Foundation (EFF), last updated 2022, https://ssd.eff.org/en.

BIBLIOGRAPHY

American Civil Liberties Union (ACLU). "FAQ on ChoicePoint: The ChoicePoint ID Theft Case: What it Means." Last updated 2022. https://www.aclu.org/other/faq-choicepoint.

Ben Shahar, Omri. "Privacy is the new money, thanks to big data." *Forbes* (April 1, 2016). https://www.forbes.com/sites/omribenshahar/2016/04/01/privacy-is-the-new-money-thanks-to-big-data/?sh=307f2b263fa2.

BioIntelliSense. "Home." Last updated 2022. https://biointellisense.com/.

Clarivate. "Clarivate Successfully Completes Acquisition of ProQuest." December 1, 2021. https://clarivate.com/news/clarivate-successfully-completes-acquisition-of-proquest/?utm_campaign=EM_Global_CA_ThumbBt_Customer_Announcement_XBU_Global_2021_EN&utm_medium=email&utm_source=Eloqua&elqTrackId=82fd75ad29514e7c96e010fd966d16a7&elq=8b8dc4fd9eb-f49bbb944d74867b04d23&elqaid=18764&elqat=1&elqCampaignId=8085.

———. "Real World Data." Last updated 2022. https://clarivate.com/products/real-world-data/.

Ding, Jennifer, with Jan Diehm and Michelle McGhee. "Can Data Die? Tracking the Lenna Image." The Pudding. October 2021. https://pudding.cool/2021/10/lenna/.

Epsilon. "The industry's most advanced data-driven marketing." Last updated 2018. http://us.epsilon.com.

Electronic Frontier Foundation (EFF). "Surveillance Self-Defense: Tips, Tools and How-tos for Safer Online Communications." Last updated 2022. https://ssd.eff.org/en.

Foster, John Bellamy, and Robert W. McChesney. "Surveillance capitalism: Monopoly finance capital, the military-industrial complex, and the digital age." *Monthly Review* (July 1, 2014). https://monthlyreview.org/2014/07/01/surveillance-capitalism/.

Hagve, Martin. "The money behind academic publishing." *Tidsskrift Den norske legeforening.* August 17, 2020. https://tidsskriftet.no/en/2020/08/kronikk/money-behind-academic-publishing.

Herb, Ulrich. "Steering science through Output Indicators & Data Capitalism." *Proceedings of the 23rd Congress of the European Society of Veterinary and Comparative Nutrition,* Turin, 2019. https://digitalcommons.unl.edu/scholcom/125/.

Hilburn, Jessica. "Big Data Clashes With Patron Privacy: OverDrive's Digipalooza 2021." *Information Today, Inc.* (August 10, 2021). http://newsbreaks.infotoday.com/NewsBreaks/Big-Data-Clashes-With-Patron-Privacy-OverDrives-Digipalooza--148369.asp.

Kant, Tanya. "A history of the data tracked user." *The MIT Press Reader* (October 8, 2021). https://thereader.mitpress.mit.edu/a-history-of-the-data-tracked-user/?utm_source=pocket-newtab.

Knuth, Rebecca. *Libricide: the Regime-Sponsored Destruction of Books and Libraries in the Twentieth Century*. Westport, CT: Praeger, 2003.

Lamdan, Sarah. "Librarianship at the crossroads of ICE surveillance." *In the Library with the Lead Pipe* (November 13, 2019). https://www.inthelibrarywiththeleadpipe.org/2019/ice-surveillance/.

Mangan, Katherine. "The surveilled student." *The Chronicle of Higher Education* (February 15, 2021). https://www.chronicle.com/article/the-surveilled-student?utm_source=Iterable&utm_medium=email&utm_campaign=campaign_3492351_nl_Academe-Today_date_20220107&cid=at&source=ams&sourceid=.

Marthews, Alex, and Catherine Tucker. "Government Surveillance and Internet Search Behavior." *SSRN Electronic Journal* (2014). doi: 10.2139/ssrn.2412564.

Melendez, Steven, and Alex Pasternack. "The data brokers quietly buying and selling your personal information." *Fast Company* (March 2, 2019). https://www.fastcompany.com/90310803/here-are-the-data-brokers-quietly-buying-and-selling-your-personal-information.

Morton, Timothy. *Hyperobjects: Philosophy and Ecology after the End of the World*. Minneapolis: University of Minnesota Press, 2013.

Noble, Safiya Umoja. *Algorithms of Oppression: How Search Engines Reinforce Racism*. New York: New York University Press, 2018.

Penney, Jonathon. "Chilling Effects: Online Surveillance and Wikipedia Use," *Berkeley Technology Law Journal* 31, no. 1 (2016). https://ssrn.com/abstract=2769645.

Proctorio. "Proctorio: Securing the integrity of your online assessments," Last updated 2022. https://proctorio.com/.

Respondus. "Respondus Monitor." Last updated 2022. https://web.respondus.com/he/monitor/.

Rogers, A. Robert. "Censorship and Libraries in the Soviet Union." *Journal of Library History, Philosophy, and Comparative Librarianship* 8, no. 1 (1973): 22–29.

Shattuck, Roger. *Forbidden Knowledge: From Prometheus to Pornography*. New York: St. Martin's Press, 1996.

Shumaker, Dave. "Librarians Can't Be Neutral in the War on Information." *Information Today, Inc.* (April 12, 2022). http://newsbreaks.infotoday.com/NewsBreaks/Librarians-Cant-Be-Neutral-in-the-War-on-Information-152307.asp.

Singer, Natasha, and Brian X. Chen. "In a Post-Roe World, the Future of Digital Privacy Looks Even Grimmer." *The New York Times* (July 13, 2022). https://www.nytimes.com/2022/07/13/technology/personaltech/abortion-privacy-roe-surveillance.html.

St. Jean, Beth, Ursual Gorham, and Elizabeth Bonsignore. *Understanding Human Information Behavior: When, How, and Why People Interact with Information.* Lanham, MD: Rowman & Littlefield, 2021.

Swaak, Taylor. "A Vulnerability in Proctoring Software Should Worry Colleges, Experts Say." *The Chronicle of Higher Education* (January 6, 2022). https://www.chronicle.com/article/a-vulnerability-in-proctoring-software-should-worry-colleges-experts-say.

Weiss, Andrew. *Big Data Shocks: An Introduction to Big Data for Librarians and Information Professionals.* Blue Ridge Summit: Rowman & Littlefield Publishers, 2018.

Weiss, Andrew, with Ryan James. *Using Massive Digital Libraries: A LITA Guide.* Chicago, IL: ALA TechSource, 2014.

Wolfie, Christl. "Corporate Surveillance in everyday life: How companies collect, combine, analyze, trade, and use personal data on billions." Vienna, Austria: Cracked Labs. Last updated 2022. https://crackedlabs.org/en/corporate-surveillance/infographics.

Zuboff, Shoshana. "Big Other: Surveillance Capitalism and the prospects of an information civilization." *Journal of Information Technology* 30, no. 1 (March 1, 2015): 75–89. doi: 10.1057/jit.2015.5

———. *The Age of Surveillance Capitalism: The Fight for a Human Future at the New Frontier of Power.* New York: Public Affairs, 2019.

PART III
Educating About Privacy

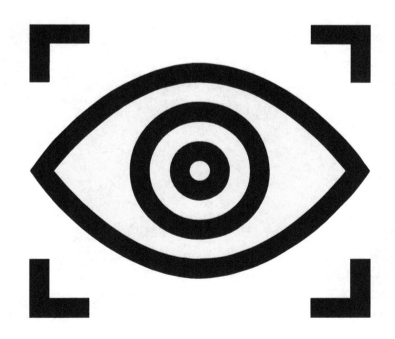

CHAPTER 7

THE PROMISE OF THEORY-INFORMED PEDAGOGY:
Building a Privacy Literacy Program

Alexandria Chisholm and Sarah Hartman-Caverly

INTRODUCTION: PRIVACY LITERACY, A STATE OF BECOMING

As an emerging literacy,[1] privacy literacy (PL) is in a state of becoming. While early works provide waypoints in the PL landscape,[2] it remains largely uncharted territory open for exploration. PL instruction provides a compelling forum for praxis—recursively theorizing and applying theories to pedagogical practice.

Privacy has become intricately entangled with technology as automation bleeds into all facets of modern life and individuals' information flows are increasingly surveilled and monetized. This conflation, while undeniable, leads to intimidated educators who fear they lack the technological expertise to lead PL initiatives.

Furthermore, PL instruction is steeped in the uncertainty of constant technological advances, creating barriers for those who feel it is impossible to stay current.

The authors believe that effective PL pedagogy is grounded in theory—both privacy and pedagogical—and that sustainable PL programs can be achieved through a theory-informed lens. This chapter recounts a theory-informed approach to teaching a successful co-curricular PL program. The literature review examines pedagogical and theoretical considerations for a simultaneously theory-informed and student-centered PL practice. The chapter demonstrates how pedagogy and theory are united in theory-informed PL instruction in four recurring workshops and outlines plans for expanding programming into new disciplinary, topical, and audience contexts.

THEORY-INFORMED PRIVACY LITERACY PEDAGOGY

Early theorizing on PL defined it explicitly in terms of data privacy, information and communications technology, and privacy settings. Rotman explores PL in the context of social media, describing PL as "a subcategory of data literacy, or as a complementary literacy" and asserting that

> a privacy-literate user should be educated to distinguish between different facets of *personal information*; familiar with the settings in which he/she will readily relinquish personal information and those in which personal information should not be disclosed; understand the limitations of *online anonymity*; aware of the threats - immediate and prospective - that may stem from information disclosure, and take precautions against overexposure (emphasis added).[3]

Building on this, Wissinger explains that "privacy literacy education can help users of social media sites assess the risks of sharing their private information online."[4] Wissinger expands Rotman's framework for PL, mapping it to critical thinking practices and applying it to instruction on the professional use of social media by healthcare providers. Such approaches can actually engender a false sense of (data) security in students, enticing them to disclose more than they otherwise would, and thus undermining the intended application of PL—a phenomenon known as the control paradox.[5] These first-generation approaches reflect Hagendorff's critique of PL, including a focus on front-end technology features, a presumption of the ability of users to make free and rational decisions with respect to their privacy, and a shift of responsibility for privacy to users and away from platform, corporate, and state actors.[6]

One approach that melds theoretical and skills-based treatments of PL is informed learning pedagogy, theorized by Bruce and Hughes, which introduces students to procedural and declarative knowledge simultaneously and in a mutually reinforcing way, through learning experiences that contextualize procedural skills within a discipline.[7] Students build skills while using information in an authentic and embedded context, instead of as discrete and isolated outcomes.[8] Informed learning is guided by three principles: incorporation of reflection or metacognition to promote knowledge retention and transferability,[9] prioritization of the simultaneity of information use and disciplinary context,[10] and delivering students with an experience using information as well as with the subject or discipline.[11]

In Lloyd's literacies of information, the emphasis in information literacy shifts from attainment of skills-based learning outcomes to the enactment of ongoing information practices constituted by action.[12] Such practices, Lloyd explains, are "relational, embodied, material, consequential, recursive."[13] These attributes map well to PL, as the experience of privacy is likewise inherently social, embodied, material, consequential, and evolving. In PL, active learning experiences paired with opportunities for group discussion and independent metacognitive reflection result in workshop sessions tailored to the distinct experiences, interests, concerns, and values of participating students, enabling them to transcend rote data privacy skill development with its overreliance on technosolutionism and to enact practices informed by privacy considerations. Through praxis, practitioners can infuse learning design with theory and reflect on the effectiveness of theory-informed activities for student learning. According to Flierl and Maybee, engaging with theory answers the *why* of undertaking information literacy (or PL) work, carrying the added benefit of communicating the value of such efforts with other institutional stakeholders.[14]

STUDENT-CENTERED PRIVACY LITERACY PEDAGOGY

Student-centered teaching methods emerged in information literacy pedagogy in the 1990s with the introduction of digital research tools and the transition from the more didactic bibliographic instruction.[15] Active learning, in which students apply concepts through hands-on learning activities and then reflect on their learning experience, is a popular student-centered pedagogy in library instruction. Active learning has many benefits cited within the literature, including that it enhances student engagement, motivation, and knowledge retention. However, Hicks and Sinkinson assert that it requires intentional scaffolding and thoughtful learning design to achieve its constructivist aim of building new knowledge on students' prior experiences.[16]

Hicks and Sinkinson's critiques of active learning pedagogy are particularly apt for PL instruction. First, they observe that it can unintentionally compel the interaction and participation of learners.[17] Students belonging to already marginalized communities are particularly vulnerable to alienation resulting from compelled participation; additionally, this is a form of compelled speech and a violation of students' intellectual freedom. They further problematize active learning's emphasis on observable, participatory learning activities, which can be at the expense of nonobservable engagement, such as solitary reading and private reflection.[18]

The reality that active learning pedagogies subject students' intellectual activities to potential surveillance by instructors and classmates alike should be given serious consideration in any instructional design—but *especially* PL. Learning activities should be flexible to avoid subjecting students to the disparate impacts of intellectual, behavioral, and social surveillance and should offer multiple modes of participation that enable—or negate the need for—students' self-protective information behaviors.[19] Activities that allow for anonymous participation, or an opt-in basis, should be prioritized.

In light of these considerations, active learning nevertheless remains a useful pedagogical construct for PL learning design. Hands-on activities are valuable for conveying complex and abstract privacy concepts, and opportunities for reflection attend to students' affective states as described by Cahoy and Schroeder, including their values, motivations, and self-efficacy with respect to privacy considerations.[20] Practically speaking, because active learning is strongly implied in ACRL's *Framework for Information Literacy for Higher Education*,[21] PL programs incorporating these principles are better situated to align and integrate with existing information literacy programming. Finally, active learning's emphasis on dialogic and social learning provides linkages to critical pedagogy and critical information literacy.[22] With its focus on power structures in the information environment, as detailed by Tewell, critical information literacy is another useful framework for PL learning design to address topics like information asymmetries, surveillance, disparate impacts, algorithmic bias, and the New Jim Code.[23]

A HUMBLE NOTE ON HUMILITY IN TEACHING

Privacy is a complex, multifaceted concept with roots in numerous disciplines. One could spend their entire life studying privacy and still not know all there is to know. But the futility of achieving expert status on privacy should not discourage the pursuit of expertise nor dampen one's self-efficacy with respect to PL. Its complex nature means that privacy provides many points of entry, and exploration is encouraged where it naturally intersects with practitioners' other interests and areas of practice.

Humility in teaching is a useful orientation for PL instruction. Simply understood as "respect for students," humility in teaching is often identified as a key characteristic of great teachers.[24] Waks reports that humble teachers "bring out and guide the aim-directed actions of learners rather than imposing external ends and controlling their behaviors."[25] This pedagogical philosophy resonates with the approach to PL practiced by Chisholm and Hartman-Caverly, which prioritizes students' autonomy, values, lived experiences, and intellectual freedom.[26] Humility in teaching is expressed in their learning design which engages students in active learning experiences paired with opportunities for reflection and discussion that enable them to interpret their own individual experiences, express their values, and act on their priorities.

Waks outlines two paths of positive humility in teaching: analytical (or self-critical) humility, and transpersonal (or immersive) humility. Teachers who practice analytical humility are self-aware, open-minded critical thinkers. They exhibit a willingness to listen, to consider the merits of opposing viewpoints, and to learn—especially from students.[27] Analytical humility requires that teachers share the reasoning underlying their content claims and learning objectives with students so that they are subject to students' evaluations of their merit.

Teachers who practice transpersonal humility are willing to suspend the boundary between self and another to experience and participate in a unified whole. They cultivate a classroom culture of open sharing, cooperation, and celebration of commonalities.[28] Transpersonal humility pedagogy attends to the whole student, including affective learning, and situates teachers as co-learners with their students.[29] Practiced together, analytical and transpersonal humility in teaching provide a constructive orientation to PL pedagogy.

WORKSHOP SERIES: CONSTRUCTING THEORY-INFORMED PRIVACY LITERACY

Hartman-Caverly and Chisholm redefine PL as "a suite of knowledge, behaviors, and critical dispositions regarding the information constructs of self-hood, expressive activities, and relationships,"[30] positing a definition that intentionally shifts the focus of privacy away from data and technology by recentering people. While first-generation PL efforts primarily addressed data privacy, Hartman-Caverly and Chisholm place a greater emphasis on autonomy privacy,[31] asserting that "privacy is about respect for persons, not just protection for data."[32] This positive case for privacy opens new space for the introduction of privacy theories and practices that are independent of specific technological trends, resulting in evergreen learning experiences that are responsive to students' interests and concerns.

Chisholm and Hartman-Caverly's flagship privacy workshop series comprises four workshops: Privacy, Digital Leadership, Digital Shred, and Digital Wellness. Their series is composed of both curricularly integrated and co-curricular workshops meant to operate as both standalone and scaffolded learning experiences.[33] These workshops share a temporal component: Privacy examines privacy issues of the immediate present, Digital Leadership considers privacy implications for the future, Digital Shred repairs privacy harms of the past, and Digital Wellness nurtures privacy awareness across the lifespan, as illustrated in figure 7.1.

The series is informed by the authors' original Six Private I's Privacy Conceptual Model, the control paradox, Zuboff's concept of surveillance capitalism, and Ip's

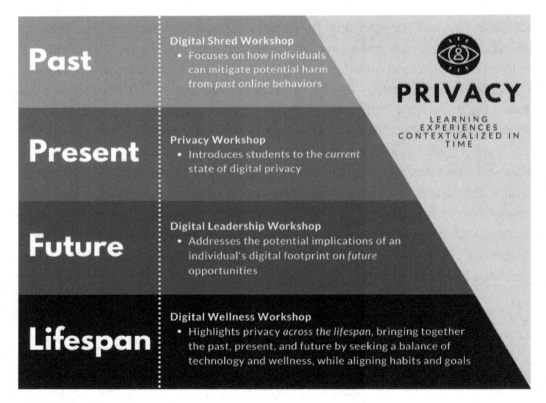

FIGURE 7.1
Privacy learning experiences contextualized in time, illustrating the temporal focus of each workshop within the Penn State Berks Privacy Workshop Series.

three types of data, which fortify the learning experiences on common ground.[34] These shared theoretical underpinnings create a cohesive message to connect the workshops, whether participants attend one or all options.

Beyond theory-informed content, the series embraces a philosophy of respect and humility by creating activities that recognize student agency and autonomy through several approaches. For one, providing ample time for guided reflections allows students the space to consider new concepts and ideas and apply them to their lived experiences. Due to the sensitive nature of topics that privacy discussions can evoke, it is vital to create opportunities to share thoughts and ideas in a safe space that respects everyone's comfort level. Building a variety of possibilities to participate, such as small group discussions, large group debriefs, as well as anonymous feedback options, encourages active engagement without the risk of compelled or coerced participation. Finally, designing activities to assist participants in applying their privacy preferences to individual solutions avoids prescriptive or proscriptive approaches that dictate actions.

PRIVACY WORKSHOP: LAYING THE GROUNDWORK

Within the series, the Privacy Workshop operates as the foundational learning experience upon which all others are scaffolded.[35] Embedded within a first-year experience course, the workshop introduces students to the current state of digital privacy as well as surveillance capitalist data collection practices and applications. As the present-oriented workshop, it considers privacy's role in what Cohen calls each individual's "capacity for self-determination."[36] The Privacy Workshop examines Ip's three types of data—consciously given, automatically monitored (metadata), and modeled.[37] This workshop also introduces Hartman-Caverly and Chisholm's Six Private I's, an onion model depicting concentric zones of personal and social privacy comprising *identity*, *intellect*, bodily and contextual *integrity*, *intimacy*, and social *interaction* and voluntary *isolation*.[38] Individual frames explored in this workshop are examined in greater depth in subsequent workshops.

Opening with a series of reflection questions, students are encouraged to share their existing thoughts and practices regarding technology and privacy. Prompts include:
- Where have you left data tracks today?
- What data do you think is collected about you regularly?
- What apps do you use daily? Weekly?
- What steps do you already take to protect your data?

- What does privacy mean to you?

This serves as both a warmup and a method of formative assessment that builds rapport and gauges knowledge. Facilitating a post-activity large group discussion of participant responses allows instructors to customize classes to each group's unique experiences and interests. Additionally, expressing curiosity about technologies and techniques which may be unfamiliar is an opportunity to embody humility in teaching as well as honor and learn from student expertise. It is also a great way to break the ice and encourage active participation.

This debrief seamlessly transitions into the micro-lecture content by utilizing student-supplied definitions of privacy from the final prompt to introduce the positive case for privacy, accomplished through a brief introduction of the authors' original Six Private I's Privacy Conceptual Model. By briefly surveying the various spheres of privacy, facilitators can begin to expand participants' understanding of privacy from one of secrecy to something that enables individual identity, intellect, contextual and bodily integrity, intimacy, and interaction/isolation. The intent is not to create a theory-laden lecture wrought with definitions but rather to shift perceptions of what privacy is and can do for individuals through a theory-informed examination.

After the micro-lecture, the workshop transitions into an exploration of personal data collection. Students are provided with a curated set of links to garner a better understanding of what metadata is regularly collected about their online behaviors and activities. Gamified tools such as ClickClickClick allow hands-on investigation of the types of behaviors websites are tracking, while links to individual ad profiles allow reflection of the application of such data collection.[39] Participants are invited to share anonymously about their ad profiles and website tracking while exploring the links. This is followed by a large group discussion where facilitators can once again build trust and exhibit humility by sharing details of their own experiences and profiles for full transparency.

To transition into the final activity, instructors provide a brief overview of the three types of data (consciously given, automatically monitored, and modeled) to frame the workshop by connecting previous exercises and introducing the culminating activity on modeled data,[40] as illustrated in figure 7.2. Students can be split into small groups and assigned a topic (e.g., location services, health data, criminal justice, and consumer profiling) from which to select a case study article from curated lists. After reading their article about how automatically monitored data is collected and modeled in a variety of contexts, groups must brainstorm one positive or negative impact of the practices on individuals or society. A final class discussion is facilitated to discuss case studies and each group's thoughts.

Privacy Workshop Data Level Framing

DATA LEVEL	EXPLANATION	LEARNING ACTIVITY
CONSCIOUSLY GIVEN	Your name, email, date of birth	Reflection stations
AUTOMATICALLY MONITORED	Where you log in from, what time you do it, where else you visit on the web	Personal data collection exploration (i.e. ClickClickClick, ad profiles, etc.)
MODELED	Predicted from other data, such as your quantified attractiveness or trustworthiness.	Case study investigation

FIGURE 7.2
Organization and framing of Privacy Workshop activities based on Ip's three types of data.

In closing, students are introduced to the Personal Data Plan as a takeaway activity, which provides tools including websites to help interpret the legalese of privacy policies and a framework to conduct a cost-benefit analysis of technology adoption.

Overall, the Privacy Workshop provides a solid foundation of personal data collection practices and applications. By grounding hands-on, gamified activities about current data collection and profiling practices in positive case privacy theory, this learning experience allows students to broaden their preconceived notions of privacy. This workshop lays the groundwork of surveillance capitalism and the current landscape of digital privacy on which all other workshops within the series are built.

DIGITAL LEADERSHIP WORKSHOP: BLUEPRINTS FOR THE FUTURE

The Digital Leadership Workshop, a co-curricular learning experience delivered in collaboration with Career Services, addresses the potential implications of an individual's digital footprint on future opportunities.[41] Intended for students beginning to plan for post-graduation prospects, this experience is all about contemplating and setting goals. Special consideration is given to how current and past online activity have major impacts on goal achievement due to surveillance capitalism and the data collection practices covered in the Privacy Workshop.

As the future-facing workshop, Digital Leadership presents privacy as necessary to what Zuboff termed a *"right to the future tense, which accounts for the individual's ability to imagine, intend, promise, and construct a future"* (emphasis in original).[42] In this workshop, Nissenbaum's theory of contextual integrity and its corollary, context collapse, is applied to unpack the *integrity* frame of the Six Private I's and guide students' thinking of how their digital activities impact their future selves.[43]

To begin the workshop with a clear perception of their personal digital leadership philosophy (or lack thereof), students are asked to respond to reflection questions intended to prompt an examination of their online behaviors in juxtaposition with personal and professional aspirations. Facilitating a debrief discussion allows instructors to establish the group's current practices and future goals as well as identify distinct concerns, interests, and any commonalities.

This opening exercise feeds into the micro-lecture by introducing a few examples of "digital leadership fails," or instances of social media behaviors having real-world impact on employment and life prospects. As these topics sometimes feel grim, a helpful tip is to provide a variety of serious and relatable examples alongside humorous ones to help establish credibility while maintaining a certain amount of levity.[44] These examples lead to a summary of statistics related to how social media is utilized in grad school admissions and various employment scenarios, illustrating current applications of individuals' digital footprints. These concrete, practical stories hook students' attention and emphasize the relevance and value of the workshop.

At this point the theoretical underpinning of the workshop is integrated through an overview of danah boyd's four properties of web data explaining how personal data is *persistent*, *searchable*, *replicable*, and *scalable*,[45] as shown in figure 7.3. boyd's scholarship exposes how online activities create vulnerabilities and

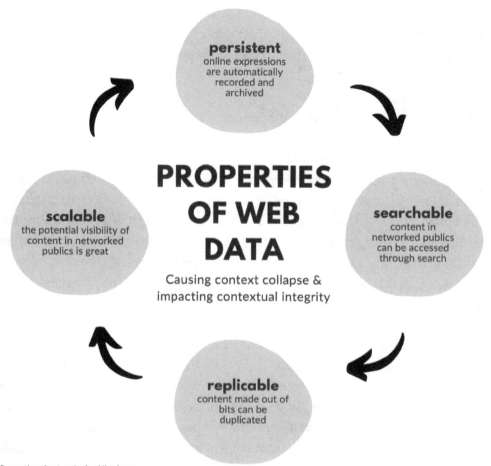

Properties of networked publics from:
danah boyd, "Taken Out of Context: American Teen Sociality in Networked Publics" (PhD diss., University of California Berkeley, 2008), 27.

FIGURE 7.3

Properties of web data (persistence, scalability, searchability, and replicability) that contribute to context collapse and contextual integrity as theorized by danah boyd.

embodies the adage "the internet is forever." After establishing the permanency of web data, the workshop is scaffolded and connected to the rest of the series through a brief overview of the Six Private I's, spotlighting contextual integrity, or the appropriate distribution and flow of personal information within contexts.[46] This transitions into the theory of a new universal human experience, context collapse—the blurring of social roles disconnected from time and space that must coexist in a single environment due to ubiquitous connectivity.[47] With the internet, individuals must present themselves in a way that is appropriate for *all potential future contexts* as opposed to expectations of clear boundaries or explicit communication within distinct social groups.

Shifting to a social media policy review, students explore a series of curated links and identify a policy relevant to their career goals or major. After selecting an applicable link, they review the social media guidelines and respond to the following reflection questions:
- What surprised you?
- How do your current behaviors and actions on social media hold up in comparison?
- What will you continue? What will you alter/change?

Once students complete their reflections, facilitators can lead a class discussion about social media policies and implications for current and future practices.

The closing exercise directs participants to draft a digital leadership motto, asking them what they want to think about before they post. Finally, the session concludes with group discourse of their mottos and takeaways.

Digital Leadership offers a new theory-informed approach to online reputation management. Framing the workshop content around theories of context collapse and contextual integrity frees instructors from the typical didactic approaches to digital citizenship and appropriate online conduct. Using informed learning pedagogy to mix privacy theory, practical exploration of real-world artifacts (i.e., social media policies and expectations within professional contexts) and ample time for reflection on future implications of online behavior, students are able to align their plans and online activity within the context of their future profession and model constructive behaviors as student leaders and impending professionals.

DIGITAL SHRED WORKSHOP: REPAIRING PAST HARMS

After establishing the current landscape of digital privacy and reflecting on the potential impact of behavioral data collection on future opportunities, Digital Shred turns focus to mitigating potential harm from past online behaviors.[48] Of all workshops in the series, Digital Shred functions as the most traditional privacy workshop—one where participants explore practical tools and techniques to safeguard their online privacy. While this type of learning experience is essential in addressing digital privacy concerns, the authors' philosophical commitment to realistic representations of privacy-protecting technologies precludes typical technosolutionist approaches. As such, the control paradox plays heavily in the fundamental design of this workshop. Despite participants' desire for solution-based answers, the authors instead embrace the complexity of the current technological landscape in their pledge to theory-informed PL. A bonus to this pedagogical style is embracing transpersonal humility, where the instructor is no longer concerned with being a "sage on the stage" and instead trudges through the frustrating complexity and nuance of our surveillance capitalist ecosystem with students as peers. Thus, with the control paradox in mind, the authors avoid instilling a false sense of security or overconfidence in privacy-protecting tools and techniques that could cause further harm.[49]

As the past-focused workshop, students determine how their consciously given and automatically monitored data are collected as behavioral surplus from their online activities and analyzed through machine learning and other artificial intelligence applications, resulting in their modeled data or data double.[50] Students learn "digital shred" strategies to assert what Burkell describes as their "right to be forgotten" in order to limit the past's ability to construct their identity (as outlined in the Six Private I's) and determine their future.[51]

The session opens with a gamified prior knowledge check used to scaffold Digital Shred for participants who may not have attended the foundational workshop. The fact or fiction game includes statements that cover the basics of digital privacy and online behavioral data collection with brief explanations. Using this gamified modality engages participants at all knowledge levels.

Once the game is completed, instructors briefly define *digital shred* as "the act of managing privacy by curating digital records for purposes of data governance, risk management, and storage efficiency,"[52] opening the micro-lecture. Theories from the Digital Shred Conceptual Framework, illustrated in figure 7.4, are introduced to underpin the strategies and subsequent learning activities of the workshop. The framework is built upon the principles of data governance to achieve data minimization and storage efficiency, emphasizing the importance of thoughtful, scheduled data maintenance. The micro-lecture closes by connecting digital shred practices to the management of an individual's "data double" using the metaphor of secure file shredding for the proactive management of one's digital dossier.

Shifting to an active learning approach, the workshop applies theoretical concepts of the Digital Shred Conceptual Framework to "shredding" past behaviors and digital data. Rather than emphasize concrete techniques—such as browser plugins, VPNs, and other front-end features—the authors concentrate on decision-making frameworks that embrace individual participants' lived experiences and personal priorities.

Preparing for a deeper examination of their digital footprint, students are asked to reflect on how to craft a "burner account." The Idea Portfolio worksheet prompts, "If you were creating a perfect account (or a fake burner account to do private research on a crush), what would you choose to make it a perfect account?"

Digital Shred Conceptual Framework

CONCEPT	STRATEGY	DATA LEVEL	LEARNING ACTIVITY
RISK MANAGEMENT	Reputation management	Data double (modeled data) derived from consciously given & behavioral surplus	Damage Assessment
DATA GOVERNANCE	Routine privacy audits	Consciously given & behavioral surplus	Personal Data Integrity Plan
STORAGE EFFICIENCY	Secure deletion tips & tools	Consciously given	Digital Shred Privacy Literacy Toolkit

FIGURE 7.4
The Digital Shred Conceptual Framework illustrates the workshop's theoretical underpinnings and their application to concrete strategies and learning activities.

The guided worksheet includes questions about various reputation management considerations. After a brief class discussion, students are introduced to the Damage Assessment worksheet, adapted from a real-life artifact, Intelligence Community Directive 732 (ICD 732).[53] This activity asks students to evaluate actual or potential damage resulting from infiltration or exfiltration, identify systemic vulnerabilities, and develop a corrective action plan. While opportunities for large group discussions are always encouraged, the authors caution against coercing student responses to these activities as topics can veer into sensitive details. As such, the authors have personal examples that they are comfortable sharing to transition and wrap up the activity.

Finally, the Personal Data Integrity Plan is introduced, asking students to use their Ideal Portfolio and Damage Assessment responses to reflect on their digital accounts, apps, and smart products which may pose privacy threats. The worksheet serves as a tool for students to plan and make routine the process of auditing and updating their digital dossier and online presence. In lieu of homegrown how-to resources, the worksheet instead links to curated, categorized lists of existing artifacts. The authors leverage their Digital Shred Privacy Literacy Toolkit, updated on a regular basis with published step-by-step guides on maintaining digital privacy.[54]

The workshop closes with "snowball confessions" where participants respond anonymously to the relevant reflection questions. The responses are written on scraps of paper, tossed into the center of the room, and read aloud by instructors or participants as a way of concluding the session.

Overall, Digital Shred is an opportunity for students to identify their privacy priorities and values and apply theory-informed decision-making frameworks to "shred" their digital footprint and mitigate past harms. This is accomplished while maintaining an understanding of the limitations of such practices, grounded in boyd's properties of web data and the control paradox.[55]

DIGITAL WELLNESS WORKSHOP: REMODELING BEHAVIORS TO LIVE LIFE TO THE FULLEST

As the final workshop within the series, Digital Wellness highlights privacy across the lifespan, bringing together the past, present, and future by seeking a balance of technology and wellness, while aligning habits and goals.[56] Offered in collaboration with campus Counseling Services and Student Affairs, this co-curricular workshop is geared toward students interested in the intersection of technology, wellness, and privacy.

In Digital Wellness, students engage with Vanden Abeele's construct of digital well-being, which strives for an optimal balance between connectivity and offline life that preserves autonomy and maximizes the benefits of digital participation while monitoring and minimizing its harms, as explicated by Chisholm and Hartman-Caverly.[57] Privacy is explored as it relates to various dimensions of wellness, including physical, intellectual, social (*interaction* and *isolation*), emotional/spiritual, financial, and recreational. Particular focus is given to attention engineering, attention autonomy, and conscientious connectivity[58] as they relate to *intellectual* privacy. Because digital well-being is dynamic across the lifespan, students apply their own values and principles to exploring privacy and digital wellness strategies that offer what Hildebrandt termed "protection of the incomputable self."[59]

To establish baseline perceptions of wellness, the workshop opens with the following reflection questions:
- What does wellness mean to you?
- List examples of healthy habits.
- What are your wellness priorities?
- Identify barriers to your well-being goals.

- What are your "imbalance indicators" that signal you are going off-track?

By design, prompts omit all reference to technology to spotlight general wellness at the beginning of the session and transition into technology's influence during the micro-lecture. After students respond, instructors facilitate a large group discussion to establish current wellness practices and concerns. As with all workshops in the series, participant responses and interests should steer the direction of the learning experience.

Discussion of wellness practices and goals naturally segues into the micro-lecture, opening with a summary of statistics related to the intersection of technology and wellness. These data should reflect major changes that have occurred over the last two decades, illustrating increased technology use, shifts in active leisure, and transformation of social interactions. Next, workshop content is scaffolded and connected to the rest of the series through a brief introduction to the authors' Six Private I's, concentrating on the hidden harms of technologies on intellectual activities and behavior.[60] An overview of considerations for achieving tech-wellness balance pivots to the Digital Wellness Wheel activity.

Using the real-world artifact of the wellness wheel, the Digital Wellness Wheel prompts special consideration of technology's influence on various spheres of wellness. Students are asked to identify three personal wellness priorities from the wheel and reflect on how technology is negatively or positively impacting those areas of their wellness. After identifying impacts, they consider how to leverage or cut out technology to improve their wellness and what steps can be taken to change habits. Informed by conscientious connectivity and attentional autonomy, the activity focuses on providing students with a decision-making framework to identify their personal wellness priorities and goals as opposed to providing prescribed solutions.[61]

To support the Digital Wellness Wheel activity, the authors present a curated list of categorized case studies on technology's role/influence on various spheres of wellness. Students are asked to anonymously share their findings regarding one case study they explored during the session. These responses feed into the final discussion with class takeaways to close the workshop.

While the authors have their own opinions on technology's influence on individual well-being, they acknowledge students' autonomy and recognize that their lived experiences and priorities may vastly differ from their own. As with all workshops in the series, the authors strive to respect students' agency and prioritize informing and empowering over imposing solutions.

BUILDING ADDITIONS: CREATING FLEXIBLE FORMATS AND NEW DIRECTIONS FOR THEORY-INFORMED PRIVACY LITERACY

Linked but adjacent to the Penn State Berks Privacy Workshop Series is #ForYou: Algorithms and the Attention Economy.[62] Integrated into first-year experience programming alongside the Privacy Workshop, #ForYou puts a new spin on media literacy by moving beyond fake news to examine the algorithms that shape individuals' online experiences and how they encounter information in their everyday lives. Taking a deep dive into machine learning algorithms and the attention economy, the workshop explores personalization and persuasive design techniques and their impact on identity formation, intellectual curiosity, and social relationships. Complementing Digital Wellness, it uses decision-making frameworks informed by conscientious connectivity and attention autonomy.[63]

A co-curricular workshop, Private Bits: Privacy, Intimacy, and Consent, is offered in partnership with the campus Wellness Center to explore privacy as it relates to healthy relationships, sexuality, consent, and safety.[64] Private Bits introduces the consentful tech framework to consider the topic of consent as it applies to technology use and contemplate the role of technology in intimate relationships.[65] This workshop takes a deeper look at how technology can both nurture and threaten intimacy, sexuality, and relationships while referencing Mozilla's *privacy not included ratings for dating apps[66] to reflect on what it means to share our most intimate and vulnerable moments with some of the world's most powerful adtech corporations and data brokers.

Privacy programming can also be tailored to specific audiences. The workshop Privacy+, designed for community entrepreneurs as well as business students and delivered through the Berks Launchbox and Flemming CEED Center for Creativity, Entrepreneurship, and Economic Development, outlines the positive case for privacy for businesses and their clients.[67] In Privacy+, the Six Private I's is applied to the business context, with a survey of case studies demonstrating the role privacy plays in entrepreneurial and corporate identity; intellectual property; data integrity and governance; confidentiality, non-disclosure agreements, and trade secrets; board recruitment; and entrepreneurial vision.

International students are another cohort for whom privacy takes on unique salience. Privacy programming for international students, as well as students preparing to travel abroad, can review privacy rights and risks at US border crossings,[68] compare privacy legal frameworks around the world,[69] and critically examine the global surveillance grid.[70] Such programming may consider the aspiration and limitations of privacy as a human right[71] and how the Six Private I's frames of contextual integrity and interaction/isolation inform our thinking about privacy beyond borders. A privacy workshop for international students can be implemented in co-curricular programming.

PL learning experiences need not be restricted to one-shot sessions or hour-long workshops. PL programming is as flexible in form as it is rich in conceptual content. In fact, PL programs can benefit greatly from creative modalities, which support students in learning privacy concepts while also processing the sometimes difficult affective experiences that they raise.[72] Gamification offers creative experiential learning opportunities that engage students in exploring privacy concepts through familiar gameplay conventions. Two examples currently under development are Surveillance Capitalism Monopoly and Obfuscation!, an impossible-to-escape room. In Surveillance Capitalism Monopoly, students acquire familiar players in the surveillance architecture industry, including ad tech companies, luxury surveillance brands, data brokerages, and government agencies. They exchange terabytes of data while navigating a data minefield of surveillance and behavioral surplus data capture. Obfuscation! uses choose-your-own-adventure style scenarios to introduce students to a wide range of practices in surveillance, data capture, data brokerage, and data profiling. While players select maneuvers to obfuscate their true identities, they will learn that there's no way to truly escape the all-pervasive panopticon. As with other gamified learning, gamified PL is most effective when student-players engage in reflection or metacognition about the concepts, such as through large-group debriefing discussions or guided personal reflection worksheets.

Micro-tutorials offer another flexible format with which to deliver PL instruction. Ironically, the theory of microlearning was developed in response to the heavily distracted information ecosystem individuals find themselves in because of many of the PL concepts discussed in this and other chapters. This emerging pedagogical theory "offers a new way of designing and organizing learning, like learning in small steps and small units of content, with structure and classification created by the learner."[73] As many of the topics addressed in PL instruction are highly technical and complex, it makes sense to utilize microlearning to break down content that librarians would otherwise be unable to integrate into information literacy instruction. The flexibility of micro-tutorials lies in their self-directed, scalable digital format, which can easily be embedded and customized for various courses and learning scenarios. Examples of micro-tutorials under development are lessons on facial recognition, deep fakes, dark patterns, and student surveillance. These microlearning experiences will leverage the many active learning activities developed by scholars, activists, and artists working in the privacy and surveillance space, alleviating the burden on the educator to create original, homegrown activities and materials.[74]

EMPOWERED PEDAGOGY: A THEORY-INFORMED PATH FORWARD

Privacy issues touch upon every individual's life, span all disciplines, and intersect with some of the world's most pressing issues. With early PL dialogue initially centered solely around data privacy, information and communications technology, and privacy settings, it is no wonder that library workers have been, and continue to be, intimidated by the prospect of integrating these issues into their teaching repertoire. When framed as a purely technological literacy, the natural inclination of the non-expert is to take simple, straightforward approaches that reduce content to a manageable level.

This chapter, however, lays out a vision of PL that frees library workers from the burden of absolute knowledge and expertise and creates a path toward a theory-informed pedagogy. By approaching PL as humble teachers, adjusting active learning to account for critiques of compelled participation and the adoption of informed learning pedagogy, library workers can develop meaningful, engaging learning experiences for students. Eliminating the burden of technological expertise by removing focus on technosolutionist approaches opens the door to instruction that concentrates on students' knowledge, behaviors, and critical dispositions. Pedagogy grounded in theory tackles common critiques of PL and recenters individual persons at the heart of the learning experience. With constant developments in surveillance capitalism, it is essential that librarians move forward with intent, focused pedagogy that engages students as partners in the learning process.

ACKNOWLEDGMENTS

First and foremost, we want to thank our students for continually inspiring us to grow as educators and privacy advocates—and for tirelessly keeping us old Millennials up to date. A special thank you to Alexandrea Glenn who collaborated with us in the development of the Digital Shred Workshop. Finally, we are incredibly grateful to Adam Beauchamp and Scott W. H. Young for their discerning and meticulous feedback which greatly improved our chapter's clarity and focus.

NOTES

1. "2021 Environmental Scan," Association of College & Research Libraries Research Planning and Review Committee, last modified April 2021, 17, https://www.ala.org/acrl/sites/ala.org.acrl/files/content/publications/whitepapers/EnvironmentalScan2021.pdf.
2. Dana Rotman, "Are You Looking At Me?: Social Media and Privacy Literacy," iConference 2009, 1-3 [2], available online at https://www.ideals.illinois.edu/handle/2142/15339, accessed January 4, 2022; Christina L. Wissinger, "Privacy Literacy: From Theory to Practice," *Communications in Information Literacy* 11, no. 2 (2017): 379.
3. Rotman, "Are You Looking At Me?," 2.
4. Wissinger, "Privacy Literacy," 379.
5. Laura Brandimarte, Alessandro Acquisti, and George Loewenstein, "Misplaced Confidences: Privacy and the Control Paradox," *Social Psychology and Personality Science* 4, no. 3 (2017): 345.
6. Thilo Hagendorff, "Privacy Literacy and Its Problems," *Journal of Information Ethics* 27, no. 2 (2018): 130.
7. Christine Bruce and Hilary Hughes, "Informed Learning: A Pedagogical Construct Attending Simultaneously to Information Use and Learning," *Library & Information Science Research* 32 (2010): A2-A8 [A2]; Michael Flierl and Clarence Maybee, "Refining Information Literacy Practice: Examining the Foundations of Information Literacy Theory," *IFLA Journal* 46, no. 2 (2020): 127.
8. Hilary Hughes and Christine Bruce, "Snapshots of Informed Learning: LIS and Beyond," *Education for Information* 29, no. 3 (September 2012): 255, https://doi.org/10.3233/EFI-130940; Bruce and Hughes, "Informed Learning," A3.
9. Bruce and Hughes, "Informed Learning," A4.
10. Ibid., A3.
11. Hughes and Bruce, "Snapshots of Informed Learning," 255.
12. Lloyd, "Information Literacy and Literacies of Information," 96.
13. Ibid., 98.
14. Flierl and Maybee, "Refining Information Literacy Practice," 130.
15. Alison Hicks and Caroline Sinkinson, "Participation and Presence: Interrogating Active Learning," *portal: Libraries and the Academy* 21, no. 4 (2021): 752.
16. Hicks and Sinkinson, "Participation and Presence," 749, 750, 753.
17. Ibid., 756.
18. Ibid.
19. Ibid., 755; Solon Barocas and Andrew B. Selbst, "Big Data's Disparate Impact," *California Law Review* 104, no. 671 (2016): 674.
20. Ellysa Cahoy and Robert Schroeder, "Embedding Affective Learning Outcomes in Library Instruction," *Communications in Information Literacy* 6, no. 1 (2012): 75.
21. Hicks and Sinkinson, "Participation and Presence," 754.
22. Ibid., 750; Deborah Schachter, "Theory into Practice: Challenges and Implications for Information Literacy Teaching," *IFLA Journal* 46, no. 2 (2020): 134; Eamon Tewell, "A Decade of Critical Information Literacy: A Review of the Literature," *Communications in Information Literacy* 9, no. 1 (2015): 25.
23. Ruha Benjamin, *Race After Technology: Abolitionist Tools for the New Jim Code* (Cambridge: Polity, 2019), 5.
24. Leonard J. Waks, "Humility in Teaching," *Educational Theory* 68, no. 4-5 (2018): 427–42 [428].
25. Waks, "Humility in Teaching," 428.
26. Sarah Hartman-Caverly and Alexandria Chisholm, "Privacy Literacy Instruction Practices in Academic Libraries: Past, Present, and Possibilities," *IFLA Journal* 46, no. 4 (2020): 316.
27. Waks, "Humility in Teaching," 431; Wayne Bivens-Tatum, "Scholarly Conversations, Intellectual Virtues, and Virtue Information Literacy," *Library Philosophy and Practice* (2021): 25.
28. Waks, "Humility in Teaching," 434.

29. Ibid., 440.
30. Hartman-Caverly and Chisholm, "Privacy Literacy Instruction Practices," 306.
31. Lisa Ho, "Privacy vs. Privacy," *EDUCAUSE Review* (February 25, 2015), accessed January 5, 2022, https://er.educause.edu/blogs/2015/2/privacy-vs-privacy.
32. Sarah Hartman-Caverly and Alexandria Chisholm, "Transforming Privacy Literacy Instruction: From Surveillance Theory to Teaching Practice," LOEX 2021, 2, https://doi.org/10.26207/417p-p335.
33. Alexandria Chisholm and Sarah Hartman-Caverly, "Privacy Workshop Series," Penn State University Libraries, accessed January 11, 2022, https://guides.libraries.psu.edu/berks/privacyseries.
34. Hartman-Caverly and Chisholm, "Privacy Literacy Instruction Practices," 306–07; Sarah Hartman-Caverly and Alexandria Chisholm, "Privacy as Respect for Persons," in *Practicing Privacy Literacy in Academic Libraries*, eds. Sarah Hartman-Caverly and Alexandria Chisholm (Chicago: ACRL, 2023); Brandimarte, Acquisti, and Loewenstein, "Misplaced Confidences," 340–47; Hagendorff, "Privacy Literacy and Its Problems"; Shoshana Zuboff, *The Age of Surveillance Capitalism: The Fight for a Human Future at the New Frontier of Power* (New York: Public Affairs, 2019); Chris Ip, "Who Controls Your Data?," Engadget, accessed January 14, 2022, https://www.engadget.com/2018-09-04-who-controls-your-data.html.
35. Alexandria Chisholm and Sarah Hartman-Caverly, "Privacy Workshop," ACRL Framework for Information Literacy Sandbox, December 7, 2018, https://sandbox.acrl.org/library-collection/privacy-workshop; Hartman-Caverly and Chisholm, "Privacy Literacy Practices," 315–17.
36. Julie E. Cohen, "What Privacy is For," *Harvard Law Review* 126, no. 7 (May 2013): 1904.
37. Ip, "Who Controls Your Data?"
38. Hartman-Caverly and Chisholm, "Privacy Literacy Instruction Practices," 307; Hartman-Caverly and Chisholm, "Privacy as Respect for Persons."
39. "Clickclickclick," Moniker, accessed January 11, 2022, https://clickclickclick.click/.
40. Ip, "Who controls your data?"
41. Alexandria Chisholm and Sarah Hartman-Caverly, "Digital Leadership Workshop," ACRL Framework for Information Literacy Sandbox, October 14, 2020, https://sandbox.acrl.org/library-collection/digital-leadership-workshop.
42. Zuboff, *The Age of Surveillance Capitalism*, 20.
43. Helen Nissenbaum, "Privacy As Contextual Integrity," *Washington Law Review* 79, no. 119 (2004): 124, https://digitalcommons.law.uw.edu/wlr/vol79/iss1/10; Michael Wesch, "YouTube and You: Experiences of Self Awareness in the Context Collapse of the Recording Webcam," *Explorations in Media Ecology* (2009): 23, https://krex.k-state.edu/dspace/bitstream/handle/2097/6302/WeschEME2009.pdf.
44. Sarah Hartman-Caverly and Alexandria Chisholm, "Ok Doomer: Privacy Instruction Strategies to Lighten the Mood – and Your Workload" (lightning talk from Penn State University Libraries, May 2021), https://doi.org/10.26207/5mq6-1y46.
45. danah boyd, "Taken Out of Context: American Teen Sociality in Networked Publics" (PhD diss., University of California Berkeley, 2008).
46. Nissenbaum, "Privacy as Contextual Integrity," 119.
47. boyd, "Taken Out of Context"; Mariek Vanden Abeele, Ralf De Wolf, and Rich Ling, "Mobile Media and Social Space: How Anytime, Anyplace Connectivity Structures Everyday Life," *Media and Communication* 6, no. 2 (2018): 5–8, https://doi.org/10.17645/mac.v6i2.1399.
48. Alexandria Chisholm, Sarah Hartman-Caverly, and Alexandrea Glenn, "Digital Shred Workshop," ACRL Framework for Information Literacy Sandbox, November 12, 2019, https://sandbox.acrl.org/library-collection/digital-shred-workshop; Sarah Hartman-Caverly, Alexandria Chisholm, and Alexandrea Glenn, "Digital Shred: Case Study of a Remote Privacy Literacy Collaboration," *College & Research Libraries* 84, no. 2 (2023).
49. Hagendorff, "Privacy Literacy and Its Problems"; Brandimarte, Acquisti, and Loewenstein, "Misplaced Confidences."
50. Zuboff, *Age of Surveillance Capitalism*, 70.

51. Jacquelyn A. Burkell, "Big Data, Individual Identity, and the Psychological Necessity of Forgetting," *Ethics and Information Technology* 18 (2016), 20, http://dx.doi.org/10.1007/s10676-016-9393-1.
52. Hartman-Caverly, Chisholm, and Glenn, "Digital Shred."
53. "Intelligence Community Directive 732," Office of the Director of National Intelligence, June 27, 2014, https://www.dni.gov/files/documents/ICD/ICD%20732.pdf.
54. Alexandria Chisholm and Sarah Hartman-Caverly, Digital Shred Privacy Literacy Toolkit, 2022, https://sites.psu.edu/digitalshred/.
55. boyd, "Taken Out of Context"; Hagendorff, "Privacy Literacy and Its Problems"; Brandimarte, Acquisti, and Loewenstein, "Misplaced Confidences."
56. Alexandria Chisholm and Sarah Hartman-Caverly, "Digital Wellness Workshop," ACRL Framework for Information Literacy Sandbox, March 23, 2020, https://sandbox.acrl.org/library-collection/digital-wellness-workshop; Alexandria Chisholm and Sarah Hartman-Caverly, "Privacy Literacy: From Doomscrolling to Digital Wellness," *portal: Libraries and the Academy* 22, no. 1 (2022), 62–71.
57. Mariek M. P. Vanden Abeele, "Digital Wellbeing as a Dynamic Construct," *Communication Theory* 31 (2021): 938, https://doi.org/10.1093/ct/qtaa024; Chisholm and Hartman-Caverly, "Privacy Literacy: From Doomscrolling to Digital Wellness."
58. Howard Rheingold, "Attention and Other 21st-Century Social Media Literacies," *EDUCAUSE Review* (October 7, 2010), 16, https://er.educause.edu/articles/2010/10/attention-and-other-21stcentury-social-media-literacies; Carrie James, *Disconnected: Youth, New Media, and the Ethics Gap* (Cambridge: MIT Press, 2014), 140–45.
59. Mireille Hildebrandt, "Privacy as Protection of the Incomputable Self: From Agnostic to Agonistic Machine Learning," *Theoretical Inquiries in Law* 20, no. 1 (2019), 84, https://doi.org/10.1515/til-2019-0004.
60. Chisholm and Hartman-Caverly, "Privacy Literacy: Doomscrolling to Digital Wellness," 62–63.
61. James, *Disconnected*; Rheingold, "Attention and Other 21st-Century."
62. Alexandria Chisholm, "#ForYou: Algorithms & the Attention Economy," ACRL Framework for Information Literacy Sandbox, October 4, 2021, https://sandbox.acrl.org/library-collection/foryou-algorithms-attention-economy.
63. James, *Disconnected*; Rheingold, "Attention and Other 21st-Century."
64. Sarah Hartman-Caverly and Alexandria Chisholm, "Private Bits: Privacy, Intimacy, and Consent," ACRL Framework for Information Literacy Sandbox, February 2023, https://sandbox.acrl.org/library-collection/private-bits-privacy-intimacy-and-consent.
65. "What Is Consentful Tech?," The Consentful Tech Project, accessed January 10, 2022, https://www.consentfultech.io/.
66. "*Privacy Not Included: Dating Apps," Mozilla Foundation, accessed January 10, 2022, https://foundation.mozilla.org/en/privacynotincluded/categories/dating-apps/.
67. Sarah Hartman-Caverly, "Privacy+: The Positive Case for Privacy - For Your Clients, and For Your Business," accessed January 10, 2022, https://doi.org/10.26207/m2yk-8g42.
68. "Privacy at Borders and Checkpoints," ACLU, accessed January 10, 2022, https://www.aclu.org/search/%20?f%5B0%5D=field_issues%3A109; Sophia Cope, Amul Kalia, Seth Schoen, and Adam Schwartz, "Digital Privacy at the U.S. Border: Protecting the Data On Your Devices," *Electronic Frontier Foundation*, accessed January 10, 2022, https://www.eff.org/wp/digital-privacy-us-border-2017.
69. "Data Protection Laws of the World," DLA Piper, accessed January 10, 2022, https://www.dlapiperdataprotection.com/; i-Sight, "A Practical Guide to Data Privacy Laws By Country [2021]," accessed January 10, 2022, https://www.i-sight.com/resources/a-practical-guide-to-data-privacy-laws-by-country/; "Comparing Privacy Laws," OneTrust Data Guidance, accessed January 10, 2022, https://www.dataguidance.com/comparisons/comparing-privacy-laws.
70. "The Global Surveillance Industry," Privacy International, accessed January 10, 2022, https://privacyinternational.org/explainer/1632/global-surveillance-industry.

71. "Universal Declaration of Human Rights," United Nations, accessed January 10, 2022, https://www.un.org/en/about-us/universal-declaration-of-human-rights.
72. Hartman-Caverly and Chisholm, "Ok Doomer."
73. Despina Kamilali and Ch Sofianopoulou, "Lifelong Learning and Web 2.0: Microlearning and Self Directed Learning," in *Proceedings of EDULEARN13 Conference* (2013), 0361.
74. Alexandria Chisholm and Sarah Hartman-Caverly, "Teaching Materials," Digital Shred Privacy Literacy Toolkit, accessed January 14, 2022, https://sites.psu.edu/digitalshred/category/teaching-materials/.

BIBLIOGRAPHY

Association of College & Research Libraries Research Planning and Review Committee. "2021 Environmental Scan." Last modified April 2021. https://www.ala.org/acrl/sites/ala.org.acrl/files/content/publications/whitepapers/EnvironmentalScan2021.pdf.

Barocas, Solon, and Andrew D. Selbst. "Big Data's Disparate Impact." *California Law Review* 104, no. 3 (2016): 671–732. http://www.jstor.org/stable/24758720.

Benjamin, Ruha. *Race After Technology: Abolitionist Tools for the New Jim Code*. Cambridge: Polity, 2019.

Bivens-Tatum, Wayne. "Scholarly Conversations, Intellectual Virtues, and Virtue Information Literacy." *Library Philosophy and Practice* (2021): 1–30.

boyd, danah. "Taken Out of Context: American Teen Sociality in Networked Publics." PhD diss., University of California Berkeley, 2008.

Brandimarte, Laura, Alessandro Acquisti, and George Loewenstein. "Misplaced Confidences: Privacy and the Control Paradox." *Social Psychology and Personality Science* 4, no. 3 (2017): 340–47.

Bruce, Christine, and Hilary Hughes. "Informed Learning: A Pedagogical Construct Attending Simultaneously to Information Use and Learning." *Library & Information Science Research* 32 (2010): A2–A8.

Burkell, Jacquelyn A. "Big Data, Individual Identity, and the Psychological Necessity of Forgetting." *Ethics and Information Technology* 18 (2016): 17–23. http://dx.doi.org/10.1007/s10676-016-9393-1.

Cahoy, Ellysa, and Robert Schroeder. "Embedding Affective Learning Outcomes in Library Instruction." *Communications in Information Literacy* 6, no. 1 (2012): 73–90.

Chisholm, Alexandria. "#ForYou: Algorithms & the Attention Economy." ACRL Framework for Information Literacy Sandbox. October 4, 2021. https://sandbox.acrl.org/library-collection/foryou-algorithms-attention-economy.

Chisholm, Alexandria, and Sarah Hartman-Caverly. "Privacy Literacy: From Doomscrolling to Digital Wellness." *portal: Libraries and the Academy* 22, no. 1 (2022): 53–79. http://doi.org/10.1353/pla.2022.0009.

———. "Privacy Workshop Series." Penn State University Libraries. Accessed January 11, 2022. https://guides.libraries.psu.edu/berks/privacyseries.

———. "Privacy Workshop." ACRL Framework for Information Literacy Sandbox. December 7, 2018. https://sandbox.acrl.org/library-collection/privacy-workshop.

———. "Digital Leadership Workshop." ACRL Framework for Information Literacy Sandbox. October 14, 2020. https://sandbox.acrl.org/library-collection/digital-leadership-workshop.

———. "Digital Wellness Workshop." ACRL Framework for Information Literacy Sandbox. March 23, 2020. https://sandbox.acrl.org/library-collection/digital-wellness-workshop.

———. Digital Shred Privacy Literacy Toolkit. Accessed January 14, 2022. https://sites.psu.edu/digitalshred/.

Chisholm, Alexandria, Sarah Hartman-Caverly, and Alexandrea Glenn. "Digital Shred Workshop." ACRL Framework for Information Literacy Sandbox. November 12, 2019. https://sandbox.acrl.org/library-collection/digital-shred-workshop.

Cohen, Julie E. "What Privacy is For." *Harvard Law Review* 126, no. 7 (May 2013), 1904–33.

Flierl, Michael, and Clarence Maybee. "Refining Information Literacy Practice: Examining the Foundations of Information Literacy Theory." *IFLA Journal* 46, no. 2 (2020): 124–32.

Hagendorff, Thilo, "Privacy Literacy and Its Problems," *Journal of Information Ethics* 27, no. 2 (2018): 127–45.

Hartman-Caverly, Sarah, Alexandria Chisholm, and Alexandrea Glenn. "Digital Shred: Case Study of a Remote Privacy Literacy Collaboration." *College & Research Libraries* 84, no. 2 (2023).

Hartman-Caverly, Sarah, and Alexandria Chisholm. "Ok Doomer: Privacy Instruction Strategies to Lighten the Mood – and Your Workload." Lightning talk from Penn State University Libraries. May 2021. https://doi.org/10.26207/5mq6-1y46.

———. "Privacy as Respect for Persons." In *Practicing Privacy Literacy in Academic Libraries*, edited by Sarah Hartman-Caverly and Alexandria Chisholm. Chicago: ACRL, 2023.

———. "Privacy Literacy Instruction Practices in Academic Libraries: Past, Present, and Possibilities." *IFLA Journal* 46, no. 4 (2020): 305–27.

———. "Private Bits: Privacy, Intimacy, and Consent." ACRL Framework for Information Literacy Sandbox. February 2023. https://sandbox.acrl.org/library-collection/private-bits-privacy-intimacy-and-consent.

———. "Transforming Privacy Literacy Instruction: From Surveillance Theory to Teaching Practice." LOEX 2021, 1–8. https://doi.org/10.26207/417p-p335.

Hicks, Alison, and Caroline Sinkinson. "Participation and Presence: Interrogating Active Learning." *portal: Libraries and the Academy* 21, no. 4 (2021): 749–71.

Hildebrandt, Mireille. "Privacy as Protection of the Incomputable Self: From Agnostic to Agonistic Machine Learning." *Theoretical Inquiries in Law* 20, no. 1 (2019): 83–121. https://doi.org/10.1515/til-2019-0004.

Ho, Lisa. "Privacy vs. Privacy." *EDUCAUSE Review* (February 25, 2015). Accessed January 5, 2022. https://er.educause.edu/blogs/2015/2/privacy-vs-privacy.

Hughes, Hilary, and Christine Bruce. "Snapshots of Informed Learning: LIS and Beyond." *Education for Information* 29, no. 3 (September 2012): 253–69. https://doi.org/10.3233/EFI-130940.

Ip, Chris. "Who Controls Your Data?" Engadget. Accessed January 14, 2022. https://www.engadget.com/2018-09-04-who-controls-your-data.html.

James, Carrie. *Disconnected: Youth, New Media, and the Ethics Gap*. Cambridge: MIT Press, 2014.

Kamilali, Despina, and Ch Sofianopoulou. "Lifelong Learning and Web 2.0: Microlearning and Self Directed Learning." In *Proceedings of EDULEARN13 Conference*, 2013, 0361-0366.

Lloyd, Annemaree. "Information Literacy and Literacies of Information: A Mid-Range Theory and Model." *Journal of Information Literacy* 11, no. 1 (2017): 91–105.

Moniker. "Clickclickclick." Accessed January 11, 2022. https://clickclickclick.click/.

Nissenbaum, Helen. "Privacy as Contextual Integrity." *Washington Law Review* 79, no. 119 (2004): 119–58. https://digitalcommons.law.uw.edu/wlr/vol79/iss1/10.

Office of the Director of National Intelligence. "Intelligence Community Directive 732." Last modified June 27, 2014. https://www.dni.gov/files/documents/ICD/ICD%20732.pdf.

Rheingold, Howard. "Attention and Other 21st-Century Social Media Literacies." *EDUCAUSE Review* (October 7, 2010): 14–24. https://er.educause.edu/articles/2010/10/attention-and-other-21stcentury-social-media-literacies.

Rotman, Dana. "Are You Looking At Me?: Social Media and Privacy Literacy." iConference 2009, 1–3. Accessed January 4, 2022. https://www.ideals.illinois.edu/handle/2142/15339.

Schachter, Deborah. "Theory into Practice: Challenges and Implications for Information Literacy Teaching." *IFLA Journal* 46, no. 2 (2020): 133–42.

Tewell, Eamon. "A Decade of Critical Information Literacy: A Review of the Literature." *Communications in Information Literacy* 9, no. 1 (2015): 24–43.

Vanden Abeele, Mariek M. P. "Digital Wellbeing as a Dynamic Construct." *Communication Theory* 31 (2021): 932–55. https://doi.org/10.1093/ct/qtaa024.

Vanden Abeele, Marikek, Ralf De Wolf, and Rich Ling. "Mobile Media and Social Space: How Anytime, Anyplace Connectivity Structures Everyday Life." *Media and Communication* 6, no. 2 (2018): 5–8, https://doi.org/10.17645/mac.v6i2.1399.

Waks, Leonard J. "Humility in Teaching." *Educational Theory* 68, no. 4-5 (2018): 427–42.

Wesch, Michael. "YouTube and You: Experiences of Self Awareness in the Context Collapse of the Recording Webcam." *Explorations in Media Ecology* (2009): 19–34. https://krex.k-state.edu/dspace/bitstream/handle/2097/6302/WeschEME2009.pdf.

Wissinger, Christina. "Privacy Literacy: From Theory to Practice." *Communications in Information Literacy* 11, no. 2 (2017): 378–89.

Zuboff, Shoshana. *The Age of Surveillance Capitalism: The Fight for a Human Future at the New Frontier of Power*. New York: Public Affairs, 2019.

CHAPTER 8

PREPARING THE NEXT GENERATION OF PRIVACY LEADERS?

The Intersection of Business Ethics and Privacy Education

Emily Mross

INTRODUCTION

Library professionals consider patron privacy core to our work. It is codified for library workers in the ALA Code of Ethics and for library users in the Library Bill of Rights.[1] Beyond library spaces, however, privacy becomes murkier. The amount of data gathered about us by others, with and without our express consent, grows exponentially each year. For many businesses, gathering, packaging, analyzing, and selling this data is the foundation of their business models.[2] There are no similar profession-wide codes of ethics that guide what businesses should or should not do with our data; a Consumer Privacy Bill of Rights, proposed by the Obama administration, was never adopted.[3] In the United States, very few legal protections or guidelines act as safeguards. Instead, consumers must often rely on their own understanding of privacy protections

151

and hope that the businesses they interact with are collecting and using their data ethically.

But as we reel from an era of businesses collecting all the consumer data they can while moving fast and breaking things, it seems privacy is likely not at the forefront of ethical discussions in the boardroom. If it were, many recent scandals, which have violated consumer trust, if not any actual laws, might not have occurred.[4] Including and further emphasizing privacy ethics in the business ethics curriculum may help build a generation of business leaders who highly value safeguarding their customers' data. This change, as a complement to greater individual privacy literacy, can build a more secure future for consumers. In this chapter, we explore the state of consumer privacy laws, perceptions of privacy in business ethics education from the literature, and the role of the library in privacy education within a case study of a large research university's business ethics curriculum. This case study explores the current status of undergraduate business ethics education at Penn State, including course offerings and content, faculty perspectives, and supplemental business ethics offerings.

PRIVACY LAWS AND PROTECTIONS

Unlike the European Union, which adopted the General Data Protection Regulation (GDPR) in 2018, the United States does not have a uniform law that protects consumer data.[5] Federal privacy laws instead cover very specific types of data, like health or education records, and sometimes specific methods of conveying this data. Instead, consumers must rely on protections given by a patchwork of state laws, which, of course, only apply to the residents of each state. As of 2021, only three states—California, Colorado, and Virginia—have laws that give the consumer a level of control over personal data collection by companies; even so, the laws could be generally considered weak in terms of consumer protections with more favor toward business interests.[6] In contrast, GDPR is written so that companies "must consider the data protection principles in the design of any new product or activity," and those violating GDPR face high fines and can be sued by harmed individuals.[7] While some protections are better than none, relatively toothless and state-bound regulations mean that consumers must rely on their own knowledge of increasingly complex data landscapes and the goodwill of the companies and technologies they interact with on a daily basis in order to keep their data secure. Unfortunately, both intentional and unintentional data-related scandals show just how risky trusting a company can be.[8] The biggest players in the technology sphere, Facebook/Meta Platforms, Inc. chief among them, have shown time and again that data exposure is a cost of doing business.[9] It will continue unless we make significant improvements in business ethics and consumer legal protections, something many groups in the US have failed to do meaningfully for decades.

BUSINESS AND PRIVACY ETHICS IN PRACTICE

A new buyer beware adage has emerged in recent years: if the product is free, you are the product. Apps and websites facilitate our work and social lives. Generally, we do not pay for them with money. Instead, we pay for them with our time and any data we give them—knowingly or unknowingly. By packaging and selling this data to advertisers and other groups, they make money. Many of today's business students will work at or start companies with business models centered on selling customer data but do not appear to receive significant instruction on the ethics of data privacy. It must be stressed again that selling consumer data and most perceived misdeeds related to this practice are not illegal. They are unethical, exploitative, and many other things. But US law does not prohibit this, nor does it give the consumer a recourse to avoid having their data collected and sold without truly informed consent aside from swearing off technology forever or taking complex steps to cover their tracks.

Most Americans know the feeling of being exposed online. Nearly 145 million Americans had personally identifiable information exposed in the 2017 Equifax data breach.[10] More than 11 billion online accounts are "pwned" (internet parlance for being compromised), according to haveibeenpwned.com, which maintains a searchable database of hacked email addresses, phone numbers, and passwords exposed in data breaches.[11] Of course, these exposures are of the illegal variety. Legal data selling can still be just as devastating.

Dating apps, therapy apps, and substance abuse treatment apps—the latter two generally being paid apps that facilitate medical treatment—have been observed selling or sharing identifiable information about their customers with third parties.[12] This information can be used to develop targeted advertising and could be used for more nefarious means depending on who buys or receives it. In the fallout of the US Supreme Court decision *Dobbs v. Jackson Women's Health Organization*, which overturned *Roe v. Wade* and a constitutionally protected right to abortion under the auspices of a federal right to privacy, further concerns are being raised about user privacy for apps that track menstrual cycles or even game apps that track one's location, since such information could theoretically be used to prosecute someone for seeking an abortion.[13] Further, the Health Insurance Portability and Accountability Act of 1996 (HIPAA), which regulates the privacy of medical records, may not protect health information shared or stored on these apps, which sometimes involves very sensitive information like HIV status, mental illness diagnoses, and other data most would prefer to (and assume would be) kept private.[14]

Following exposure of ethical lapses, companies promise they will do better. But do they? In 2014, Cambridge Analytica, a voter psychology firm, began improperly exporting Facebook user data to build tools for campaigns, most notably the Trump 2016 presidential campaign, that would influence voters.[15] This was only exposed following a *New York Times/Guardian* investigation in 2018.[16] It would be days before Facebook responded, following mounting pressure from governments and users alike. The company's valuation tanked, and celebrities began deleting their accounts while encouraging others to do the same.[17] The following month, Facebook CEO Mark Zuckerberg was called before Congress to account for what went wrong.[18] The scandal violated Facebook's own rules but went unnoticed and/or unacknowledged until the debacle became public.[19] It may have also potentially violated US election laws by involving foreigners and foreign money in American elections, as Cambridge Analytica is based in England and had contracts with Russian entities.[20] In 2019, Facebook was fined $5 billion by the Federal Trade Commission (FTC) for violating a 2012 order that required the company to be more transparent about privacy settings and to secure users' data in alignment with their chosen privacy settings, but no other privacy laws were in place to protect US consumers' online data on a larger scale.[21] The absence of laws requires company ethics and culture to safeguard user data and privacy, which can be difficult to instill. In the intervening years, additional scandals relating to user data continue to plague Facebook. The company was accused by a whistleblower of ignoring evidence that a user-data-driven change to its algorithm, which promoted higher-interaction posts, led to an increase in controversial, divisive, and factually inaccurate content in users' feeds, among other harmful effects of its products.[22] Facebook executives have blamed these problems on users—not their technology or their use of user data.[23]

The behavior of technology executives has shown that ethics are not their main concern. As they compete for more of our time, having such high ambitions as to completely immerse us in their technology in the future, it is clear that both laws and ethical standards must evolve to ensure that history does not repeat itself on grander and grander scales with increasingly higher stakes. Business ethics tend to be reactive. They have to start reacting faster, and the curriculum may need to change in order to further change business's views on customer privacy.

BUSINESS AND PRIVACY ETHICS IN THE LITERATURE

Business researchers have investigated corporate handling of information privacy for more than two decades, from the infancy of the web to our current online society, raising concerns about the lack of rules along the way. However, there are no new federal laws in the United States that provide blanket protections or standards of practice for protecting the privacy of consumers as they engage with commercial technology, though devices, websites, and applications that have become more essential to daily life since this area was first explored. The most recent US federal law regarding online privacy was passed in 1998 and specifically protects the data of children under the age of thirteen.[24] Some existing laws, such as the Federal Trade Commission Act, can be used to prosecute companies that violate their own privacy policies, but this only applies following harm.[25] There are no federal laws in the US that preemptively spell out protections for consumers and their data to be incorporated as technology is developed. Thus, the consumer is largely at the ethical whims of business, which, in the area of privacy, are often found lacking.

A comprehensive exploration of privacy as a corporate social responsibility (CSR) for ninety-five large information technology companies found that only thirty mentioned privacy in their CSR documents, and only thirteen explained why they were motivated to protect privacy.[26] This study, published in 2011, did not evaluate other types of companies because the author did not consider data and information to be "at the core of their activities."[27] However, just two years later, a business case was published examining the ethics of a 2012 marketing mishap at Target involving predictive analytics, which led to the company mailing pregnancy-related coupons to a teen girl whose parents had no idea their daughter was expecting—but based on her purchasing habits, the company did.[28] Much has changed in eleven years related to data and information and the types of companies that collect, sell, and use consumer data as part of their core business strategies, but the lack of oversight has not changed. In October 2021, the FTC reported that internet service providers (ISP)—which have consolidated into six companies that control 98 percent of the US mobile internet market—collect, store, and use scads of sensitive data about their users that is unrelated to their primary business purpose: providing internet access.[29] Under current rules, such collection is legal, but the report raises alarms that consumer privacy is at risk, that the idea of consumer choice and informed consent in such matters is generally an illusion, and that ISPs engage in many of the same problematic data and privacy practices as companies like Google and Facebook.

We hope that businesses will behave ethically because "it is the noble way for corporations to behave," but we should know better than to rely on this ideal.[30] Instead, there generally must be more compelling reasons for social responsibility in the business realm. These reasons are various avenues of self-interest, which still require reliance on laws and acting nobly to some degree; we need both to maintain our society, but noble ethics weigh heavier because one can always find ways around a law.[31] In upholding corporate social responsibility (CSR), companies should make profits while fulfilling their legal responsibilities and while striving to be ethical, avoid harm, and improve quality of life.[32] These concepts can only be legislated to a certain degree. Instead, they must be a part of individual employee character and company culture, which are generally not principles born by chance but are developed through education and exploration.

Given the increasingly global and digital nature of business, especially as it pertains to consumer data, there should be more intense company commitment to CSR, corporate citizenship, and community stakeholders.[33] At the dawn of the modern internet, however, some felt that there seemed to not be room for technology companies to practice CSR and corporate citizenship due to the pace of the business.[34] Google can tell us they strive to not be evil,[35] but as we look around the digital landscape, such mottos seem to fall more on the side of Facebook's pre-2014 motto: move fast and break things.

Companies collecting consumer data may see no real incentive in curbing their practices or offering users more control given current narratives. The privacy paradox, in which users say they value their privacy while continuing to share their information with products and platforms works in corporate favor, but it may not be real; even after consumers have shared information, they feel it should be protected and not shared or sold with third parties.[36] The consumer may think that such third parties are focused on targeted advertising, but our data is not just sold to marketing companies to deliver better ads. It is used to teach algorithms to curate the content we consume, and we do not know how these algorithms work nor how our data is fed to or manipulated by them.[37] This places the consumer in situations where they cannot give true informed consent, a standard required before data disclosure in many other settings.[38] Achieving better privacy ethics will require compromise. Companies must weigh tradeoffs between data collection and privacy in terms of impacts on their profits and logistics but also with regard to consumer trust and transparency.[39] As CSR scholars have noted for decades, the customer is a key stakeholder who should be considered in important decisions and informed about the impacts. They should not be treated as afterthoughts in the pursuit of profits at any cost.

Still, most consumers and scholars tend to present the issue of privacy in the business ethics arena as closely related to marketing. Though marketing educators first raised the issue of a "privacy gap" in the education of their students, little progress has been made in transforming marketing education to include data privacy ethics as a key component of the curriculum, though others continue to advocate for and propose models of privacy education for marketing students.[40] It should be noted that this transformation is of particular need in the marketing curriculum, as analysis of consumer data is a key skill for most contemporary marketing jobs. However, privacy ethics do not apply only to the marketing realm. While marketing and advertising may be major areas for data collection and sales, it permeates all areas of business and should not be relegated to one particular area within the discipline. As Waldman notes, a chief privacy officer does not an ethical company make. If one executive advocates for privacy but the multitudes of other employees who design the products do not operate with privacy in mind, then is privacy truly a central ethic for the corporation?[41]

CASE STUDY: BUSINESS ETHICS AND PRIVACY AT PENN STATE

Background

Pennsylvania State University (PSU) is ranked as a top provider of undergraduate and graduate business education.[42] In the past five years, PSU has granted more than 30,000 undergraduate and graduate degrees across all business programs at its twenty-four campuses.[43] Students from all majors may also participate in the Entrepreneurship and Innovation minor, which uses a core set of business classes to complement entrepreneurial skills in various disciplines.[44] PSU has four AACSB International (AACSB) accredited business schools: Smeal College of Business at University Park, Black School of Business at Behrend, the School of Business Administration at Harrisburg, and the School of Graduate Professional Studies at Great Valley.[45] Each offers MBAs, and all except for Great Valley offer undergraduate business degrees as well. AACSB accreditation is recognized as the standard in business education, and their guidelines place high emphasis on ethics and integrity, listing it first on their Guiding Principles and Expectations for Accredited Schools; they also expect that accredited programs will demonstrate that business education is a force for good in society.[46] Given these standards and that most business schools maintain or seek to attain AACSB accreditation, it stands to reason, considering current events and research in privacy and business ethics, that ethics is a key component of business education. Further, customer privacy should be included in education and training related to business ethics in order to have a positive impact on the future of data-driven business.

The University Libraries' Role in Instruction

At Penn State, librarians typically provide non-credit, course-related instruction at the invitation of the instructor of record for a given course. The consistency with which any particular course is reached varies from campus to campus based on many factors, such as librarian capacity, course offerings, and faculty awareness of library services. In addition to course-related instruction, many librarians provide supplemental workshops focused on research and literacy skills that are tailored to specific majors or related to current trends or events. At Penn State Harrisburg, the business librarian conducts one-shot instruction for business writing each semester, which is a curriculum requirement and addresses basic business research methods. Other undergraduate business courses with regular, though not mandated, library instruction include introductory marketing and management courses and business and society courses.

PSU Undergraduate Business Ethics Courses

Regardless of campus, each undergraduate student in a business program will take at least one course focused on business ethics, though the course may vary by campus. While twelve courses mentioning business ethics appear in the undergraduate bulletin, only five are taught regularly across the twenty campuses offering undergraduate business degrees and are included in the required curriculum for undergraduate business students.[47]

Faculty have great latitude within their courses to include various readings and topics as long as the ultimate outcomes of the course are met. Faculty made an effort to collect as many syllabi as possible for each course, however, the range of syllabi received ranged from one (Business Administration (BA) 242, BA 342) to eight (Management (MGMT) 451) per course. In the instance of BA 342, it is only taught at one campus, University Park, and all professors use a standard syllabus. In addition to collecting syllabi and reviewing course materials, faculty from each course were interviewed about the role of privacy ethics within their course and within business education in general. An overview of the courses, main topics, textbooks, and privacy topics addressed is in table 8.1.

TABLE 8.1

Overview of common business ethics courses at PSU

COURSE NUMBER AND TITLE	CAMPUS(ES)	MAIN TOPICS	TEXTBOOK(S)	PRIVACY/ETHICS TOPIC(S)
BA 242: Social and Ethical Environment of Business	Altoona, Harrisburg, DuBois, Erie, Greater Allegheny, Hazleton,	Social and ethical environments of business, ethical decision making, business law	Introduction to Business Ethics (Desjardins) Dynamic Business Law (Kubasek) Honest Work (Ciulla) Business Law: Principles for Today's Commercial Environment (Twomey)	Torts: invasion of privacy
BA 243: Social, Legal, and Ethical Environment of Business	Lehigh Valley, Berks, Beaver, Mont Alto, Abington, Scranton, World Campus, Wilkes-Barre, Shenango, New Kensington, York, Schuylkill, Fayette, Brandywine	Ethical, social, legal, regulatory, and technological environments of business; demographic diversity	Business Law (Miller) Legal Environment of Business (Melvin) Business Ethics Now (Ghillger) Anderson's Business Law and the Legal Environment (Twomey) Business and Society (Lawrence) Legal and Regulatory Environment of Business (Pagnattaro) Business: Its Legal, Ethical, and Global Environment (Jennings) Business Law (Morgan)	Moral theory in marketing; privacy and internet ethics
BA 342: Socially Responsible, Sustainable, and Ethical Environment of Business	University Park	Corporate global citizenship, environmental sustainability, economic stability, corporate rights, responsibilities, and relationships with stakeholders	Business & Society (Carroll)	Ethics and technology; data security and hacking; US privacy laws

TABLE 8.1

Overview of common business ethics courses at PSU

COURSE NUMBER AND TITLE	CAMPUS(ES)	MAIN TOPICS	TEXTBOOK(S)	PRIVACY/ETHICS TOPIC(S)
BA 364: International Business and Society	Abington, Harrisburg, Berks, Altoona, World Campus	Sociocultural environment of business, corporate responsibility, international/multinational business environments	Global Business Today (Hill) Business & Society (Carroll) Business and Society (Lawrence)	Ethics and technology; data security and hacking; US privacy laws
MGMT 451: Business, Ethics, and Society	University Park, Mont Alto, Berks, Abington, Brandywine, Hazleton, Schuylkill, Wilkes-Barre, Lehigh Valley, Greater Allegheny	Social, ethical, legal, economic, equity, environmental, public policy, and political influences on managerial decisions and strategies.	Managing Business Ethics (Trevino) Applied Business Ethics (Bredeson) Wall Street Journal	User data in business models; ethics and user data; ethics in marketing/sales

Privacy Topics in the Syllabus and Textbooks

Privacy topics appear to some degree within the syllabus for each course, though they do not appear to be a central theme throughout the semester. BA 242 specifically mentions invasion of privacy as a topic for the first week of the course; however, upon examination of the course text, this appears to be limited to business tort law and the rights of the corporation and individual harm rather than the ambiguous world of data privacy.[48] In reviewing BA 243, one syllabus includes units on marketing and moral theory as well as privacy, responsibility, and the internet. The latter unit also involves a case study on privacy and internet ethics. Other BA 243 syllabi do not explicitly mention privacy as a topic of ethics beyond business torts, and the assigned textbook focuses primarily on traditional business law, with no exploration of privacy beyond the definitions and example cases of invasion of privacy in a business context.

BA 342, taught only at University Park's Smeal College of Business, has a stronger focus on ethics and corporate social responsibility than BA 242 and BA 243, which are taught across the university. The course includes one week on ethics and technology, within the module on ethical decision-making. The third and final module focuses on a stakeholder model of corporate social responsibility, which includes several course sessions on the consumer as a stakeholder. The course text, written by prominent researcher in corporate social responsibility, Archie Carroll, devotes a chapter to business ethics and technology, though the text tends to focus more on legal questions than true ethical questions involving privacy and data.[49] Instead, there is a greater focus on the legal or ethical use of company technology, effectively securing customer data and ethical responses to illegal data breaches, and biotechnology ethics. Approximately two pages of the twenty-seven-page chapter present an overview of the lack of digital privacy laws in the US, information on corporate privacy policies and chief privacy officers, and the aforementioned discussion of data privacy, with a focus on illegal hacking.

Another course with a greater emphasis on ethics and corporate social responsibility, as opposed to business law is BA 364, taught at several campuses but not at University Park. This course incorporates international cultures and is writing intensive. Some sections use Carroll's *Business and Society* text and include the chapter on ethics and technology in the course. Others use a textbook also called *Business & Society* by Anne Lawrence. This text includes two relevant chapters—the first on the role of technology in business and the second on regulation and management of business technology.[50] The first chapter provides an example of all of the data that might be collected about an individual by the various websites, technology, and apps one uses; it prompts students to consider the loss of privacy and the ethical challenges related to corporate collection and use of such data; however, the primary focus remains on illegal access of such data. In the regulation chapter, emphasis is placed largely on cybercrime, hacking, and piracy as well as discussion about internet censorship in authoritarian nations.

MGMT 451 is a writing-intensive capstone ethics course for management students. University Park sections utilize a standard syllabus and textbook authored by a Smeal faculty member who designed the course; the text specifically calls out Facebook for promising to protect user data while operating on a business model of selling this data.[51] Students at Smeal participate in ethical challenges throughout the semester in the course; one case involves a biotech company in a conundrum about the sale of its customer data. Throughout the course, current news appears on the syllabus which directly addresses corporate collection and monetization of customer data. The Mont Alto section includes a week on data ethics and another on ethics in selling, marketing, and advertising. Their textbook includes a specific module on the use of customer data.[52] Sections at other campuses do not appear to have specific units or modules that involve privacy ethics or customer data.

However, these sections appear to have student-selected case studies as final projects; students could potentially select privacy-related cases to examine.

Overall, most of the ethics courses appear to have some connection to privacy within the realm of business ethics. It is more pronounced in the courses, which focus more specifically on corporate social responsibility and which are writing intensive. The legal-focused courses are more concerned with business torts, which generally overlook data privacy as the laws have not yet caught up with this nuanced issue. Inclusion of privacy ethics seems to lie mostly at the feet of the instructor of record for each section—the professor is ultimately the person who chooses the readings, speakers, and assignments. To better understand their perspectives, some agreed to be interviewed about the role of privacy as a business ethic in their courses and in the discipline at large.

Perspectives of Business Ethics Faculty

Attempts were made to speak with faculty who teach these courses at each campus. The greatest response was from faculty teaching MGMT 451 at University Park's Smeal College of Business; an additional faculty member from Berks was also able to meet for an interview. In total, six faculty members spoke about the role of privacy within their business ethics instruction. Interviews were conducted during the fall 2021 semester, and demands of course loads as well as managing multiple instructional modes related to COVID-19 protocols may have contributed to a lower response rate for interviews. Though faculty perspectives are an important factor in understanding the importance of privacy within the course, coverage of privacy topics should be somewhat evident from reviews of the syllabus and textbook, which were conducted for each course, regardless of interview participation. Faculty interviewees were asked to speak about any privacy topics addressed within their course, their views on the role of privacy as part of business ethics, and their opinions regarding the inclusion of privacy education within the business curriculum. As part of this question, the idea of a business ethics-focused privacy workshop was presented for their feedback.

Generally, Smeal faculty seemed to echo the literature in that they felt such conversations about data privacy and ethics would be most suited to the marketing curriculum. However, each identified ways that ethical questions related to data privacy are incorporated into the curriculum through the ethical challenges and the aforementioned biotech case in Managing Business Ethics.[53] In faculty estimation, students seem most interested in biotech questions but may not see a direct connection to privacy ethics when discussing the topic. Students also may not yet be fully cognizant of how much data they give up with the various technologies they use daily, from a big-picture perspective. One faculty member mentioned she focuses on Kantian ethics in her courses, which centers on respecting the rights of the individual. In many of the courses, students are able to select ethical topics of interest for final projects or other written assignments. Privacy does not seem to be a common choice for these assignments, but faculty felt that it could become more popular over time.

Overall, the Smeal faculty spoke to the culture of ethics embedded in their curriculum. Student groups focus on ethics and students can become certified integrity advocates. Workshops related to ethics and integrity at Smeal regularly attract students, with attendance sometimes in the hundreds, according to faculty. Ethics and integrity are threaded throughout many courses, not only those designated as ethics classes. Smeal also has an honor code that community members are invited to sign each semester, committing themselves to upholding the highest ethical standards at school and in their careers.[54] The college is home to the Tarriff Center for Business Ethics and Social Responsibility, which hosts business ethics and integrity case challenges, ethical literacy and ethical leadership programs, and a mentoring program to guide students as they develop into ethical business leaders.[55]

A Berks faculty member reported incorporating privacy as a moral issue throughout his course. He has a background in philosophy which motivates him to have in-depth and challenging conversations with students about ethics and morals beyond standard business ethics, exploring the connections between capitalism, democracy, privacy, and autonomy. He finds his students to be interested in the topic and feels they are savvy about privacy. Librarians at this campus have worked toward creating a culture of privacy literacy through the implementation of a workshop series as part of the campus first-year experience program.[56] The success of this program may contribute to the interest and enthusiasm students show for privacy in the business ethics course.

AN OPPORTUNITY: PRIVACY WORKSHOPS

Privacy workshops initially conceived by the Thun Library at Berks campus have been successfully implemented at the Harrisburg campus over the past four years. Students, faculty, and staff attend, and survey feedback has been positive. Harrisburg offered the first workshop in the series, which primarily focuses on developing an understanding of personal data collection and use by others and discussing the steps and resources necessary to make informed decisions about sharing and safeguarding personal data online.[57]

In conversations with faculty, the option of creating new privacy workshops focused on data privacy as a business ethic was presented. Faculty reception was positive from Smeal faculty and Berks faculty. Smeal students have demonstrated an interest in past ethics workshops, and Berks students showed keen interest in privacy topics in class. This is a promising sign that such workshops might be welcomed at other campuses as well. Such a workshop could be designed with input from business faculty to include topics not covered in class or to provide additional space for exploring data privacy issues that are time-constrained in the curriculum. Potential learning outcomes could include analyzing a company privacy policy for areas of concern as a consumer, drafting a consumer bill of privacy rights, and debating the balance between company goals and customer privacy.

To maintain the interactivity and active learning modes of the existing privacy workshops, a business ethics privacy workshop would likely incorporate reflection stations that ask students to discuss a time when they felt their privacy was violated by a company, regardless of whether this violation was illegal, like a hack, or legal, such as selling data to a third party. This reflection station would open a conversation about the differences between ethics and laws, prompt a discussion of the current legal status of data privacy protections, and would serve as a lead-in to evaluating a privacy policy and drafting ideas for the proposed consumer bill of privacy rights. As made evident by both the literature review and faculty interviews, students as consumers do not understand the privacy they give away to companies each day by interacting with their technology. The outcomes and related activities would encourage students to more deeply consider the people behind the data and the idea of informed consent as it applies to data collection. This would be facilitated through small group conversations and large group reportouts. Students would break into groups to review and discuss articles selected from areas of interest, such as ethics education, legal reform, the role of the chief privacy officer, customer privacy autonomy, privacy policies, big data analytics and ethics, and other related categories.

Ultimately, the session would conclude with the groups making a proposal for the best way for corporations to move ahead ethically, using their consumer privacy bill of rights. They should discuss what changes should be made, by whom and at what level, and identify the stakeholders who should be involved. If students are particularly passionate about a certain company's privacy policy (or lack thereof), or by government inaction on this ongoing problem, they might be encouraged to share their ideas in a formal business letter—a skill that is part of the business writing curriculum.

CONCLUSION

The literature indicates that something must be done in the United States to strengthen consumer privacy protections for everyone. Businesses generally have shown that their own ethics do not go far enough to gain informed consent from their customers with regard to data collection and use, nor do they exercise the restraint necessary to stop collecting unnecessary data. Similarly, conversations with faculty and course materials reviews revealed that ethics should be more about doing—exploring, discussing, and creating—than lecture. If students are empowered to develop the changes they would like to see, perhaps they will be the ones to go into the world and actually make them.

That is currently what we need: educated, ethical, and empowered business leaders who will not only implement and uphold high standards within their own organizations but who will also call upon and work with legislators and regulators to develop a legal framework that will assist in accountability and enforcement. As business and technology researchers have discussed for decades, a two-pronged approach is needed. Corporations must think more about how they should protect privacy rather than focusing on all the ways they could collect and monetize data, and government must install and enforce meaningful guardrails. Small steps, such as increasing exploration of consumer privacy as a part of business ethics, could be a start.

ACKNOWLEDGMENTS

I would like to thank the stalwart librarians of the Penn State University Libraries, especially those at Thun Library and the Schreyer Business Library, as well as the business faculty at Penn State Harrisburg, Penn State Berks, and the Smeal College of Business for their assistance and contributions to this chapter.

NOTES

1. "Privacy," American Library Association, Advocacy, Legislation & Issues, October 2021, https://www.ala.org/advocacy/privacy.
2. "A Look at What ISPs Know About You: Examining the Privacy Practices of Six Major Internet Service Providers," Federal Trade Commission, October 21, 2021, https://www.ftc.gov/reports/look-what-isps-know-about-you-examining-privacy-practices-six-major-internet-service-providers; Sara Morrison, "Meta Is Getting Data about You from Some Surprising Places," Vox (June 17, 2022), https://www.vox.com/recode/23172691/meta-tracking-privacy-hospitals.

3. Natasha Singer, "Why a Push for Online Privacy Is Bogged Down in Washington," *The New York Times* (February 28, 2016), sec. Technology, https://www.nytimes.com/2016/02/29/technology/obamas-effort-on-consumer-privacy-falls-short-critics-say.html.
4. "The Facebook Files," *The Wall Street Journal* (October 1, 2021), https://www.wsj.com/articles/the-facebook-files-11631713039; Robinson Meyer, "Everything We Know About Facebook's Secret Mood-Manipulation Experiment," *The Atlantic* (June 28, 2014), https://www.theatlantic.com/technology/archive/2014/06/everything-we-know-about-facebooks-secret-mood-manipulation-experiment/373648/.
5. Thorin Klosowski, "The State of Consumer Data Privacy Laws in the US (And Why It Matters)," *The New York Times*, sec. Wirecutter (September 2021), https://www.nytimes.com/wirecutter/blog/state-of-privacy-laws-in-us/.
6. Klosowski, "The State of Consumer."
7. Ben Wolfard, "What Is GDPR, the EU's New Data Protection Law?," GDPR.eu, November 7, 2018, https://gdpr.eu/what-is-gdpr/.
8. Kyle Barr, "TikTok's In-App Browser Has Code to Track Users' Inputs and Activity," Gizmodo, August 19, 2022, https://gizmodo.com/tiktok-keylogging-privacy-meta-1849433690; Felix Krause, "IOS Privacy: Instagram and Facebook Can Track Anything You Do on Any Website in Their in-App Browser," *KrauseFx* (blog), August 10, 2022, https://krausefx.com/blog/ios-privacy-instagram-and-facebook-can-track-anything-you-do-on-any-website-in-their-in-app-browser.
9. Dan Milmo, "Facebook 'Overpaid in Data Settlement to Avoid Naming Zuckerberg,'" *The Guardian* (September 24, 2021), https://www.theguardian.com/technology/2021/sep/24/facebook-overpaid-in-data-settlement-to-avoid-naming-zuckerberg.
10. "Chinese Hackers Charged in Equifax Breach," Federal Bureau of Investigation, February 2020, https://www.fbi.gov/news/stories/chinese-hackers-charged-in-equifax-breach-021020.
11. "Have I Been Pwned?," n.d., https://haveibeenpwned.com/.
12. Sarah Morrison, "A Priest's Resignation after His Phone Location Data Leaked Shows the Urgent Need for Data Privacy Laws," Vox, July 2021, https://www.vox.com/recode/22587248/grindr-app-location-data-outed-priest-jeffrey-burrill-pillar-data-harvesting; Carly Page, "Opioid Addiction Treatment Apps Found Sharing Sensitive Data with Third Parties," TechCrunch, July 2021, https://techcrunch.com/2021/07/07/opioid-addiction-treatment-apps-found-sharing-sensitive-data-with-third-parties/; Thomas Germain, "Mental Health Apps and User Privacy," *Consumer Reports* (March 2021), https://www.consumerreports.org/health-privacy/mental-health-apps-and-user-privacy-a7415198244/.
13. Rina Torchinsky, "How Period Tracking Apps and Data Privacy Fit into a Post-Roe v. Wade Climate," NPR, June 24, 2022, https://www.npr.org/2022/05/10/1097482967/roe-v-wade-supreme-court-abortion-period-apps.
14. Germain, "Mental Health Apps and User Privacy."
15. Matthew Rosenberg, Nicholas Confessore, and Carole Cadwalladr, "How Trump Consultants Exploited the Facebook Data of Millions," *The New York Times* (March 2018), https://www.nytimes.com/2018/03/17/us/politics/cambridge-analytica-trump-campaign.html.
16. Keith Collins and Gabriel J. X. Dance, "How Researchers Learned to Use Facebook 'Likes' to Sway Your Thinking," *The New York Times* (March 2018), https://www.nytimes.com/2018/03/20/technology/facebook-cambridge-behavior-model.html.
17. Cecilia Kang, "Facebook Faces Growing Pressure Over Data and Privacy Inquiries," *The New York Times* (March 2018), https://www.nytimes.com/2018/03/20/business/ftc-facebook-privacy-investigation.html.
18. Kang, "Facebook Faces Growing Pressure."
19. Nicholas Confessore, "Cambridge Analytica and Facebook: The Scandal and the Fallout So Far," *The New York Times* (April 2018), https://www.nytimes.com/2018/04/04/us/politics/cambridge-analytica-scandal-fallout.html.

20. Confessore, "Cambridge Analytica and Facebook."
21. "FTC Imposes $5 Billion Penalty and Sweeping New Privacy Restrictions on Facebook," Federal Trade Commission, July 2019, https://www.ftc.gov/news-events/press-releases/2019/07/ftc-imposes-5-billion-penalty-sweeping-new-privacy-restrictions.
22. Jeff Horwitz and Deepa Seetharaman, "Facebook Executives Shut Down Efforts to Make the Site Less Divisive," *The Wall Street Journal* (May 2020), https://www.wsj.com/articles/facebook-knows-it-encourages-division-top-executives-nixed-solutions-11590507499.
23. Jason Aten, "The Head of Facebook's Metaverse Project Says Users Are to Blame for Its Misinformation Problem, Not Facebook," *Inc.* (November 2021), https://www.inc.com/jason-aten/the-head-of-facebooks-metaverse-project-andrew-bosworth-says-users-are-to-blame-for-its-misinformation-problem-not-facebook.html.
24. "Children's Online Privacy Protection Rule ('COPPA')," Federal Trade Commission, Rules, 1998, https://www.ftc.gov/enforcement/rules/rulemaking-regulatory-reform-proceedings/childrens-online-privacy-protection-rule.
25. Klosowski, "The State of Consumer Data Privacy Laws."
26. Irene Pollach, "Online Privacy as a Corporate Social Responsibility: An Empirical Study," *Business Ethics: A European Review* 20, no. 1 (January 2011): 88–102, https://doi.org/10.1111/J.1467-8608.2010.01611.X.
27. Pollach, "Online Privacy as a Corporate Social Responsibility."
28. Brett Belock et al., "Target Corporation: Predictive Analytics and Customer Privacy," in *Sage Business Cases* (2013), https://sk-sagepub-com.ezaccess.libraries.psu.edu/cases/target-corporation-predictive-analytics-and-customer-privacy?utm_source=ss360&utm_medium=discovery-provider#i223.
29. "A Look at What ISPs Know About You: Examining the Privacy Practices of Six Major Internet Service Providers," Federal Trade Commission, October 21, 2021, https://www.ftc.gov/reports/look-what-isps-know-about-you-examining-privacy-practices-six-major-internet-service-providers.
30. Henry Mintzberg, "The Case for Corporate Social Responsibility," *Journal of Business Strategy* 4, no. October (1983): 3.
31. Mintzberg, "The Case for Corporate Social Responsibility."
32. Archie B. Carroll, "The Pyramid of Corporate Social Responsibility: Toward the Moral Management of Organizational Stakeholders," *Business Horizons* 34, no. 4 (July 1991): 39–48, https://doi.org/10.1016/0007-6813(91)90005-G.
33. James E. Post, "Moving from Geographic to Virtual Communities: Global Corporate Citizenship in a Dot.Com World," *Business and Society Review* 105, no. 1 (2000): 26–46, https://doi.org/10.1111/0045-3609.00063.
34. Post, "Moving from Geographic to Virtual Communities."
35. Shirin Ghaffary, "'Don't Be Evil' Isn't a Normal Company Value. But Google Isn't a Normal Company." Vox, February 16, 2021, https://www.vox.com/recode/2021/2/16/22280502/google-dont-be-evil-land-of-the-giants-podcast.
36. Kirsten Martin, "Breaking the Privacy Paradox: The Value of Privacy and Associated Duty of Firms," *Business Ethics Quarterly* 30, no. 1 (January 2020): 65–96, https://doi.org/10.1017/BEQ.2019.24.
37. Tae Wan Kim and Bryan R. Routledge, "Why a Right to an Explanation of Algorithmic Decision-Making Should Exist: A Trust-Based Approach," *Business Ethics Quarterly* (May 2021): 1–28, https://doi.org/10.1017/BEQ.2021.3.
38. Adam J. Andreotta, Nin Kirkham, and Marco Rizzi, "AI, Big Data, and the Future of Consent," *AI & SOCIETY 2021* 1 (August 2021): 1–14, https://doi.org/10.1007/S00146-021-01262-5.
39. Pollach, "Online Privacy as a Corporate Social Responsibility."
40. James W. Peltier et al., "Teaching Information Privacy in Marketing Courses: Key Educational Issues for Principles of Marketing and Elective Marketing Courses," *Journal of Marketing Education* 32, no. 2 (2010): 224–46, https://doi.org/10.1177/0273475309360164; Kristen L. Walker and Nora Moran, "Consumer Information for Data-Driven Decision Making: Teaching Socially Responsible

Use of Data," *Journal of Marketing Education* 41, no. 2 (2019): 109–26; Lauren I. Labrecque, Ereni Markos, and Aron Darmody, "Addressing Online Behavioral Advertising and Privacy Implications: A Comparison of Passive Versus Active Learning Approaches," *Journal of Marketing Education* 43, no. 1 (2021): 43–58.
41. Ari Ezra Waldman, "Designing without Privacy," *Houston Law Review* 55, no. 3 (2018): 659–728.
42. "University Rankings," Penn State University, Facts and Rankings, 2021, https://www.psu.edu/this-is-penn-state/facts-and-rankings/.
43. "Degrees Awarded," Assessment and Institutional Research Penn State Planning, *Data Digest* (2021), https://datadigest.psu.edu/degrees-awarded/.
44. Center for Penn State Student Entrepreneurship, Penn State, accessed January 14, 2022, https://cpsse.psu.edu/enti.
45. "AACSB-Accredited Schools," AACSB, n.d., https://www.aacsb.edu/accredited.
46. "2020 Guiding Principles and Standards for Business Accreditation," AACSB, 2021, https://www.aacsb.edu/-/media/documents/accreditation/2020-aacsb-business-accreditation-standards-july-2021.pdf?rev=80b0db4090ad4d6db60a34e975a73b1b&hash=D210346C64043CC2297E8658F676AF94.
47. "Undergraduate Bulletin," Penn State, 2021, n.d., https://bulletins.psu.edu/undergraduate/.
48. David P. Twomey, Marianne Jennings, and Stephanie M. Greene, *Business Law Principles for Today's Commercial Environment*, 5th ed. (Boston: Cengage Learning, 2016).
49. Archie B. Carroll, Jill A. Brown, and Ann K. Buchholtz, *Business & Society: Ethics, Sustainability, and Stakeholder Management*, 10th ed. (Boston: Cengage Learning, 2017).
50. Anne T. Lawrence and James Weber, *Business and Society: Stakeholders, Ethics, Public Policy*, 16th ed. (New York: McGraw Hill, 2019).
51. Linda Klebe Treviño and Katherine A. Nelson, *Managing Business Ethics: Straight Talk about How to Do It Right*, 7th ed. (New York: Wiley, 2017).
52. Dean Bredeson, *Applied Business Ethics*, 1st ed. (Boston: Cengage Learning, 2012).
53. Treviño and Nelson, *Managing Business Ethics*.
54. "Integrity at Smeal," Smeal College of Business, 2022, https://www.smeal.psu.edu/integrity.
55. "Tarriff Center for Business Ethics and Social Responsibility," Smeal College of Business, 2022, https://www.smeal.psu.edu/tarriff-center.
56. Sarah Hartman-Caverly and Alexandria Chisholm, "Privacy Literacy Instruction Practices in Academic Libraries: Past, Present, and Possibilities," *IFLA Journal* 46, no. 4 (2020): 305–27, https://doi.org/10.1177/0340035220956804.
57. Alexandria Chisholm and Sarah Hartman-Caverly, "Privacy Workshop," Privacy Workshop, n.d., https://guides.libraries.psu.edu/berks/privacy.

BIBLIOGRAPHY

AACSB. "2020 Guiding Principles and Standards for Business Accreditation," 2021. https://www.aacsb.edu/-/media/documents/accreditation/2020-aacsb-business-accreditation-standards-july-2021.pdf?rev=80b0db4090ad4d6db60a34e975a73b1b&hash=D210346C64043CC2297E8658F676AF94.

———. "AACSB-Accredited Schools." n.d. https://www.aacsb.edu/accredited.

American Library Association. "Privacy." Advocacy, Legislation & Issues. October 2021. https://www.ala.org/advocacy/privacy.

Andreotta, Adam J., Nin Kirkham, and Marco Rizzi. "AI, Big Data, and the Future of Consent." AI & SOCIETY 2021 1 (August 2021): 1–14. https://doi.org/10.1007/S00146-021-01262-5.

Aten, Jason. "The Head of Facebook's Metaverse Project Says Users Are to Blame for Its Misinformation Problem, Not Facebook." *Inc.* (November 2021). https://www.inc.com/jason-aten/the-head-of-facebooks-metaverse-project-andrew-bosworth-says-users-are-to-blame-for-its-misinformation-problem-not-facebook.html.

Barr, Kyle. "TikTok's In-App Browser Has Code to Track Users' Inputs and Activity." Gizmodo. August 19, 2022. https://gizmodo.com/tiktok-keylogging-privacy-meta-1849433690.

Belock, Brett, Firas Fasheh, Anna McKeever, and James S. O'Rourke. "Target Corporation: Predictive Analytics and Customer Privacy." In *Sage Business Cases*. 2013. https://sk-sagepub-com.ezaccess.libraries.psu.edu/cases/target-corporation-predictive-analytics-and-customer-privacy?utm_source=ss360&utm_medium=discovery-provider#i223.

Bredeson, Dean. *Applied Business Ethics*. 1st ed. Boston: Cengage Learning, 2012.

Carroll, Archie B. "The Pyramid of Corporate Social Responsibility: Toward the Moral Management of Organizational Stakeholders." *Business Horizons* 34, no. 4 (July 1991): 39–48. https://doi.org/10.1016/0007-6813(91)90005-G.

Carroll, Archie B., Jill A. Brown, and Ann K. Buchholtz. *Business & Society: Ethics, Sustainability, and Stakeholder Management*. 10th ed. Boston: Cengage Learning, 2017.

Center for Penn State Student Entrepreneurship. Accessed January 14, 2022. https://cpsse.psu.edu/enti.

Chisholm, Alexandria, and Sarah Hartman-Caverly. "Privacy Workshop." Privacy Workshop. n.d. https://guides.libraries.psu.edu/berks/privacy.

Collins, Keith, and Gabriel J.X. Dance. "How Researchers Learned to Use Facebook 'Likes' to Sway Your Thinking." *The New York Times* (March 2018). https://www.nytimes.com/2018/03/20/technology/facebook-cambridge-behavior-model.html.

Confessore, Nicholas. "Cambridge Analytica and Facebook: The Scandal and the Fallout So Far." *The New York Times* (April 2018). https://www.nytimes.com/2018/04/04/us/politics/cambridge-analytica-scandal-fallout.html.

Federal Bureau of Investigation. "Chinese Hackers Charged in Equifax Breach." February 2020. https://www.fbi.gov/news/stories/chinese-hackers-charged-in-equifax-breach-021020.

Federal Trade Commission. "A Look at What ISPs Know About You: Examining the Privacy Practices of Six Major Internet Service Providers." October 21, 2021. https://www.ftc.gov/reports/look-what-isps-know-about-you-examining-privacy-practices-six-major-internet-service-providers.

———. "Children's Online Privacy Protection Rule ('COPPA')." Rules. 1998. https://www.ftc.gov/enforcement/rules/rulemaking-regulatory-reform-proceedings/childrens-online-privacy-protection-rule.

———. "FTC Imposes $5 Billion Penalty and Sweeping New Privacy Restrictions on Facebook." July 2019. https://www.ftc.gov/news-events/press-releases/2019/07/ftc-imposes-5-billion-penalty-sweeping-new-privacy-restrictions.

Germain, Thomas. "Mental Health Apps and User Privacy." *Consumer Reports* (March 2021). https://www.consumerreports.org/health-privacy/mental-health-apps-and-user-privacy-a7415198244/.

Ghaffary, Shirin. "'Don't Be Evil' Isn't a Normal Company Value. But Google Isn't a Normal Company." Vox. February 16, 2021. https://www.vox.com/recode/2021/2/16/22280502/google-dont-be-evil-land-of-the-giants-podcast.

Hartman-Caverly, Sarah, and Alexandria Chisholm. "Privacy Literacy Instruction Practices in Academic Libraries: Past, Present, and Possibilities." *IFLA Journal* 46, no. 4 (2020): 305–27. https://doi.org/10.1177/0340035220956804.

Have I Been Pwned? n.d. https://haveibeenpwned.com/.

Horwitz, Jeff, and Deepa Seetharaman. "Facebook Executives Shut Down Efforts to Make the Site Less Divisive." *The Wall Street Journal* (May 2020). https://www.wsj.com/articles/facebook-knows-it-encourages-division-top-executives-nixed-solutions-11590507499.

Kang, Cecilia. "Facebook Faces Growing Pressure Over Data and Privacy Inquiries." *The New York Times* (March 2018). https://www.nytimes.com/2018/03/20/business/ftc-facebook-privacy-investigation.html.

Kim, Tae Wan, and Bryan R. Routledge. "Why a Right to an Explanation of Algorithmic Decision-Making Should Exist: A Trust-Based Approach." *Business Ethics Quarterly* (May 2021): 1–28. https://doi.org/10.1017/BEQ.2021.3.

Klosowski, Thorin. "The State of Consumer Data Privacy Laws in the US (And Why It Matters)." *The New York Times*, sec. Wirecutter (September 2021). https://www.nytimes.com/wirecutter/blog/state-of-privacy-laws-in-us/.

Krause, Felix. "IOS Privacy: Instagram and Facebook Can Track Anything You Do on Any Website in Their in-App Browser." *KrauseFx* (blog), August 10, 2022. https://krausefx.com/blog/ios-privacy-instagram-and-facebook-can-track-anything-you-do-on-any-website-in-their-in-app-browser.

Labrecque, Lauren I., Ereni Markos, and Aron Darmody. "Addressing Online Behavioral Advertising and Privacy Implications: A Comparison of Passive Versus Active Learning Approaches." *Journal of Marketing Education* 43, no. 1 (2021): 43–58.

Lawrence, Anne T., and James Weber. *Business and Society: Stakeholders, Ethics, Public Policy*. 16th ed. New York: McGraw Hill, 2019.

Martin, Kirsten. "Breaking the Privacy Paradox: The Value of Privacy and Associated Duty of Firms." *Business Ethics Quarterly* 30, no. 1 (January 2020): 65–96. https://doi.org/10.1017/BEQ.2019.24.

Meyer, Robinson. "Everything We Know About Facebook's Secret Mood-Manipulation Experiment." *The Atlantic* (June 28, 2014). https://www.theatlantic.com/technology/archive/2014/06/everything-we-know-about-facebooks-secret-mood-manipulation-experiment/373648/.

Milmo, Dan. "Facebook 'Overpaid in Data Settlement to Avoid Naming Zuckerberg'." *The Guardian* (September 24, 2021). https://www.theguardian.com/technology/2021/sep/24/facebook-overpaid-in-data-settlement-to-avoid-naming-zuckerberg.

Mintzberg, Henry. "The Case for Corporate Social Responsibility." *Journal of Business Strategy* 4, no. October (1983): 3–15.

Morrison, Sara. "A Priest's Resignation after His Phone Location Data Leaked Shows the Urgent Need for Data Privacy Laws." Vox. July 2021. https://www.vox.com/recode/22587248/grindr-app-location-data-outed-priest-jeffrey-burrill-pillar-data-harvesting.

———. "Meta Is Getting Data about You from Some Surprising Places." Vox. June 17, 2022. https://www.vox.com/recode/23172691/meta-tracking-privacy-hospitals.

Page, Carly. "Opioid Addiction Treatment Apps Found Sharing Sensitive Data with Third Parties." TechCrunch. July 2021. https://techcrunch.com/2021/07/07/opioid-addiction-treatment-apps-found-sharing-sensitive-data-with-third-parties/.

Peltier, James W., George R. Milne, Joseph E. Phelps, and Jennifer T. Barrett. "Teaching Information Privacy in Marketing Courses: Key Educational Issues for Principles of Marketing and Elective Marketing Courses." *Journal of Marketing Education* 32, no. 2 (2010): 224–46. https://doi.org/10.1177/0273475309360164.

Penn State Planning, Assessment and Institutional Research. "Degrees Awarded." Data Digest, 2021. https://datadigest.psu.edu/degrees-awarded/.

Penn State University. "University Rankings." Facts and Rankings. 2021. https://www.psu.edu/this-is-penn-state/facts-and-rankings/.

Penn State University. "Undergraduate Bulletin." 2021. https://bulletins.psu.edu/undergraduate/.

Pollach, Irene. "Online Privacy as a Corporate Social Responsibility: An Empirical Study." *Business Ethics: A European Review* 20, no. 1 (January 2011): 88–102. https://doi.org/10.1111/J.1467-8608.2010.01611.X.

Post, James E. "Moving from Geographic to Virtual Communities: Global Corporate Citizenship in a Dot.Com World." *Business and Society Review* 105, no. 1 (2000): 26–46. https://doi.org/10.1111/0045-3609.00063.

Rosenberg, Matthew, Nicholas Confessore, and Carole Cadwalladr. "How Trump Consultants Exploited the Facebook Data of Millions." *The New York Times* (March 2018). https://www.nytimes.com/2018/03/17/us/politics/cambridge-analytica-trump-campaign.html.

Singer, Natasha. "Why a Push for Online Privacy Is Bogged Down in Washington." *The New York Times* (February 28, 2016). https://www.nytimes.com/2016/02/29/technology/obamas-effort-on-consumer-privacy-falls-short-critics-say.html.

Smeal College of Business. "Integrity at Smeal." 2022. https://www.smeal.psu.edu/integrity.
———. "Tarriff Center for Business Ethics and Social Responsibility." 2022. https://www.smeal.psu.edu/tarriff-center.
Torchinsky, Rina. "How Period Tracking Apps and Data Privacy Fit into a Post-Roe v. Wade Climate." NPR. June 24, 2022. https://www.npr.org/2022/05/10/1097482967/roe-v-wade-supreme-court-abortion-period-apps.
Treviño, Linda Klebe, and Katherine A. Nelson. *Managing Business Ethics: Straight Talk about How to Do It Right*. 7th ed. New York: Wiley, 2017.
Twomey, David P., Marianne Jennings, and Stephanie M. Greene. *Business Law Principles for Today's Commercial Environment*. 5th ed. Boston: Cengage Learning, 2016.
Waldman, Ari Ezra. "Designing without Privacy." *Houston Law Review* 55, no. 3 (2018): 659–728.
Walker, Kristen L., and Nora Moran. "Consumer Information for Data-Driven Decision Making: Teaching Socially Responsible Use of Data." *Journal of Marketing Education* 41, no. 2 (2019): 109–26.
The Wall Street Journal. "The Facebook Files." *The Wall Street Journal* (October 1, 2021). https://www.wsj.com/articles/the-facebook-files-11631713039.
Wolfard, Ben. "What Is GDPR, the EU's New Data Protection Law?" GDPR.eu. November 7, 2018. https://gdpr.eu/what-is-gdpr/.

CHAPTER 9

OUR STUDENTS ARE ONLINE CONSUMERS:
Using Privacy Literacy to Challenge Price Discrimination

Joshua Becker

INTRODUCTION

When a consumer goes to purchase an item online, they often assume that the price they are charged will be the same for everyone. They would be wrong; many retailers provide differential pricing to consumers. This is true even if two identical goods are purchased from the same retailer at the same time. Differential pricing is given many names: dynamic pricing, algorithmic pricing, price optimization, and price discrimination. This practice is extremely common and, in most cases, perfectly legal. Most online retailers determine prices based on the consumer's online data, of which there is plenty. This makes price discrimination more than just an economic and ethical issue, it is a privacy issue as well. As pervasive as this problem is, there are remedies. This chapter discusses a process librarians can implement to empower students to combat price discrimination while protecting their personal data. As librarians move to expand beyond traditional notions of library instruction, this long-overlooked problem provides an opportunity to collaborate with a broad group of campus stakeholders.

PRICE DISCRIMINATION AND PRIVACY

As other chapters in this volume have mentioned, most of your online behavior (especially on commercial sites) is tracked. Before a price is generated on a retail site, the seller will run a potential purchaser's data through their algorithm. Retailers make price determinations based on factors as varied as preferred browser, search history, IP address, previous online purchases, credit score, age, gender, sex, zip code, Mac versus PC, and many other factors.[1] What retailers cannot mine on their site, they will supplement with help from data brokers and credit companies (e.g., Experian). Given that a company's pricing algorithm is proprietary, it's unsurprising that retailers are unwilling to share the inner workings of their invasive techniques.

Through these online practices, retailers have made consumer data vulnerable. This raises not just the issue of privacy but of security as well. Most consumers would like their personal data *and* purchase history to remain anonymous. Unfortunately, a hack on a major retailer or credit agency can often lead to widespread identity theft. While some students may be aware of these security issues, few students are aware of how price discrimination affects them.

LITERATURE REVIEW

In its most elemental form, price discrimination simply implies that different prices are offered to different purchasers. Economists like to refer to three degrees of price discrimination.[2] First-degree price discrimination is a practice where a business tries to set prices at the maximum an individual is willing to pay. Through the mining of personal data, corporations can use information about purchasing habits and preferences to set the highest optimized price that the consumer will agree to pay.[3] This practice has become very prevalent in online retail settings. The second degree of price discrimination, quantity discounts; and the third degree, segmented or group pricing, have a much smaller impact and are not the focus of this chapter.

Nearly 80 percent of youth purchase something online, and during the recent pandemic, it has become increasingly rare to purchase goods and services without relying in part on online retailers.[4,5] Differential pricing predates the internet, though the practice has existed online since at least 2000[6] when a consumer noticed that an item on Amazon was priced differently based on the browser that was used. Since that time, price discrimination has become much more sophisticated, and it now affects the prices of many common goods and services, including groceries, apparel, hotel rooms, airline tickets, and rideshare services.[7] The differences can be stark. One item by a major retailer can vary significantly from one consumer to another.[8] Surge pricing has been employed by Uber, Lyft, and others, resulting in them being sued for price gouging and banned in some locales.[9]

While differential pricing has long been controversial, there is little legislative oversight. The Robinson Patman Act was enacted in 1936 to protect against collusion and price fixing by corporations.[10] At the time, there was an active concern over creating monopolies. No significant federal legislation has been passed since that time to restrict corporations from setting prices for most goods and services. At the state level, there have been some recent legal victories in instances where companies set prices based on age and race.[11] Perhaps the most promising change doesn't deal directly with pricing. The *California Privacy Rights Act of 2020* was enacted to help safeguard an individual's data.[12] Without that data, price optimization becomes far more difficult for corporations.

Although price discrimination may not be a pressing legal issue, it is an ethical one. Scholars and policymakers have long questioned the fairness of this practice. In a democratic society, where everyone should receive equal treatment under the law, shouldn't we pay the same prices for common goods and services? Alexi Marcoux believed it violates the "golden rule" and equal treatment mores.[13] In 1785, Immanuel Kant strongly condemned charging individuals different prices.

> That a dealer should not overcharge an inexperienced purchaser certainly accords with [the] duty [the moral duty of the good will]; and where there is much commerce, the prudent merchant does not overcharge but keeps to a fixed price for everyone in general, so that a child may buy from him just as well as everyone else may. Thus customers are honestly served....[14]

Ethical issues aside, many entrepreneurs believe businesses have the right to set their own prices. Economists have conflicting views about the market utility of price discrimination. A recent paper appears to suggest that obtaining user data can lead to diminished corporate profits, while corporations that do not collect user data may be *better off* financially.[15] Other research finds that company profits are higher without consumer privacy.[16] Some policymakers believe that by charging certain consumers less for goods and services, these practices may help reduce the current economic disparities in our society.[17,18]

Price discrimination has long been very unpopular with the public. When asked about this practice, survey after survey have revealed significant displeasure at this practice. According to an Annenberg Survey from 2005: 76 percent of respondents *agree(d)* that, "it would bother me to learn that other people pay less than I do for the same products; 87 percent *disagreed* with the statement, "It's OK if an online store I use charges people different prices for the same products during the same hour."[19] More recent survey results indicate that 88 percent of respondents thought online companies should be more transparent about the customer data they collect, use, or share,[20] while a different survey revealed that 75 percent of respondents felt it was unacceptable to charge Apple users higher prices than other users on hotel rooms.[21]

Setting aside these ethical and economic arguments, consumers should be aware that companies buy and sell this information to others, often without their permission.[22] This information may also be hacked, which poses security threats. Raising consumer awareness of these practices is the first step toward empowerment. When consumers are made aware of the potential for identity theft, unequal pricing, and the loss of anonymity, they see a compelling rationale to safeguard their privacy. Despite this rationale, price optimization remains under the radar and will likely remain popular among retailers for the foreseeable future.

Fortunately, there are technologies that can help circumvent these corporate practices. Virtual private networks (VPN) offer a search experience that offers significantly more anonymity. A VPN uses a different set of servers to "direct your data through an encrypted tunnel."[23] As a result, it is very difficult for search engines to know your location and thus charge prices based on your location.[24] While legitimate questions are raised about the efficacy and security of individual VPNs,[25] there is agreement that they often make a user's online searching more difficult to track.

TEACHING PRICE DISCRIMINATION AND PRIVACY

Despite the real impact of this issue on our students' lives, price discrimination has been largely ignored in the undergraduate curriculum. Although this concept is consistently taught in economics, it is only occasionally taught in the business curriculum or other disciplines. Given price optimization's reliance on user data, this issue is inextricably linked to privacy and security. Librarians have an opportunity to mitigate the effects of price discrimination and help safeguard personal data in the bargain.

In my information ethics class, an elective course open to all undergraduates, students are exposed to the realities of price discrimination and learn privacy techniques to diminish those influences. This instruction takes place over two class sessions and students have readings and homework assignments tied to this theme. This lesson consists of five steps, each of which is explained below. While this lesson appeared in a course that I designed and created, I believe this lesson could work equally as a mini-unit in many courses.

Both differential pricing and online privacy can be very technical topics. As a writer with a novice understanding of economics and computer science, it was necessary to build up my expertise over time. Several resources proved invaluable in my planning. *Big Data and Differential Pricing Offered*[26] from the White House offered an excellent introduction to the topic. CBC's exposé from 2017, *Exposing Price Discrimination in Online Shopping*,[27] was very informative and provided an initial template for how I wanted to structure this unit. Finally, Akiva Miller offered a painstaking look at many of the contemporary and historical ethical and legal issues involving price discrimination.[28]

For a look at how businesses use personal data, Stuart Lacey's 2015 TEDx talk[29] is very sobering. When selecting materials for students I wanted the readings and clips to be succinct and accessible. Neil Howe's article in *Forbes*, "A Special Price Just for You,"[30] was very well received. Similarly, there were many news clips on YouTube that provocatively introduced students to price discrimination.

I approach teaching students about price discrimination and privacy by breaking the process down into five separate steps: (1) students will be introduced to the concepts of price discrimination; (2) after learning about that concept, students will research ways that price discrimination affects potential online purchases; (3) to curtail price discrimination, and safeguard their privacy, students will install a virtual private network or VPN; (4) once the VPN is installed, students will determine how effectively this software works when comparing the online prices from step two; and (5) finally, students will learn about ways to check for VPN updates as well as additional techniques to combat price discrimination. I will explain each of these steps in more detail.

Understanding Price Discrimination – Step 1

To introduce the topic of price discrimination, students are given a series of readings and video examples. This may be introduced in class or read in advance. Three or four short articles on price discrimination from popular sources typically work best (e.g., *The New York Times*, *Scientific American*, *USA Today*, etc.). After reading these articles, students realize that corporations utilize consumer information to help determine the "ideal price" for goods and services. Students then read about the role of Virtual Private Networks (VPNs) and how this technology can be used to circumvent price discrimination. A couple of video clips can be used as a complement or alternative to the readings based on available time. A thoughtful discussion of price discrimination can easily take twenty to thirty minutes.

Once students are aware of price discrimination, it is important for them to see how it affects them personally. A few students may have direct experiences with price discrimination; when that occurs, they are often willing to share these events with the class. In three years of discussing this topic with students, the result is almost inevitably surprise followed by disgust.

Initial Pricing Log – Step 2

After students are introduced to the topic, they partner with another student and look for various products from popular online retailers (Amazon.com, Hotels.com, etc.). In addition to common items, students also price out experiences such as airline tickets and hotel reservations. Students then compare the results and notice the variation in prices. This occurs even though they are both looking for the same product at the same time! In the past, students have also considered possible reasons (past purchases, search history, preferred browser, Mac vs. PC, etc.) why these prices are different.

At my institution, all students are required to own a laptop and nearly everyone brings their laptop to class. This allows students to quickly price out various items and compare those prices with their classmates. I have turned this into an assignment where students log this information on a worksheet and compare their prices with classmates. This log will also come in helpful during step 4.

The worksheet compares prices for items such as airline tickets, hotel rooms, candy bars, blue jeans, and noise-canceling headphones. Students were asked to compare using at least two different browsers: Chrome, Firefox, Microsoft Edge, or Safari. After completing the price comparison, students were also asked to compare their prices with their classmates and theorize why those prices might be different. This activity is valuable because students are looking for the same items in the same location at the same time, yet the pricing is different. I would give students between twenty-five and thirty-five minutes to complete this worksheet individually and then engage in group discussion. This worksheet could easily be modified to incorporate many different types of consumer goods (see appendix).

Installing a Virtual Private Network – Step 3

After students have seen the direct effects of price optimization, I show students how to set up a VPN. There are many different VPNs to choose from. My institution has its own VPN as do many of the major web browsers. As mentioned earlier, some VPNs are not completely secure, while others become less effective over time.[31] Viruses are rare, but they happen. Some students may initially be hesitant to download this software on their machines. Librarians should contact Information Technology for guidance and recommendations on VPNs. Information Technology can also provide insights about updating VPNs as needed. Ten to twenty minutes may be appropriate to complete this step during class.

Adding VPN Results to the Pricing Log – Step 4

Once students have installed a VPN, the class returns to the worksheet and searches and records prices for each of the items in question in the gold column. In essence, they repeat step 2, but this step should go much more rapidly. Students quickly notice any disparities between their initial searches and using the VPN. Students will once again be asked to compare their results with their peers. Given the differences in VPNs, students notice there are usually considerable variations in the final column as well.

Additional Techniques to Prevent Corporate Tracking – Step 5

While installing a VPN can be highly effective in ensuring personal privacy,[32] there are several other precautions that often prove successful in getting competitive prices and thwarting corporate use of personal data. Some of these techniques include using multiple devices, finding multiple retailers, using incognito windows, disabling cookies, using different browsers, and setting up price alerts. Students learn about these techniques and have the opportunity to apply them to the pricing log. Students are also encouraged to update their software regularly, maintain strict antivirus settings, and remain vigilant. At this stage, a member of Information Technology could briefly talk to students about online safety and answer questions they have about privacy and security. By the end of this step, students should feel much more confident about limited price discrimination and protecting their online data. This step may take longer than step 4 (twenty minutes or so should suffice), but it is an effective way to end the unit.

DISCUSSION

At first glance, price discrimination may seem very far removed from traditional discussions of information literacy. While this topic will not address issues of scholarship or the research process, it will expand student understanding of the information landscape. Our personal data is a commodity that businesses use to their advantage. In that way this unit addresses the ACRL frame, Information Has Value.[33]

While price discrimination is very much a social justice issue, revealing ageism, gender bias, and racial inequality, there are other reasons it should be considered a part of the greater academic library curriculum. Knowledge of corporate practices leads to a thoughtful discussion of how corporations exploit personal data. If privacy literacy is going to become a mainstay in library instruction, price discrimination is a very effective introduction to this topic. As our society spends more of its time online, it is critical that librarians dispel any student notions of benign corporations. The online reality is far more troubling than most students imagine; serious legal remedies to these practices (should they ever occur) appear years in the future.

The process laid out in this chapter goes far beyond obtaining a competitive price on goods and services. Students are given clear ways to keep their personal data safe and secure from corporations. By implementing these privacy safeguards, students can see tangible results almost immediately. After completing this process, students should have a greater appreciation of the complex online information landscape.

Given the time that my students spend online, their reactions of surprise and then disgust were understandable perhaps because it was also an ethics class and students felt that differential pricing online violated their sense of fairness. The class engaged in these exercises with a sense of enthusiasm and a desire to level the playing field as consumers. Students were surprised and shocked to see the variation in pricing for the same objects throughout the class. Their disgust mirrored earlier surveys on price discrimination and made students very open to installing a VPN on their devices.

Of the five steps in the process, I imagined installing the VPN would be the most challenging. It was not; nearly every student agreed to install the software on the laptops. While students shared their laptop pricing in class, I regret not offering students extra credit to track the prices they found through their cell phones. That assignment would have made this unit even more relevant. Similarly, while I received positive student feedback on this unit, I intend to incorporate larger and more formal assessments in future iterations of this course.

My collaboration from outside the library proved valuable as well, I enjoyed making additional connections with Information Technology on campus. The office wants to protect every member of the community from online attacks. Working with this department helped inform my instruction beyond just this course.

Given the background readings, videos, class discussions, and activities that are part of this five-step process, it would be very difficult to teach all these concepts in a one-shot instruction setting. One potential solution would be to eliminate most of the readings and class discussions on price discrimination and online privacy. A brief reading or short video on each topic could take less than fifteen minutes and allow the bulk of the class to focus squarely on steps 2 through 5. In this setting, students would complete a streamlined worksheet and install a pre-selected VPN. While the student experience would be different, this activity could certainly be worthwhile.

NEXT STEPS

Students are often painfully unaware of how corporate interests abuse their personal data. By following these steps, students should be able to reduce the price they spend on many online purchases and keep much of their personal information out of corporate hands. While differential pricing and privacy literacy are complex topics, this lesson should provide an effective student foundation. Given its immediate success, I plan to retain this unit on price discrimination and privacy in my information ethics course.

I feel privileged to be able to design and teach a semester-long elective course devoted to information ethics. At the same time, I feel price discrimination and privacy is relevant to all students. I have worked to provide outreach to different disciplines where this unit would complement existing curricula. With slight modifications, this unit could dovetail well with a course on financial literacy. Financial literacy courses are becoming more popular, and an examination of price discrimination and user privacy would be a valuable addition to such a course. Similarly, many classes in information technology or computer science would care about the ethical and practical issues surrounding data privacy. Courses on ethics and business would also provide a strong fit for a small unit or class devoted to these themes. In the coming years, I plan to work with a variety of campus partners to expand these topics to a student population.

In addition to students, I believe other members of the institution would find this a valuable workshop topic. I'd look to work with campus events and the offices for faculty and staff development to raise awareness of this issue. I value the connection I made with the Office of Information Technology, and I hope to foster similar collaborations on campus.

ACKNOWLEDGMENTS

I would like to acknowledge and thank the students in my Information Ethics class at Southern New Hampshire University.

APPENDIX
PRICE DISCRIMINATION WORKSHEET

Name

Date and Time

Price Discrimination Worksheet

Let's compare prices via browsers, dates, and locations. Complete every section, **except the VPN column in gray. The VPN column will be completed after class discussion.**

1. Airfare from Boston (BOS) to Seattle (SEA) on April 22 one-way on United Airlines

Browser Use at least two browsers	Chrome	Firefox	Microsoft Edge	Safari if (applicable)	VPN (please specify)
Price on United.com					
Price on Expedia.com					

2. Hotel Room in Las Vegas on April 10 for three nights at the Venetian Hotel

Browser Use at least two browsers	Chrome	Firefox	Microsoft Edge	Safari if (applicable)	VPN (please specify)
Price on https://www.venetianlasvegas.com					
Price on Expedia.com					

3. Toblerone Swiss Chocolate Gift Set, Milk Chocolate, White Chocolate & Crunchy Salted Caramelized Almond, Valentine's Day Chocolate Candy, 9 - 3.52 oz Bars

Browser Use at least two browsers	Chrome	Firefox	Microsoft Edge	Safari if (applicable)	VPN (please specify)
Price on Walmart.com					
Price on Amazon.com					

4. Heath Milk Chocolate English Toffee Candy, Bulk, 1.4 oz Bars (18 Count)

Browser Use at least two browsers	Chrome	Firefox	Microsoft Edge	Safari if (applicable)	VPN (please specify)
Price on Walmart.com					
Price on Amazon.com					

5. Levi's Men's or Women's 501 Jeans (specify the style and cut and size)

| Browser
Use at least two browsers	Chrome	Firefox	Microsoft Edge	Safari if (applicable)	VPN (please specify)
Price on Levis.com					
Price on Amazon.com					
Price on Walmart.com					

6. Sony WH-XB910N EXTRA BASS Bluetooth Wireless Noise-Cancelling Headphones – Black

| Browser
Use at least two browsers	Chrome	Firefox	Microsoft Edge	Safari if (applicable)	VPN (please specify)
Price on Target.com					
Price on Amazon.com					

7. Compare the prices you selected.
    A. Of these six products, what was the greatest difference you found between browsers?
    B. What was the greatest difference you found between different retailers?
8. Compare the prices you found with your classmates. What were some of the largest differences you noticed?
9. Do you have any theories why their prices might be different from yours?

NOTES

1. Aniko Hannak, Gary Soeller, David Lazer, and Alan Mislove, "Measuring Price Discrimination and Steering on E-Commerce Web Sites." IMC '14: Proceedings of the 2014 Conference on Internet Measurement Conference (2014): 305–18.
2. Ari Shpanya, "What is Price Discrimination and is it Ethical?," accessed January 14, 2022, https://econsultancy.com/what-is-price-discrimination-and-is-it-ethical/.
3. Shpanya, "What is Price Discrimination."
4. Shawn Carter, "80% of younger shoppers make impulse purchases online—here's how sites trick you into spending," December 11, 2018.
5. Mayumi Brewster, "E-Commerce Sales Surged During the Pandemic," April 27, 2022.
6. Rodrigo Montes, Wilfried Zantman, and Tommaso M. Valletti, "The Value of Personal Information in Markets with Endogenous Privacy," May 27, 2016.
7. Hannak, Soeller, Lazer, and Mislove, "Measuring Price Discrimination."
8. Ibid.
9. Tracey Lien, "Honolulu Lawmakers Agree to Cap Surge Pricing for Uber and Lyft," Los Angeles Times (Online), June 7, 2018.
10. "Price Discrimination: Robinson-Patman Violations," Federal Trade Commission, accessed January 14, 2022, https://www.ftc.gov/tips-advice/competition-guidance/guide-antitrust-laws/price-discrimination-robinson-patman.
11. Dami Lee, "Tinder Settles Age Discrimination Lawsuit with $11.5 Million Worth of Super Likes," accessed Jan 14, 2022, https://www.theverge.com/2019/1/25/18197575/tinder-plus-age-discrimination-lawsuit-settlement-super-likes.
12. California Consumer Privacy Act (CCPA), 2018, accessed January 14, 2022, https://oag.ca.gov/privacy/ccpa.

13. Alexei Marcoux, "Much Ado about Price Discrimination," *The Journal of Markets & Morality* 9, no. 1 (March 22, 2006): 57.
14. Immanuel Kant and James W. Ellington, *Grounding for the Metaphysics of Morals* (Cambridge, MA: Hackett Publishing Company, Inc, 1993).
15. Rosa-Branca Esteves, "Price Discrimination with Private and Imperfect Information," *The Scandinavian Journal of Economics* 116, no. 3 (July 2014): 766–96, doi: 10.1111/sjoe.12061.
16. Laussel Didier, Ngo V. Long, and Joana Resende, "The Curse of Knowledge: Having Access to Customer Information can Reduce Monopoly Profits," *The Rand Journal of Economics* 51, no. 3 (2020): 650–75, doi: 10.1111/1756-2171.12336.
17. William J. Baumöl and Daniel G. Swanson, "The New Economy and Ubiquitous Competitive Price Discrimination: Identifying Defensible Criteria of Market Power," *Antitrust Law Journal* 70, no. 3 (January 1, 2003): 661–85.
18. Michael E. Levine, "Price Discrimination without Market Power," *Yale Journal on Regulation* 19 (January 1, 2002): 1–541.
19. Joseph Turow, Lauren Feldman, and Kimberly Meltzer, "Open to Exploitation: America's Shoppers Online and Offline," *A Report from the Annenberg Public Policy Center of the University of Pennsylvania*, 2005.
20. "Exposing Price Discrimination in Online Shopping," Marketplace, CBC, 2017.
21. Joost Poort and Borgesius Zuiderveen, "Does Everyone have a Price? Understanding People's Attitude Towards Online and Offline Price Discrimination," *Internet Policy Review* 8, no. 1 (2019): 1–20, doi: 10.14763/2019.1.1383.
22. Rodrigo Montes, Wilfried Zantman, and Tommaso M. Valletti, "The Value of Personal Information in Markets with Endogenous Privacy," AACSB, May 27, 2016.
23. Yael Grauer, "Mullvad, IVPN, and Mozilla VPN Top Consumer Reports' VPN Testing," *Consumer Reports* (December 7, 2021).
24. Shachar Shamir, "2 huge reasons you should be using a VPN," The Next Web, May 4, 2016.
25. Yael Grauer, "VPN Testing Reveals Poor Privacy and Security Practices, Hyperbolic Claims," *Consumer Reports*, December 7, 2021.
26. "Big Data and Differential Pricing," Executive Office of the President of the United States, 2015.
27. "Exposing Price Discrimination," Marketplace.
28. Akiva Miller, "What Do We Worry About When We Worry About Price Discrimination? The Law and Ethics of Using Personal Information for Pricing," *Journal of Technology Law & Policy* 19 (September 13, 2014).
29. "The Future of Your Personal Data – Privacy vs Monetization," Anonymous, 2015.
30. Neil Howe, "A Special Price just for You," *Forbes* (November 17, 2017).
31. Yael Grauer, "Should You Use a VPN?," *Consumer Reports* (December 7, 2021).
32. Grauer, "Should You Use a VPN?"
33. "Framework for Information Literacy for Higher Education," Association of College and Research Libraries, 2016.

BIBLIOGRAPHY

ACRL Board. *Framework for Information Literacy for Higher Education*. January 11, 2016.

Baumöl, William J., and Daniel G. Swanson. "The New Economy and Ubiquitous Competitive Price Discrimination: Identifying Defensible Criteria of Market Power." *Antitrust Law Journal* 70, no. 3 (January 1, 2003): 661–85.

Brewster, Mayumi. "E-Commerce Sales Surged during the Pandemic." Accessed September 22, 2022. https://www.census.gov/library/stories/2022/04/ecommerce-sales-surged-during-pandemic.html.

California Consumer Privacy Act (CCPA). 2018.

Carter, Shawn. "80% of Younger Shoppers Make Impulse Purchases Online—Here's How Sites Trick You into Spending." Accessed September 22, 2022. https://www.cnbc.com/2018/12/11/80percent-of-young-people-made-an-impulse-buy-online-this-yearheres-why.html.

Esteves, Rosa-Branca. "Price Discrimination with Private and Imperfect Information." *The Scandinavian Journal of Economics* 116, no. 3 (July 2014): 766–96. https://api.istex.fr/ark:/67375/WNG-JD-NR568H-T/fulltext.pdf.

Executive Office of the President of the United States. "Big Data and Differential Pricing Offered." 2015.

"Exposing Price Discrimination in Online Shopping (Marketplace)." Anonymous. 2017.

Federal Trade Commission. "Price Discrimination: Robinson-Patman Violations." Accessed January 14, 2022. https://www.ftc.gov/tips-advice/competition-guidance/guide-antitrust-laws/price-discrimination-robinson-patman.

"The Future of Your Personal Data – Privacy vs Monetization. Anonymous. 2015.

Grauer, Yael. "Mullvad, IVPN, and Mozilla VPN Top Consumer Reports' VPN Testing." *Consumer Reports* (December 7, 2021).

———. "Should You Use a VPN?" *Consumer Reports* (December 7, 2021).

———. "VPN Testing Reveals Poor Privacy and Security Practices, Hyperbolic Claims." *Consumer Reports* (December 7, 2021).

Hannak, Aniko, Gary Soeller, David Lazer, Alan Mislove, and Christo Wilson. "Measuring Price Discrimination and Steering on E-Commerce Web Sites." *IMC '14: Proceedings of the 2014 Conference on Internet Measurement Conference* (2014): 305–18.

Howe, Neil. "A Special Price just for You." *Forbes* (November 17, 2017).

Kant, Immanuel, and James W. Ellington. *Grounding for the Metaphysics of Morals.* Cambridge, MA: Hackett Publishing Company, Inc, 1993.

Laussel, Didier, Ngo V. Long, and Joana Resende. "The Curse of Knowledge: Having Access to Customer Information Can Reduce Monopoly Profits." *The Rand Journal of Economics* 51, no. 3 (2020): 650–75. doi: 10.1111/1756-2171.12336.

Lee, Dami. "Tinder Settles Age Discrimination Lawsuit with $11.5 Million Worth of Super Likes." Accessed January 14, 2022. https://www.theverge.com/2019/1/25/18197575/tinder-plus-age-discrimination-lawsuit-settlement-super-likes.

Marcoux, Alexei M. "Much Ado about Price Discrimination." *The Journal of Markets & Morality* 9, no. 1 (March 22, 2006): 57.

Michael E. Levine. "Price Discrimination without Market Power." *Yale Journal on Regulation* 19 (January 1, 2002): 1–541.

Miller, Akiva. "What Do We Worry About When We Worry About Price Discrimination? The Law and Ethics of Using Personal Information for Pricing." *Journal of Technology Law & Policy* 19 (September 13, 2014).

Miller, Alex, and Kartik Hosanagar. "How Targeted Adds and Dynamic Pricing Can Perpetuate Bias." *Harvard Business Review* (2019). https://hbr.org/2019/11/how-targeted-ads-and-dynamic-pricing-can-perpetuate-bias.

Montes, Rodrigo, Wilfried Zantman, and Tommaso M. Valletti. "The Value of Personal Information in Markets with Endogenous Privacy." AACSB. May 27, 2016. https://wwws.law.northwestern.edu/research-faculty/clbe/events/internet/documents/sand-zantman_privacy270516.pdf.

Poort, J., and F. J. Zuiderveen Borgesius. "Does Everyone Have a Price? Understanding People's Attitude Towards Online and Offline Price Discrimination." *Internet Policy Review* 8, no. 1 (2019): 1–20. https://www.narcis.nl/publication/RecordID/oai:repository.ubn.ru.nl:2066%2F214976.

Shamir, Shachar. "2 Huge Reasons You Should Be Using a VPN." Accessed September 22, 2022. https://thenextweb.com/news/reasons-need-vpn.

Shpanya, A. "What is Price Discrimination and is it Ethical?" Econsultancy. https://econsultancy.com/what-is-price-discrimination-and-is-it-ethical/.

Tracey Lien. "Honolulu Lawmakers Agree to Cap Surge Pricing for Uber and Lyft." *Los Angeles Times (Online)* (June 7, 2018).

Turow, J., L. Feldman, and K. Meltzer. "Open to Exploitation: America's Shoppers Online and Offline." *A Report from the Annenberg Public Policy Center of the University of Pennsylvania.* 2005.

CHAPTER 10

PRIVACY LITERACY IN ENGINEERING

Paul McMonigle and Lori Lysiak

INTRODUCTION

A paper presented at the American Society for Engineering Education (ASEE) Conference in 2007 asks the question "Whose job is it?" in reference to teaching people about the effects of technology on society.[1] With respect to privacy and technology, we believe that the engineers who create the tech have a responsibility to ensure that it is used properly. Teaching privacy literacy to engineering students in the twenty-first century has two primary goals. The first is the same as teaching the topic to anyone: what it is and how students can protect their own privacy. The second, as many of the students will be responsible for creating technology that collects the data of its users, is understanding how to create "built-in" privacy protection in their potential products.

This chapter looks at several ways academic librarians focused on engineering fields can assist their patrons in achieving both goals. Several topics related to privacy literacy in engineering librarianship are covered in addition to current trends and practices in privacy education as well as examples of privacy-focused courses. These topics include instruction based on the Association of College and Research Libraries (ACRL) *Framework for Information Literacy for Higher Education*, privacy and intellectual property (IP), privacy safeguards in the course syllabi, and models for privacy literacy in instruction.

CURRENT TRENDS AND PRACTICES WITH PRIVACY IN ENGINEERING

Privacy is an emerging consideration in engineering and STEM education, research, and practice. In engineering education, there has been research into the engineering design process and how to incorporate (and engage with) privacy literacy. Thompson, Di, and Daugherty provide a model for teaching students about radio frequency identification (RFID) and how to incorporate the technology into their projects, with the intention of keeping data security and privacy in mind.[2] Meanwhile, another group of researchers in Morocco has investigated the use of blockchain technology, including teaching students how to use it to manage and secure personal data as well as how universities can use the tech for their own data needs.[3] Additionally, in an article about senior-year engineering students' perspectives on the impact of technology, the authors discovered that matters of privacy ranked remarkably high on the list of concerns. It was expressed that one of the major threats of recent technology was how it affects the privacy and safety of users. Students were able to reflect on their own practices and develop ways to improve their projects to incorporate privacy protection.[4]

The push for "open science" and data sharing in engineering and STEM research has also led to increased consideration of privacy issues. A group of researchers looked at issues of privacy and open science, which revolves around making all research and its data available to everyone by using ACRL's new *Framework for Information Literacy for Higher Education*. One of the major challenges they found was reconciling privacy with open data management practices.[5] Diving further into data sharing and management, a grant from the National Science Foundation (NSF) in 2016 was used to conduct a variety of collaborative research on data sharing in engineering education. An entire issue of the journal *Advances in Engineering Education* was dedicated to the results, with two articles of particular interest for privacy literacy. The first used a survey of engineering education researchers across North America to discover what practices they incorporate when sharing their data. One issue that came up was the fact that only 20 percent of respondents had any formal training in data management.[6] A full third of those surveyed replied that it would be "not fair" for them to be required to get legal permission to use other people's data, while more respondents were concerned about the "confusing IRB process" than with the preservation of data privacy.[7] If this survey reflects the thinking of the average engineering education researcher, then there is a serious deficiency in privacy literacy in the field that needs to be overcome.

On the other hand, the second article on intentional design of shared data sets ensures that privacy was at the forefront of the design process. There are several steps within the creation of the data set where researchers must pause and follow specific procedures to protect privacy and the confidentiality of their research subjects. Of course, the focus on including privacy in the design may be a side-product of having an engineering librarian on the design team.[8]

Privacy-related specifications are also increasingly of interest in engineering practice. Vasalou et al. conducted research into how users engage with technology and how they attempt to maintain their privacy during these interactions. They have found that many consumers lack the motivation necessary to maintain their privacy and believe that technology should be better designed to remind people at constant intervals of the terms they agreed to when using products and software, which they refer to as "engagement theory."[9] Hoel and Chen write about the differences in the expectation of privacy in different cultures, recognizing that most studies into privacy literacy are from the standpoint of North American/European views. Engineers working in an increasingly interconnected world need to understand these differences to ensure that the products they create can follow all the varying rules and regulations that exist across the globe.[10] Engineering standards regarding privacy design will increasingly inform best practices worldwide as the first ISO for privacy information management systems was published in 2019.[11]

PRIVACY LITERACY IN ENGINEERING LIBRARIANSHIP

Our discussion now turns to rationales and strategies for integrating privacy literacy into engineering library instruction and reference practices. Hartman-Caverly and Chisholm's recent article included the results of a survey on current practices by academic librarians regarding privacy literacy. They found that over a third of respondents do not teach about it at all.[12] Most instruction that does occur is not based on a need to teach privacy literacy but to combat fake news or as a "critical librarianship" initiative. The remarks of several STEM librarians were included, but the results were not broken down by subject group.[13]

Hagendorff offers a comprehensive overview of privacy literacy and its challenges. The author notes that the privacy-literate person needs to have a range of competencies and abilities to control their information, supporting the need for a library collection with the depth and breadth to allow individuals and designers of products access to the necessary knowledge. He continues by discounting the notion that most users make informed decisions based on the risks and rewards of using online services. He criticizes current privacy literacy practices as most focus on front-end features, such as changing privacy settings, removing posts, and deleting personal information, although many privacy risks are in the backend of the services, such as data capture, search tracking, and so forth. His last major point is that even the privacy-literate individual cannot regulate companies or update and strengthen privacy legislation as this is the role of the government. These points support the wide variation of items that are needed for an effective privacy literacy program.[14]

As librarians guided by the principles found in the ACRL Framework, we can connect privacy literacy to the knowledge practices of two of the frames—Authority is Constructed and Contextual and Information Has Value. Among the six knowledge practices of Authority is Constructed and Contextual, learners come to acknowledge their own authoritative voices and recognize their personal responsibilities, including seeking accuracy and reliability, respecting intellectual property, and participating in communities of practice. With Information Has Value, two of the eight knowledge practices can be applied. Learners come to understand that intellectual property is a legal and social construct that varies by culture, and learners develop their skills to make informed choices regarding their online actions in full awareness of privacy issues and the commodification of personal information.[15] The question now is: How do engineering librarians put these various concepts into practice at the reference desk and in the classroom when teaching privacy literacy?

One place to turn for guidance is engineering education accreditation standards and criteria. The Accreditation Board for Engineering and Technology (ABET) annual "Criteria for Accrediting Engineering Programs" for 2022–2023 has two expected outcomes of undergraduate engineering education that deal with privacy and ethics: Criterion 3.2 and Criterion 3.4. It is apparent that ABET considers this issue important enough to mention it twice.[16] In contrast, ASEE does not mention the word "privacy" in its engineering education criteria; however, the "criteria" includes a section on "understanding of professional and ethical responsibility." We can easily see how privacy issues can fall under the heading of ethical responsibility.[17]

Integrating privacy literacy into engineering ethics education is important, as research finds that engineering students differ from non-engineering students with respect to their privacy expectations and how to prioritize them in engineering design. A 2021 Israeli study considered how computing systems violated privacy norms among undergraduates in engineering and non-engineering fields. Ayalon and Toch discovered that students with prior engineering-related work experience were less critical than comparatively inexperienced students in their evaluation of system design with respect to privacy. The authors conclude that privacy norms among engineers and end users differ and that engineers cannot assume that their privacy preferences are representative of those of users. They further posited that *privacy-by-design* methods propose a design and development framework that helped produce privacy-respectful systems.[18]

Including ethics in the education of future engineers is of high interest to educators seeking to position ethical principles and critical thinking about ethical dilemmas in the curriculum. Popa and Popescu's overview of engineering ethics trends revealed that

> students must be taught to evaluate the risks and the implications of developing or using different scientific approaches, technologies or information over peoples' life, economy, and business practices. For instance, the ethical aspects related to conducting experiments, performing tests and using their results, to legal issues on using digital data, safety aspects, intellectual property rights, etc. should all be considered by engineers as technology developers.[19]

As librarians, we can raise students' ethical awareness while educating them about a certain technology and advocating for including privacy considerations in the engineering curriculum.

PRIVACY LITERACY AND INTELLECTUAL PROPERTY

Librarians can use patents, the manifestation of IP, as the key to transforming student research ideas into economically viable technical solutions sought by engineering industries. Engineering students and researchers are often encouraged to capture their ideas as patents and use patent databases to research innovative ideas and to avoid infringement on existing patents. But while students might understand privacy literacy to the extent of protecting their personal information, they may not realize or understand the implications of protecting their IP in higher education.

Patent and IP are a specific set of literacies for which librarians can unveil the complexities for instructors and students learning how to find and use this specialized information. Patent and IP may be considered from three perspectives: the learning outcomes of a course, the level of student literacy in IP, and the unique characteristics of various engineering fields. As an example, Meier describes that in an introductory course, the "learning outcomes likely will focus only on an awareness of different IP types where another course may focus specifically on patents as they are involved in a project or paper." Meier further illustrates that engineering requires unique patent information and that an "engineering design course may be interested in patent drawings alone and the process involved in producing them."[20] Yet, as we consider the intersection of privacy literacy, information literacy, and engineering coursework, the protection of students' IP rights balanced with ethical considerations for users of students' designs should be critically examined. What does it mean for undergraduate engineering students to create unique designs? Are those designs protected? Are there ethical concerns related to external users of students' designs?

If undergraduate students must reveal their original designs as part of their coursework, the United States Patent & Trademark Office (USPTO) patent laws on public disclosure will have a direct impact. Once a student's work has been made public through a class presentation, as one example, their original designs (i.e., their IP) have been made public. Technically speaking, anyone else can then legitimately take the student's design idea and apply for a patent in their own name. While this nuance of public disclosure laws may seem unethical, it is further compounded by the "First Inventor to File Provision." This provision permits anyone present during a public disclosure of a new and novel idea to file for a patent of that idea before the inventor—and it is considered ethical![21]

If a student plans to patent their original designs, they must do so within one year of public disclosure because once disclosure has been made, all ideas are no longer regarded as a "novelty"—a key ingredient needed to file a new patent. Should a student wait more than one year to file a new patent, their design ideas will fall under "prior art," rendering them ineligible for patent protection.[22] Fortunately, there are safeguards that students may take to protect their patentable design ideas and IP. If a student must deliver a presentation about their design ideas, they should include content that describes that the information presented is confidential and should not be shared outside of the classroom. Students may also protect themselves by having classmates sign a non-disclosure agreement. Such documentation should be kept on file with the original research and patent application materials. These measures should satisfy the USPTO provided students file for a new patent within one year of public disclosure. Otherwise, any external user may ethically lay claim to a student's design idea.

In addition to public disclosure and non-disclosure agreements, further studies and surveys illustrate instructional models designed to help students understand practical privacy considerations for future users of their IP. One case study explored the need for effective teaching and learning methods related to IP. To teach engineering students about the privacy implications of their own projects and research, Rowlinson et al. took instruction out of the classroom and described the impact of turning to the NSF/ASEE Innovation Corps for Learning (I-Corps L) program and its associated evidence-based entrepreneurship methodology. This 2019 experience put the students in the mindset of customers, thereby shifting how engineering students learn about design and IP. This was an innovative shift from the technical steps of patent writing and the process needed to protect ideas to protecting the external users of those ideas. The real-world experience of a customer-centered approach allowed students to identify who would use an idea and in what form and promoted translating ideas into innovations.[23]

PRIVACY LITERACY, THE SYLLABI, AND LEARNING EXPERIENCES

Librarians can collaborate with engineering instructors on syllabi design best practices to include student privacy and instructional learning experiences related to privacy. We'll first look at syllabi design. Privacy safeguards are most aptly placed in course syllabi since they are the central documents that outline the instructors' values, discipline measures, course content, and learning outcomes. As an instructional tool, the syllabi outline how to access content and use technologies, and as a policy instrument, syllabi detail academic rules, behavioral expectations, and student rights. Instructors who discuss student privacy in syllabi statements have an opportunity to reflect genuine caring as well as privacy policies. A 2019 study conducted by Jones and Van Scoy investigated how instructors discuss student data and information privacy in these critical documents and how librarians may train both instructors and students in privacy safeguards. The authors stated that the:

> challenges associated with data privacy issues include accurately explaining privacy concepts and ensuring that students have adequate privacy literacy. Facilitating reflection and discussion among instructors about student data privacy in the syllabi may help to alleviate some of these challenges and strengthen the syllabi as useful documents in empowering students to value and protect their own data privacy.[24]

Additionally, instructors may increase student understanding vis-à-vis student privacy by directly addressing ownership of IP in their syllabi.

Institutional policy on IP should be briefly outlined and linked for full access to information in the syllabi of engineering courses where patents and IP are a learning outcome. Moreover, if students are positioned by the nature of the course to create original designs that could be marketed or patented, institutional policy and key resources on IP are needed at the topmost level—the syllabi. While Diaz and Nathans-Kelly assert that "many universities state that they will not make any claims on undergraduate work if it is the normal outcome of a course,"[25] it is not a given that undergraduate students are aware of institutional policy much less the intricacies of federal IP law. By also linking institutional IP offices in the syllabi, students will be a step ahead in knowing where to seek assistance to interpret their rights and to learn which instances, such as receipt of grant funding and using institutional facilities and equipment, will permit institutions to lay claim to the patentable work. Diaz and Nathans-Kelly agree that "Instructors who have students create design ideas…who have students conduct research and present it in a classroom, at a research fair, or hang a poster in a hallway, need to understand how ideas are treated on their campus and how to help students protect their ideas."[26]

Turning to engineering learning experiences, librarians may collaborate with instructors on selecting topics and assignments related to privacy that would be fruitful to students. At the same time, these collaborations can help the librarian determine collection needs. For example, library instruction for the entry-level Engineering Design courses at Penn State Altoona provides tips and tools for basic patent searching to support their cornerstone project, but it also includes a significant component on how the Penn State University Libraries, as an official Patent and Trademark Resource Center (PTRC), may help them in their research. This naturally leads to further discussions on how to find university partners, such as the Penn State Law IP Clinic, that offer assistance and advice on IP rights and other legal matters. In addition to the PTRC librarian at the main University Park location, select librarians at campus locations throughout the commonwealth have received training at the USPTO. These librarians tailor their instruction to the unique learning experiences at their locations while at the same time pointing students to centralized resources and experts at University Park. The librarians are also able to see where core titles should be purchased for their respective locations. While interlibrary loan is a viable option among the twenty-four Penn State library locations, many have robust entrepreneurship programs in addition to engineering design courses. This demand necessitates having core patent and trademark titles at individual locations.

The cornerstone projects previously mentioned are examined with IP in mind to prevent the inadvertent disclosure of ideas. These projects seek to explore groundbreaking outcomes, such as designing a model train system using rapid prototyping or designing alternative-powered solutions that enable zero emissions on the railroad network. With these projects, students may be asked to sign a non-disclosure agreement. But prior to implementing these cornerstone project models, a typical course assignment had students create a design idea and describe their idea in a business letter mailed to a company. On some occasions, a company engineer would ethically respond with comments and usually state that they were not allowed to accept ideas from outside sources. There were at least two inherent issues with this assignment:

1. There was an apparent lack of awareness on the part of the instructor to adequately inform students of public disclosure and their IP rights. A better approach would have been to have students write but not submit their business letters to a bona fide company. A peer review of classmates' business letters would have cemented the desired outcomes without triggering the public disclosure clock.
2. The submitted business letters were public disclosure of design ideas. Even if a company ethically could not and did not accept and use ideas from outside sources, the ideas were nonetheless made public and the clock for filing a patent began ticking. In this case, students were not thinking about their IP. They were not trained to understand the value of protecting their ideas and how those ideas can be sold or traded. They did not know how to implement a non-disclosure agreement or understand the legality of the document.

With that said, it can be argued that a general education course in engineering design could be implemented to provide foundational information on IP. At Penn State University, the general education model is structured to help students "acquire skills, knowledge, and experiences for living in interconnected contexts; making life better for themselves, others, and the larger world."[27] A general education course structured around IP would enable undergraduate students to be better prepared in the current iteration of engineering design courses to confidently create robust projects while protecting their ideas. It would also allow the librarian to shift instruction to more advanced research applications, knowing that the foundational studies on IP have been completed.

In the meantime, instructors must be on the alert to help students protect their ideas. Librarians may lay the groundwork with instructors on what institutional resources are available. They can assist in pointing instructors to the right units and key individuals that work with IP routinely and are available by appointment to evaluate ideas and offer direction. Diaz and Nathans-Kelley suggest that instructors should attend meetings with their students to learn as much as possible and to be able to "discern the difference in a good business idea that can't be protected, an idea that needs patent protection, and an idea that might fall under trade secret." They also suggest developing an action plan to "establish parameters about how to handle the idea for the rest of the semester."[28] These are excellent measures to safeguard the IP of students new to the complex intersection of privacy and engineering.

POTENTIAL MODELS FOR ENGINEERING PRIVACY LITERACY INSTRUCTION

ASEE does not have specific guidelines for incorporating privacy literacy into the engineering curriculum, but the organization has given three specific tasks for engineering educators to accomplish:

- Make students aware of the problem and how to recognize it.
- Help students understand that their projects affect people in both good and bad ways and that they need to understand and anticipate all effects.
- Show students that they are responsible for developing solutions to ethical problems as they arise.

The two methods mentioned to integrate the topic into the curriculum are either by a full semester course or adding privacy and ethics into preexisting courses (via "one-shot" instruction or built into long-term projects).[29]

Using the example of biometrics, Chinchilla has created two different instructional models based on the ASEE guidance. Biometrics is an excellent example to use because of the different privacy issues that can arise from misuse, including possible theft of information and the use of facial recognition to surveil people. The information is taught either through a one-shot lecture seminar with students writing a "field report" afterward on specific uses of biometrics around campus or via a special section on "Biometric Ethics" in preexisting engineering ethics courses. In the second method, the emphasis is placed on learning from case studies.[30] Librarians can assist these types of sessions by ensuring easy access to a collection of several case studies and even coming in as a guest instructor for the ethics course.

Cote and Branzan Albu initiated a privacy session in a senior-year electrical and computer engineering course. Students had an in-class discussion on facial recognition technologies and how they affect privacy. They then were given an essay assignment investigating the socio-cultural implications of a new technology of their choice. The essays touched on a wide variety of topics; however, privacy/

anonymity was the third most popular (twenty-two essays in a three-year period). Students were able to use reflective thinking skills about technologies that they were interested in. The activity allowed them to learn more about the impact on society of that technology along with its technical aspects. The authors plan on integrating this activity into several capstone courses for other engineering disciplines.[31] Librarians can easily provide support for the essay assignment by helping students with the research process through research consultations or course-integrated research instruction.

More recently, Drev and Delak have proposed a different standard for engineering privacy literacy which they call "the conceptual model of privacy by design." This model has three sets, which must be followed in the proper order:

- Legal elements. The purpose of data processing must be clearly defined in advance and data must be collected in a lawful manner. People need to be informed beforehand as to how their data will be used.
- Security features. Confidentiality, integrity, and availability of the data must be constantly maintained. Records must be kept tracking who processed what data when. (ISO/IEC 27001)
- Data protection by design and default. Systems should be designed and constructed in a way to avoid or minimize the amount of data processed. It is easier to include privacy controls at the beginning of a project rather than attach them as an afterthought at the end.

The model is general enough to be implemented in a variety of ways while still being specific enough for instructors to understand its implementation.[32] Engineering librarians can deliver research instruction and consultation as well as provide access to relevant engineering standards and legal frameworks.

Another model, this time based on overall data literacy, comes from Germany and is designed to help undergraduate engineering students understand the responsibilities they have in creating products and solutions that comply with the European Union's General Data Protection Regulation. Like the privacy-by-design model, there are three components that make up data literacy: statistics, programming, and transparency/awareness. Instead of trying to combine all that information into one class, the authors scaffolded the three topics across the entire undergraduate engineering curriculum.[33] Since both statistics and programming were well covered in the existing courses, the focus of their model was on the final component—transparency and awareness. They broke the topic into three "pillars": legal, technical, and ethical.[34] In this model, engineering librarians can provide case studies of real-world examples along with research instruction and consultation to support student projects.

The previous examples are just some of the methods that librarians and other instructors have used to help their engineering students understand the importance of remembering consumer privacy when designing products and solutions to engineering problems.

CONCLUSION

It is easy to see that privacy literacy is an essential component of a healthy life by protecting an individual's social and economic privacy. Privacy literacy, despite its importance, is in its infancy. Engineering students will play a major role in creating future technologies that can either protect or expose the private data of consumers. As librarians are often the leaders in protecting our patrons, it is the authors' hope that this chapter will spur reactions to greater awareness of the need to model and teach privacy literacy in engineering students' personal and professional lives.

ACKNOWLEDGMENTS

The authors wish to gratefully acknowledge Beth Thomsett-Scott, former head of the Engineering Library at Penn State University, for contributing her expertise in the development of this chapter.

NOTES

1. Shayna Stanton and Michael Bailey, "Whose Job Is It? Technological Literacy in Society," American Society for Engineering Education Annual Conference and Exhibition (paper # AC 2007-1316, Honolulu, Hawaii, 2007).
2. Dale R. Thompson, Jia Di, and Michael K. Daugherty, "Teaching RFID Information Systems Security," *IEEE Transactions on Education* 57, no. 1 (February 2014): 42–47.
3. Attari Nabil, Khalid Nafil, and Fouad Mounir, "Blockchain Security and Privacy in Education: A Systematic Mapping Study," in *Trends and Innovations in Information Systems and Technologies* (Geneva: Springer, 2020), 253–62.
4. Melissa Cote and Alexandra Branzan Albu, "Teaching Computer Vision and Its Societal Effects: A Look at Privacy and Security Issues from the Students' Perspective," *IEEE Computer Society Conference on Computer Vision and Pattern Recognition Workshops* (2017): 1385.
5. Carlos Lopes, Maria da Luz Antunes, and Tatiana Sanches, "Information Literacy and Open Science: Before and After the New ACRL Framework," in *Communications in Computer and Information Science* 989 (February 20, 2019): 247–52.
6. Aditya Johri et.al., "Perceptions and Practices of Data Sharing in Engineering Education," *Advances in Engineering Education* 5, no. 2 (2016): 8.
7. Johri et al., "Perceptions and Practices," 10–13.
8. Robin S. Adams, David Radcliffe, and Michael Fosmire, "Designing for Global Data Sharing, Designing for Educational Transformation," *Advances in Engineering Education* 5, no. 2 (2016): 6, 11.
9. Asimina Vasalou et al., "Understanding Engagement with The Privacy Domain Through Design Research," *Journal of the Association for Information Science and Technology* 66, no. 6 (2015): 1263–73.

10. Tore Hoel and Weiqin Chen, "Privacy Engineering for Learning Analytics in a Global Market – Defining a Point of Reference," *International Journal of Information and Learning Technology* 36, no. 4 (2019): 288–98.
11. Clare Naden, "Tacking Privacy Information Management Head On: First International Standard Just Published," ISO, last modified August 6, 2019, https://www.iso.org/news/ref2419.html.
12. Sarah Hartman-Caverly and Alexandria Chisholm, "Privacy Literacy Instruction Practices in Academic Libraries: Past, Present, and Possibilities," *International Federation of Library Associations and Institutions* 46, no. 4 (2020): 313.
13. Hartman-Caverly and Chisholm, "Privacy Literacy Instruction Practices," 315.
14. Thilo Hagendorff, "Privacy Literacy and Its Problems," *Journal of Information Ethics* 27, no. 2 (2018): 127–45.
15. *Framework for Information Literacy for Higher Education*, Association of College & Research Libraries, accessed April 8, 2021, https://www.ala.org/acrl/standards/ilframework.
16. "Criteria for Accrediting Engineering Programs, 2022 – 2023," ABET, accessed July 15, 2022, https://www.abet.org/accreditation/accreditation-criteria/criteria-for-accrediting-engineering-programs-2022-2023/.
17. "Ethics in Engineering Education," American Society for Engineering Education, accessed July 15, 2022, https://www.asee.org/about-us/who-we-are/our-vision-mission-and-goals/statements/ethics-in-engineering-education.
18. Oshrat Ayalon and Eran Toch, "User-Centered Privacy-by-Design: Evaluating the Appropriateness of Design Prototypes," *International Journal of Human-Computer Studies* (2021): 102641.
19. Diana Mariana Popa and Diana Popescu, "An Overview of Past and Current Engineering Ethics Research Trends," *Research and Science Today* (2019): 102–11.
20. John Meier, "Intellectual Property: Patents," in *The Busy Librarian's Guide to Information Literacy in Science and Engineering*, ed. Katherine O'Clair and Jeanne R. Davison (Chicago: ALA, 2012), 99.
21. "Examination Guidelines for Implementing the First Inventor to File Provisions of the Leahy-Smith America Invents Act," United States Patent and Trademark Office, Department of Commerce, Federal Register, last modified February 14, 2013, https://www.federalregister.gov/documents/2013/02/14/2013-03450/examination-guidelines-for-implementing-the-first-inventor-to-file-provisions-of-the-leahy-smith.
22. "Appendix L - Patent Laws," United States Patent and Trademark Office, USPTO.GOV, last modified June 25, 2020, https://www.uspto.gov/web/offices/pac/mpep/mpep-9015-appx-l.html.
23. Sarah C. Rowlinson et al., "Enhancing the Academic Innovation Culture by Incorporation of Customer-Centric Practices," *Technology and Innovation* 21, no. 1 (2019): 63–74.
24. Kyle M. L. Jones and Amy Van Scoy, "The Syllabus as a Student Privacy Document in an Age of Learning Analytics," *Journal of Documentation* 75, no. 6 (2019): 1333–55.
25. Charlsye S. Diaz and Traci M. Nathans-Kelly, "Whose Idea Is It Anyway? Students Communicating Innovative and Entrepreneurial Work and the Quagmire of Ownership at the University Level," *2016 IEEE International Professional Communication Conference (IPCC)*, (2016): 1.
26. Diaz and Nathans-Kelly, "Whose Idea Is It Anyway?," 4.
27. "Office for General Education," Penn State Undergraduate Education, https://gened.psu.edu/.
28. Diaz and Nathans-Kelly, "Whose Idea is it Anyway?," 6–7.
29. "Ethics in Engineering Education," ASEE.
30. Rigoberto Chinchilla, "Ethical and Social Consequences of Biometric Technologies in the US: Implementation in Engineering Curriculum," *American Society for Engineering Education Annual Conference and Exhibition* (paper # AC 2012-3498, San Antonio, TX, 2012).
31. Melissa Cote and Alexandra Branzan Albu, "Teaching Socio-Cultural Impacts of Technology in Advanced Technical Courses: A Case Study," *European Journal of Engineering Education* 44, no. 5 (November 2018): 688–701.

32. Matjaz Drev and Bostjan Delak, "Conceptual Model of Privacy by Design," *Journal of Computer Information Systems* (July 2021): 1–8.
33. Tim G. Giese, Martin Wende, Serdar Bulut, and Reiner Anderl, "Introduction of Data Literacy in the Undergraduate Engineering Curriculum," *IEEE Global Engineering Education Conference (EDUCON)*, 1237–45, Porto, Portugal, 2020.
34. Giese, Wende, Bulut, and Anderl, "Introduction of Data Literacy."

BIBLIOGRAPHY

ABET. "Criteria for Accrediting Engineering Programs, 2022–2023." Accessed on July 15, 2022. https://www.abet.org/accreditation/accreditation-criteria/criteria-for-accrediting-engineering-programs-2022-2023/.

Adams, Robin S., David Radcliffe, and Michael Fosmire. "Designing for Global Data Sharing, Designing for Educational Transformation." *Advances in Engineering Education* 5, no. 2 (2016): 1–24. http://advances.asee.org/wp-content/uploads/vol05/issue02/Papers/AEE-18-Adams.pdf.

American Society for Engineering Education. "Ethics in Engineering Education." Last modified January 31, 1999. https://www.asee.org/about-us/who-we-are/our-vision-mission-and-goals/statements/ethics-in-engineering-education.

Association of College & Research Libraries. *Framework for Information Literacy for Higher Education*. Accessed April 8, 2021. https://www.ala.org/acrl/standards/ilframework.

Ayalon, Oshrat, and Eran Toch. "User-Centered Privacy-by-Design: Evaluating the Appropriateness of Design Prototypes." *International Journal of Human-Computer Studies* (2021). https://doi.org/10.1016/j.ijhcs.2021.102641.

Chinchilla, Rigoberto. "Ethical and Social Consequences of Biometric Technologies in the US: Implementation in Engineering Curriculum." *American Society for Engineering Education Annual Conference and Exhibition*. Paper # AC 2012-3498, San Antonio, TX, 2012. https://peer.asee.org/21340.

Cote, Melissa, and Alexandra Branzan Albu. "Teaching Socio-Cultural Impacts of Technology in Advanced Technical Courses: A Case Study." *European Journal of Engineering Education* 44, no. 5 (November 2018): 688–701. https://doi.org/10.1080/03043797.2018.1551329.

———. "Teaching Computer Vision and Its Societal Effects: A Look at Privacy and Security Issues from the Students' Perspective." *IEEE Computer Society Conference on Computer Vision and Pattern Recognition Workshops* (2017): 1378–86. http://dx.doi.org/10.1109/CVPRW.2017.180.

Diaz, Charlsye S., and Traci M. Nathans-Kelly. "Whose Idea is it Anyway? Students Communicating Innovative and Entrepreneurial Work and the Quagmire of Ownership at the University Level." *IEEE International Professional Communication Conference (IPCC)*, Austin, TX, USA, 2016: 1–8. https://doi.org/10.1109/IPCC.2016.7740537.

Drev, Matjaz, and Bostjan Delak. "Conceptual Model of Privacy by Design." *Journal of Computer Information Systems* (July 2021): 1–8. https://doi.org/10.1080/08874417.2021.1939197.

Fitzgerald, Rachel, and Hayley Henderson-Martin. "Transforming the First Year Experience (HE) With Digital Literacy via Techno-Social Engagement and Evaluation." *European Conference on e-Learning* (2015): 199–205.

Giese, Tim G., Martin Wende, Serdar Bulut, and Reiner Anderl. "Introduction of Data Literacy in the Undergraduate Engineering Curriculum." *IEEE Global Engineering Education Conference (EDUCON)*. Porto, Portugal, 2020: 1237–45. https://doi.org/10.1109/EDUCON45650.2020.9125212.

Hagendorff, Thilo. "Privacy Literacy and Its Problems." *Journal of Information Ethics* 27, no. 2 (2018): 127–45.

Hartman-Caverly, Sarah, and Alexandria Chisholm. "Privacy Literacy Instruction Practices in Academic Libraries: Past, Present, and Possibilities." *International Federation of Library Associations and Institutions* 46, no. 4 (2020): 305–27. http://dx.doi.org/10.1177/0340035220956804.

Hoel, Tore, and Weiqin Chen. "Privacy Engineering for Learning Analytics in a Global Market – Defining a Point of Reference." *International Journal of Information and Learning Technology* 36, no. 4 (2019): 288–98. https://dx.doi.org/10.1108/IJILT-02-2019-0025.

Johri, Aditya, Seungwon Yang, Mihaela Vorvoreanu, and Krishna Madhavan. "Perceptions and Practices of Data Sharing in Engineering Education." *Advances in Engineering Education* 5, no. 2 (2016): 1–25. http://dx.doi.org/10.1371/journal.pone.0021101.s001.

Jones, Kyle M. L., and Amy Van Scoy. "The Syllabus as a Student Privacy Document in an Age of Learning Analytics." *Journal of Documentation* 75, no. 6 (2019): 1333–55. http://dx.doi.org/10.1108/JD-12-2018-0202.

Lopes, Carlos, Maria da Luz Antunes, and Tatiana Sanches. "Information Literacy and Open Science: Before and After the New ACRL Framework." In *Communications in Computer and Information Science* 989 (February 20, 2019): 244–53. Geneva: Springer, 2019. https://dx.doi.org/10.1007/978-3-030-13472-3_23.

Meier, John. "Intellectual Property: Patents." In *The Busy Librarian's Guide to Information Literacy in Science and Engineering*, edited by Katherine O'Clair and Jeanne R. Davison. Chicago: ALA, 2012.

Nabil, Attari, Khalid Nafil, and Fouad Mounir. "Blockchain Security and Privacy in Education: A Systematic Mapping Study." In *Trends and Innovations in Information Systems and Technologies* 3, 253–62. Geneva: Springer, 2020. https://dx.doi.org/10.1007/978-3-030-45697-9_25.

Naden, Claire. "Tacking Privacy Information Management Head On: First International Standard Just Published." ISO. Last modified August 6, 2019. https://www.iso.org/news/ref2419.html.

Pennsylvania State University Undergraduate Education, The. "Office for General Education." Penn State. https://gened.psu.edu/.

Popa, Diana Mariana, and Diana Popescu. "An Overview of Past and Current Engineering Ethics Research Trends." *Research and Science Today Supplement* 1 (2019): 102–111.

Rege, Aunshul, Alyssa Mendlein, and Katorah Williams. "Security and Privacy Education for STEM Undergraduates: A Shoulder Surfing Course Project." *IEEE Frontiers in Education Conference*. Cincinnati, OH, 2019. https://doi.org/10.1109/FIE43999.2019.9028560.

Robertshaw, M. Brooke, and Andrew Asher. "Unethical Numbers? A Meta-Analysis of Library Learning Analytics Studies." *Library Trends* 68, no. 1 (2019): 76–101.

Rowlinson, Sarah C., Timothy C. Burg, William C. Bridges Jr., and Karen J. L. Burg. "Enhancing the Academic Innovation Culture by Incorporation of Customer-Centric Practices." *Technology and Innovation* 21 (2019): 63–74. http://dx.doi.org/10.21300/21.1.2019.63.

Stanton, Shayna, and Michael Bailey. "Whose Job Is It? Technological Literacy in Society." *American Society for Engineering Education Annual Conference and Exhibition*. Paper # AC 2007-1316, Honolulu, HI, 2007. https://peer.asee.org/2217.

Thompson, Dale R., Jia Di, and Michael K. Daugherty. "Teaching RFID Information Systems Security." *IEEE Transactions on Education* 57, no. 1 (February 2014): 42–47. https://doi.org/10.1109/TE.2013.2264289.

United States Patent and Trademark Office. "Appendix L - Patent Laws." USPTO.GOV. Last modified June 25, 2020. https://www.uspto.gov/web/offices/pac/mpep/mpep-9015-appx-l.html.

———. "Examination Guidelines for Implementing the First Inventor to File Provisions of the Leahy-Smith America Invents Act." Federal Register. Last modified February 14, 2013. https://www.federalregister.gov/documents/2013/02/14/2013-03450/examination-guidelines-for-implementing-the-first-inventor-to-file-provisions-of-the-leahy-smith.

Vasalou, Asimina, Anne-Marie Oostveen, Chris Bowers, and Russell Beale. "Understanding Engagement with The Privacy Domain Through Design Research." *Journal of the Association for Information Science and Technology* 66, no. 6 (2015): 1263–73.

CHAPTER 11

TEACHING PRIVACY USING LEARNER-CENTERED PRACTICES IN A CREDIT-BEARING CONTEXT

Scott W. H. Young and Sara Mannheimer

INTRODUCTION

This chapter describes practices of teaching privacy to undergraduate students in a credit-bearing context. The chapter features a discussion of a semester-long course, Information Ethics and Privacy in the Age of Big Data. This chapter opens by briefly outlining three points of consideration for approaching a semester-long course. We then highlight three assignments from the course that we think are particularly useful and adaptable for teaching privacy. We include excerpts from course materials and student feedback to illustrate specific points. The chapter concludes with a self-reflective assessment of our experience as teachers.

We co-taught the course with a pedagogical viewpoint of learner-centered participation and trust, an approach that we have previously discussed in detail.[1]

The course was built around reflective and co-creative activities that make space for students to bring their own experiences and perspectives into the classroom, including self-evaluation, student-led discussion sessions, small-group discussions, creative activities, and hands-on projects.

We intend for the assignments and topics of this chapter to be used beyond a credit-bearing context. Librarians teach in so many different contexts. With that in mind, we offer points of consideration for adapting our assignments for other settings, like workshops, one-shot instruction, or a sequence of course-embedded instruction to be completed over two or three class sessions.

APPROACHES

This chapter is focused on the practical aspects of teaching privacy. As such, this literature review is not presented as a scholarly analysis but rather as a set of practical considerations for approaching an instructional project, particularly from a credit-bearing perspective. We focus on presenting and discussing select resources that we found useful in designing and delivering our course. We focused on three main areas: librarian/teacher identity, learner-centered pedagogies, and assessment.

Librarians as Teachers

First, we confronted questions related to librarians assuming the role of teacher in a credit-bearing context. The professional duties of an academic librarian don't typically involve such teaching, yet the main teaching function on a university campus is credit-bearing instruction. The topic of librarians-as-teachers has been a part of our professional conversation for many years. Douglas, for instance, writing in 1999 about the many benefits of teaching semester-long courses, encourages librarians to move more toward the role of "librarian professor."[2] Loesch amplifies this message of the librarian as professor, writing of "innovative opportunities to teach beyond library instruction or information literacy."[3] Such opportunities to teach in credit-bearing contexts exist as an expansion of or complement to traditional library instruction and should be approached with a consideration of any attendant challenges. One important challenge is that of professional identity and professional practice. In a study of librarian identity and teaching, Walter states, "Few professions are as sensitive to issues of professional identity and public perception as that of librarianship."[4] Walter addresses a few key issues that complicate the identity of teacher-librarian: the importance of administrative support, stress of multiple job duties, professional education that doesn't include pedagogy, and misconceptions based on stereotype. Despite these challenges, Walter ultimately sees the rise of the teacher-librarian to be a welcome response to broader efforts to expand instruction on college campuses—that is, more academic professionals of all stripes across campus are now engaging in credit-bearing instruction, librarians included. Importantly, Walter rejects the idea that librarians-as-teachers represent a grasping for higher status, as our professional literature has previously claimed.[5] Pagowsky and DeFrain similarly discuss the librarian turn from service provider to educator, remarking in particular on stereotype and self-identity as leading issues.[6] As Drabinski helps us understand, taking the time to engage with these questions of professional practice and identity is professional practice itself.[7] We decided to take on the task of teaching this credit-bearing course as a pilot project, in a sense, as a way to discover for ourselves how teaching in this setting would change or advance our own professional practice.

Learner-centered Pedagogies

Next, we wanted to understand together as a teaching cohort how we would approach our classroom environment. We each had prior experience conducting privacy-oriented projects from a user-centered perspective.[8] We wanted to further the values of user-centeredness in the classroom, and this took the form of a student-centered, or learner-driven, pedagogy. In the context of our course, we applied learner-driven pedagogy through the assignments and the assessments. To accomplish this, we offered semi-structured directions for students in completing their assignments, but we left the completion of the work open-ended so that the students could bring their own viewpoints and values into the assignment.[9] Such an approach can lead to more engaged learning, greater trust among teachers and students, and a more empowering student experience.

Assessment

Finally, we needed to address grading. All courses must include a final letter grade, and faculty have discretion as to the means of arriving at the final grade. In keeping with our learner-centered pedagogical approach, we implemented a contract grading system.[10] This approach makes clear the expectations for achieving certain grades and helps students chart their own way through the course.[11] To determine the final grade for the course, we asked students to complete a reflective self-evaluation.[12] We provided reflective prompts for the students, who then provide a narrative that includes a letter grade with justification. This approach critically addresses the power that teachers hold over students in unilaterally determining grades. In approaching grading in this way, we were inspired by movements in education to critically address traditional grade paradigms, such as ungrading, minimal grading, and compassionate grading.[13] In our experience, the grade that a student self-assigns is nearly always the grade that we ourselves would have assigned. In the few instances in which the grades are misaligned, it is the student who typically grades themselves more harshly than we would have. In these cases, we take the opportunity to boost the student up by reminding them of their performance in the course and the learning that was accomplished. This process fosters self-reflection, trust, and communication.

Student-centered self-evaluation is particularly apt for teaching about privacy, as the topic of privacy involves issues of trust and communication, especially involving information related to the self. In the self-evaluations—given at the midpoint and end of the semester— students are asked to consider how their thinking and practices related to technology use and privacy have changed over the course of the semester, what new skills or concepts particularly resonated with them, and to self-grade their participation and contributions. In providing our own feedback to the students, we offer dialogue-oriented narrative feedback that approaches students as learners empowered in their own grading and assessment. This models a vision of technology and privacy whereby users or citizens are empowered in their own use of technology and personal data.

COURSE OVERVIEW

This chapter focuses on a four-credit, upper-division seminar that was taught in the spring term of 2018, entitled Information Ethics and Privacy in the Age of Big Data. Course enrollment included eleven undergraduate juniors and seniors from the Honors College at Montana State University. The course was taught by the authors of this chapter. We are each faculty librarians at Montana State University. The syllabus is available online.[14]

The learning outcomes for the course included the following:
- Evaluate networked technologies, including algorithms, artificial intelligence, the web, and social media.
- Apply and critique strategies for personal privacy protection.
- Critically analyze and evaluate the contribution of networked technologies to societal structures of control, power, and oppression, especially for marginalized communities.
- Develop practical responses to ethical challenges relating to information and data from discrete disciplinary perspectives.

In the sections below, we describe three learner-centered assignments that support the learning outcomes above. Each section below is organized into three subsections: key points, description, and assessment.

COURSE ASSIGNMENTS

In the credit-bearing instructional context in which we were the primary instructors, we were in a position to design and deliver several learner-driven assignments that focused on privacy in both theory and practice. In this section, we describe three assignments: a diary study, value-sensitive design discussion, and a privacy awareness campaign. These three assignments can be remixed and reused in different contexts, including credit-bearing courses, but also other instructional environments such as workshops and traditional library instruction sessions.

Diary Study

Key points

Learning outcome

- Evaluate networked technologies, including algorithms, artificial intelligence, the web, and social media.

When to use

- Semester-long credited course instruction: It worked well for us to assign this project near the beginning of the semester to support the foundational ideas of the course.

- Course-embedded instruction. This assignment may work best if the librarian has the benefit of working with students over two sessions. The librarian can assign the diary in the first session and then discuss results in the second session.

- Virtual instruction. This assignment could be adapted for a virtual environment. Asynchronously, students could read and respond to each other's diary studies. Synchronously, students could meet in small virtual breakout rooms to discuss diary studies.

How to assess

- Students create a group report describing patterns and identifying key takeaways.

Description

A "diary study" is a research method in which participants create "logs (diaries) of daily activities as they occur [to] give contextual insights about real-time user behaviors and needs."[15] We adapted the diary study method as a way to record, demonstrate, and discuss daily technology usage among the students. For this assignment, students recorded daily logs that highlighted their own personal position within today's networked technologies. This assignment aimed to support students in data-driven inquiry into how technology affects everyday life. Appendix A contains the full assignment for the diary study.

We provided students with a structured "diary" in which they recorded their daily activities relating to browsing the web, interacting on social media, and using apps on mobile devices. The diary took the form of a simple spreadsheet. We provided a set of typical technologies across different categories and asked the students to mark days in which a given technology was used. For example, we offered the following options for web browsers: Chrome, Firefox, Firefox Focus, Safari, and Edge. Students then marked their daily usage of each browser.

After students submitted their diaries, we aggregated the data and created some visualizations to prompt discussion in class. For example, figure 11.1 shows the aggregate results for web browsers.

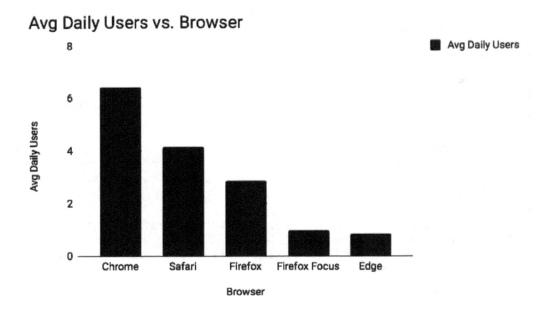

FIGURE 11.1
Average daily users of each web browser.

We can see from this chart that Chrome and Safari are the top two browsers in terms of daily usage. We used this data to discuss the different privacy settings and capabilities of each browser and the cost-benefit of each browser in terms of service and privacy. Students were able to offer their own perspectives as to why they choose one browser over another, or, in other cases, why they didn't really consider the choice. From this discussion, students became more informed and capable about their technology choices.

Students also recorded their emotional response to technology usage, using the Self-Assessment Manikin (SAM) framework, "a non-verbal pictorial assessment technique that directly measures the pleasure, arousal, and dominance associated with a person's affective reaction to a wide variety of stimuli."[16] The SAM scale, illustrated in figure 11.2, helps students assess their levels of "pleasantness" (top row), "frustration" (middle row), and "control" (bottom row).

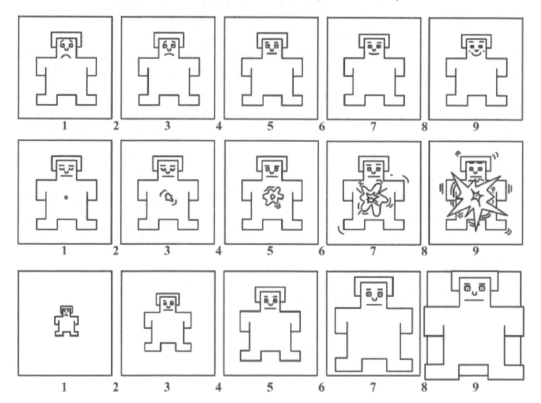

FIGURE 11.2
Self-Assessment Manikin.

This assignment happened relatively early in the semester, so many students reported that they didn't feel especially concerned about online tracking or privacy.

The emotional response patterns that students identified were that of pleasantness as it related to control—that is, when technology works as it should, they felt pleasantness and in control. When technology malfunctioned, their frustration rose. This assignment was an opportunity to set the stage for the remainder of the semester, as it established a baseline of technology usage, privacy thinking, and emotional response. When sharing the reports, we as librarians were able to highlight how pervasive technology and social media are in students' lives and how the features and functions of these technologies can affect their well-being.

The diary study is particularly adaptable for course-embedded instruction. If a librarian has the benefit of working with students over two or three sessions, the librarian could assign the diary in the first session and then discuss results in the second session.

Assessment: How to Know That the Assignment Was Successful

We wanted this assignment to help students evaluate different technologies through a privacy lens. After completing the weeklong diary process, students were divided into groups of two or three to analyze their collective diaries and their diary reports, with a view toward detecting patterns and connections. In the reports, students discussed the similarities and differences between each of their experiences, including the technology they used, their emotional response, privacy considerations, and any patterns they identified.

These group reports were the main assessment strategy for the diary study assignment. Students submitted these reports alongside their diaries and diary reports, and these reports showed how the students had synthesized the information.

Value-sensitive Design Discussion

Key points

Learning outcome

- Critically analyze and evaluate the contribution of networked technologies to societal structures of control, power, and oppression, especially for marginalized communities.

When to use

- Semester-long credited course instruction. This activity is well-suited as a structured, small-group discussion occurring within a single class session.

- Course-embedded instruction. This assignment could be developed in collaboration with another faculty member, with the assignment completed by students during a single library instruction session.
- Virtual instruction. Breakout rooms would be well-suited as a way to organize students into small-group discussions.

How to assess

- During the class session, student observation and conversation can reveal engagement with the topic. Later in the semester, specific questions in self-evaluations can prompt students to think back and reflect on how this assignment has integrated into their overall learning.

Description

For this assignment, students worked in small groups to think ethically about the uses and possibilities of different technologies in their areas of study. We used the Envisioning Cards, a values-based design tool created by researchers at the University of Washington School of Information.[17] Privacy can sometimes be a dense and abstract topic to explore. Tools like the Envisioning Cards help focus the conversation around one technology and one ethical point of consideration.

We introduced an activity using the Envisioning Cards as a way to prompt students' critical thinking around the potential consequences of a technology. This activity occurred toward the end of the first half of the course, while we were still building an understanding of technology ethics and society. The designers of the Envisioning Cards suggest the following use with students: "Have your students select a few Envisioning Cards to help guide them during a design project." Each Envisioning Card features a future-oriented consideration, such as "Crossing National Boundaries." For example, to complete this suggested activity, students consider a new technology that they might be designing, and then they imagine that the technology would cross national boundaries. Reflective prompts printed on each card help the students think through potential outcomes, as with the card dealing with national boundaries: "Nations have different rules, customs, and infrastructure that affect the use of a technology. What challenges will be encountered by your system if it is used in other countries?" Another Envisioning Card features the consideration of "Non-targeted Use," with the following reflective prompt: "Technologies are not always used in ways that the designers intended. Who might use the system for unplanned or nefarious purposes (e.g., frustrated stakeholders or an identity thief)? In what ways?" The Envisioning Cards contain thirty-two different considerations, including Diverse Geographies, Widespread Use, and Variation of Human Ability.

For our particular application of this ethical design tool, the students in our class showed an interest in image-based artificial intelligence (AI), so we built this assignment around that interest. We asked students to imagine a new "Image recognition AI system." Students were grouped into groups of three, and we randomly distributed cards to each group. We spent thirty minutes in this small-group discussion activity, where students cycled through the cards and discussed this new technology in light of each ethical consideration. As instructors, we moved from group to group to observe the conversation and add our own thoughts when appropriate. Following the small-group activity, we re-convened together as a full class to share and discuss our insights.

This Envisioning Card activity can be replicated in a full-semester course, and it's also especially suited to workshops and library instruction sessions focusing on privacy. The cards can be quickly understood and deployed to generate dialogue among students and faculty, and they are designed specifically to prompt values-based, ethical discussion around technology. In this context, privacy can be centerstage in the conversation. In a stand-alone workshop setting, for example, attendees can nominate an everyday technology to examine with the Envisioning Cards, such as Twitter and other social networking services, Face ID and other biometrics, or always-on location services that are active on many mobile phones. The Envisioning Cards can then structure a discussion of the potential uses and misuses of these technologies, which can then give rise to further discussions about how these technologies can be redesigned with ethics and privacy more in mind for the ultimate benefit of the real people who use the technologies.

Assessment: How to Know That the Assignment Was Successful

This assignment can be assessed both during the class session and later in the semester. As a formative assessment, the in-class assessment can take the shape of observations and conversations with students in their small groups. Interacting directly with the student discussions can reveal their engagement with the topic, including their personal insights and connections as well as any sticking points or questions that arise. In terms of an overall summative assessment, our course applied self-evaluation as a means of connecting all the dots of our class. If you are able to design and apply your own self-evaluation for the students, the self-evaluation questions can include prompts related to this assignment specifically to integrate the work of this assignment into the overall learning reflections of the students.

Privacy Awareness Campaign

Key points

Learning outcome

- Apply and critique strategies for personal privacy protection.

When to use

- Semester-long credited course instruction. For our course, this assignment was used as a closing assignment for the privacy unit. The assignment supports students' communicating the knowledge they had gained during the unit.

- Course-embedded instruction. This assignment may work best if the librarian has the benefit of working with students over two sessions. The librarian can assign the infographic in the first session and then guide the infographic presentations and peer review in the second session.

- Virtual instruction. For virtual instruction, the librarian could choose to keep the group aspect of this assignment or adapt the assignment so that each student creates their own infographic. Peer review could be completed asynchronously through written comments or synchronously via virtual breakout rooms or chat rooms.

How to assess

- We used peer review to assess this project. Students took notes during peer review sessions and then revised their infographics in response to the peer review.

Description

For this assignment, we asked students to design a privacy awareness campaign, with the goal of communicating about information privacy through an engaging and accessible campaign, in the form of an infographic. Students were paired into groups of two, and each pair was asked to provide an answer to the question, "How do you get your friends to care about privacy?" This assignment aimed to prompt students to apply and critique strategies for personal privacy protection and to communicate ideas using data visualization and infographics to build compelling, evidence-driven arguments. In class, we provided examples of relevant infographics and discussed what makes a compelling infographic—design, sources, and data visualization. Students had fun with this assignment and took it in many different directions. Some pairs focused on online tracking, others focused on specific social media platforms or technologies.

Appendix B contains the full assignment for the privacy awareness campaign.

Assessment: How to Know That the Assignment Was Successful

Once the infographics were finished, each pair of students presented their infographic in small groups (groups of four to six students, comprising two or three pairs). By presenting in pairs to a small group, we tried to ease the pressure on the students, while supporting peer feedback and sharing.

As preparatory reading, we provided students with resources on thoughtful peer review, and we asked students to respond with questions and comments after each infographic presentation. We suggested some prompts, such as:
- Is the information identified important and compelling?
- Is the infographic convincing? Does it provide information about the topic while piquing your interest to learn more?
- Does the infographic speak clearly to its intended audience (your friends and families)?
- Do the visual elements clearly and concisely communicate key concepts, essential information, and compelling knowledge?
- Are the sources credible and clearly cited?

Students took notes during their peer review sessions, and then each pair of students revised their infographic in response to the peer feedback.

INSTRUCTOR REFLECTIONS

We would like to close with a self-reflective assessment that looks back on our experience as teachers. We apply a version of self-reflective assessment previously discussed, involving dialogue and shared perspectives, with a view toward understanding and improving our experience as teachers.[18] We focused our reflection on three thematic areas: the rewards of teaching, the relationship between credit-bearing teaching and library work, and student experiences. We offer these reflections as points of reference in planning credit-bearing courses or implementing privacy-focused assignments.

Rewards of Teaching

Academic librarianship affords the opportunity to develop meaningful pedagogical relationships with students. By teaching a semester-long course, we felt the reward of this opportunity. Our students brought a curiosity and creativity to the course topics, and we felt energized to work directly with students over a sustained period. In addition to the in-class experience and connection with students, we also found curriculum development to be a rewarding challenge. We taught a new course of our own design, involving learning outcomes, assignments, assessments, readings, and syllabus design. As we developed and taught the course together, we also found co-teaching to be a rewarding experience. We co-created ideas for the course, collaborating with each other and the students to cultivate a shared classroom experience. We deployed a number of hands-on activities with the students that dovetailed with our library practice. As librarianship is a collaborative, practice-based profession, teaching a course in a similar way was a suitable and fulfilling extension of our expertise. The new pursuits of credit-based instruction were stimulating, but they also came with a set of barriers that should be acknowledged and addressed.

Credit-bearing Courses and Library Work

The main barrier we experienced was a tension between credit-bearing instruction and the practice of everyday library work. While some librarians regularly teach semester-long, credit-based courses, this type of work is not commonly represented in the job duties of most librarians. And librarian workdays are typically structured more according to the needs of library operations and less to the needs of course schedules. The five-day-a-week work structure that characterizes librarianship—comprising a steady flow of meetings, emails, projects, and collaborations—doesn't naturally lend itself to the work structure of credit-based courses, which center on short, intensive class sessions that occur every other day. In some important structural ways, our credit-based teaching was in tension with the duties and expectations of our ongoing and regular library projects. Most critically, the class necessarily became our top priority in terms of time and effort. The class sessions each week functioned as intense, high-stakes meetings that could not be missed. There was preparation and a debrief before and after each session, along with evaluation and feedback for the students. We needed to balance these new high-priority tasks with our ongoing library projects and collaborations, and this meant that projects were delayed so that we could accommodate the needs of the course and the students. We attempted to communicate early and clearly with our collaborators and supervisors about the shifting workload that teaching necessitates. But practically, we found it an ongoing challenge to balance the workloads of teaching and librarianship. When we next approach this work, we will follow a thorough and careful planning process that accommodates ongoing duties, workloads, and expectations before, during, and after the semester. In light of these questions around the integration and sustainability of credit-based teaching, we were motivated in this chapter to reframe our assignments as stand-alone activities that can be applied in different settings more common to library teachers, such as workshops and course-embedded instruction.

We also reflected on how teaching this course affected perceptions of the library at our university. We found that teaching the course served to promote the library's interest and expertise in privacy. Credit-bearing courses are widely understood across campus, and our course was seen by many other faculty and administrators as it underwent the extensive review process for approving the course. But there is a double edge that we reflected upon. The library, as a unique entity on campus, can often be misunderstood. Our wide-ranging and diverse areas of responsibility—from collections to spaces to metadata to scholarly communication—do not conform to templates readily available to other degree-granting units whose faculty mainly teach courses. By presenting ourselves as teaching credit-based courses, we could lead others to assume that we in the library also mainly teach courses or that we should be teaching even more credit-bearing courses. In an environment where we wish to present the unique contributions of the library as a strength and a value that we uniquely provide to the university—indeed, no other campus unit does the work of the library—we were cognizant of the possibility that teaching credit-based courses could potentially confuse non-librarians as to the work of the library. With that in mind, a thoughtful outreach message could be crafted that positions credit-based courses as a complement to the full suite of library activities, thereby enriching the story of the library by expanding the ground on which we work.

Student Responses

Finally, we reflect on the student experience. Through student self-evaluations, we learned that students experienced a sense of community in the class. As we aimed for this outcome through our small-group, dialogue-based, interactive activities, we viewed this as a positive outcome. Students also shared that their privacy skills and know-how improved over the semester, an outcome that also met our teaching goals. A few students expressed a desire to learn more about the historical and legal issues of privacy. In the future, we may consider integrating more readings and discussions about court decisions and the cultural history of privacy in America and the West, drawing particularly from a recent volume on the subject.[19]

One aspect that we especially noted involved the emotional impact of learning about privacy. Many students were not aware of the extensive tracking, data sharing, and other privacy-violating practices that are built into everyday software and hardware. At a point early in the semester, after we had discussed the socially harmful aspects of technology—thereby complicated existing ideas of technology as an inherent good—students found themselves in a valley of despair, unsure of how to proceed with this new knowledge about their favorite devices and websites. We realized that we needed to attend to this experience and carefully bring students back to a balanced place of using technology but with a more aware and responsible application. In retrospect, we could have provided a softer landing and further guidance for students as they came to a fuller realization of technology's positive and negative aspects.

We'd like to close this reflection by sharing excerpts from student feedback that illustrate the student experience:

- "I learned plenty of privacy and ethics skills along the way in this class. Of course I learned the more practical skills, like downloading ad blockers, adjusting Facebook privacy settings. But the most interesting things to learn were the deeper principles behind privacy policies and technology ethics. When we discussed how privacy violations impacted populations differently, we were able to delve into how to define a right and where those rights come from."
- "Building community with my classmates was a great joy. The class was full of interesting people with very cool input."
- "As an emerging computer scientist …to have this ethical discussion with me for the rest of my career will likely change the way I may view some of the code I have to write."
- "Before taking this class, I had no idea how little control I had over my privacy or how at-risk my everyday actions put me."
- "One of my biggest lightbulb moments this semester was learning about the information that big data corporations collect on the average citizen."
- "This semester, I developed ethics and privacy skills that assist me in making informed decisions about my privacy and how I choose to treat the privacy of others."

CONCLUSION

In this chapter we presented a brief discussion of key points of consideration for approaching a credit-bearing instructional context: librarian-teacher identity, student-centered pedagogies, and assessment. We also described three student assignments that can be remixed and reused in different settings for teaching about privacy. First, a diary study guides students through the evaluation of networked technologies, including algorithms, artificial intelligence, the web, and social media. Second, a value-sensitive design discussion supports critical analysis and evaluation of the contribution of networked technologies to societal structures of control, power, and oppression, especially for marginalized communities. Third, a student-designed privacy awareness campaign gives students an opportunity to apply and critique strategies for personal privacy protection. Altogether, these assignments help encourage students to engage critically and practically with today's technologies from a viewpoint of privacy. The content of our course is applicable in many different instructional contexts, including credit-bearing courses, one-time instructional sessions or workshops, multi-session course-embedded instruction, and virtual settings. By designing assignments around a learner-centered pedagogy, students are able to engage deeply and think critically about the landscape of privacy. Assessment strategies are also focused on learner-centered outcomes; we suggest that instructors observe and converse with students, and we also suggest student self-evaluation and student peer review as key assessment measures. We concluded with a self-reflective assessment of our experience as teachers. The assignments described in this chapter can support students' individual privacy protection, as well as emphasize the complexities of privacy in our data-driven society, encouraging students to think beyond individual privacy protections toward bigger-picture, community-oriented privacy advocacy.

ACKNOWLEDGMENTS

We wish to express gratitude to MT Regan, an essential collaborator on library instruction and assessment. And we thank the students enrolled in our course for their interest and curiosity in privacy and ethics.

APPENDIX A
ASSIGNMENT INSTRUCTIONS FOR THE DIARY STUDY

Instructions for Students, Part 1

For a period of one week, please record your daily technology usage, using the diary template spreadsheet provided by the instructors (See Appendix X).

- There is a row for each technology and a column for each day, along with a set of rows that will record your emotional response to technology usage.
- We have created a list of some common technologies. Please add to the list as necessary by adding a row to the spreadsheet.
- At the end of each day, you will record two main entries:
  o Technology usage: make an X in the spreadsheet beside each technology that you used that day.
  o Emotional response: using the visual scale linked in the spreadsheet, record from 1–9 how you felt that day using technology.
    - Pleasantness: How pleasant was your technology usage that day?
    - Frustration: How frustrated did you feel when using technology that day?
    - Control: How in control did you feel when using technology that day?
  o Please feel free to take notes that provide further context for your responses.
- After you complete your diary study, we will share, analyze, and discuss your diaries in class—both in small groups and as a whole class. We will look for patterns and reflect on individual and collective technology usage.

Instructions for Students, Part 2

Overview

- What was your overall experience tracking your networked technology usage?
- How did your technology usage factor into your emotional responses each day?

Technology usage

- What did you learn from tracking your networked technology use?
- How prevalent are networked technologies in your life?
- Did the act of tracking your networked technology use affect your technology use?
- Are there technologies that you're more or less comfortable using?
- Are there technologies that caused more emotional response than others?
- How did your use of networked technologies compare to your partner and to that of your aggregated classmates?
- What algorithms did you encounter throughout the week? How did they shape or direct your behavior?

Emotional response

- What factors contributed to the feelings of pleasantness, frustration, and control when you were using technology?
- Were there some days that were outliers on the scale for pleasantness, frustration, and control (higher or lower emotional response to technology)? What caused these?
- How do your emotions surrounding technology affect your technology use—both immediately and over the course of the week?

Privacy

- How did some of (or all of) the networked technologies you use track your usage?
- Did you read privacy policies or terms of service agreements to fully understand and consent to data collection?

- How do you feel about your privacy as related to each of the networked technologies that you used this week?
- Why do you or don't you use privacy-protecting technologies?

Patterns

- Technology usage: Describe the key patterns that appear in your technology usage, both in relation to your partner and to the class. Describe why you used or didn't use each technology.
- Emotional response: Describe key patterns that appear in your emotional response, both in relation to your partner and to the class. Describe why you felt pleasantness, frustration, or control on each day.
- Privacy protection: Describe key patterns that appear in your privacy practice. How do you or don't you achieve privacy? What are the key drivers of your behavior?
- What patterns do you see in the data as a whole, both in your diary and in the aggregated class data?
- What patterns do you see within each category of technology?

APPENDIX B
ASSIGNMENT INSTRUCTIONS FOR THE PRIVACY AWARENESS CAMPAIGN

1. Research

    - Familiarize yourself with the infographics genre. Explore other infographics related to topics we've discussed in class to better understand which elements and layouts are important for creating a visually appealing, compelling, and clear message.
    - Explore the topic by reading a variety of sources regarding networked technologies, big data, and privacy.
    - Include references to at least 5 sources. These sources should include:
        o 2 peer-reviewed articles
            - Library guide about finding sources: Search for Articles, Books, & More - MSU Library Research Guide (https://guides.lib.montana.edu/libraryresearch/findsources)
            - When using CatSearch (the main search on https://www.lib.montana.edu/), use the options on the right to select only Peer Reviewed Journals.
            - Academic Search Complete is a good all-purpose database, and it has a box you can check to limit your results to only peer-reviewed articles (https://guides.lib.montana.edu/asc).
        o 3 other sources such as news articles, reports, podcasts, and videos

2. Synthesis

    - What essential information about the topic do you want your audience to understand? What are the most compelling pieces of knowledge about your topic? Write down the key concepts and compelling information about your selected topic. Your infographic will include visual elements to clearly and concisely communicate key concepts, essential information, and compelling knowledge to your audience of friends and family—make sure that the information you identify is the most important and most compelling.

3. Sketch

- Before you begin creating your infographic with the infographic software of your choice (see 4. Design for some options), it is a useful conceptual exercise to sketch your infographic. What is the story you are going to tell? Grab a pen, pencil, crayons, or other writing implements and visually organize your key concepts on paper. Draw a flowchart that shows what order the data should be presented.
    o Begin with a compelling title that tells your story or conveys your message.
    o Identify the main issue.
    o Present persuasive facts and figures.

Discuss strategies to address the issue. 4. Design

- Log into your infographics app and familiarize yourself with the tool.
    o Some app options (but feel free to choose a different app if there's one you like better)
        - Canva (https://www.canva.com/create/infographics/)
        - Piktochart (https://piktochart.com/formats/infographics/)
        - Visme (https://www.visme.co/make-infographics/)
- Modify an existing template or begin with a blank canvas.
- Search for new graphical elements to include (e.g., charts, maps, icons, pictures, tables) that are well-matched with the information you've researched and synthesized about the topic.
- Design constraints: 3–5 visual elements and less than 250 words. All of your visual elements should not just be images; instead, please create at least 1–2 data visualizations such as charts, graphs, word clouds, or other figures. These visuals should provide evidence that supports the ideas of the infographic.

5. Submit and share

- Please submit a PDF version of your infographic.
- We will print your infographics for sharing and discussing in class.

NOTES

1. Matthew T. Regan, Scott W. H. Young, and Sara Mannheimer, "Improving Learner-Driven Teaching Practices through Reflective Assessment," *Evidence Based Library and Information Practice* 15, no. 3 (September 15, 2020): 59–77.
2. Gretchen V. Douglas, "Professor Librarian: A Model of the Teaching Librarian of the Future," *Computers in Libraries; Westport* 19, no. 10 (December 1999): 24–30.
3. Martha Fallahay Loesch, "Librarian as Professor: A Dynamic New Role Model," *Education Libraries* 33, no. 1 (2010): 31–37.
4. Scott Walter, "Librarians as Teachers: A Qualitative Inquiry into Professional Identity," *College & Research Libraries* 69, no. 1 (January 1, 2008): 51–71.
5. Pauline Wilson, "Librarians as Teachers: The Study of an Organization Fiction," *The Library Quarterly* 49, no. 2 (1979): 146–62.
6. Nicole Pagowsky and Erica DeFrain, "Ice Ice Baby: Are Librarian Stereotypes Freezing Us out of Instruction?," *In The Library With The Lead Pipe* (June 2014).
7. Emily Drabinski, "Becoming Librarians, Becoming Teachers: Kairos and Professional Identity / Devenir Bibliothécaire, Devenir Enseignant : Le Kairos et l'identité Professionnelle," *Canadian Journal of Information and Library Science* 40, no. 1 (2016): 27–36.
8. Scott W. H. Young, Paige Walker, Shea Swauger, Michelle J. Gibeault, Sara Mannheimer, and Jason A. Clark, "Participatory Approaches for Designing and Sustaining Privacy-Oriented Library Services," *Journal of Intellectual Freedom & Privacy* 4, no. 4 (July 31, 2020): 3–18.
9. Regan, Young, and Mannheimer, "Improving Learner-Driven Teaching Practices."
10. Jane Danielewicz and Peter Elbow, "A Unilateral Grading Contract to Improve Learning and Teaching," *College Composition and Communication* 61, no. 2 (2009): 244–68.
11. Miriam Posner, "Contract Grading," *Miriam Posner's Blog: Digital Humanities, Data, Labor, and Information* (blog), 2015.
12. Anne Jumonville Graf and Benjamin R. Harris, "Reflective Assessment: Opportunities and Challenges," *Reference Services Review* 44, no. 1 (February 8, 2016): 38–47; Lyda Fontes McCartin and Rachel Dineen, *Toward a Critical-Inclusive Assessment Practice for Library Instruction* (Sacramento, CA: Library Juice Press, 2018).
13. Jesse Stommel, "Compassionate Grading Policies," *Jesse Stommel* (blog), January 3, 2022.
14. Scott W. H. Young and Sara Mannheimer, "Information Ethics and Privacy in the Age of Big Data – Syllabus," Montana State University, 2018.
15. Kim Salazar, "Diary Studies: Understanding Long-Term User Behavior and Experiences," Nielsen Norman Group, June 5, 2016.
16. Margaret M. Bradley and Peter J. Lang, "Measuring Emotion: The Self-Assessment Manikin and the Semantic Differential," *Journal of Behavior Therapy and Experimental Psychiatry* 25, no. 1 (March 1994): 49–59.
17. Batya Friedman, Lisa Nathan, Shaun Kane, and John Lin, "Envisioning Cards," Value Sensitive Design Research Lab at the Information School at the University of Washington, 2011.
18. Regan, Young, and Mannheimer, "Improving Learner-Driven Teaching Practices."
19. Sarah E. Igo, *The Known Citizen: A History of Privacy in Modern America* (Harvard University Press, 2018).

BIBLIOGRAPHY

Bradley, Margaret M., and Peter J. Lang. "Measuring Emotion: The Self-Assessment Manikin and the Semantic Differential." *Journal of Behavior Therapy and Experimental Psychiatry* 25, no. 1 (March 1994): 49–59. https://doi.org/10.1016/0005-7916(94)90063-9.

Danielewicz, Jane, and Peter Elbow. "A Unilateral Grading Contract to Improve Learning and Teaching." *College Composition and Communication* 61, no. 2 (2009): 244–68.

Douglas, Gretchen V. "Professor Librarian: A Model of the Teaching Librarian of the Future." *Computers in Libraries; Westport* 19, no. 10 (December 1999): 24–30.

Drabinski, Emily. "Becoming Librarians, Becoming Teachers: Kairos and Professional Identity / Devenir Bibliothécaire, Devenir Enseignant : Le Kairos et l'identité Professionnelle." *Canadian Journal of Information and Library Science* 40, no. 1 (2016): 27–36.

Friedman, Batya, Lisa Nathan, Shaun Kane, and John Lin. "Envisioning Cards." Value Sensitive Design Research Lab at the Information School at the University of Washington, 2011. http://www.envisioningcards.com/.

Graf, Anne Jumonville, and Benjamin R. Harris. "Reflective Assessment: Opportunities and Challenges." *Reference Services Review* 44, no. 1 (February 8, 2016): 38–47. https://doi.org/10.1108/RSR-06-2015-0027.

Igo, Sarah E. *The Known Citizen: A History of Privacy in Modern America*. Harvard University Press, 2018.

Loesch, Martha Fallahay. "Librarian as Professor: A Dynamic New Role Model." *Education Libraries* 33, no. 1 (2010): 31–37. https://doi.org/10.26443/el.v33i1.287.

McCartin, Lyda Fontes, and Rachel Dineen. *Toward a Critical-Inclusive Assessment Practice for Library Instruction*. Sacramento, CA: Library Juice Press, 2018. https://litwinbooks.com/books/toward-a-critical-inclusive-assessment-practice-for-library-instruction/.

Pagowsky, Nicole, and Erica DeFrain. "Ice Ice Baby: Are Librarian Stereotypes Freezing Us out of Instruction?" *In The Library With The Lead Pipe* (June 2014). https://www.inthelibrarywiththeleadpipe.org/2014/ice-ice-baby-2/.

Posner, Miriam. "Contract Grading." *Miriam Posner's Blog: Digital Humanities, Data, Labor, and Information* (blog), 2015. http://web.archive.org/web/20171225153005/https://miriamposner.com/dh150w15/contract-grading/.

Regan, Matthew T., Scott W. H. Young, and Sara Mannheimer. "Improving Learner-Driven Teaching Practices through Reflective Assessment." *Evidence Based Library and Information Practice* 15, no. 3 (September 15, 2020): 59–77. https://doi.org/10.18438/eblip29729.

Salazar, Kim. "Diary Studies: Understanding Long-Term User Behavior and Experiences." Nielsen Norman Group. June 5, 2016. https://www.nngroup.com/articles/diary-studies/.

Stommel, Jesse. "Compassionate Grading Policies." *Jesse Stommel* (blog), January 3, 2022. http://web.archive.org/web/20220104024158/https://www.jessestommel.com/compassionate-grading-policies/.

Walter, Scott. "Librarians as Teachers: A Qualitative Inquiry into Professional Identity." *College & Research Libraries* 69, no. 1 (January 1, 2008): 51–71. https://doi.org/10.5860/crl.69.1.51.

Wilson, Pauline. "Librarians as Teachers: The Study of an Organization Fiction." *The Library Quarterly* 49, no. 2 (1979): 146–62. https://doi.org/10.1086/630131.

Young, Scott W. H., and Sara Mannheimer. "Information Ethics and Privacy in the Age of Big Data – Syllabus." Montana State University. 2018. https://scottwhyoung.com/teaching/information-ethics-privacy-spring-2018.

Young, Scott W. H., Paige Walker, Shea Swauger, Michelle J. Gibeault, Sara Mannheimer, and Jason A. Clark. "Participatory Approaches for Designing and Sustaining Privacy-Oriented Library Services." *Journal of Intellectual Freedom & Privacy* 4, no. 4 (July 31, 2020): 3–18. https://doi.org/10.5860/jifp.v4i4.7134.

CHAPTER 12

AMPLIFYING STUDENT VOICES:
Developing a Privacy Literacy Conversation

Melissa N. Mallon and Andrew Wesolek

INTRODUCTION AND UNIVERSITY BACKGROUND

New online research environments make the discovery and consumption of information easier than ever. However, these environments often threaten privacy and intellectual freedom by relying on surveillance economies and architectures. While students may be tangentially aware of these issues through course discussions, sensationalized news stories, or even sparked by their own interests, rarely do they have a platform to critically investigate, research, and/or discuss these issues. Rather than provide a one-sided library workshop series or lecture related to privacy and surveillance, we wanted to go deeper. We wanted to provide undergraduate students with opportunities to explore the intersection of privacy and intellectual freedom and the surveillance logics that influence online research and communication practices. To accomplish this, we developed an immersive, semester-long library fellowship, which provided the perfect opportunity for undergraduate students to not only develop their privacy literacy but also to synthesize research and contribute to the conversation on privacy and surveillance by producing their own podcasts.

Vanderbilt University is a Carnegie-classified R1 research institution located in Nashville, Tennessee. Vanderbilt consists of nearly 14,000 students, roughly equally divided between graduate and undergraduate populations. A highly selective university, Vanderbilt is ranked number fourteen on the *US News and World Report*'s ranking of national universities. The university prioritizes immersive, transdisciplinary, and residential learning experiences among undergraduates. The Jean and Alexander Heard Libraries (Vanderbilt Libraries) at Vanderbilt University is well-positioned to support these efforts through its nine campus and divisional libraries. The libraries partner with faculty and students to encourage the development of informed scholars and engaged citizens through a number of instructional activities, including a Vanderbilt Library Fellows program.

BUCHANAN LIBRARY FELLOWSHIP

The Vanderbilt Library Fellows program began in 2012 as a way for students to engage more deeply with library resources. In 2018, a generous endowment by Poppy and Richard Buchanan further developed the fellows program, resulting in the Poppy Pickering Buchanan and Richard D. Buchanan Library Fellows Fund (the Buchanan Library Fellowship). The fellowship provides students with immersive and experiential learning opportunities, allowing them the chance to work closely with librarians and Vanderbilt faculty as they critically explore information from different angles. Fellowships range from creating tactile and digital exhibits using the libraries' Special Collections to text analysis and GIS projects to exploring the challenges and opportunities of contemporary information environments. The Buchanan Library Fellowship also ties in nicely with several Vanderbilt initiatives, including the University Strategic Plan, with its emphasis on unique, on-campus student experiences and transdisciplinary learning and research. Similarly, the fellowship is one of the primary ways the Vanderbilt Libraries contribute to the Immersion Vanderbilt initiative, which "provides undergraduate students with the opportunity to pursue their passions and cultivate intellectual interests through experiential learning."[1] Each Buchanan Library Fellowship is taught by "mentors," often librarians and, many times, faculty, and the fellowships are open to all undergraduate students. Interested students must complete an online application, including a cover letter addressing their interest in the particular fellowship as well as submit a recommendation from a faculty member. Once accepted, fellows are required to attend all "seminar" sessions (usually held weekly over the course of a semester) and to complete a project at the end of the fellowship, which is displayed on the library's website and shared with other fellows. If they complete these requirements, they earn a stipend, funded by the Buchanan Fellowship Fund.

Several years ago, we collaborated to develop and teach a fellowship with two of our colleagues, Bobby Smiley and Sarah Burriss, focused on the ethics of information, of which privacy and surveillance were integral components. Students responded positively to this fellowship, but we learned that the topic was broad enough, and the research interests of the mentors divergent enough, to warrant several future fellowships on more focused topics, all converging within the general space of the ethics of information. Our aim, then, was to develop a series of fellowships that built upon one another, leveraging student final projects over the course of several semesters to offer a deeper understanding of the ethics of information than one cohort could achieve in a single semester. Due to our research interests, and the positive reaction of the initial ethics of information fellows, we decided to launch a more focused fellowship on privacy and surveillance.

So, in the fall of 2020, we took a deep dive into this space and developed a new Buchanan Library Fellowship, Privacy, Surveillance, and Intellectual Freedom (subsequently shortened to Privacy Fellowship). The Privacy Fellowship's description advertised an opportunity for students to investigate issues related to the ethical considerations of surveillance and privacy concerns. Our intent was to engage students in a critical interrogation of the role technology plays in information consumption and what our roles are, as participants in this ecosystem, to both question and change current practices.

A total of six undergraduates were accepted to the Privacy Fellowship. The fellows ranged from first years to seniors and represented a diverse set of majors, spanning from Environmental Studies to Spanish to Political Science, Gender Studies, History, Computer Science, and Cognitive Studies. As is typical at Vanderbilt, many students double or sometimes triple major. In the first meeting, we asked fellows what drew them to this fellowship. Responses included passionate dedication to preserving civil liberties to healthy criticality of government surveillance to curiosity of policy regarding cyber security and the criminal justice system. One fellow was interested in the role of social media—specifically, TikTok—on intellectual property, and yet another fellow wanted to explore corporate surveillance of environmental activists on social media. The range of interests and interdisciplinarity of the fellows resulted in robust and engaging conversations throughout the semester. We were particularly pleased when they connected weekly fellowship readings and discussions to their experiences in their other classes. Such connections bore fruit in both our synchronous discussions and asynchronous communications on the fellowship course site. We'll discuss this more in the following sections.

THE PRIVACY FELLOWSHIP
Fellowship Structure

As we developed the content and structure for the Privacy, Surveillance, and Intellectual Freedom Fellowship, we were cognizant of the fact that this is by no means a narrow topic, and we would need to draw some boundaries around what we chose to cover in lectures, readings, and student projects. To help define our scope, we started by brainstorming a series of questions that addressed our own interests and inquiries related to privacy, surveillance, and information ethics. We then narrowed those questions down to a list that would encourage students to consider these same issues from transdisciplinary academic and social lenses, as well as inspire proactivity and action in their own lives. The following guiding questions then helped us develop the content of the Privacy Fellowship:

- How is surveillance technology operative (and often invisible) in our daily lives, and what opportunities do we have for opting in/out?
- What are the relationships between privacy, surveillance, and intellectual freedom?
- What opportunities for resistance and/or change do we see?

We encouraged fellows to consider these questions as we moved through the semester and used them as guideposts as students started brainstorming their final projects. Articulating guiding principles for the fellowship is key for initiating learning transfer, which, according to Thomas, "must be viewed as fundamental to the overall learning process and it is a cornerstone for the success of the total learning experience."[2] The guiding questions are also designed to help fellows make explicit connections with the fellowship topic and their lives outside of the classroom. Through the readings and weekly discussions, we intentionally encouraged them to consider the guiding questions both from a macro scale, through their role as citizens of the United States and the world, and from a micro perspective, thinking about their academic experiences and, in particular, their enrollment at an elite private university. By facilitating these connections, we successfully completed the transfer of learning.

Fostering Community and Collaboration

Due to the ongoing COVID-19 pandemic, and the fact that at least one of our fellows was remote during the fall 2020 semester, we decided to hold our weekly synchronous sessions via Zoom. We used our university's Learning Management System (LMS), Brightspace, to post readings and have a "home base" for the fellowship. We provided fellows with a syllabus (see appendix) with readings and videos to provide some structure for our weekly meetings. We selected readings from a diverse pool, from Neil Richard's *Intellectual Privacy: Rethinking Civil Liberties in the Digital Age*[3] to Foucault's *Panopticon*.[4] We also asked students to engage with several virtual privacy projects, including the Data Detox Kit,[5] the Glass Room,[6] and Digital Shred.[7]

Since our synchronous meetings were held just once per week and took place virtually, we were committed to creating additional opportunities for fellows to continue conversations and build community outside of our weekly meetings. In online learning environments, and asynchronous courses in particular, where instructors may come across as talking heads and students may be coming from diverse backgrounds and locations, creating a more "humanizing" environment results in more engagement and increased student success.[8] To facilitate this, we identified several opportunities for fellows to connect asynchronously, outside of our weekly meetings. We share more about this connection shortly.

Bridging Theory to Practice

Building on our goals to humanize the learning environment, we used these opportunities for asynchronous communication to encourage fellows to draw connections between the rather theoretical readings to current events impacting online privacy. In addition to the weekly required readings for the fellowship (see appendix), which tended toward the abstract or more theoretical perspectives, we sought to encourage connections from the theoretical to the practical. By doing so over the course of each week, our hope was that fellows would be prompted to think about the ways in which surveillance technology is operative in their daily lives and then communicate this with their peers.

To this end, in addition to weekly readings in theory, one fellow, on a rotating basis, would select a news article that aligned well with that week's readings. Articles were selected and distributed to the class five days prior to our weekly meeting, and fellows were expected to discuss the connections between the weekly readings and the selected article both in person and online. To facilitate asynchronous annotation and conversation related to the articles, we relied on the web annotation tool, Hypothes.is.[9] After creating a free account with Hypothes.is, each fellow was invited to a group consisting of all fellows and mentors. Within this group, fellows could annotate news articles, highlight relevant sections, ask questions, or otherwise draw connections to the readings. This asynchronous annotation created a foundation on which we could develop in-person dialog at each meeting. We were consistently impressed by the connections drawn and the students' engagement with the platform.

We structured the syllabus to connect seemingly abstract aspects of the logics of surveillance to both lived and easily imagined experiences. For example, most students would not have previous experience with critical theory in general or Foucault in particular prior to joining the fellowship, so we paired Foucault's *Panopticon* with an episode of *Black Mirror*, "Nosedive." This allowed students to connect how surveillance logics might be operative in their lives through tools—social media in this case—with which they were familiar. Similarly, in a module exploring the quasi-interdependent relationship between data and personhood, we paired critical readings about the quantified self and the role of algorithmically recommended memories, with a lived experience—*The Great Hack*, which outlined the role of data targeting and manipulation in the 2016 US presidential election.[10]

Additionally, we sought to connect theoretical perspectives to practical privacy-defending practices. Through Alison Macrina at the Library Freedom Project,[11] we were connected with a local privacy technology expert, Bryan Jones, at the Nashville Public Library. Bryan agreed to guest lecture one session of the fellowship, during which he focused on a digital self-defense toolkit of open source technologies. Bryan introduced fellows to the Privacy Tools Github repository,[12] walking them through a variety of options and providing insight into the features and drawbacks of a number of the tools. Much of the literature we had read in class might have come across as dire, and so fellows reacted very positively to this wealth of tools that they could employ to enhance their personal online privacy. In addition, the students encouraged the fellowship group, mentors included, to begin using Signal,[13] an encrypted messaging platform, for all future fellowship communications.

FINAL PROJECTS

As per the endowment that established the Buchanan Library Fellowship program, fellows were to build on these readings and discussions in support of a culminating final project that integrated the material that they learned throughout the semester. Initially, the mentors proposed that the fellows manage a privacy fair designed to educate their colleagues on both threats to privacy and tips and tricks for digital self-defense.

This project was to be a continuation of a privacy-focused event held at the Vanderbilt Libraries in March of 2019. This inaugural event took a practical approach, equipping attendees with skills for encrypting online activity. At the 2019 event, Alison Macrina, founding director of the Library Freedom Project, delivered a keynote session exploring the implications of the normalization of online surveillance and the links between privacy and intellectual freedom. Attendees were encouraged to bring their laptops and smartphones to the event in order to participate in a subsequent privacy fair. Here, campus partners staffed tables to walk attendees through installing password managers, using Tor, understanding location data tracking via smartphones, and making use of secured encrypted communication.

This inaugural event was both well attended and well received by the Vanderbilt community. However, the organizers noted that while participation was strong among faculty and staff, few students were present. With this in mind, we designed the initial final project for our Privacy Fellowship along similar lines as the inaugural privacy fair. It was to feature a keynote speaker and a series of staffed tables to assist attendees in installing privacy-protecting software. The Buchanan Fellows, though, were charged with leading this event to make it by students and for students. Our hope was that our core group of fellows could better communicate privacy threats and solutions to their peers, thus continuing the conversation within the Vanderbilt student population.

Unfortunately, due to the persistence of the ongoing coronavirus pandemic, this privacy fair was not to be. We did still, though, want to harness student voices as we remained firm in the belief that the fellows themselves were best able to communicate privacy threats to their peers. As a result, we worked with them to launch a podcast series in which they were to speak to their peers, as peers, about issues they explored in the Privacy Fellowship.

Podcasts

This revised podcast project also afforded us the opportunity to work with the fellows to develop additional digital literacy and technology skills. As these podcasts would rely on the use of existing media, such as background music and sound effects, the mentors worked with fellows to develop additional digital literacy skills focused on better understanding online intellectual property regimes. In one session of the fellowship, for example, we engaged fellows in discussions to better understand the ways in which copyright is operative in online environments, where "free to read" is the norm. This included brief instruction on the essentials of understanding copyright as well as creative commons licenses and where to find and how to use open digital content.

For the technical aspects of the podcast project, we spent one session delving into how to record and edit podcasts. To help us plan the session, we consulted with our colleagues in the Vanderbilt Center for Teaching; the executive director, Derek Bruff, is very active in student-produced podcasts on campus and provided some helpful pedagogical suggestions. Likewise, our colleague Rhett McDaniel, a fantastic media producer, shared some handouts and editing guides that we added to our fellowship Brightspace site. Since all students were remote, we encouraged them to use Zoom to record their podcasts and then use Audacity to edit the audio. One or two fellows had prior experience creating podcasts for other classes, so they served as peer mentors. We also held several open "work times" where they could meet virtually to collaboratively edit and ask us questions. In addition to the five- to seven-minute podcast each group produced, we also required them to submit a transcript for accessibility purposes and a list of resources consulted and used.

We encouraged the fellows to choose the topics on which they wanted to address in their podcasts. We firmly believe that this type of personalization is an effective way to allow students to align their projects with their own interests and prior experiences.[14] However, as Kucirkova, Gerard, and Linn note, this type of personalization can also cause difficulties, particularly when trying to balance customization of learning for individual students at the possible expense of the group.[15] This can also cause issues with equity and student agency. We did find that leaving the topic selection fully up to our fellows resulted in us having to guide students to narrow their topics, much like helping students winnow down a research paper topic, and that some students' preferences didn't necessarily mesh with those of their peers. To counteract this, while we required each fellow to collaboratively produce and edit *at least one* podcast for their final project, we also encouraged them to explore additional topics solo, should they have the time and interest. This allowed students the agency to explore topics fully aligned with their experiences and interests. To help fellows narrow down their topics to a manageable size that could be covered in the shorter (five- to seven-minute) podcast, we engaged them in a process of brainstorming conversations during our weekly meetings, facilitated by collaborative work on a Google Doc.

Eventually, the fellows self-sorted into three groups of two, deciding to record podcasts on the following areas: activism and surveillance, surveillance capitalism and corporations (a two-parter), and historical progression of privacy and philosophy (also a two-parter), which explored the philosophical evolution of privacy through the lens of Facebook's development and analyzed the definition of privacy in relation to technological innovations and ethical controversies, including the Cambridge Analytica scandal, Twitter's handling of the 2014 Ferguson Black Lives Matter Protest, and more. One fellow did end up producing an additional solo podcast, focusing on the legal applications of privacy, which investigated the history and development of federal statutes governing digital information, providing a foundational understanding of relevant law. Perhaps not surprisingly, this fellow was a senior and pre-law. We combined the fellows' edited podcasts along with their supplementary materials and a description of the fellowship onto a publicly available research guide.[16]

REFLECTIONS AND CONCLUSIONS
Fellow Reflections

In addition to their final projects, Buchanan Fellows are also asked to provide statements reflecting on their experience throughout the semester; these statements are used in donor reports and as advertising for the Buchanan Library Fellowship program. Our privacy fellows provided statements that were representative of their engagement in the fellowship; it was gratifying to see that they felt as happy and passionate about their experience as we did.[17]

As mentioned, one of the major goals of the Buchanan Library Fellowship program is to foster a connection between undergraduates and the library. Happily, our Privacy Fellowship seemed to accomplish this. In their reflection, a first-year student noted, "I learned so much about privacy and surveillance and the impacts it has on our lives. I hope to continue to engage with the library and staff in different ways, especially since Andrew and Melissa were so nice and imparted so much knowledge to us, and the book recommendations especially were so helpful!" One of the best things about this takeaway is that this fellow now associates the library with privacy advocacy and will hopefully make continued associations between the work we do and the conversation on privacy.

Fellows also made connections to the interests and passions they initially brought into the fellowship. As a nice "closing the loop" statement to the comments made at our very first meeting, one fellow, an environmental studies major, explained how the privacy fellowship helped them meet their academic and professional goals:

> The Privacy Fellowship not only allowed myself [sic] to immerse myself in the literature of privacy and surveillance, but served as the basis for an independent study that allowed me to explore this topic within my area of interest: environmental sociology. In the fellowship we delved into contemporary examples of surveillance structures in action through discussion of current events, documentaries, and examination of a

weekly newspaper article that each student was able to choose. By exploring these tangents, we were able to debate topics such as algorithmic bias, the benefits and downfalls of surveillance, and how to be proactive in our own online security.

It was also interesting to see that some fellows commented on the community and collaboration we worked hard to foster, despite the pandemic circumstances we were all living in. According to one fellow, "Our class discussions were always fruitful and would often lead us down paths that weren't originally planned for the day's seminar." Yet another reflected on how the readings and discussions contributed to their understanding of the fellowship content: "I am profoundly appreciative of my experience as a Buchanan fellow. The fellowship offered me the opportunity to engage with content of intellectual interest which falls outside of my major. It enabled me to pursue in-depth research on the exceedingly relevant and widely applicable topic of data privacy and surveillance. I am incredibly thankful for our project mentors, Andy and Melissa, who provided invaluable individualized guidance which facilitated my exploration and discovery of the political significance of intellectual freedom."

Since this was the first semester to include the podcasts, we also wanted to get a sense of how satisfied the fellows were with this final project. One summed up their experience with the podcasts: "As the semester drew to a close, I crafted a podcast with a classmate, one which surveyed privacy through its philosophical underpinnings. Immersing myself in the theories of Kant and Locke, while simultaneously studying entities like Facebook and Google, sure made this Fellowship one exciting ride!" This same fellow went on to say, "The Buchanan Library Fellowship combines the very best of a Vanderbilt education: immersion and discussion. By analyzing a variety of texts—historical, philosophical, economic—I was able to gain an interdisciplinary understanding of privacy in the digital age." This kind of enthusiasm is everything we would hope for in providing these undergraduate fellowship opportunities. We were gratified to hear from our fellows even several semesters after offering the Privacy Fellowship, asking us to serve as references for their job searches and letting us know how they have explored the topics we discussed in other ways throughout their academic career, including as a launch point for an Immersion Vanderbilt project.

Mentor Reflections

Along with the fellows, we, the mentors, learned a great deal over the course of this semester. First, we learned that at least some undergraduates really care about privacy! It is often assumed that younger generations, saturated in social media and raised in increasingly surveilled environments, do not care about privacy concerns. However, our fellows were clearly passionate about these issues and their positive outlook buoyed the admittedly occasionally pessimistic view of the future of privacy held by the mentors.

Moreover, the podcast series was initially developed as a contingency due to the persistence of the pandemic. However, we were so impressed with the time, energy, and thoughtfulness fellows gave their podcasts that we wanted to build on the momentum they developed. As a result, this podcast project served as the foundation for an ongoing podcast series featuring student voices exploring issues at the intersection of information, media, and society.[18] Subsequent fellowships led by the mentors and our collaborator Bobby Smiley, feature podcasts as final projects. Learning from this fellowship, we built additional time in subsequent curricula to help fellows refine their audio-production skills and better understand intellectual property in online environments.

Student engagement with hypothes.is also exceeded our expectations. We built this component into future fellowships as a valuable tool in connecting theory to practice. During the Privacy Fellowship, we had occasional concerns that using hypothes.is as a communication tool might lead to tangential conversations that fellows might find uninteresting. However, as confirmed by their reflections, the flexibility in discussion topics led to a more personalized learning experience and deeper connections to the fellows' own disciplinary backgrounds. We did have some reservations about the privacy policies of the platform, but these did not outweigh the benefits of conversation it helped to generate.

We also remain firmly committed to the essentiality of diverse student backgrounds and disciplinary perspectives for this and subsequent Buchanan Fellowships. Issues around privacy, surveillance, and intellectual freedom are transdisciplinary in nature and can be explored much more richly with a diversity of disciplinary perspectives present. The diversity of perspectives on these issues allowed for the growth of peer mentoring within the fellowship in addition to prompting the mentors to think about these issues from new perspectives. Additionally, the range of grade levels enhanced this diversity, adding to the peer-mentoring opportunities and fostering the development of a community of student-scholars that extended beyond the fellowship.

Not all aspects of the fellowship exceeded our expectations, however. This was the first fellowship we mentored in which we encouraged fellows to create podcasts. Upon completion of them, however, we noticed that the production quality was not quite as polished as we had anticipated. Granted, the podcasts were offered as a final project as a contingency plan due to the persistent pandemic, but we did learn that future fellowships should include additional time and instruction devoted to the technical aspects of podcast production. In future fellowships we offered, we carved out time for this instruction toward the beginning of the semester to give students the space to experiment and ask questions as the semester progressed. This resulted in podcasts with higher production values.

We also want to be intentional in recognizing our privilege in this opportunity; we are fortunate to work at a prestigious institution with a healthy endowment. While this financial support admittedly does not always make its way to the library, we are grateful for families like the Buchanans that see the value in experiential learning and undergraduate research, and, even more importantly, see the value of these initiatives as directly connected to academic libraries. However, a library need not have a similarly funded fellowship structure to take advantage of the lessons we learned through this case study. Librarians can apply different aspects of our Privacy Fellowship to their own institutional contexts, particularly with a bit of creativity and thinking outside the box. We recommend connecting with student advocacy groups and other student-led organizations to align the topics covered with their goals and activities. For example, any student group that centers on privacy, ethics, or freedom of information might be willing to host a special workshop or discussion group, housed in the library. The different modules we covered within our fellowship (see appendix) can also be packaged into individual lessons that can either be delivered in a workshop format, through select course curriculum (look for relevant courses in computer sciences, political science, sociology, and/or communication studies), or via asynchronous modules that can either be self-paced or embedded into courses. Similarly, the podcast project might be replicated through a library contest or similar incentive-based structure for undergraduates. Regardless of the campus environment and institutional context, the projects and content in this Privacy Fellowship are extremely transferable and relevant for students of all types.

The Buchanan Library Fellowship focusing on Privacy, Surveillance, and Intellectual Freedom was a rewarding experience for both fellows and mentors. We all had much to learn from each other and created connections that have extended well beyond the semester in which the fellowship occurred. Fellows carried the conversation forward among their peers through the podcasts, future independent studies, and campus activism work, while mentors were reinvigorated by the enthusiasm of the fellows. Privacy advocacy can be a challenge, but working directly with undergraduates to develop and share the conversation proved both fruitful and inspiring.

APPENDIX
FELLOWSHIP SYLLABUS

Buchanan Library Fellowship Course
Jean & Alexander Heard Libraries, Vanderbilt University
Fall 2020
Privacy, Surveillance, and Intellectual Freedom
Thursdays, 4:00–5:00 p.m. | Zoom

Instructors

Melissa Mallon (she/her/hers), Associate University Librarian for Teaching & Learning, Vanderbilt Libraries, melissa.mallon@vanderbilt.edu
Andrew Wesolek (he/him/his), Director of Digital Scholarship & Communications, Vanderbilt Libraries, andrew.j.wesolek@vanderbilt.edu
All virtual office hours by appointment

Course Description

New online research environments have made the discovery and consumption of information easier than ever. However, these environments often threaten privacy and intellectual freedom by relying on surveillance economies and architectures. In this seminar, fellows will explore the intersection of privacy and intellectual freedom and the surveillance logics that influence online research and communication practices. Using a variety of formats (such as a podcast, presentation, or video public service announcement), fellows will create final projects that analyze issues related to technology and privacy.

Guiding Questions for the Course

- How is surveillance technology operative (and often invisible) in our daily lives, and what opportunities do we have for opting in/out?
- What are the relationships between privacy, surveillance, and intellectual freedom?
- What opportunities for resistance and/or change do we see?

Projects and Assignments

Privacy and Surveillance Podcasts and Resource Guide

As a group, we will collaboratively produce a series of podcasts and additional resources designed to raise awareness of issues surrounding privacy and surveillance as well as steps students can take to mitigate challenges. You will work in pairs to record a podcast conversation around an area of interest related to the course topics. To accompany your podcast, you will gather a list of additional resources (websites, readings, etc.). Andy and Melissa will combine the podcasts and resources into a publicly available resource guide.

Privacy in the News

On a weekly basis, we will find a contemporary news article addressing issues of privacy and/or surveillance. Be prepared to discuss the article both in Brightspace and through the social annotation extension Hypothes.is (note, you will need to register in advance for a free account). More information will be available in Brightspace.

Brightspace and Course Materials

Materials are posted on Brightspace (*Privacy, Surveillance, & Intellectual Freedom*: 2020F). Please familiarize yourself with the Brightspace page and let us know if you have any difficulty accessing course content. Please also feel free to post and share resources for our class in the discussion board or email us to post in the supplementary materials section. Brightspace does track and collect information about your use of the site and materials on it. We will discuss this on the first day of class.

Course Calendar *(schedule and content subject to changes)*

Week 1, *Introduction to the Course*
    Introductions and Syllabus
    Brightspace and logistics
    Discuss course content and topic areas
    Overview of course projects

Week 2, *What do we talk about when we talk about "Privacy?"*
    Read before class (on Brightspace)
- *Privacy as Trust*: p. 13-34
- *Known Citizen*: p. 1-16

- *Intellectual Privacy*: p. 1-12

Week 3, *What do we talk about when we talk about "Surveillance?"*
   Read before class (on Brightspace)
   - *Introduction to Surveillance Studies: XIX-XXXIV*
   - *Surveillance Studies: An Overview: p. 18-21*
   - *The Panoptic Sort: p. 9-13*

Week 4, *The Logics of Surveillance*
   Read before class
   - "Account," Serpell
   - "Panopticism," Foucault
   - "Postscript on Societies of Control," Deleuze

   Watch before class
   - "Nosedive," *Black Mirror* (season 3, episode 1) Available on Netflix or on reserve at Central Library

Week 5, *Data and Personhood*
   Watch before class
   - *The Great Hack* (Netflix)

   Read before class
   - Algorithmic Harms Beyond Facebook and Google
   - Psychographic Profiling and Cambridge Analytica
   - The Digital Madeleine (Simanowski)
   - New Hybrid Beings (Lupton)

Week 6, *Podcasting 101*
   - Introduce podcasting project
   - Share podcast teams & topics

   Explore before class
   - https://my.vanderbilt.edu/podcasting/

Week 7, *Algorithmic Bias*

Week 8, *Surveillance Capitalism*
   Watch before class
   - "Shoshana Zuboff on surveillance capitalism" (documentary)

   Read before class
   - *Big other: Surveillance Capitalism and the Prospects of an Information Civilization*, Zuboff

Week 9, *Digital Self Defense*
   Check in on podcast scripts/progress
   Explore before class

- *Privacy Libguide*
- *Repository of Privacy Tools*
- *CryptoParty*
- *Data Detox Kit*
- *The Glass Room*
- *Library Freedom Project Resources*
- *Digital Shred*

Week 10, *Work on Projects*
- Send podcasts scripts to Andy & Melissa
- Worktime in breakout rooms

Week 11, *Work on Projects*
- Melissa/Andy office hours
- Worktime in breakout rooms

Week 12, *Wrap-up*
- Present and listen to podcasts

Fellowship Readings:

- Foucault, M. *Discipline and Punish: The Birth of the Prison*. New York: Random, House, 1979.
- Igo, S. E. *The Known Citizen: A History of Privacy in Modern America*. Cambridge: Harvard University Press, 2018.
- Lupton, D. *The Quantified Self: A Sociology of Self-tracking*. Cambridge: Polity Press, 2016.
- Monahan, T., and D. M. Wood. *Surveillance Studies: A Reader*. New York: Oxford University Press, 2018.
- Richards, N. *Intellectual Privacy: Rethinking Civil Liberties in the Digital Age*. New York: Oxford University Press, 2017.
- Simanowski, R. *Waste: A New Media Primer*. Cambridge: The MIT Press, 2018.
- Waldman, A. E. *Privacy as Trust: Information Privacy for an Information Age*. Cambridge: Cambridge University Press, 2018.

Course Policies
Contacting the Instructors
Please refer to the email addresses on the first page of the syllabus for contacting us electronically. Please note that all office hours are by appointment and will be conducted virtually.

Academic Integrity
We expect all students to live to the letter and the intent of the university Honor Code. Please refer to the Honor System. This includes respect for others' intellectual property. When in doubt, ask the instructor.

Special Needs
If you have a physical, psychiatric, or learning need, please let us know early in the semester so that we can make any necessary accommodations or meet your learning needs. **We know that this semester is highly unusual, and things may happen that are out of your control. Keep in contact with us, and we will work with you to make this a successful experience!**

Time Commitment
Outside of the scheduled seminar time, plan to spend about two to three hours per week on assigned readings, assignments, and/or engaging with your final project. Let us know as soon as possible if you are having difficulty keeping up with the course activities.

Participation
You are expected to be an active participant in the class learning environment. Please come to class having completed the readings and assignments and be ready to discuss your thoughts.

Any readings will be posted in Brightspace in the weekly folders—please read for class on the week it is posted—this will help facilitate conversations.

NOTES
1. "Immersion Vanderbilt," Vanderbilt University, accessed August 29, 2022, https://www.vanderbilt.edu/immersion/.

2. Earl Thomas, "Thoughtful Planning Fosters Learning Transfer," *Adult Learning* 18, no. 3 (Summer 2007): 5.
3. Neil M. Richards, *Intellectual Privacy: Rethinking Civil Liberties in the Digital Age* (New York: Oxford University Press, 2017).
4. Michel Foucault, *Discipline and Punish: The Birth of the Prison* (New York: Random House, 1979).
5. "Data Detox Kit," Tactical Tech, accessed August 29, 2022, https://datadetoxkit.org/en/privacy.
6. "The Glass Room," Tactical Tech, accessed August 29, 2022, https://www.theglassroom.org/.
7. Alexandria Chisholm and Sarah Hartman-Caverly, "Digital Shred: Privacy Literacy Toolkit," accessed August 29, 2022, https://sites.psu.edu/digitalshred/.
8. Michelle Pacansky-Brock, Michael Smedshammer, and Kim Vincent-Layton, "Humanizing Online Teaching to Equitize Higher Education," *Current Issues in Education* 21, no. 2 (2020).
9. Hypothes.is, accessed August 29, 2022, https://web.hypothes.is/.
10. Jehane Noujaim and Karim Amer, *The Great Hack*, 2019, https://www.netflix.com/title/80117542.
11. Alison Macrina, "Library Freedom Project, accessed August 29, 2022, https://libraryfreedom.org/.
12. "Privacy Tools: Software Alternatives and Encryption," Privacy Tools, accessed August 29, 2022, https://www.privacytools.io/.
13. "Signal," accessed August 29, 2022, https://signal.org/en/.
14. Natalia Kucirkova, Libby Gerard, and Marcia C. Linn, "Designing Personalised Instruction: A Research and Design Framework," *British Journal of Educational Technology* 52, no. 5 (2021): 1839–61, http://dx.doi.org/10.1111/bjet.13119.
15. Kucirkova, Gerard, and Linn, "Designing Personalised Instruction."
16. Student podcasts and accompanying materials are available at https://researchguides.library.vanderbilt.edu/buchananfellows/privacy.
17. Student comments are taken from their end of semester reflection statements and purposefully left anonymous.
18. Information, Media, & Society guide, https://researchguides.library.vanderbilt.edu/buchananfellows/.

BIBLIOGRAPHY

Chisholm, Alexandria, and Sarah Hartman-Caverly. "Digital Shred: Privacy Literacy Toolkit." Accessed August 29, 2022. https://sites.psu.edu/digitalshred/.

Foucault, Michel. *Discipline and Punish: The Birth of the Prison*. New York: Random House, 1979.

Hypothes.is. Accessed August 29, 2022. https://web.hypothes.is/.

Igo, Sarah E. *The Known Citizen: A History of Privacy in Modern America*. Cambridge: Harvard University Press, 2018.

Kucirkova, Natalia, Libby Gerard, and Marcia C. Linn. "Designing Personalised Instruction: A Research and Design Framework." *British Journal of Educational Technology* 52, no. 5 (2021): 1839–61. http://dx.doi.org/10.1111/bjet.13119.

Lupton, Deborah. *The Quantified Self: A Sociology of Self-Tracking*. Cambridge: Polity Press, 2016.

Macrina, Alison. "Library Freedom Project." Accessed August 29, 2022. https://libraryfreedom.org/.

Monahan, Torin, and David Murakami Wood. *Surveillance Studies: A Reader*. New York: Oxford University Press, 2018.

Noujaim, Jehane, and Karim Amer. *The Great Hack*. 2019. https://www.netflix.com/title/80117542.

Pacansky-Brock, Michelle, Michael Smedshammer, and Kim Vincent-Layton. "Humanizing Online Teaching to Equitize Higher Education." *Current Issues in Education* 21, no. 2 (2020).

Privacy Tools. "Privacy Tools: Software Alternatives and Encryption." Accessed August 29, 2022. https://www.privacytools.io/.

Richards, Neil M. *Intellectual Privacy: Rethinking Civil Liberties in the Digital Age*. New York: Oxford University Press, 2017.

Signal. Accessed August 29, 2022. https://signal.org/en/.

Simanowski, Roberto. *Waste: A New Media Primer*. Cambridge: The MIT Press, 2018.
Tactical Tech. "Data Detox Kit." Accessed August 29, 2022. https://datadetoxkit.org/en/privacy.
———. "The Glass Room." Accessed August 29, 2022. https://www.theglassroom.org/.
Thomas, Earl. "Thoughtful Planning Fosters Learning Transfer." *Adult Learning* 18, no. 3 (Summer 2007): 4–8.
Waldman, Ari Ezra. *Privacy as Trust: Information Privacy for an Information Age*. Cambridge: Cambridge University Press, 2018.
Vanderbilt University. "Immersion Vanderbilt." Accessed August 29, 2022. https://www.vanderbilt.edu/immersion/.

PART IV
Advocating for Privacy

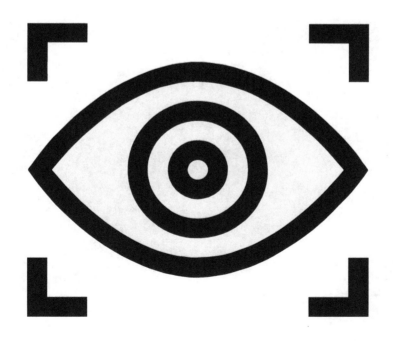

CHAPTER 13

UNDERSTANDING STUDENT PERSPECTIVES ON LEARNING ANALYTICS TO ENABLE PRIVACY ADVOCACY AND POLICY DESIGN

Michael R. Perry, Andrew D. Asher, Kristin A. Briney, Mariana Regalado, Abigail Goben, Maura A. Smale, Dorothea Salo, and Kyle M. L. Jones

PROJECT OVERVIEW

The rise of computing infrastructure and data collection in higher education has opened the door for colleges and universities to begin large-scale data analytics projects, commonly known as learning analytics (LA). These initiatives are defined as the "measurement, collection, analysis, and reporting of [student and other data] for the purposes of understanding and optimizing learning and the environments in which it occurs."[1] Historically, academic libraries have collected data, such as circulation statistics, without reference to specific users. The extensive data collected by library and higher-education programs and networks now regularly include personal information. More academic libraries are being asked to engage in learning analytics projects or to share data with campus units[2] to demonstrate how library use may correlate with student success measures such as GPA, retention, and time to graduation. Literature in 2018 at the time of the team's grant application[3] showed a distinct lack of research around student perceptions of LA and library participation. This gap was the driving goal of the research team's project to understand student perceptions through an IMLS-funded study of undergraduate students at eight institutions. While the researchers hold expertise in the areas of data ethics and privacy, data management, library assessment, qualitative and quantitative research methods, and survey design, they were not involved in the practical application of learning analytics at their various universities. To begin, the team conducted a literature review[4] that brought together the ethical challenges of library participation in LA with respect to librarianship's professional values, especially privacy. This informed the overall design of the study, which was conducted in three phases: semi-structured interviews, a survey, and finally a series of LA scenario-based focus groups. The initial literature review was used as the basis for the interview protocol of the first phase. The findings from the interviews were then used to develop the survey instrument for the second phase. The results of the survey were subsequently leveraged to develop the focus group scenarios. Due to the COVID-19 pandemic, the project was extended to May 2022 and focus groups were conducted virtually rather than in person.

While the goal of this research project has been to give voice to student perceptions of privacy and trust related to LA and library participation, the findings should also be useful to librarians being asked to collect or provide data, library administrators being asked to participate in campus-level initiatives, or campus leaders designing those initiatives. This chapter outlines each of the three research phases with an overview of the methodology and findings as well as the challenges in conducting that research. While the findings represent a variety of campus contexts, it is often important that institutions conduct local research, especially when the results will inform advocacy. The research team has made our tools and findings openly available to enable others to explore what students think about LA, privacy, and academic libraries on their own campuses. Finally, this chapter discusses how some members of the research team have engaged their own campuses via project data and findings as well as the potential value of using these methods to understand more specific local issues. We hope this can lead libraries that choose to participate in LA initiatives to ensure that their participation reflects professional values and actively engages with students regarding their privacy and autonomy as it relates to the use of their student data.

RESEARCH TOOLS AND DATA

The research team wanted to not only share the findings of our research but also the materials used for each of the research phases so that the methods could be replicated at any institution. To this end, the researchers established an Open Science Framework (OSF) site[5] to document the bibliographies, publication and presentation materials, and research tools for each phase. For phase one, the semi-structured interviews, the site contains the recruitment materials, consent forms, interview protocol, and the coding guides and documentation. Phase two materials include the survey text, question response distributions, and statistical test results. The phase three materials include recruitment materials, consent forms, scenario documentation, and the slides used for each scenario. Access to the full consent and administrative documents necessary to conduct similar research is intended to aid other schools in submission to their local Institutional Review Boards (IRB).

The research team also produced data management plans for each phase of research to standardize file organization and naming as well as to track documents as they moved through the analysis workflows. Detailed instructions and organization were critical to coordinating a team of distributed researchers across eight institutions that were each responsible for producing research that would be ultimately merged. This was vital for not only the completion of the project but also to ensure the security and integrity of the research data.

PHASE ONE – SEMI-STRUCTURED INTERVIEWS

The initial phase of the research entailed semi-structured interviews with undergraduate students at each research site to understand student reactions to data mining and analytic practices generally and, more specifically, those practices in higher education and academic libraries. The research team recruited undergraduate students over the age of eighteen years from eight US institutions:
- Indiana University-Bloomington, Bloomington, IN

- Indiana University-Indianapolis (IUPUI), Indianapolis, IN
- Linn-Benton Community College, Albany, OR
- Northwestern University, Evanston, IL
- Oregon State University, Corvallis, OR
- University of Illinois Chicago, Chicago, IL
- University of Wisconsin-Madison, Madison, WI
- University of Wisconsin-Milwaukee, Milwaukee, WI

Students were recruited using a variety of sampling methods, including random, quota, convenience, and snowball, with the goal of conducting fifteen interviews at each site. This number has been demonstrated to reveal over 90 percent of subsequently coded topics in qualitative interviews, or "saturation," the point at which gathering additional data is unlikely to yield new information.[6] Participants who completed interviews were provided a $10 Amazon gift card as an incentive. The protocol was reviewed at each research site by the local IRB and classified as exempt.

Each participant was first asked three core questions covering societal, student, and library privacy generally. For example, the library privacy question asked:

> College and university libraries are supporting learning analytics practices. They collect and analyze when individual students use library services and spaces, along with physical and electronic collections, such as books, articles, and databases. What are your reactions to this, and what do you think are the privacy implications, if any?

Participants were then asked a set of questions related to one of the following themes. Included below are two examples of questions for each theme. The full interview protocol is available at the OSF site.

- Privacy
    - Does your institution have a responsibility to inform you about how they will share data and information about you?
    - Who do you think owns the data you create as a student?
- Data sharing and use
    - Finish this sentence: I expect my institution to use data and information about me to…
    - Would you be willing to share data and information about you if it led to a personalized educational experience?
- Data protections
    - Different groups often feel the need for more or less data protection;

how do you think that your expectations of data protections differ from others?
    ○ What data protection practices should your institution take to safeguard data about you?
- Awareness of and reactions to LA
    ○ Learning analytics are informed by what are sometimes called "digital trails" or "breadcrumbs," pieces of data you leave when you interact with your university's websites, applications, e-mail systems, sensors, and other things. What do you think about this practice?
    ○ Learning analytics systems can attempt to predict your future success or failure in courses and programs of study. How might these predictions benefit or harm you?
- Libraries and LA
    ○ How would you feel about the library sharing your library usage information with the broader campus? Is there some information you are comfortable sharing and other information you aren't?
    ○ What do you think the privacy standard should be for libraries?

In total, the team completed 112 interviews. A thorough review of interview transcripts caused removal of seven interviews from the final data set over quality control issues, for a total of 105 usable interviews. The removal of those interviews did not have an impact on the reliability of the results and ensured the overall quality of data collected.

The transcripts were loaded into Dedoose, a qualitative data analysis application, for coding and review. A subteam of three researchers utilized a modified version of grounded theory to develop a codebook using a sample of the transcription data and an open coding technique. This resulted in a final codebook that included seventy-nine codes grouped into seven thematic areas: affect, data, data practices, learning analytics, people, things, and privacy. The full team then completed closed coding, using the codebook to ensure code consistency across the dataset. Researchers analyzed nearly 11,000 code applications by examining code counts, co-occurrence counts, and heatmaps to determine the most frequent combinations of codes.

The researchers found that students lacked data and privacy literacy, leading to an inability to express privacy preferences and concerns unprompted. This led the students to speculate about what LA could achieve and whether it justified data collection. Students did express more nuanced arguments about when data should be restricted and often observed that their preference should not determine the rights of their peers. Researchers also found a deep sense of trust in their institutions as well as their libraries, which often led students to be more comfortable with data collection and analysis in a university setting compared to a corporate one. Full findings can be found in the *Journal of the Association for Information Science and Technology*.[7]

This method of research allowed the team to cover a wide variety of topics and would be straightforward to replicate at any institution as a means of engaging students in discussion of LA, privacy, and libraries. The majority of researcher time in developing this phase of the research was spent creating and testing the interview protocol and codebook, both of which the team has made openly available for reuse. IRB review of the project and recruitment of participants requires some planning as well as funding for an incentive for participation. Interviews will also need to be recorded and transcribed for analysis. Coding will likely represent the most time-intensive activity for researchers adopting this method. If the results of the research are done for specific campus advocacy or student engagement, however, this process can be far more targeted than the comprehensive approach of this research team.

The insights gleaned in this phase from talking with students about privacy, learning analytics, and higher education informed not only subsequent phases of research but also the researchers' own perspectives on their local institutions. Privacy is a core value of librarianship, and it cannot be overstated how impactful talking with an actual student user about those issues can be. Semi-structured interviews do so in a controlled and reproducible way.

PHASE TWO – UNDERGRADUATE SURVEY

Building on the findings of the initial interviews, the research team conducted a survey of undergraduate students to better understand the themes and compare findings across demographic groups. The team developed a survey of twenty-five questions with 154 unique responses. These responses were grouped into seven thematic modules outlined below with two sample questions and possible answers for each module included. The full survey instrument is available at the OSF site:

- Knowledge about learning analytics
    - [University Name]'s libraries use my personally identifiable information to identify the services I use (e.g. library help desk, electronic library resources). - Yes/No/Unsure
    - [University Name]'s libraries can give your personally identifiable information to other offices affiliated with my university. — Yes/No/Unsure
- Data sharing and use

- I think other campus offices share personally identifiable information about me with the library. — Yes/No/Unsure
        - I think personally identifiable information about me will be centralized and accessible by any campus office. — Yes/No/Unsure
- Data access and limits
    - How private do you consider the following types of your information to be? Building/room access (e.g. via student ID card or other key). — Completely Private/Sometimes Public and Sometimes Private/Completely Public
    - I expect to be able to access the following personally identifiable information about me that is held by my university: Activities within a learning management system like Blackboard, Canvas, or Moodle. — Yes/No/Unsure
- Data rights
    - I think that I should have ownership rights to personally identifiable information I create within my university's websites. — Yes/No/Unsure
    - I think that I should have ownership rights to personally identifiable information I create within commercial websites (e.g., Amazon). — Yes/No/Unsure
- Consent
    - With respect to my personally identifiable information, I expect my university to inform me about how they will use it. — Yes/No/Unsure
    - With respect to my personally identifiable information, I expect my university to inform me about how they will share it. — Yes/No/Unsure
- Privacy
    - Privacy with respect to my personally identifiable information is: — Not important to me/Slightly important to me/Important to me/Very important to me
    - Privacy is important for me as a student to develop intellectual ideas. — Yes/No/Unsure
- Trust
    - How likely do you think it is that [University name] shares personally identifiable information about me with other universities. — Likely/Somewhat likely/Unlikely/Unsure
    - How likely do you think it is that [University name] sells personally

identifiable information about me with other universities. — Likely/Somewhat likely/Unlikely/Unsure

The survey closed with a set of demographic questions. Demographic data was self-reported (rather than using institutional data) to best respect the privacy of participants and to give students the opportunity to choose whether and how they were identified for each question. A pilot test of the survey was conducted at Northwestern University before the instrument was submitted to each institutional IRB, and a sample of 4,000–5,000 student emails were requested at each of the following institutions:

- Brooklyn College, CUNY, New York, NY
- Indiana University-Bloomington, Bloomington, IN
- Indiana University-Indianapolis (IUPUI), Indianapolis, IN
- Linn-Benton Community College, Albany, OR
- Northwestern University, Evanston, IL
- University of Illinois at Chicago, Chicago, IL
- University of Wisconsin-Madison, Madison, WI
- University of Wisconsin-Milwaukee, Milwaukee, WI

In total, 35,598 recruitment emails were sent with an overall response rate of 6 percent. Across all participating institutions, 1,908 students completed the entire survey, while another 338 completed at least nineteen questions (equivalent to the length of the first survey module) for a total of 2,246 participants.

Researchers found that almost all undergraduate students considered privacy to be important, specifically to protect against intrusions in their life (94 percent) and to develop their identity (79 percent), and to a lesser degree to develop intellectual ideas (71 percent) and personal relationships (68 percent). The research team also found that students made many assumptions, some false, about library collection of personally identifiable information as well as libraries' willingness to share that information. For example, 47 percent of students said the library can share PII with "other offices affiliated with my university" and 44 percent with "law enforcement officials" while only 14 percent thought their PII could be shared with "outside businesses and advertisers." The nature of most vendor library systems now requires some personally identifiable information to be shared with those outside business. The researchers also inquired about how the students would feel if different kinds of university staff accessed their personally identifiable and de-identified information. In a headline result, 70 percent of students responded yes when asked, "If the following type of university employee (librarians) had access to my PII, I would feel that my privacy was violated." Full results from the survey can be found in *Library Quarterly*.[8]

The development, testing, and validation of the survey instrument represented a vast amount of work and technical expertise, as did the analysis of the resulting data. The research team has made the survey questions and response summary data available for researchers. Despite this, fielding the survey locally will still require IRB approval, recruitment logistics, and data analysis that may not be feasible for all institutions. Ensuring that a survey delivers quality results is dependent on having a representative sample that will have to be obtained from campus. While an open survey link distributed via email, listserv, or social media is far easier to administer, it will impact this sampling. Obtaining a sample of students will vary from institution to institution but will often be done through an Office of Institutional Research or through the Registrar's Office. This variance may impact the requirements or ability to obtain a sample and convenience sampling may be required. Though a survey will allow for a broader and possibly more representative response, other research methods may be better suited to identify local themes and provide context to researchers. If possible, however, this type of research can uncover local campus themes and especially allow for analysis of differences in privacy expectations across demographic groups. Understanding such differences can be especially important for campuses with a majority of underserved student populations.

PHASE THREE – SCENARIO-BASED FOCUS GROUPS

Having identified broader themes via semi-structured interviews and expanded that knowledge via the survey, the researchers then developed a focus group instrument presenting undergraduate students with three scenarios that reflected current practices and potential futures of LA work but were still understandable to students: library service integration into the learning management system (LMS), data centralization via a library data warehouse, and geolocation data tracking. The scenarios were evaluated for their connection to libraries and participant comprehensibility and then for their potential benefit and privacy risks. Scenarios were then tested with a group of students to ensure they were clear and comprehensible.

Each scenario began with a brief description of the technology; for example, the LMS scenario was described as follows:

> Your university library is planning to integrate library services and resources into the learning management system (LMS), Canvas or Blackboard. This means data about your use of

library services and resources through Canvas or Blackboard will be collected and made accessible for analysis purposes.

Examples of data used in the scenario were then presented. For the LMS example, this included the following:
- time-on-page tracking (e.g., how long you viewed a discussion forum);
- communications between users (e.g., librarians and students);
- submitted assignments;
- grades; and
- names of books, articles, and equipment you have looked at, downloaded, or checked out.

Next, the facilitator outlined the goals of the technology and what the university hoped to achieve with it. For the LMS scenario, these goals were:
- improve access to course and library materials for students;
- increase access to librarians; and
- better its ability to track material usage.

Finally, each scenario provided a rationale for the technology and outlined why the university is using the technology. Using the LMS scenario as an example:
- increase student awareness and use of library resources;
- seamless access to resources and expertise;
- make more informed library purchasing decisions; and
- assess readings and assignments.

While the focus groups were originally envisioned as in-person activities, they needed to be conducted online because of the COVID-19 pandemic.[9] This greatly increased the logistical difficulty of conducting the focus groups but did allow for researchers to observe focus groups at other research sites. Recruitment was done via a sample of 3,000 email addresses at each research site:
- Brooklyn College, CUNY, Brooklyn, NY
- Borough of Manhattan Community College, CUNY, New York, NY
- Indiana University-Bloomington, Bloomington, IN
- Indiana University-Indianapolis (IUPUI), Indianapolis, IN
- Northwestern University, Evanston, IL
- University of Illinois at Chicago, Chicago, IL
- University of Wisconsin-Madison, Madison, WI

Survey reminders were sent until ten participants were registered for each of the three focus groups at each site. In total, twenty-one focus groups were conducted across seven sites with 116 total participants. The focus group transcriptions and videos were loaded into MaxQDA for analysis as the research team found this software to be better able to meet the team's needs. Descriptive coding was completed and then a modified version of initial phase one codebook was used to code the transcripts.

Initial findings for the focus groups match themes found in the earlier phases. Most notably, there was broad agreement that granular consent was essential for LA systems to ensure that students feel their privacy and trust are being honored. There was also a desire to have LA to be used solely for educational purposes with clearly stated goals. Students also expressed the desire to audit or review data and clearly understand the nature of LA data uses.

Some of the most impactful findings often included specifically local context or history. One focus group discussed at length the institution's previous use of personally identifiable information (PII) for disciplinary purposes and how this eroded their trust in the institution's use of PII for educational purposes. Another focus group discussed the specifics of learning management system email nudges and their dislike of them. These issues are tied into specifics of local LMS configurations and represent potential practical findings from this type of research. These localized and specific issues are a core reason to reproduce similar research locally. The scenario descriptions and tools the researchers used have been made available for reuse. While the researchers used a random sample to recruit, convenience sampling can be used to minimize administrative overhead. The pivot to virtual focus groups also demonstrates how focus groups can be done either remotely or in person. The focus group format also allows researchers to witness the ways students can inform and learn from each other about real-world data practices and specific privacy concerns. The full results from this study will soon be published in *portal: Libraries and the Academy*.[10]

RESEARCH AS USER AND LIBRARY ADVOCACY

Library LA initiatives largely began as a means of demonstrating the value of libraries to higher education. The Value of Academic Libraries (VAL)[11] and Assessment in Action (AiA)[12] initiatives encouraged data capture and integration with campus data as well as demographic data. There remain open issues with the ethics of our profession, as articulated by the ALA Code of Ethics third principle, "We protect each library user's right to privacy and confidentiality with respect to information sought or received and resources consulted, borrowed, acquired or transmitted."[13] This focus on privacy and confidentiality seems at odds with the technical requirements of LA projects that require broad data collection as well as linking that data to other systems or data points such as GPA or retention. This research project sought to respond to these trends and the gap between them and library professional ethics as outlined by the ALA Code of Ethics by amplifying the voice of students and articulating their thoughts on LA and academic libraries. What researchers found were students who were able to detail nuanced arguments about the value of privacy in their lives, especially in a focus group setting with their peers. They also expressed a clear desire to be informed about the nature of data collection as well as the goals of LA projects. Students also wanted a means of consenting to data collection, use, and sharing. These findings illustrate the current gap between some library LA practices and interests when compared with students' views of library LA, similar to the gap in library professional values and LA practices.[14]

Conducting research like this captures local issues and context that might differ from the campuses studied in this research; it also creates advocacy opportunities for libraries' professional values. It has also developed local partnerships between Data Doubles researchers and other campus entities interested in LA. The results of our research have allowed Northwestern University Library to become involved in campus-level data governance committees. This has uniquely positioned both the researcher and library to give voice to the important role privacy plays in the intellectual development of students as well as the concerns brought up by students throughout the research process. The rigor apparent in the research has also opened the door to begin exploring the adaptation of the focus group scenario techniques to study the role of campus data stewards. Understanding the expectations of data stewards as it relates to data use and especially sharing can help to establish norms across campus units and bring additional structure and consistency to currently siloed systems. By showing the results of our student research as well as the adaptability of the methods to other constituencies, the libraries on this campus have become a crucial partner in campus data policy. University of Illinois at Chicago has been able to share the research and findings of the team with multiple campus stakeholder groups as a way of not only talking about student perspectives of LA and privacy but also the research output of faculty librarians.

Pursuing local research on student privacy perspectives also allows libraries to understand student data and privacy literacy needs. The research team's findings show clear gaps in students' ability to understand the complexities of library and higher-education systems and their potential for data capture as well as the ability to model threats that data collection and use cause. These issues tie clearly to library information literacy efforts as well as filling a clear gap in student understanding. Digital Shred creators, Sarah Hartman-Caverly and Alex Chisholm, have created a robust set of teaching and learning tools to aid in privacy instruction.[15]

While the need for a student- and privacy-focused voice in the development of LA initiatives seems clear, and libraries' focus on information literacy and privacy makes them likely candidates to be this voice, it does not change the power imbalance many libraries face. The initial goal of VAL and AiA was to demonstrate the value of academic libraries to justify and potentially increase investment in academic libraries. This goal can make it difficult if not impossible for libraries to push back on data collection and sharing as part of larger campus LA initiatives. This power imbalance and inability to use research to set a student-focused LA agenda have been documented.[16] If libraries are required to participate in LA, the input of both librarians and students can be valuable to help articulate clear goals for LA projects and transparency in the process and data collection.

CONCLUSION

This project sought to provide a comprehensive look at student perceptions of LA and the privacy issues tied to library participation in LA. To identify broad themes, the team began by conducting semi-structured interviews with students. These interviews are easily replicable in a local context, but findings may require more detailed analysis. To expand on those themes, researchers developed a survey to collect a larger data set, but this technique does require more specialized knowledge. Finally, the research team developed scenario-based focus groups to explore potential LA projects. This research is easily replicated and new scenarios can be developed and explored. This technique also provides a great template for actual LA project development. To identify potential issues with potential LA projects, libraries can, with minimum cost, explore the project with students via a focus group. This can help to clarify the goals of the project as well as areas where transparency is valued by students such as data sharing or retention.

The various research methods outlined above each carry with them different requirements or skills to replicate. The researchers hope that by making all the research materials available, more librarians might consider replicating the studies at their own institutions. Novice researchers with the interview protocol, survey instrument, or focus group scenarios need only process the IRB paperwork and obtain a student sample from the Office of Institutional Research or Registrar's Office and can then conduct the study. Analysis of resulting data may be a challenge, especially for the survey, which requires statistical analysis. However, both the interviews and focus groups will provide data that is easily read and can be summarized for internal use without much difficulty.

It may be crucial for sites to replicate these studies as views of students around privacy and institutional data use are closely tied to the history and past actions of the institution itself. A data breach or hack of university systems will obviously have a profound effect on institutional trust. The researchers found an incident at Northwestern University related to the use of pictures to identify student protesters[17] to have a profound effect on the willingness of students to trust the university to use their data in good faith. While the researcher was aware of this incident, the connection to overall institutional trust only became clear as a result of conducting the focus group study.

One of the most consistent themes the research team found across phases was the desire among students to be able to consent to data collection and use for LA. While a consent process imposes technical and logistical difficulties, for example, focus groups often had difficulty articulating when and where consent should happen and they do not diminish the clear desire from students to understand how their data was being collected and used. Transparency in data collection and use is an achievable goal for libraries participating in LA. The research team believes that this transparency, coupled with student engagement through research, can help to better define the goals of any specific LA project and help to deliver outcomes that will truly impact student learning. By making students partners in this research as opposed to subjects, libraries may start to see some of the suggested benefits of LA materialize.

ACKNOWLEDGMENTS

This project was made possible in part by the Institute of Museum and Library Services (LG-96-18-0044-18). The views, findings, conclusions, or recommendations expressed in this article do not necessarily represent those of the Institute of Museum and Library Services.

NOTES

1. George Siemens, "Learning Analytics: Envisioning a Research Discipline and a Domain of Practice," in *Proceedings of the 2nd International Conference on Learning Analytics and Knowledge*, 4–8 (New York: ACM, 2012), https://doi.org/10.1145/2330601.2330605.
2. Michael R. Perry, Kristin A. Briney, Abigail Goben, Andrew Asher, Kyle M. L. Jones, M. Brooke Robertshaw, and Dorothea Salo, "Spec Kit 360: Learning Analytics," Association of Research Libraries, September 4, 2018, https://doi.org/10.29242/spec.360.
3. "LG-96-18-0044-18," Institute of Museum and Library Services, accessed January 11, 2022, http://www.imls.gov/grants/awarded/lg-96-18-0044-18.

4. Kyle M. L. Jones, Kristin A. Briney, Abigail Goben, Dorothea Salo, Andrew Asher, and Michael R. Perry, "A Comprehensive Primer to Library Learning Analytics Practices, Initiatives, and Privacy Issues," *College & Research Libraries* 81, no. 3 (2020): 570–91, https://doi.org/10.5860/crl.81.3.570.
5. Kyle M. L. Jones, Andrew Asher, Kristin Briney, Abigail H. Goben, Michael Perry, Mariana Regalado, Dorothea Salo, and Maura Smale, "Data Doubles Open Science Framework Site," OSF, March 1, 2019, https://osf.io/d7f3g/.
6. Greg Guest, Arwen Bunce, and Laura Johnson, "How Many Interviews Are Enough? An Experiment with Data Saturation and Variability," *Field Methods* 18, no. 1 (2006): 59–82.
7. Kyle M. L. Jones, Andrew Asher, Abigail Goben, Michael R. Perry, Dorothea Salo, Kristin A. Briney, and M. Brooke Robertshaw, "'We're Being Tracked at All Times': Student Perspectives of Their Privacy in Relation to Learning Analytics in Higher Education," *Journal of the Association for Information Science and Technology* 71, no. 9 (2020): 1044–59, https://doi.org/10.1002/asi.24358.
8. Andrew Asher, Kristin A. Briney, Kyle M. L. Jones, Mariana Regalado, Michael R. Perry, Abigail Goben, Maura A. Smale, and Dorothea Salo, "Questions of Trust: A Survey of Student Expectations and Perspectives on Library Learning Analytics," *Library Quarterly* 92, no. 2 (2022): 151–71, https://doi.org/10.1086/718605.
9. Kyle M. L. Jones, Michael R. Perry, and Mariana Regalado, "'You're on Mute': A Reflective Case Study of Conducting Scenario-Based Online Focus Groups on Student Privacy," *SAGE Research Methods Doing Research Online* (2022), 1–12, https://doi.org/10.4135/9781529799415.
10. Kyle M. L. Jones, Abigail H. Goben, Michael Perry, Mariana Regalado, Dorothea Salo, Andrew Asher, Maura Smale, and Kristin Briney, "Transparency and Consent: Student Perspectives on Educational Data Analytics Scenarios," *portal: Libraries and the Academy* (n.d.).
11. Megan Oakleaf, "Value of Academic Libraries Report: A Comprehensive Research Review and Report," Association of College & Research Libraries, September 2010, http://www.ala.org/acrl/sites/ala.org.acrl/files/content/issues/value/val_report.pdf.
12. "Assessment in Action: Final Narrative," Association of College and Research Libraries, September 30, 2015, http://www.ala.org/acrl/sites/ala.org.acrl/files/content/AiA%20final%20report%20to%20IMLS%20FINAL%20no%20cover.pdf.
13. "Code of Ethics of the American Library Association," American Library Association, 2008, https://www.ala.org/tools/ethics.
14. Kyle M. L. Jones and Dorothea Salo, "Learning Analytics and the Academic Library: Professional Ethics Commitments at a Crossroads," *College & Research Libraries* 79, no. 3 (2018): 304–23, https://doi.org/10.5860/crl.79.3.304.
15. Sarah Hartman-Caverly and Alex Chisholm, "Digital Shred: Privacy Literacy Toolkit," accessed October 8, 2019, https://sites.psu.edu/digitalshred/.
16. Sarah Cohn, "Professional Ethics and Learning Analytics: A Reflection on a Cross-Departmental Assessment Project," *Urban Library Journal* 27, no. 1 (January 1, 2021), https://academicworks.cuny.edu/ulj/vol27/iss1/1.
17. Eva Herscowitz, "Northwestern Students Protest Jeff Sessions' Speech, Police Presence," *The Daily Northwestern* (blog), November 6, 2019, https://dailynorthwestern.com/2019/11/06/campus/students-protest-jeff-sessions-speech-police-presence/.

BIBLIOGRAPHY

American Library Association. "Code of Ethics of the American Library Association." 2008. https://www.ala.org/tools/ethics.

Asher, Andrew, Kristin A. Briney, Kyle M. L. Jones, Mariana Regalado, Michael R. Perry, Abigail Goben, Maura A. Smale, and Dorothea Salo. "Questions of Trust: A Survey of Student Expectations and Perspectives on Library Learning Analytics." *Library Quarterly* 92, no. 2 (2022): 151–71. https://doi.org/10.1086/718605.

Association of College and Research Libraries. "Assessment in Action: Final Narrative." September 30, 2015. http://www.ala.org/acrl/sites/ala.org.acrl/files/content/AiA%20final%20report%20to%20IMLS%20FINAL%20no%20cover.pdf.

Cohn, Sarah. "Professional Ethics and Learning Analytics: A Reflection on a Cross-Departmental Assessment Project." *Urban Library Journal* 27, no. 1 (January 1, 2021). https://academicworks.cuny.edu/ulj/vol27/iss1/1.

Guest, Greg, Arwen Bunce, and Laura Johnson. "How Many Interviews Are Enough? An Experiment with Data Saturation and Variability." *Field Methods* 18, no. 1 (2006): 59–82.

Hartman-Caverly, Sarah, and Alex Chisholm. "Digital Shred: Privacy Literacy Toolkit." Accessed October 8, 2019. https://sites.psu.edu/digitalshred/.

Herscowitz, Eva. "Northwestern Students Protest Jeff Sessions' Speech, Police Presence." *The Daily Northwestern* (blog), November 6, 2019. https://dailynorthwestern.com/2019/11/06/campus/students-protest-jeff-sessions-speech-police-presence/.

Institute of Museum and Library Services. "LG-96-18-0044-18." Accessed January 11, 2022. http://www.imls.gov/grants/awarded/lg-96-18-0044-18.

Jones, Kyle M. L., Andrew Asher, Kristin Briney, Abigail H. Goben, Michael Perry, Mariana Regalado, Dorothea Salo, and Maura Smale. "Data Doubles Open Science Framework Site." OSF. March 1, 2019. https://osf.io/d7f3g/.

Jones, Kyle M. L., Andrew Asher, Abigail Goben, Michael R. Perry, Dorothea Salo, Kristin A. Briney, and M. Brooke Robertshaw. "'We're Being Tracked at All Times': Student Perspectives of Their Privacy in Relation to Learning Analytics in Higher Education." *Journal of the Association for Information Science and Technology* 71, no. 9 (2020): 1044–59. https://doi.org/10.1002/asi.24358.

Jones, Kyle M. L., Kristin A. Briney, Abigail Goben, Dorothea Salo, Andrew Asher, and Michael R. Perry. "A Comprehensive Primer to Library Learning Analytics Practices, Initiatives, and Privacy Issues." *College & Research Libraries* 81, no. 3 (2020): 570–91. https://doi.org/10.5860/crl.81.3.570.

Jones, Kyle M. L., Abigail H. Goben, Michael Perry, Mariana Regalado, Dorothea Salo, Andrew Asher, Maura Smale, and Kristin Briney. "Transparency and Consent: Student Perspectives on Educational Data Analytics Scenarios." *portal: Libraries and the Academy* (n.d.).

Jones, Kyle M. L., Michael R. Perry, and Mariana Regalado. "'You're on Mute': A Reflective Case Study of Conducting Scenario-Based Online Focus Groups on Student Privacy." *SAGE Research Methods Doing Research Online* (2022), 1–12. https://doi.org/10.4135/9781529799415.

Jones, Kyle M. L., and Dorothea Salo. "Learning Analytics and the Academic Library: Professional Ethics Commitments at a Crossroads." *College & Research Libraries* 79, no. 3 (2018): 304–23. https://doi.org/10.5860/crl.79.3.304.

Oakleaf, Megan. "Value of Academic Libraries Report: A Comprehensive Research Review and Report." September 2010. http://www.ala.org/acrl/sites/ala.org.acrl/files/content/issues/value/val_report.pdf.

Perry, Michael R., Kristin A. Briney, Abigail Goben, Andrew Asher, Kyle M. L. Jones, M. Brooke Robertshaw, and Dorothea Salo. "Spec Kit 360: Learning Analytics." Association of Research Libraries. September 4, 2018. https://doi.org/10.29242/spec.360.

Siemens, George. "Learning Analytics: Envisioning a Research Discipline and a Domain of Practice." In *Proceedings of the 2nd International Conference on Learning Analytics and Knowledge*. New York: ACM, 2012, 4–8. https://doi.org/10.1145/2330601.2330605.

CHAPTER 14

BUILDING A CULTURE OF PRIVACY THROUGH COLLABORATIVE POLICY DEVELOPMENT

Margaret Heller

INTRODUCTION

Plenty of resources exist for understanding and protecting patron privacy in libraries. So too does governmental pressure, particularly for institutions subject to the European Union's General Data Protection Regulation (GDPR) or similar US state laws. While at some levels there are clearly articulated visions around the privacy of library users, the implementation of privacy practices at the local level remains spotty. Some of this is due to limited time or resources, but some of it is a lack of culture around privacy norms within institutions. Building that culture will mean that every decision someone makes at their job in the library will consider patron privacy to some degree, even if individuals disagree on appropriate measures. Like all cultural shifts, it takes time and empathy to help people to see the benefits and

265

requirements of new ways of thinking, and creating tangible exercises for working through these challenges is one way to address them.

I suggest ways of building and maintaining a culture of privacy through the act of writing and revising a privacy policy based on my experience at Loyola University Chicago. When approached as a holistic project to understand why decisions have been made a certain way in the past and how to shift—or radically transform—that decision-making, rewriting policy can be transformative for institutions. The process is certainly no panacea, but with a document in place and widely accepted, the process of periodic review and revision can maintain practices throughout time. More than the specific items to include in a policy, which are well-covered by many resources, this chapter guides you in how to think about decision-making as part of building or maintaining privacy culture through a case study of writing this specific policy.

LITERATURE REVIEW

In planning a project to create a culture of privacy, it is important to consider the role of staff across the library in planning and implementing policy, why privacy can be different from other aspects of library practice, and particular considerations for academic libraries in the age of learning analytics.

Changing institutional practices and professional norms requires a healthy organizational culture that can lead to overall culture shifts in the library. Understanding how organizational culture functions in libraries has been an ongoing topic of research, recently with a particular focus on the dysfunctional elements of library culture that lead to low morale and disengagement as people are not able to effect real change in areas they value. Kaetrena Davis Kendrick's 2017 work demonstrates that one way that low morale manifests for faculty librarians is a lack of the type of collaboration and professional development that would lead to cultural change, particularly at the larger institutional level.[1] That scholarship did not include staff working in academic libraries who are critical in making privacy decisions. The 2022 study by Glusker and colleagues built on Kendrick's work to look specifically at staff. While many of the participants in this study had reasonably good morale, they found the most powerful impact on staff morale was a librarian/staff divide, where staff found themselves blocked from influencing library policy, even when they have direct interactions with students.[2] Including people at all levels of institutional power in decision-making in a real way is part of maintaining a healthy culture, particularly when it comes to privacy issues.

Patron record management tends to have more legal requirements or external policies that libraries must follow than other areas of library service, but inclusive cultures can improve privacy practices at all levels. In many cases, the specific requirements around privacy may be set at a state level and interact with other education privacy regulations like FERPA. While institutions may wish to leave such decisions in the hands of institutional lawyers, individuals will still have to face daily decisions about their work. This includes front-line library workers like circulation desk clerks who may not know policy and may not understand the reasons for privacy in library records unless they have been involved in active training or had a say in the policy. This has been the case for decades, of course. In the 1970s and '80s, a government surveillance program involved the Internal Revenue Service looking for circulation records to find potential readers on subversive topics, to which Bruce S. Johnson responded in a 1989 article. Johnson argues that a 1970 ALA statement, "Advisory Statement to U.S. Libraries from the American Library Association," established a strong precedent for privacy before any case law established legal precedent and led to the end of the IRS program.[3] In this pre-internet age, Johnson lays out the thought experiment of the circulation clerk who is asked by law enforcement to share borrowing records and the role that library administrators must play in informing and empowering all staff members to resist non-lawful governmental or other requests for patron records (for example, from journalists).[4]

Over the following years, the increasing role of the internet and then the PATRIOT Act created a flurry of calls for privacy policies and a greater understanding of privacy in libraries, especially as the ALA produced the original versions of the Privacy Tool Kit in 2002. Karen Coombs noted in 2004 that libraries were just beginning to work to implement the Privacy Tool Kit but that technological advances made policies irrelevant quickly.[5] By 2007, when Stacey Voeller analyzed existing privacy policies at academic libraries, she found the majority were either nonexistent or cursory and did not reflect ALA recommendations.[6] The worry in the early 2000s was that libraries would no longer be trusted with privacy the way they had been due to the threats from the PATRIOT Act without close attention to professional standards and conduct, including a privacy audit.[7] Over the past decade, the issues have shifted somewhat to focus more on potential social or big data analytics use of library data, which has, of course, also expanded exponentially beyond borrowing records. A 2012 study by Michael Zimmer indicated that there was reason to be concerned that attitudes toward privacy were loosening compared to 2008 as the overall culture changed and perhaps was related to younger librarians who were less concerned about online privacy.[8] While a cultural move to social media seems here to stay, recent work by Kyle M. L. Jones et al. indicates that rather than governmental oversight, the current generation of students is far more concerned about privacy in social media and the commercial realm and generally trusts libraries and universities, though without necessarily knowing what data they are collecting or fully understanding the purpose of this data collection.[9]

Yet that study also found that for students, the modern university may be perceived to be a place where intellectual curiosity or questioning is subject to oversight.[10] What academic libraries choose to do with data collection has a lot to do with library culture as well as overall institutional culture. One of the major problems with privacy in academia is that it has not always been a concern at an institutional level. It does limited good for the library to protect users if every other unit on campus is gathering and compiling data about student use of other systems on campus, such as learning management platforms. Library staff can advocate for more limited data collection, even if they cannot prevent it. Working together across areas not always considered in the privacy discussion, such as collection management and instruction, is more likely to create a staff who is knowledgeable about the privacy ecosystem and able to have these conversations with campus partners.[11] This is an issue for faculty as well. Traditionally, academic freedom purports to protect individuals' research interests, but this has only ever applied really to a small number of people, and with tenure-track positions now in the minority, there are even fewer people who will feel completely comfortable with their research interests not being protected until they are ready to make it public.[12]

The culture of privacy in libraries is not monolithic. For example, in a 2019 editorial, Russell Michalak and Monica Rysavy made an argument that gathering personally identifying information about individuals is part of the library's mission to improve service. In the editorial, they have a wish list for even more information at the vendor level about which individuals are using which features.[13] Jones et al. question this level of tracking without meaningful education and co-creation of procedures with students.[14] Such tensions point to the need for open discussions about privacy in libraries.

Despite a recent cultural trend to talk about social media and learning analytics, the threat from government oversight over what libraries buy and patrons choose to read has not disappeared, particularly at the state and local level, and this requires ongoing attention. In mid-2022, we have once again found an inflection point in the role of libraries in privacy with the *Dobbs v. Jackson Women's Health Organization* case, which made abortion immediately illegal in several states. Law enforcement used mobile search data to arrest a woman for allegedly purchasing abortion pills.[15] Ensuring that libraries remain a place where people can seek information without fear of arrest has become a focus of professional concern again, as an August 2022 statement by the ALA Executive Board stating their commitment to protecting patrons from "unwanted surveillance" in researching reproductive health.[16] Beyond abortion, numerous news stories about censorship in schools and public libraries show that a renewed focus on providing an open yet private environment for research is critical.

CASE STUDY OF LOYOLA UNIVERSITY CHICAGO

Creating a Privacy Policy

Loyola University Chicago is a private doctoral-granting university with an enrollment of about 17,000 students, the majority of whom are undergraduates. Starting in fall 2017, I co-chaired a library privacy policy task force. This section describes that work and how we experienced the policy in action while implementing new tools and services.

At Loyola, when we set out to write the policy, our main concern was a push for learning analytics and data warehousing at a campus level. We knew that we had to get ahead of the inevitable push for collating and using library data. At the time, we were barely even aware of the critical role of a policy itself; we just knew we wanted to get the staff talking about privacy and learning what to do, and the release of the ALA Library Privacy Checklists made the work seem more possible. Initially, the Scholarly Communications Committee had discussions that led to the formation of a group. It became clear that to create a comprehensive privacy policy that covered all areas of the library, members from diverse areas with different experiences and expertise would be needed to ensure that all practices and needs were captured. For Loyola, the size of the library staff and its well-established cross-departmental collaborative culture made it straightforward to work with department heads and recruit a member from each department, with some conversations to make sure representatives had a mix of background experience. The team purposely had a mix of department heads, faculty librarians, and staff and had nine members, including two co-chairs. No one from library administration was on the team, but the administration had numerous opportunities to learn about work in progress and had final approval on the policy.

We wrote a formal charge for the group, which was called the "Patron Privacy Task Force," and created a formal project plan to keep on track, given the short timeline of August to December 2017. The project plan defined the stages of work and committee member roles. Initial stages included a reading list of articles (all of which are cited in this chapter) and resources, such as privacy policies from other libraries, to help committee members get up to speed and create a list of questions that occurred to committee members that we could take into our work. We then conducted an inventory of systems and a privacy audit of those systems. The systems inventory was not intended to suggest that privacy was a technology problem only but rather helped the team identify how data could be jeopardized as it passed between systems. The team structure shone here. For example, we discussed user purchase requests, where we discovered that deleting the user request records from the back end of the catalog is only marginally helpful for privacy since the request was submitted via email to an inbox to which many people have access. The subject liaison knew how faculty wish to request books and have them put on hold, and the acquisitions assistant knew how the orders are placed and tracked. Together, these two understood what needs to happen to make book request records more private in a way that neither could do alone. Discussing these workflows was a critical piece of writing policy since it helped catch easy fixes to privacy problems before we described them in the policy.

We took existing lists of types of systems created by Karen Coyle for privacy audits and filled in the names of our specific software in each category as well as the primary manager for the software. In a few cases, we had elements of library services that used paper forms. We used the ALA Library Privacy Checklists level 1 priorities to create lists of practices that should be addressed. (See the appendix for more on available resources.) While it was straightforward to determine where we had immediate major gaps—for example, we did not have a privacy policy—some projects were more abstract or required coordination with other campus units. In these cases, when we wrote the policy, we tried to be honest about what our limitations were, but this became something we could record as a practice to work toward change.

One of the goals for this project that was not successful was to create an interactive procedures manual that would allow departments to map their procedures to levels of privacy as defined by the Library Privacy Checklist priority actions, which started with steps that all libraries could take and then moved on to more challenging projects. Ultimately, we were only able to review Priority 1 actions, and the interactive procedure manual was too complicated to implement.

Writing the policy was relatively straightforward. My co-chair and I used existing templates and examples from other institutions in the same jurisdiction and type to ensure that the policy was not missing any important features. We knew few people would read a privacy policy, so headings and bullet points helped people to locate the specific information they need. Committee members provided feedback after discussions in their departments. We also asked a colleague outside the library to read a draft to check for jargon. One other issue to settle before making the policy public was determining our library privacy officer, which is a role suggested by the ALA Privacy Checklists. Ideally, this would be a person with the institutional authority to make decisions or exceptions to policy but with a strong understanding of privacy issues as well. In the case of Loyola, the person selected for this role was not on the committee but had the institutional authority to take complaints and had a general understanding of the issues.

For Loyola, highlighting our new library privacy policy was an important moment that created new opportunities. Presenting the policy at a standing academic technology review committee showcased the library as a resource for privacy questions. Almost immediately, the library received invitations to present to other groups (such as academic departments) and to consult on privacy practices at other campus units. The library was then invited to join a campus information technology-level committee on information security, which since then has had a real impact on privacy on a campus level. One of the strengths of the team was that it was not always the department member on the committee who became the privacy expert for their department; in at least one case, another department member found the process so appealing that they went on to learn more and pursue additional privacy-related projects.

Applying the Privacy Policy

The policy that Loyola created in 2017 positioned the library staff to ask questions about the choices they were making going forward. A yearly review of a policy is warranted, but privacy becomes a de facto question in all projects so the library will be able to make decisions that will not need to be undone at the next review period. Policy revision is a balance: does one change procedures to conform to a better policy or does the policy serve as an aspirational document? Ideally, both should be true. The act of writing and interpreting the policy as a team created an impetus to consider changes to procedures, especially in the moments of crisis that we all experienced throughout the pandemic with a need to reinvent services quickly and do more tracking of users for contact tracing and de-densification. In the normal course of providing library services, we need to balance convenience and privacy for both users and staff.

Two examples from Loyola's experience illustrate this. One is pandemic-based, the other is not. Both took place in 2020 when Loyola adopted OpenAthens as a federated authentication solution while at the same time creating a contactless pickup service—two completely different types of projects involving different groups within the library but both requiring privacy conversations informed by the privacy policy process.

Adopting a new technology like OpenAthens, and fully evaluating the privacy options and settings, required a great deal of new technical learning and provided opportunities to question privacy practices and needs across our electronic resources as we learned the technology better. We began working on the project well before the pandemic, but the switch to remote work and instruction across campus highlighted the challenges inherent in using solely IP-based authentication, especially one that is locally hosted. EZProxy, our proxy server, is highly configurable to make logging usage more private, but to make it practical for troubleshooting ends up creating logs with very specific information about users and their access, particularly when everyone who uses resources is logging in through the proxy server because no one is in the library's IP range. While we still use EZProxy concurrently for certain resources, we found the process of moving to OpenAthens provided a chance to understand the realities of federated access and attributes.

Federated authentication has the potential to be much more private, but only if it is configured to do so. A proxy server requires running all traffic through a central point, so libraries can and do collect data about what resources particular users are viewing and when. While some of that is useful for troubleshooting, it creates a toxic dataset that without proper maintenance is ripe for misuse. An IP-based authorization solution can be more private, certainly, when users are on campus, but in an environment where few if any people are in the IP range, the proxy server is always in the way. A federated solution, on the other hand, separates the identification and authentication of a user from what they are authorized to do and can provide relative anonymity for users from both the library and the vendor, but only if the information passed between entities is not identifiable.

OpenAthens itself has a relatively privacy-forward outlook, but it is possible to configure data collection in such a way that could identify individuals.[17] At Loyola, this sort of individual tracking is not part of our library's privacy policy or in its guiding principles; tracking the usage of resources and platform features helps us make general decisions about what to improve. If we desired to find out more about individual needs around the library, we would design a study and have it approved by the Institutional Review Board, which would ensure that we were collecting and reviewing data in an appropriate manner. The concept of collecting everything "just in case" is an overwhelming prospect for how we would go about safely storing that data and analyzing it.

That said, for cost-sharing decisions, it would be helpful to track usage by school or department, but we have found it difficult to release the appropriate attributes in such a way that they would be useful to OpenAthens reporting. The more data that is released, the easier it is to re-aggregate. Releasing personal attributes in a way that a user cannot see is sometimes necessary for access to individual databases such as Elsevier and O'Reilly (among others), but OpenAthens makes it easy to set which attributes are available for authorization versus reporting.

The "go live" date for OpenAthens was in August 2020, but it took almost a year before we felt we had the technology working well enough and had a good enough understanding to revise the privacy policy. This means that at that time, our privacy policy was inaccurate, and that was an uncomfortable feeling. Knowing the technology well enough to understand where privacy leakage can occur takes time, however, and should be an understood part of long-term technical projects.

The time-limited projects of pandemic service warrant close attention to privacy. While the service provided during the pandemic was never going to be exactly the same, it was important to not place people in an even more difficult situation. Establishing a contactless pickup service was one such event—how to balance the need to allow people to pick up books without interacting with staff but also not to make it obvious who was picking up what when. Of course, removing friction from an already potentially stressful situation was necessary. The original plan was very privacy-focused: place books in bags identified only by the last four digits of the patron barcode. Reality very quickly changed this plan: not all students had a barcode on their IDs, and even patrons who did found it difficult to locate their bag on the shelf. This made it necessary for them to talk to the staff in the building for help, which was antithetical to the aims of the project. For that reason, we shifted to last name and barcode for identification. After an introductory period, patron complaints indicated that the bags themselves were a problem. Some people were uncomfortable with the number of plastic bags that they were using in frequent book pickups. Staff found a new solution: reusable bags and a return box for people to return the bags after they had picked up their books.

While we were able to use our 2017 policy for ongoing decision-making, it became clear in early 2021 that a policy rewrite was overdue since it did not accurately reflect the new technical infrastructure of OpenAthens and other procedural changes. We determined that the policy needed to be revised in the summer of 2021. The challenge here was to get people motivated to do the work. With so many projects and competing priorities, the privacy policy was not top of people's minds. In the end, none of the original committee members from 2017 were available, but we were able to create a new small group that reached out to all the library departments for review and updates.

The tools used in creating the privacy policy can and should be reused in revision. Departments should build a periodic review of the systems they are using that collect personal information, and those can be used to update system inventories. Because we had asked department heads to identify items on the privacy project wish list for annual department goals, there were at least attempts to change practices to meet higher standards. Most practices did and will remain unchanged without external pressures, such as a new system like OpenAthens, or the massive reset that the pandemic required. Rather than feeling despondent about this inertia, a culture of privacy means that even if people are not undertaking big projects to fix privacy problems, they are making a few small decisions that will aid privacy over time or not choosing a new practice that will negatively impact privacy. One example is that Google Analytics released version 4 in October 2020, which is designed to work across the web and apps. The problem is that the limited privacy controls available in earlier versions are no longer available in this version. Thus, a review of the new version showed that upgrading was not necessary and would be deleterious. Google recently announced that it would stop support for the current version, so we will implement Matomo Analytics. These small inflection points create opportunities for knowledge and growth.

BUILDING A PRIVACY CULTURE WITH OR WITHOUT POLICY

While I believe the act of writing a policy can help establish privacy culture, if approached as an inclusive research and education project, libraries can follow the same process to come to a shared privacy understanding, even if the outcome is an internal document or a set of guiding principles rather than a policy. This may be more politically feasible than setting out to write a policy. When it comes down to it, a person with a commitment to privacy will be more efficacious than someone half-heartedly following a policy. As new technology and new challenges to intellectual freedom arise, a written document describing a policy is important, but it is not the only approach. The calls for more training and commitment to privacy have been consistent in the literature, but surveys of actual practice find that institutional follow-through is inconsistent. Technology seems to trend toward more tracking and surveillance, as does higher education. There are few external pressures on libraries to actually "fix" privacy, so we are less likely to apply a lot of resources to do so.

The good news is that privacy is about values and mindset, and a process that instills these will ultimately be more likely to succeed. The library profession is not a monolith when considering privacy. Some want lots of user data, others want none, and most fall in the middle. Privacy advocates may not feel that we have yet earned the right as a profession to be optimistic about the future of privacy in libraries. But creating a core set of staff who feel comfortable with privacy language and decision-making goes a long way to creating an environment at individual institutions where optimism is possible. Such efforts can filter throughout the profession.

Creating that core group of staff who feel empowered starts with culture. Culture is important because it will help when library workers cannot or do not know how to apply legal frameworks to the question of privacy. Most of us receive a cursory overview of privacy laws at some point in our training and may have to undergo more specific training. Understanding how we translate those laws into practical decisions, and where we may need to reject something that feels convenient or necessary in order to protect privacy, is an ongoing set of decisions. Positioning the library as a privacy expert and advocate will help enhance privacy across the institution.

Whether you are starting fresh with no privacy policy at all or revising an old one, a successful culture-building process starts with an inclusive and well-considered team. These will be the people who will understand the policy and be able to adapt procedures to comply with it. Teams should have a mix of perspectives, both in the type of expertise and staff role. A department manager in a public services area and an hourly worker in technical services would both be ideal members of the same team since they will each understand different areas of the library workflow to achieve the same result.

With all such work, questions of authority and ownership may crop up. For some libraries, policy created from grassroots efforts would be a problem. If this is the case at your library and you are not in library administration, your first task will be to find an administrative ally. This may be an area of interest for library leadership, but they may lack knowledge or time to pursue it and will be supportive of others heading up the work. If leadership is not supportive, you might be able to start a learning club or working group to investigate privacy issues and have conversations with colleagues in the same way you would in writing an effective policy. The outcome of this work could lead to more official documents in the future while still building a stronger privacy culture.

A related issue in deciding how to approach your policy is how it sits within a larger legal framework. For example, if your state has specific laws regarding library privacy, your policy must follow these laws. Certainly, at the very least it should refer to them for individuals to review. Your institution may have additional requirements. For example, some institutions may not allow individual units to create a privacy policy different from the institutional privacy policy. In such cases, it may be possible to write guidelines about specific ways in which the library follows the institutional privacy policy. If it varies significantly, that would be a point of negotiation with the institution.

If a policy per se is not permissible due to campus requirements or other restrictions, a team to investigate privacy best practices and ensure compliance will still help. Either way, you may find that a more experimental and informal process helps to plan the project initially, particularly if there is a lack of existing or up-to-date knowledge. Starting with a systems inventory and privacy audit is a practical way to get into the more theoretical or technical aspects of privacy. Working through a checklist of systems helps a team think across departments about how users interact with different services, leaving their information across systems. As gaps are discovered, the team can create a privacy project wish list to inform future work, which can be revisited on a yearly basis or whenever the library makes a change to technical infrastructure.

Academic governance and policymaking are often left to who shows up and does the work, for better or worse. Proactive policy development by the library can make this for the better. When the university chooses a new technical solution to meet a perceived educational technology need, people with knowledge about privacy must be there to question the tool and push back on usage that is overly prone to surveillance. Taking the time to educate staff and students on privacy gives everyone the tools to see systems through a lens of privacy and to think through issues in a more holistic way. One example of this is with the shift to widespread remote education in 2020, students suddenly had to allow their professors, classmates, and institutions into their private spaces. Students needed advocates for their privacy during that time, and the library is a natural advocate in educational technology spaces on campus if they have already positioned themselves as such or can take the opportunity to do so.

The reality of the work it takes to position the library and its staff as an ally to privacy on campus is not minimal. Creating a collaborative policy is a way to begin this effort, but maintaining the culture of privacy over time is more of a challenge. As with many efforts in planning and administration, without dedicated personnel assigned to the task, work is lodged with ad hoc groups or individuals, and as those individuals develop new interests or leave the library, no one maintains the policy. Regularly updating policies should be part of library work, but with a culture of privacy, there can be many opportunities for creating better procedures. In an ideal world, the privacy policy will be reviewed yearly or upon the adoption of a new system. The group that reviews it need not be a standing committee but should continue to reflect staff across the library and in different types of roles. Department heads, administrators, and external partners, such as campus IT, should be part of the conversation. Departments can "own" their part of the policy, but given the siloed nature of academic libraries, it will be necessary to make sure that some unit or group "owns" the writing of the policy, with the expectation that the cultural norms may need to be invigorated or enforced over time.

CONCLUSION

It was not until 1938 that the "Code of Ethics for Librarians" explicitly mentioned privacy as a professional library value.[18] In the following years of the twentieth century, changes in overall culture and technology made privacy an even more specific value. Still, given the threats to privacy in the library that have manifested in the last fifty years, many library workers are only dimly aware of these risks, and many libraries have not taken stock of the situation by creating a policy or even guidelines. While there are many legal requirements at the state, federal, and international levels that may affect academic libraries and require them to provide privacy protections, history indicates that the legal threat is not enough. Individuals who value privacy are not enough. They must find collaborators and build a team to begin to change the culture of their libraries and ensure this is a value that does not disappear.

APPENDIX

This is a small selection of the many resources that are available and will help institutions to learn about privacy and create a policy. Choosing the right approach for your context among these resources will take some thought and experimentation.

- "Creating a Privacy Policy from the Ground Up," ACRL TechConnect Blog, https://acrl.ala.org/techconnect/post/creating-a-privacy-policy-from-the-ground-up/. Find more resources and information about this project in this 2018 blog post.
- American Library Association Privacy Advocacy, https://www.ala.org/advocacy/privacy. The American Library Association (ALA) and its divisions have developed several resources to guide the privacy process. These date from the early 2000s in their original form but have been updated and expanded over the years. In recent years, these resources have expanded to become even more accessible, in particular the Privacy Field Guides project, funded by IMLS and led by Erin Berman and Bonnie Tijerina,[19] has created visually appealing and easy-to-understand short guides to every stage of the process and should be a first stop in planning your process and a deeper dive into the additional ALA resources.
- A National Forum on Web Privacy and Web Analytics, https://www.lib.montana.edu/privacy-forum/. The National Forum on Web Privacy and Web Analytics in 2018 was a catalyst for many projects and resources around privacy. The Action Handbook[20] is a useful toolkit for understanding different attitudes to privacy and provides many additional resources for how to gather data responsibly for library planning.
- Digital Library Federation Privacy & Ethics in Technology, https://wiki.diglib.org/Privacy_and_Ethics_in_Technology. This working group has created a number of reports and toolkits[21] to understand privacy in libraries in different areas, and their work is ongoing. Many members of this group also participated in the National Forum on Web Privacy and Web Analytics and have written about the participatory nature of both groups and the challenges and opportunities.[22]

ACKNOWLEDGMENTS

I would like to thank Niamh McGuigan, now at Brown University, who co-chaired the original Patron Privacy Task Force and co-wrote the policy with me. I would also like to thank Hong Ma, Head of Library Systems, and the entire Loyola

University Chicago Systems team who have helped with many of the planning and technical elements of privacy projects.

NOTES

1. Kaetrena Davis Kendrick, "The Low Morale Experience of Academic Librarians: A Phenomenological Study," *Journal of Library Administration* 57, no. 8 (November 17, 2017): 861, https://doi.org/10.1080/01930826.2017.1368325.
2. Ann Glusker et al., "'Viewed as Equals': The Impacts of Library Organizational Cultures and Management on Library Staff Morale," *Journal of Library Administration* 62, no. 2 (February 17, 2022): 167–68, https://doi.org/10.1080/01930826.2022.2026119.
3. Bruce S. Johnson, "A More Cooperative Clerk: The Confidentiality of Library Records," *Law Library Journal* 81, no. 4 (1989): 776.
4. Johnson, "A More Cooperative Clerk," 800–801.
5. Karen A. Coombs, "Walking a Tightrope: Academic Libraries and Privacy," *The Journal of Academic Librarianship* 30, no. 6 (November 1, 2004): 493–94, https://doi.org/10.1016/j.acalib.2004.08.003.
6. Stacy Voeller, "Privacy Policy Assessment for the Livingston Lord Library at Minnesota State University Moorhead," *Library Philosophy & Practice* (November 2007): 9–10.
7. Chris Matz, "Libraries and the USA PATRIOT Act: Values in Conflict," *Journal of Library Administration* 47, no. 3–4 (May 2008): 84, https://doi.org/10.1080/01930820802186399.
8. Michael Zimmer, "Librarians' Attitudes Regarding Information and Internet Privacy," *The Library Quarterly: Information, Community, Policy* 84, no. 2 (2014): 147, https://doi.org/10.1086/675329.
9. Kyle M. L. Jones et al., "'We're Being Tracked at All Times': Student Perspectives of Their Privacy in Relation to Learning Analytics in Higher Education," *Journal of the Association for Information Science and Technology* 71, no. 9 (2020): 1053, https://doi.org/10.1002/asi.24358.
10. Jones et al., "'We're Being Tracked at All Times,'" 1052.
11. Emily Singley, "A Holistic Approach to User Privacy in Academic Libraries," *The Journal of Academic Librarianship* 46, no. 3 (May 1, 2020): 2, https://doi.org/10.1016/j.acalib.2020.102151.
12. "The Annual Report on the Economic Status of the Profession, 2020-21," American Association of University Professors, AAUP, June 28, 2021, 14, https://www.aaup.org/report/annual-report-economic-status-profession-2021-22.
13. Monica D. T. Rysavy and Russell Michalak, "Data Privacy and Academic Libraries: Non-PII, PII, and Librarians' Reflections (Part 1)," *Journal of Library Administration* 59, no. 5 (July 4, 2019): 532–47, https://doi.org/10.1080/01930826.2019.1616973.
14. Jones et al., "'We're Being Tracked at All Times,'" 1055.
15. Patricia Hurtado and Francesa Maglione, "In a Post-Roe World, More Miscarriage and Stillbirth Prosecutions Await Women," Bloomberg.com, July 5, 2022, https://www.bloomberg.com/news/articles/2022-07-05/miscarriage-stillbirth-prosecutions-await-women-post-roe.
16. "American Library Association (ALA) Condemns Proposed State Legislation Limiting Access to Information on Reproductive Health," American Library Association, News and Press Center, August 9, 2022, https://www.ala.org/news/press-releases/2022/08/american-library-association-ala-condemns-proposed-state-legislation-limiting.
17. "About Reports and Privacy," OpenAthens, OpenAthens Documentation, accessed January 14, 2022, https://docs.openathens.net/libraries/about-reports-and-privacy.
18. Johnson, "A More Cooperative Clerk," 774.
19. "Privacy Advocacy Guides for Libraries," 2019, https://www.imls.gov/grants/awarded/lg-36-19-0073-19.
20. "A National Forum on Web Privacy and Web Analytics: Action Handbook," Montana State University, April 30, 2019, https://doi.org/10.15788/20190416.15446.

21. "Privacy and Ethics in Technology," DLF Wiki, January 12, 2022, https://wiki.diglib.org/Privacy_and_Ethics_in_Technology.
22. Scott W. H. Young et al., "Participatory Approaches for Designing and Sustaining Privacy-Oriented Library Services," *Journal of Intellectual Freedom & Privacy* 4, no. 4 (July 31, 2020): 3–18, https://doi.org/10.5860/jifp.v4i4.7134.

BIBLIOGRAPHY

American Association of University Professors. "The Annual Report on the Economic Status of the Profession, 2020-21." AAUP. June 28, 2021. https://www.aaup.org/report/annual-report-economic-status-profession-2021-22.

American Library Association. "American Library Association (ALA) Condemns Proposed State Legislation Limiting Access to Information on Reproductive Health." News and Press Center. August 9, 2022. https://www.ala.org/news/press-releases/2022/08/american-library-association-ala-condemns-proposed-state-legislation-limiting.

———. "Library Privacy Checklists." Advocacy, Legislation & Issues. February 2, 2017. https://www.ala.org/advocacy/privacy/checklists.

Coombs, Karen A. "Walking a Tightrope: Academic Libraries and Privacy." *The Journal of Academic Librarianship* 30, no. 6 (November 1, 2004): 493–98. https://doi.org/10.1016/j.acalib.2004.08.003.

Coyle, Karen. "Library Privacy Audits." kcoyle.net. Accessed January 14, 2022. http://www.kcoyle.net/privacy_audit.html.

DLF Wiki. "Privacy and Ethics in Technology." January 12, 2022. https://wiki.diglib.org/Privacy_and_Ethics_in_Technology.

Glusker, Ann, Celia Emmelhainz, Natalia Estrada, and Bonita Dyess. "'Viewed as Equals': The Impacts of Library Organizational Cultures and Management on Library Staff Morale." *Journal of Library Administration* 62, no. 2 (February 17, 2022): 153–89. https://doi.org/10.1080/01930826.2022.2026119.

Hurtado, Patricia, and Francesca Maglione. "In a Post-Roe World, More Miscarriage and Stillbirth Prosecutions Await Women." Bloomberg.com. July 5, 2022. https://www.bloomberg.com/news/articles/2022-07-05/miscarriage-stillbirth-prosecutions-await-women-post-roe.

Institute of Museum and Library Services. "Privacy Advocacy Guides for Libraries." 2019. https://www.imls.gov/grants/awarded/lg-36-19-0073-19.

Johnson, Bruce S. "A More Cooperative Clerk: The Confidentiality of Library Records." *Law Library Journal* 81, no. 4 (1989): 769–802.

Jones, Kyle M. L., Andrew Asher, Abigail Goben, Michael R. Perry, Dorothea Salo, Kristin A. Briney, and M. Brooke Robertshaw. "'We're Being Tracked at All Times': Student Perspectives of Their Privacy in Relation to Learning Analytics in Higher Education." *Journal of the Association for Information Science and Technology* 71, no. 9 (2020): 1044–59. https://doi.org/10.1002/asi.24358.

Kendrick, Kaetrena Davis. "The Low Morale Experience of Academic Librarians: A Phenomenological Study." *Journal of Library Administration* 57, no. 8 (November 17, 2017): 846–78. https://doi.org/10.1080/01930826.2017.1368325.

Matz, Chris. "Libraries and the USA PATRIOT Act: Values in Conflict." *Journal of Library Administration* 47, no. 3–4 (May 2008): 69–87. https://doi.org/10.1080/01930820802186399.

Michalak, Russell, and Monica D. T. Rysavy. "Data Privacy and Academic Libraries: Non-PII, PII, and Librarians' Reflections (Part 2)." *Journal of Library Administration* 59, no. 7 (October 2019): 768–85. https://doi.org/10.1080/01930826.2019.1649969.

Montana State University, Scott W. H. Young, Jason A. Clark, Sara Mannheimer, Lisa Janicke Hinchliffe, and University of Illinois at Urbana-Champaign. "A National Forum on Web Privacy and Web Analytics: Action Handbook." Montana State University. April 30, 2019. https://doi.org/10.15788/20190416.15446.

Nichols Hess, Amanda, Rachelle LaPorte-Fiori, and Keith Engwall. "Preserving Patron Privacy in the 21st Century Academic Library." *The Journal of Academic Librarianship* 41, no. 1 (January 1, 2015): 105–14. https://doi.org/10.1016/j.acalib.2014.10.010.

OpenAthens. "About Reports and Privacy." OpenAthens Documentation. Accessed January 14, 2022. https://docs.openathens.net/libraries/about-reports-and-privacy.

Singley, Emily. "A Holistic Approach to User Privacy in Academic Libraries." *The Journal of Academic Librarianship* 46, no. 3 (May 1, 2020): 102151. https://doi.org/10.1016/j.acalib.2020.102151.

Voeller, Stacy. "Privacy Policy Assessment for the Livingston Lord Library at Minnesota State University Moorhead." *Library Philosophy & Practice* (November 2007): 1–29.

Young, Scott W. H., Paige Walker, Shea Swauger, Michelle J. Gibeault, Sara Mannheimer, and Jason A. Clark. "Participatory Approaches for Designing and Sustaining Privacy-Oriented Library Services." *Journal of Intellectual Freedom & Privacy* 4, no. 4 (July 31, 2020): 3–18. https://doi.org/10.5860/jifp.v4i4.7134.

Zimmer, Michael. "Librarians' Attitudes Regarding Information and Internet Privacy." *The Library Quarterly: Information, Community, Policy* 84, no. 2 (2014): 123–51. https://doi.org/10.1086/675329.

CHAPTER 15

PRIVACY PEDAGOGY:
Aligning Privacy Advocacy with Course Design Standards

Lindsey Wharton, Liz Dunne, and Adam Beauchamp

INTRODUCTION

As concerns increase over big data, loss of control of personal information, and the overarching effects of these trends on societal well-being, an integral aspect of privacy advocacy is privacy education.[1] Integrating privacy practices into course and instructional design provides a new landscape for privacy advocacy for academic librarians. Librarians are well-suited for this work, based on the perspectives and expertise we gain through our experience with information literacy and course-embedded instruction, as well as our long-standing professional commitment to privacy advocacy. Partnerships established with instructional design teams and instructors create opportunities to integrate privacy into pedagogical practices at our institutions, from development of privacy-related learning objectives within curricula to assistance with assessing risk and mitigating harms when adopting digital tools.

This chapter focuses on aligning privacy work with course design standards and pedagogy, specifically in our university-adopted Quality Matters (QM) rubric. We will begin with an overview of privacy and data protection in higher education environments as it pertains to teaching and learning as well as how privacy has been integrated into the work and advocacy for academic librarians on campus. Then, we will provide an overview of how we developed a faculty-focused workshop on privacy pedagogy grounded in the QM rubric.

As a small group of librarians at a public research-intensive university, we present a case study of our experiences with privacy pedagogy and broader privacy initiatives in order to inform practitioners of the insights we have gained. Our privacy pedagogy is built upon the broader information literacy missions of our library, an effort to further privacy advocacy through standard course design rubrics, and our professional ethics, both as librarians and as teachers.[2]

PRIVACY AND DATA PROTECTION IN HIGHER EDUCATION

Digital tools and technologies that collect vast amounts of personal data have become ubiquitous in higher education, especially in course design, information technology, and academic support units across campuses. Students' data can be collected through learning management systems, video conferencing and communication tools, apps and web-based tools, and through interactions with personal devices and ID card readers. The resulting datasets can then be aggregated collaboratively and collectively among campus units and departments.[3] As pressure grows to make educational analytics more precise, institutions are incentivized to collect more data, not only in the learning environment but also across multiple online and physical spaces.[4] The educational technology companies (EdTech) that sell these tools and platforms profit from gathering as much personal data as possible, which they then monetize by selling their claims to be able to personalize services and predict student behavior.[5] Thus, their business models depend on suppressing user privacy, which could shield valuable data from them.

All digital tools carry an element of risk, to institutions and to users, alongside their benefits, but risk assessment is often time-consuming without clear standards or training for decision-makers.[6] In some cases, EdTech also markets harmful ideas about students and learning in order to convince university administrators that such data collection is necessary. For example, anti-plagiarism software and online test proctoring services sell the idea that all students are potential cheaters, thereby justifying the need to purchase their harmful surveillance products.[7] Once these products are adopted, without proper reflection, they may become normalized and have lasting impacts on privacy with potentially discriminatory consequences.

Digital tool adoptions that introduce harm and surveillance have created an antagonistic and adversarial relationship between students and educators, especially when these technologies limit students' agency. Audrey Watters has observed that educational technologies are often "built with a belief that students shouldn't have agency but rather should be engineered and optimized," thereby curtailing students' autonomy and their ability to make decisions about their own learning.[8] Chris Gilliard further argues that "student labor is rendered invisible (and uncompensated), and student consent is not taken into account. In other words, students often provide the raw material by which ed tech is developed, improved, and instituted, but their agency is for the most part not an issue."[9]

Privacy advocates and concerned educators have questioned the amount of moral consideration offered to the growing prevalence of learning analytics and surveillance capitalism.[10] Trina Magi explores the definition and concerns around privacy, identifying fourteen reasons why privacy is integral to wide-ranging fields and cultures, benefiting individuals, relationships, and society. Many of these, such as opportunity for relaxation, allowance for creativity, and provision of space for debate, speak to an improved learning environment.[11] Within the field of instructional design and technology, learner privacy issues have consistently been identified in the literature as a concern in higher education.[12]

Privacy advocates and educators have also pushed back against the common misconception that students and younger generations do not care about privacy.[13] Daniel Solove argues that these generalized attitudes about privacy have more to do with conflated issues and flawed logic in the interest of avoiding regulation than with empirical evidence.[14] In fact, recent studies of student perspectives on data use in higher education have shown that students do indeed care about data privacy, especially concerning who uses their data and for what purposes. A 2017 study conducted at our institution by education researchers examined Facebook use in higher education and revealed that 92 percent of students who identified as Facebook users attempted to manage their privacy within the platform, through censorship or through the privacy settings, and expressed an overall interest in minimizing their digital footprint.[15] Students have also expressed a degree of situational awareness about their data, affording greater trust to educational and non-profit organizations than to for-profit commercial enterprises like most retailers and social media companies.[16]

PRIVACY AND ACADEMIC LIBRARIANSHIP

The rapid pivot to remote and online instruction during the COVID-19 pandemic increased both the prevalence of education technologies in higher education and critical scrutiny of these digital tools and platforms. Librarians, who have long been advocates for patron privacy and intellectual freedom, are well-situated to take a leadership role in policy debates and pedagogical support on these issues. As part of our professional code of ethics, we believe that protecting library patrons' privacy and keeping their reading habits confidential is essential to intellectual freedom.[17] Surveillance over what you read or download may have a chilling effect on which kinds of information you can safely access. However, the library profession's privacy advocacy has traditionally been focused internally and applied to library policies and practices. For example, librarians strive to collect the least amount of patron data possible, keep circulation records and the content of reference questions confidential, and write privacy protections into license agreements with publishers and database companies. When librarians have advocated externally for patron privacy, the focus has often been defense against government intrusion, as evidenced in librarians' opposition to the PATRIOT ACT of 2001.[18]

Librarians are also involved in some of the data-intensive technologies and practices sweeping higher education. Academic libraries have felt the pressures of outcomes-based assessment and made efforts to align their practices and programming with broader institutional efforts. For example, some libraries have attempted to connect transactional usage of library spaces and resources with measures of student success. Some within the library profession have even embraced data-intensive assessments, mostly in the form of learning analytics. Kyle Jones et al. provide a thorough review of the learning analytics literature and professional debate.[19] Through this debate, librarians find themselves already engaged in campus-wide conversations about student data and privacy, creating opportunities to share our professional concerns and ethical standards.

It was in this context of internal and external debates on the disposition of student data collection, educational technologies, and professional ethics that the librarians at Florida State University Libraries began to mobilize. Before the pandemic, FSU librarians began to debate the wisdom of our own foray into data accumulation and learning analytics projects. Mirroring the broader professional debate, some claimed that data-intensive analysis would allow librarians to more effectively intervene in the education of struggling students. Others noted the methodological flaws of such practices, rooted, at best, in a deficit model of education, and at worst, in the racist, colonialist ideologies baked into the algorithmic sorting and quantifying of human lives.[20] At the same time, FSU Libraries began to consider single sign-on (SSO) alternatives for remote authentication of electronic resources. In these discussions, some saw the potential to track individual users along with the resources they access, ostensibly to make better decisions around licensing, budgeting, and marketing of e-resources. This elicited a strong response among librarians concerned about the privacy implications of tying individual users directly to databases, journals, and even individual articles accessed.

Finally, in the spring of 2020, when the COVID-19 pandemic forced a sudden transition to remote teaching and learning, the FSU administration touted our access to Honorlock, an online remote proctoring service. As with other similar products, Honorlock accesses students' individual computer cameras and microphones to monitor and record test-takers' faces, movements, and environments, claiming that their algorithms use such surveillance to detect academic dishonesty. While Honorlock had been available before the pandemic, many students were encountering it for the first time and were justifiably horrified. As stories of remote proctoring gone terribly wrong filtered into the national news coverage, FSU students launched a petition asking FSU to refrain from promoting Honorlock as it violated students' privacy and was unfair to students who didn't have the requisite computer hardware.

Amidst the internal and external debates about privacy, surveillance, and technology, a group of FSU librarians, the present authors included, formed the Privacy Special Interest Group. This group met regularly to discuss the state of privacy on FSU's campus and to strategize how we could best advocate for students' privacy and our professional values. Over the course of that year, the group established a public-facing statement of the FSU Libraries' Privacy Principles,[21] released a blog post in direct response to the Honorlock controversy,[22] and strengthened collaborative efforts with campus partners, including the Office of Distance Learning (ODL) and the Center for the Advancement of Teaching (CAT). It was through these partnerships that the privacy advocates at FSU Libraries shifted from offering critiques of objectionable surveillance technology to offering more positive solutions through alternative pedagogies.

ESTABLISHING PRIVACY PEDAGOGY

We define privacy pedagogy as teaching about privacy while also teaching with our privacy principles. In other words, privacy is both the content and the method of instruction. This is especially important in an online course, where students and instructors interact on digital platforms and those relationships are mediated by the technologies that the instructor has invited into the course. Learning can be affected by undue surveillance. Some students might hesitate to engage in free inquiry for fear of having their mistakes or misunderstandings recorded and scrutinized. Others might hold back their creativity if only certain behaviors are tracked and rewarded by classroom technologies.[23] Librarians have ample opportunity to integrate discussions of privacy into their own instruction, often in the form of "one-shot" information literacy sessions. Others may teach for-credit courses and have more freedom to include privacy principles in both the content and teaching methods of the course. In addition to our own instruction, however, librarians are well-positioned to advocate for privacy pedagogy across our campus and to support teaching faculty in adopting their own privacy pedagogy.

Historically, literacy initiatives have been utilized as a method to promote social justice, a philosophy grounded in the great work of Paulo Freire's *Pedagogy of the Oppressed* and applicable to the problems faced in digital learning.[24] Though information and digital literacy competencies have been adapted to meet the needs of an ever-changing information environment, privacy-related literacies and instruction have only recently been explored. Raffaghelli examined data literacy and its relationship to social justice with pedagogical approaches to examine data collection, analysis, power dynamics, as well as the ethical use of educational data.[25] Data literacies that explore educational and personal data require instructors to adopt a professional and ethical position with efforts to expose "the bigger picture" in the context of the course curriculum as well as a critical consideration of building "fair data cultures."[26] Furthermore, critical digital literacy, and the instructional counterpart of critical digital pedagogy, aim to integrate privacy education and surveillance resistance into discipline-specific courses, promoting, for example, efforts to "break-up" with social media, question or resist harmful EdTech, and provide learners with the tools and skills to critically engage with data in research.[27]

Within LIS literature, case studies of privacy instruction have included online profile management, algorithmic bias, and the broader context of metaliteracy.[28] Hartman-Caverly and Chisolm broadly survey the history and landscape of privacy literacy with an exploratory survey of current instruction practices. The authors demonstrate that while academic librarians address privacy within information literacy instruction, significant barriers—namely time, expertise, and administrative support—hinder these efforts. Another significant finding from the assessment was that none of the 163 respondents indicated that privacy topics were being taught by another campus department.[29] Additionally, instructors' perceptions and measures to address student privacy have a significant impact on how privacy is addressed in online and virtual classrooms. Jones and Vascoy focused on syllabi as values-based policy and analyze if and how LIS instructors adopt these recommendations in their own syllabi. Their research findings revealed that only 2 percent of the 8,302 syllabi examined contained language specific to privacy, with 36 percent mentioning privacy when discussing tools, 35 percent when discussing communication, and 32 percent in relation to institutional policies. The authors reflected on whether this indicated that instructors do not value privacy or lack the motivation to include privacy language.[30] In a subsequent study, Jones, Vascoy, Bright, and Harding surveyed over 500 instructors and found that faculty recognize the importance of privacy on student learning, specifically through the lens of information access, though they noted that further research was needed to examine how these perceptions affect pedagogical practices.[31]

Our analysis seeks to answer these cross-disciplinary calls to action and connect the foundational work into privacy advocacy and literacy in academic librarianship, information literacy instruction and related metaliteracies, and the broader ethical and practical concerns around student data in the field of teaching and learning through an exploration into privacy pedagogy. By aligning this initiative with course design rubrics championed by our university, our team of librarians realized a natural partnership with our Office of Distance Learning, leading to a Privacy Pedagogy faculty workshop and integration of privacy pedagogy into some of our teaching and learning.

OUR EXPERIENCE ADVOCATING PRIVACY PEDAGOGY WITH QM

As part of a recent Online Quality Initiative, our institution's Office of Distance Learning (ODL) adopted the QM Higher Education Rubric to assess and improve the quality of online courses offered at the university. The Quality Matters (QM) rubric is one of the most widely recognized online course design standards, providing general and specific rubric standards as best practices for course design. Full certification requires a QM peer review. The Quality Matters standards offer multiple opportunities to consider the purpose and privacy credentials of EdTech we consider when designing online learning experiences. Given this opportunity to introduce instructors to privacy pedagogy through the QM lens, we identified the ODL as an optimal partner for promoting our efforts. Lindsey Wharton, the extended campus and distance services librarian, already maintained a fruitful working relationship with the ODL and participated in the ODL's semesterly workshop series aimed at aiding instructors with their digital instruction.

We began by analyzing the QM standards to identify opportunities for integrating privacy pedagogy into online learning. The most obvious is QM standard 6.5, which asks that we provide links to privacy policies for all external tools. But for anyone who has read a privacy policy, simply providing links may not be enough. For example, Google's privacy policy, which is written in relatively readable prose, is still a daunting thirty-one pages long. Students will likely need support in knowing what privacy protections to look for when selecting digital products and in understanding the legal language often found in these documents.

However, providing links to privacy policies and helping students to interpret them typically come at the end of the course planning process. There are opportunities much earlier in the course design process and on the QM standards to consider privacy pedagogy. As soon as we establish our learning objectives (QM 2), we begin to review and select the instructional materials and technologies that we will invite into our classroom to achieve our goals. QM standard 4 covers instructional materials, requiring, for example, that instructional materials contribute to achieving the stated learning objectives (QM 4.1), and that the relationship between selected materials and the course learning objectives is clearly explained (QM 4.2). QM standard 6 addresses course technology, including a parallel requirement that our technologies also support the learning objectives. Therefore, throughout the planning process, and at multiple points in the QM rubric, we have opportunities to inject privacy pedagogy into our practice. Thus, when we do share the privacy policies of our chosen technologies, we will be prepared to discuss our decision-making process, the privacy pros and cons of each online tool, and how these technologies support the learning outcomes of the course.

With a clearer understanding of how privacy pedagogy can be connected to multiple QM standards, we developed a synchronous session as part of the ODL's workshop series that engages instructors in the above-mentioned dialogues regarding technology and privacy in higher education. After participants situate their own teaching and learning experiences within these broader conversations, the workshop culminates in an activity in which they evaluate the privacy implications of the digital tools in their classrooms, both ethically and pedagogically. To accomplish this goal, we first considered creating a matrix of digital tools commonly used in the classroom that would include information on each tool's privacy-related features and functions. We ultimately decided that such a static resource would never be as exhaustive as we intended. Furthermore, having instructors use it to make their tool selection decisions was rather limiting and antithetical to the critical analyses we hoped to facilitate. We instead developed a set of tasks (see appendix) that instructors can work through to consider more critically the privacy implications of adopting a tool in their course and what role that tool might play in their students' learning experiences. Our departmental contacts at the ODL were receptive to our workshop proposal and offered to host two sessions of it as part of their fall 2021 workshop series.

Despite promoting the workshop via the web presence of both the ODL and the Libraries, neither session was attended. As is the case with many one-off workshops, the lack of attendance can be attributed to a number of potential factors. Perhaps the sessions were offered too late in the semester, at a time when most instructors had already designed their assignments with certain technologies in mind and felt that these pedagogical decisions were immutable at that point. Maybe the audience that regularly attends ODL-hosted workshops was not the audience our instructional content appeals to. It is also possible that the ongoing stress educators have faced due to COVID-19 has shifted their instructional priorities away from combatting privacy concerns. And as discussed further in the next section, we conclude that it is also likely that the QM rubric was in fact too narrow of an entry point to reach our intended audience and convey the breadth of our approach to privacy pedagogy.

Despite the low attendance numbers for our initial workshop offering, we remain committed to raising awareness of the threats EdTech poses to student privacy and to training instructors to consider privacy pedagogy when choosing to incorporate digital tools into their courses. As such, we will attempt other iterations of our instruction and continue seeking campus partners who will join us in championing privacy-centered course design. We plan on breaking out of the confines of the QM rubric and partnering with the Program of Instructional Excellence, an office that supports the instructional development of graduate student teaching assistants. We believe this audience will be motivated to expand their course design practices to include a privacy perspective, creating course assignments that protect learners' personal data and empowering learners to develop their own set of informed privacy principles that they can exercise both in and outside of the classroom. Aside from offering synchronous sessions of the workshop, we will also record the presentation and package it as an asynchronous resource accompanied by additional literature and activities that instructors can access as needed, hopefully alleviating the timing issues associated with scheduling workshops.

In addition to directly advancing our own education efforts, we found that offering such workshops serves another important purpose in that it markets our privacy pedagogy and facilitates connections with other parties on campus who are similarly invested in privacy in higher education. For instance, one of our colleagues at ODL later referred a faculty member from FSU's Department of Instructional Systems and Learning Technologies (ISLT) to the Libraries' Privacy Special Interest Group based on their perceived connection between our workshop content and this faculty member's teaching and research interests. This faculty member teaches courses on topics such as learning analytics to graduate students in the ISLT program, some of whom will likely go on to become instructional design practitioners in higher ed settings where they collaborate with instructors to design courses. Being able to engage such faculty in privacy-pedagogy dialogues is an integral step in increasing the likelihood that the future instructional designers and educators they train are taking learner-centered approaches to course design that prioritize the privacy of learners and foster learners' abilities to develop and abide by their own set of privacy ethics. Leveraging our workshop offerings to build ongoing relationships with faculty and staff who influence department as well as campus-wide discourse on privacy in higher education and how that impacts our teaching practices is an invaluable strategy in our advocacy efforts.

LIMITATION OF THE QM APPROACH

As alluded to above, one conclusion we draw from the lack of attendance at the synchronous workshops concerns the Quality Matters rubric as a point of entry for librarians to discuss and advocate for privacy pedagogy. We surmise that there are two reasons the QM rubric failed to capture the attention of our desired audience. First, we reflected on the extent to which Quality Matters is integrated into course design and teaching at our institution. At FSU, the QM standards are required for all online courses, which go through a formal review process, but instructors teaching in person, or even remotely during the COVID-19 pandemic, are not required to comply with the QM rubric. This limits the reach and application of the QM standards to an important but small subset of all university instruction. Furthermore, the QM review process at FSU assumes that the online course has already been created; the application form for QM review asks that instructors provide a link to their existing Canvas course (https://odl.fsu.edu/certify-my-course). Thus, the QM standards are being used as a *post hoc* compliance tool rather than a fully integrated instructional design program.

Second, the QM rubric itself may give the impression that privacy pedagogy is easy to implement and requires little effort. While we outline the many ways privacy attaches to the QM standards above, the only explicit mention of privacy in the rubric, standard 6.4, merely asks that "the course provides learners with information on protecting their data and privacy." An instructor could comply, albeit superficially, by including the URL to a technology product's terms and conditions or privacy website on their syllabus without providing any additional context, critique, or proactive effort to protect students' data. At FSU, since instructors are expected to create their online courses *before* seeking QM certification, the QM rubric is likely to be used simply as a checklist, a final hurdle to clear, rather than a means to effect meaningful pedagogical changes except by the most motivated and well-resourced instructors. If instructors can earn a QM point for simply copying and pasting a link, it seems unlikely that they would substantially alter a course that is otherwise devoid of privacy pedagogy, or even one that includes harmful technologies, in response to the QM certification process. As Burtis and Stommel noted, this sort of implementation of Quality Matters likely results in "administrative box-checking instead of actual care."[32]

While we have plans to repackage our workshop and approach new audiences with the QM-based guidance, we have also had some success advocating privacy pedagogy without QM standards through established departmental and individual relationships, such as those cultivated by subject or liaison librarians. In many academic libraries, these librarians serve as the first point of contact for faculty and other instructors, providing discipline-specific reference, instruction, and outreach services. These established relationships can provide fertile ground in which to plant the seeds of privacy pedagogy. For example, in summer 2020, after the dramatic pivot to remote instruction during the COVID-19 pandemic, an opportunity surfaced with the FSU Department of Religion to promote privacy pedagogy. Co-author Adam Beauchamp, the humanities librarian, serves as subject liaison to Religion and learned that graduate students were organizing a summer boot camp for faculty and graduate instructors to improve their online instruction in the fall. Adam reached out to the organizers to offer his expertise and joined the planning committee for the weekly series of workshops. Adam took the lead in developing and facilitating the final session, focused on effective and ethical assessment of student learning. In this session, he shared his expertise and offered advice on assessment techniques that did not require the use of academic surveillance tools like Turnitin, a plagiarism detection tool, and Honorlock, an online proctoring system. The effort was very successful, with several participants pledging during the session never to use such invasive tools in their teaching. A year later, while Adam participated in an orientation session for new graduate students in this department, the chair noted that he didn't know of anyone who used Honorlock in their classes, suggesting perhaps that this session and Adam's overall privacy advocacy had a lasting impact.

CONCLUSION

Based on our recent experiences and reflection, we will not abandon our mission to advocate for privacy on campus and within online and physical learning spaces. Librarians can use our knowledge of privacy and data concerns in higher ed, the guiding ethics of our profession, and the lens of Quality Matters to encourage instructors to investigate what tools they use in the classroom and enshrine learners' rights to privacy and privacy-related agency in their course design. Instruction librarians also have an opportunity to include privacy literacy in information literacy instruction and encourage students to think about data, privacy, and ethics as an integral part of our goal for learners to think critically about information. Librarians can and should remain privacy advocates in the higher education landscape by clearly communicating how we collect and use personal identifying information and other data, continuing to negotiate data protection and minimization strategies on our campuses, and developing privacy policies and principles to guide our work and library practices. Finally, students should always be at the center of this work. Librarians should make space for student voices and find ways to partner with them, both in their learning and in broader privacy advocacy; they should also encourage faculty to adopt student-centric teaching strategies that protect student privacy and provide opportunities for students to develop and exercise their own privacy principles. Through these efforts and collaborations, we hope that librarians will feel empowered to become privacy champions within their communities and make positive contributions toward the widespread adoption of privacy pedagogy in instruction and course design.

APPENDIX
APPLYING PRIVACY PEDAGOGY TO YOUR EDUCATIONAL TECHNOLOGIES

A. Determine how the tool serves your learning objectives.
B. Strategically read the tool's privacy policy to discern and convey what data it collects and why, how the data is stored and protected, and who owns that data and what they can do with it.
C. Investigate news surrounding the tool, paying particular attention to learners' attitudes toward it.
D. Consider how using that tool may impact learners outside of your classroom, such as whether it leads to context collapse or feeds into predictive learning analytics.
E. Explore how the tool allows for learner agency, such as whether learners can choose to create an account or remain anonymous and whether the tool allows learners to interact with one another and demonstrate their understanding of course content in diverse ways best suited to them.

ACKNOWLEDGMENTS

We would like to acknowledge our fellow Privacy Interest Group members: Matt Hunter, Theresa Haworth, Kirsten Kinsley, and Scott Schmucker.

Also, many thanks to our colleagues at the FSU Office of Distance Learning, especially Kerry Burner.

NOTES

1. Michael Zimmer, "Librarians' Attitudes Regarding Information and Internet Privacy," *The Library Quarterly* 84, no. 2 (April 1, 2014): 123–51, https://doi.org/10.1086/675329; Sarah Hartman-Caverly and Alexandria Chisholm, "Privacy Literacy Instruction Practices in Academic Libraries: Past, Present, and Possibilities," *IFLA Journal* 46, no. 4 (December 1, 2020): 305–27, https://doi.org/10.1177/0340035220956804.
2. Marian Fitzmaurice, "Voices from within: Teaching in Higher Education as a Moral Practice," *Teaching in Higher Education* 13, no. 3 (June 2008): 341–52, https://doi.org/10.1080/13562510802045386.
3. Goldie Blumenstyk, "Big Data Is Getting Bigger. So Are the Privacy and Ethical Questions," *The Chronicle of Higher Education* (July 31, 2018), http://www.chronicle.com/article/big-data-is-getting-bigger-so-are-the-privacy-and-ethical-questions/; Lee Garner, "Students Under Surveillance?," *The Chronicle of Higher Education* (October 13, 2019), http://www.chronicle.com/article/students-under-surveillance/; Roxana Marachi and Lawrence Quill, "The Case of Canvas: Longitudinal Datafication through Learning Management Systems," *Teaching in Higher Education* 25, no. 4 (May 18, 2020): 418–34, https://doi.org/10.1080/13562517.2020.1739641; Britt Paris, Rebecca Reynolds, and

3. Catherine McGowan, "Platforms Like Canvas Play Fast and Loose With Students' Data," *The Nation* (April 22, 2021), https://www.thenation.com/article/society/canvas-surveillance/.
4. Chris Sadler, "Privacy Considerations in Higher Education Online Learning," New America Open Technology Institute, October 24, 2020, http://newamerica.org/oti/reports/privacy-considerations-higher-education-online-learning/.
5. Shoshana Zuboff, *The Age of Surveillance Capitalism: The Fight for a Human Future at the New Frontier of Power* (New York: Public Affairs, 2019).
6. Lindsey Wharton, "Ethical Implications of Digital Tools and Emerging Roles for Academic Librarians," in *Applying Library Values to Emerging Technology: Decision-Making in the Age of Open Access, Maker Spaces, and the Ever-Changing Library*, ed. Peter D. Fernandez and Kelly Tilton, ACRL Publications in Librarianship, no. 72 (Chicago: Association of College and Research Libraries, a division of the American Library Association, 2018), 35–54; Jenae Cohn, "Who Chooses What Ed Tech to Buy for the College Classroom?," *The Chronicle of Higher Education* (June 3, 2021), http://www.chronicle.com/article/who-chooses-what-ed-tech-to-buy-for-the-college-classroom.
7. Chris Gilliard, "How Ed Tech Is Exploiting Students," *The Chronicle of Higher Education* (April 8, 2018), http://www.chronicle.com/article/how-ed-tech-is-exploiting-students/; Shea Swauger, "Our Bodies Encoded: Algorithmic Test Proctoring in Higher Education," *Hybrid Pedagogy* (April 2, 2020), https://hybridpedagogy.org/our-bodies-encoded-algorithmic-test-proctoring-in-higher-education/; Adam Beauchamp, "Trust Students, Suspect Algorithms," *FSU Libraries* (blog), August 21, 2020, https://fsulib.com/trust-students-suspect-algorithms/; Charles Logan, "Toward Abolishing Online Proctoring: Counter-Narratives, Deep Change, and Pedagogies of Educational Dignity," *The Journal of Interactive Technology and Pedagogy*, no. 20 (December 10, 2021), https://jitp.commons.gc.cuny.edu/?p.
8. Audrey Watters, "Ed-Tech and Trauma," *Hack Education* (blog), November 5, 2020, http://hackeducation.com/2020/11/05/trauma.
9. Gilliard, "How Ed Tech Is Exploiting Students."
10. Joel A. Howell et al., "Are We on Our Way to Becoming a 'Helicopter University'? Academics' Views on Learning Analytics," *Technology, Knowledge and Learning: Learning Mathematics, Science and the Arts in the Context of Digital Technologies* 23, no. 1 (April 2018): 1–20, http://dx.doi.org/10.1007/s10758-017-9329-9.
11. Trina J. Magi, "Fourteen Reasons Privacy Matters: A Multidisciplinary Review of Scholarly Literature," *The Library Quarterly: Information, Community, Policy* 81, no. 2 (2011): 187–209, https://doi.org/10.1086/658870.
12. Hong Lin, "The Ethics of Instructional Technology: Issues and Coping Strategies Experienced by Professional Technologists in Design and Training Situations in Higher Education," *Educational Technology Research & Development* 55, no. 5 (October 2007): 411–37, https://doi.org/10.1007/s11423-006-9029-y.
13. Kyle M. L. Jones et al., "'We're Being Tracked at All Times': Student Perspectives of Their Privacy in Relation to Learning Analytics in Higher Education," *Journal of the Association for Information Science and Technology* 71, no. 9 (2020): 1044–59, https://doi.org/10.1002/asi.24358; Alison J. Head, Barbara Fister, and Margy MacMillan, "Information Literacy in the Age of Algorithms," Project Information Literacy Research Institute, January 15, 2020, https://projectinfolit.org/publications/algorithm-study.
14. Daniel J. Solove, "The Myth of the Privacy Paradox," SSRN Scholarly Paper (Rochester, NY: Social Science Research Network, January 29, 2021), 42, https://doi.org/10.2139/ssrn.3536265.
15. Vanessa P. Dennen and Kerry J. Burner, "Identity, Context Collapse, and Facebook Use in Higher Education: Putting Presence and Privacy at Odds," *Distance Education* 38, no. 2 (May 4, 2017): 173–92, https://doi.org/10.1080/01587919.2017.1322453.

16. Jones et al., "We're Being Tracked at All Times"; Jasmine Park and Amelia Vance, "Data Privacy in Higher Education: Yes, Students Care," *Educause Review* (February 11, 2021), https://er.educause.edu/articles/2021/2/data-privacy-in-higher-education-yes-students-care.
17. "Code of Ethics of the American Library Association," American Library Association, accessed September 20, 2019, https://www.ala.org/tools/ethics.
18. Emily Drabinski, "Librarians and the Patriot Act," *The Radical Teacher*, no. 77 (2006): 12–14; Chris Matz, "Libraries and the USA PATRIOT Act: Values in Conflict," *Journal of Library Administration* 47, no. 3–4 (July 1, 2008): 69–87, https://doi.org/10.1080/01930820802186399.
19. Kyle M. L. Jones et al., "A Comprehensive Primer to Library Learning Analytics Practices, Initiatives, and Privacy Issues," *College & Research Libraries* 81, no. 3 (April 3, 2020): 570–91, https://doi.org/10.5860/crl.81.3.570.
20. Some of this internal debate appeared in professional publications and conference presentations. See Kirsten Kinsley, "One Academic Library's Approach to the Learning Analytics Backlash," *Against the Grain*, April 1, 2020, https://against-the-grain.com/2020/04/v321-one-academic-librarys-approach-to-the-learning-analytics-backlash/; Adam Beauchamp and Mallary Rawls, "In Search of a Just and Responsible Culture of Assessment: Two Critical Alternatives to Learning Analytics in Libraries" (Conference presentation, Critical Librarianship & Pedagogy Symposium, Tucson, AZ, September 9, 2020), https://www.youtube.com/watch?v=t6f_1QvAu_A&feature=youtu.be. For more on the deficit model of education, see Eamon Tewell, "The Problem with Grit: Dismantling Deficit Thinking in Library Instruction," *portal: Libraries and the Academy* 20, no. 1 (January 2020): 137–59, https://doi.org/10.1353/pla.2020.0007. For more on racism and colonialism in learning analytics and algorithms, see April Hathcock, "Learning Agency, Not Analytics," *At The Intersection* (blog), January 24, 2018, https://aprilhathcock.wordpress.com/2018/01/24/learning-agency-not-analytics/; Simone Browne, *Dark Matters: On the Surveillance of Blackness* (Duke University Press, 2015); Safiya Umoja Noble, *Algorithms of Oppression: How Search Engines Reinforce Racism* (New York: New York University Press, 2018); Ruha Benjamin, *Race after Technology: Abolitionist Tools for the New Jim Code* (Polity, 2019).
21. "FSU Libraries Privacy Principles," FSU Libraries, accessed January 14, 2022, https://www.lib.fsu.edu/about/privacy-principles.
22. Beauchamp, "Trust Students, Suspect Algorithms."
23. Sarah Hartman-Caverly, "Human Nature Is Not a Machine: On Liberty, Attention Engineering, and Learning Analytics," *Library Trends* 68, no. 1 (2019): 24–53, https://doi.org/10.1353/lib.2019.0029.
24. Paulo Freire, *Pedagogy of the Oppressed*, 30th anniversary ed. (Continuum, 2000); Antony Farag, Luke Greeley, and Andrew Swindell, "Freire 2.0: Pedagogy of the Digitally Oppressed," *Educational Philosophy and Theory* (December 2, 2021): 1–14, https://doi.org/10.1080/00131857.2021.2010541.
25. Juliana Elisa Raffaghelli, "Is Data Literacy a Catalyst of Social Justice? A Response from Nine Data Literacy Initiatives in Higher Education," *Education Sciences* 10, no. 9 (September 2020): 233, https://doi.org/10.3390/educsci10090233.
26. Juliana Elisa Raffaghelli et al., "Supporting the Development of Critical Data Literacies in Higher Education: Building Blocks for Fair Data Cultures in Society," *International Journal of Educational Technology in Higher Education* 17, no. 1 (November 24, 2020): N.PAG-N.PAG, https://doi.org/10.1186/s41239-020-00235-w.
27. Estee Beck, "Breaking up with Facebook: Untethering from the Ideological Freight of Online Surveillance," *Hybrid Pedagogy* (June 24, 2014), https://hybridpedagogy.org/breaking-facebook-untethering-ideological-freight-online-surveillance/; Charles Logan, "Refusal, Partnership, and Countering Educational Technology's Harms," *Hybrid Pedagogy* (October 21, 2020), https://hybridpedagogy.org/refusal-partnership-countering-harms/; Annette N. Markham, "Critical Pedagogy as a Response to Datafication," *Qualitative Inquiry* 25, no. 8 (October 1, 2019): 754–60, https://doi.org/10.1177/1077800418809470.

28. Lauren Magnuson, "Promoting Privacy: Online and Reputation Management as an Information Literacy Skill," *College & Research Libraries News* 72, no. 3 (2011): 137–40, https://doi.org/10.5860/crln.72.3.8525; Eamon Tewell, "Toward the Resistant Reading of Information: Google, Resistant Spectatorship, and Critical Information Literacy," *portal: Libraries and the Academy* 16, no. 2 (2016): 289–310, https://muse.jhu.edu/pub/1/article/613843; Donna Witek and Teresa Grettano, "Teaching Metaliteracy: A New Paradigm in Action," *Reference Services Review* 42, no. 2 (2014): 188–208, https://www.researchgate.net/publication/275317628_Teaching_metaliteracy_A_new_paradigm_in_action.
29. Hartman-Caverly and Chisholm, "Privacy Literacy Instruction Practices."
30. Kyle M. L. Jones and Amy VanScoy, "The Syllabus as a Student Privacy Document in an Age of Learning Analytics," *Journal of Documentation* 75, no. 6 (January 1, 2019): 1350, https://doi.org/10.1108/JD-12-2018-0202.
31. Kyle Jones et al., "Do They Even Care? Measuring Instructor Value of Student Privacy in the Context of Learning Analytics," in *Proceedings of the 54th Hawaii International Conference on System Sciences* (Hawaii International Conference on System Sciences, Honolulu, Hawaii, 2021), 1529–37, https://doi.org/10.24251/HICSS.2021.185.
32. Martha Burtis and Jesse Stommel, "The Cult of Quality Matters," *Hybrid Pedagogy* (August 10, 2021), https://hybridpedagogy.org/the-cult-of-quality-matters/.

BIBLIOGRAPHY

American Library Association. "Code of Ethics of the American Library Association." Accessed September 20, 2019. https://www.ala.org/tools/ethics.

Beauchamp, Adam. "Trust Students, Suspect Algorithms." *FSU Libraries* (blog), August 21, 2020. https://fsulib.com/trust-students-suspect-algorithms/.

Beauchamp, Adam, and Mallary Rawls. "In Search of a Just and Responsible Culture of Assessment: Two Critical Alternatives to Learning Analytics in Libraries." Conference presentation presented at the Critical Librarianship & Pedagogy Symposium, Tucson, AZ. September 9, 2020. https://www.youtube.com/watch?v=t6f_1QvAu_A&feature=youtu.be.

Beck, Estee. "Breaking up with Facebook: Untethering from the Ideological Freight of Online Surveillance." *Hybrid Pedagogy* (June 24, 2014). https://hybridpedagogy.org/breaking-facebook-untethering-ideological-freight-online-surveillance/.

Benjamin, Ruha. *Race after Technology: Abolitionist Tools for the New Jim Code*. Polity, 2019.

Blumenstyk, Goldie. "Big Data Is Getting Bigger. So Are the Privacy and Ethical Questions." *The Chronicle of Higher Education* (July 31, 2018). http://www.chronicle.com/article/big-data-is-getting-bigger-so-are-the-privacy-and-ethical-questions/.

Browne, Simone. *Dark Matters: On the Surveillance of Blackness*. Duke University Press, 2015.

Burtis, Martha, and Jesse Stommel. "The Cult of Quality Matters." *Hybrid Pedagogy* (August 10, 2021). https://hybridpedagogy.org/the-cult-of-quality-matters/.

Cohn, Jenae. "Who Chooses What Ed Tech to Buy for the College Classroom?" *The Chronicle of Higher Education* (June 3, 2021). http://www.chronicle.com/article/who-chooses-what-ed-tech-to-buy-for-the-college-classroom.

Drabinski, Emily. "Librarians and the Patriot Act." *The Radical Teacher*, no. 77 (2006): 12–14.

Dennen, Vanessa P., and Kerry J. Burner. "Identity, Context Collapse, and Facebook Use in Higher Education: Putting Presence and Privacy at Odds." *Distance Education* 38, no. 2 (May 4, 2017): 173–92. https://doi.org/10.1080/01587919.2017.1322453.

Farag, Antony, Luke Greeley, and Andrew Swindell. "Freire 2.0: Pedagogy of the Digitally Oppressed." *Educational Philosophy and Theory* (December 2, 2021): 1–14. https://doi.org/10.1080/00131857.2021.2010541.

Fitzmaurice, Marian. "Voices from within: Teaching in Higher Education as a Moral Practice." *Teaching in Higher Education* 13, no. 3 (June 2008): 341–52. https://doi.org/10.1080/13562510802045386.

Freire, Paulo. *Pedagogy of the Oppressed*. 30th Anniversary ed. Continuum, 2000.

FSU Libraries. "FSU Libraries Privacy Principles." Accessed January 14, 2022. https://www.lib.fsu.edu/about/privacy-principles.

Garner, Lee. "Students Under Surveillance?" *The Chronicle of Higher Education* (October 13, 2019). http://www.chronicle.com/article/students-under-surveillance/.

Gilliard, Chris. "How Ed Tech Is Exploiting Students." *The Chronicle of Higher Education* (April 8, 2018). http://www.chronicle.com/article/how-ed-tech-is-exploiting-students/.

Hartman-Caverly, Sarah. "Human Nature Is Not a Machine: On Liberty, Attention Engineering, and Learning Analytics." *Library Trends* 68, no. 1 (2019): 24–53. https://doi.org/10.1353/lib.2019.0029.

Hartman-Caverly, Sarah, and Alexandria Chisholm. "Privacy Literacy Instruction Practices in Academic Libraries: Past, Present, and Possibilities." *IFLA Journal* 46, no. 4 (December 1, 2020): 305–27. https://doi.org/10.1177/0340035220956804.

Hathcock, April. "Learning Agency, Not Analytics." *At The Intersection* (blog), January 24, 2018. https://aprilhathcock.wordpress.com/2018/01/24/learning-agency-not-analytics/.

Jones, Kyle M. L., Andrew Asher, Abigail Goben, Michael R. Perry, Dorothea Salo, Kristin A. Briney, and M. Brooke Robertshaw. "'We're Being Tracked at All Times': Student Perspectives of Their Privacy in Relation to Learning Analytics in Higher Education." *Journal of the Association for Information Science and Technology* 71, no. 9 (2020): 1044–59. https://doi.org/10.1002/asi.24358.

Jones, Kyle M. L., Kristin A. Briney, Abigail Goben, Dorothea Salo, Andrew Asher, and Michael R. Perry. "A Comprehensive Primer to Library Learning Analytics Practices, Initiatives, and Privacy Issues." *College & Research Libraries* 81, no. 3 (April 3, 2020): 570–91. https://doi.org/10.5860/crl.81.3.570.

Jones, Kyle M. L., and Amy VanScoy. "The Syllabus as a Student Privacy Document in an Age of Learning Analytics." *Journal of Documentation* 75, no. 6 (January 1, 2019): 1333–55. https://doi.org/10.1108/JD-12-2018-0202.

Jones, Kyle, Amy Vanscoy, Kawanna Bright, and Alison Harding. "Do They Even Care? Measuring Instructor Value of Student Privacy in the Context of Learning Analytics." In *Proceedings of the 54th Hawaii International Conference on System Sciences*, 1529–37. Honolulu, Hawaii, 2021. https://doi.org/10.24251/HICSS.2021.185.

Kinsley, Kirsten. "One Academic Library's Approach to the Learning Analytics Backlash." *Against the Grain*. April 1, 2020. https://against-the-grain.com/2020/04/v321-one-academic-librarys-approach-to-the-learning-analytics-backlash/.

Lin, Hong. "The Ethics of Instructional Technology: Issues and Coping Strategies Experienced by Professional Technologists in Design and Training Situations in Higher Education." *Educational Technology Research & Development* 55, no. 5 (October 2007): 411–37. https://doi.org/10.1007/s11423-006-9029-y.

Logan, Charles. "Refusal, Partnership, and Countering Educational Technology's Harms." *Hybrid Pedagogy* (October 21, 2020). https://hybridpedagogy.org/refusal-partnership-countering-harms/.

———. "Toward Abolishing Online Proctoring: Counter-Narratives, Deep Change, and Pedagogies of Educational Dignity." *The Journal of Interactive Technology and Pedagogy*, no. 20 (December 10, 2021). https://jitp.commons.gc.cuny.edu/?p.

Magi, Trina J. "Fourteen Reasons Privacy Matters: A Multidisciplinary Review of Scholarly Literature." *The Library Quarterly: Information, Community, Policy* 81, no. 2 (2011): 187–209. https://doi.org/10.1086/658870.

Magnuson, Lauren. "Promoting Privacy: Online and Reputation Management as an Information Literacy Skill." *College & Research Libraries News* 72, no. 3 (2011): 137–40. https://doi.org/10.5860/crln.72.3.8525.

Marachi, Roxana, and Lawrence Quill. "The Case of Canvas: Longitudinal Datafication through Learning Management Systems." *Teaching in Higher Education* 25, no. 4 (May 18, 2020): 418–34. https://doi.org/10.1080/13562517.2020.1739641.

Markham, Annette N. "Critical Pedagogy as a Response to Datafication." *Qualitative Inquiry* 25, no. 8 (October 1, 2019): 754–60. https://doi.org/10.1177/1077800418809470.

Matz, Chris. "Libraries and the USA PATRIOT Act: Values in Conflict." *Journal of Library Administration* 47, no. 3–4 (July 1, 2008): 69–87. https://doi.org/10.1080/01930820802186399.

Noble, Safiya Umoja. *Algorithms of Oppression: How Search Engines Reinforce Racism.* New York: New York University Press, 2018.

Paris, Britt, Rebecca Reynolds, and Catherine McGowan. "Platforms Like Canvas Play Fast and Loose with Students' Data." *The Nation* (April 22, 2021). https://www.thenation.com/article/society/canvas-surveillance/.

Park, Jasmine, and Amelia Vance. "Data Privacy in Higher Education: Yes, Students Care." *Educause Review* (February 11, 2021). https://er.educause.edu/articles/2021/2/data-privacy-in-higher-education-yes-students-care.

Raffaghelli, Juliana Elisa. "Is Data Literacy a Catalyst of Social Justice? A Response from Nine Data Literacy Initiatives in Higher Education." *Education Sciences* 10, no. 9 (September 2020): 233. https://doi.org/10.3390/educsci10090233.

Raffaghelli, Juliana Elisa, Stefania Manca, Bonnie Stewart, Paul Prinsloo, and Albert Sangrà. "Supporting the Development of Critical Data Literacies in Higher Education: Building Blocks for Fair Data Cultures in Society." *International Journal of Educational Technology in Higher Education* 17, no. 1 (November 24, 2020): N.PAG-N.PAG. https://doi.org/10.1186/s41239-020-00235-w.

Roberts, Lynne D., Kristen Seaman, and David C. Gibson. "Are We on Our Way to Becoming a 'Helicopter University'? Academics' Views on Learning Analytics." *Technology, Knowledge and Learning: Learning Mathematics, Science and the Arts in the Context of Digital Technologies* 23, no. 1 (April 2018): 1–20. http://dx.doi.org/10.1007/s10758-017-9329-9.

Sadler, Chris. "Privacy Considerations in Higher Education Online Learning." New America Open Technology Institute. October 24, 2020. http://newamerica.org/oti/reports/privacy-considerations-higher-education-online-learning/.

Solove, Daniel J. "The Myth of the Privacy Paradox." SSRN Scholarly Paper. Rochester, NY: Social Science Research Network, January 29, 2021. https://doi.org/10.2139/ssrn.3536265.

Swauger, Shea. "Our Bodies Encoded: Algorithmic Test Proctoring in Higher Education." *Hybrid Pedagogy* (April 2, 2020). https://hybridpedagogy.org/our-bodies-encoded-algorithmic-test-proctoring-in-higher-education/.

Tewell, Eamon. "The Problem with Grit: Dismantling Deficit Thinking in Library Instruction." *portal: Libraries and the Academy* 20, no. 1 (January 2020): 137–59. https://doi.org/10.1353/pla.2020.0007.

———. "Toward the Resistant Reading of Information: Google, Resistant Spectatorship, and Critical Information Literacy." *portal: Libraries and the Academy* 16, no. 2 (2016): 289–310. https://muse.jhu.edu/pub/1/article/613843.

Watters, Audrey. "Ed-Tech and Trauma." *Hack Education* (blog), November 5, 2020. http://hackeducation.com/2020/11/05/trauma.

Wharton, Lindsey. "Ethical Implications of Digital Tools and Emerging Roles for Academic Librarians." In *Applying Library Values to Emerging Technology: Decision-Making in the Age of Open Access, Maker Spaces, and the Ever-Changing Library*, edited by Peter D. Fernandez and Kelly Tilton, 35–54. ACRL Publications in Librarianship, no. 72. Chicago: Association of College and Research Libraries, a division of the American Library Association, 2018.

Witek, Donna, and Teresa Grettano. "Teaching Metaliteracy: A New Paradigm in Action." *Reference Services Review* 42, no. 2 (2014): 188–208. https://www.researchgate.net/publication/275317628_Teaching_metaliteracy_A_new_paradigm_in_action.

Zimmer, Michael. "Librarians' Attitudes Regarding Information and Internet Privacy." *The Library Quarterly* 84, no. 2 (April 1, 2014): 123–51. https://doi.org/10.1086/675329.

Zuboff, Shoshana. *The Age of Surveillance Capitalism: The Fight for a Human Future at the New Frontier of Power.* New York: PublicAffairs, 2019.

CHAPTER 16

WHAT SUCCESSFUL STUDENTS KNOW:
Promotes *Promoting Privacy Literacy and Positive Digital Citizenship through Credit-Bearing Courses and Co-Curricular Partnerships*

Theresa McDevitt, Crystal Machado, Melissa Calderon, Jaqueline McGinty, Jennifer McCroskey, and Ann Sesti

INTRODUCTION

Students are drawn to institutions of higher learning by the promise of opportunities to acquire skills and earn degrees that will enable them to find rewarding careers. Librarians, faculty instructors, and student support professionals intentionally plan curricular and extra-curricular experiences to help students reach their goals. Increasingly, this involves the creation of learning experiences to help students develop the skills to communicate successfully within, and contribute positively to, the challenging and always-changing online world in a productive, professional way, while still maintaining their privacy.

There is a growing need for such intervention. Cybervetting, or employers' practice of screening social media postings of job applicants, may be the "new normal." Phishing attempts are on the rise.[1] College students are damaging their career prospects, suffering economic losses, and adding to the misinformation that abounds on the internet through the inappropriate sharing of private and inappropriate information. Curricular or co-curricular educational efforts to address these success-threatening issues might help students avoid such errors. Librarians have a commitment to honor the privacy of information-seekers. They routinely work with faculty to develop information literacy assignments for their classes and support faculty development efforts with bibliographic support. They collaborate with student support professionals who provide educational outreach in library facilities. This puts them in an ideal position to start conversations and collaborations that can bring efforts together, create community around privacy literacy development, and boost the effectiveness and efficiency of efforts.

This chapter is designed for librarians who would like to help students avoid making the privacy-related errors mentioned above. It provides background and justification for action and introduces vocabulary, frameworks, and standards for addressing the issues that may assist librarians in opening privacy literacy-related discussions. It offers illustrations of how librarians, faculty, and student support professionals addressed these issues through credit-bearing classes and co-curricular outreach. The final section offers tips for finding and working with partners.

BACKGROUND AND LITERATURE REVIEW

Librarians have traditionally respected the privacy of their users and adopted practices to support them. The ALA Bill of Rights states libraries should "advocate for, educate about, and protect people's privacy, safeguarding all library use data, including personally identifiable information."[2] In practice, this has been done in a variety of ways, including by refusing to share user borrowing records or information about reference inquiries that identify individuals. Since our clients increasingly access and share information online, librarians can expand their privacy advocacy through educational opportunities, programming, and outreach to assist users in improving awareness of best practices in searching and sharing information online.

In discussing these efforts, one term that has been used is "privacy literacy." Privacy literacy can be defined as "the understanding that consumers have of the information landscape with which they interact and their responsibilities within that landscape," or "one's level of understanding and awareness of how information is tracked and used in online environments and how that information can retain or lose its private nature."[3] Privacy literacy may not be a familiar term to college faculty and student support professionals, though concern for the issues that result from lack of these skills may be universal. Often, these skills are discussed using different frameworks and standards. Understanding additional ways the same skills are discussed by colleagues in other disciplines and professions may help librarians make connections with campus partners and lead to collaborations that can improve student learning outcomes. Professors in the School of Education at Indiana University of Pennsylvania (IUP) discuss these topics under the frameworks put forth by top scholars in the field of technology in education. The following section provides a brief description of frameworks and technology standards they use in their teaching.

The International Society for Technology in Education (ISTE)

Over the years, scholars and professional organizations have made recommendations for the content and skills needed to create safe and meaningful experiences using digital technology, which have evolved in response to the rapid development of new technology. The International Society for Technology in Education (ISTE) has remained at the forefront of educational technology content and competencies for the past twenty years and outlined the content, skills, and strategies students need for equitable and effective mastery of digital tools. These roles include empowered learner, digital citizen, knowledge constructor, innovative designer, computational thinker, creative communicator, and global collaborator.[4]

Digital Citizenship

Many technology recommendations from other scholars echo the ISTE standards. These include Ribble's Digital Citizenship (DC)[5] framework and Davis's 9 Ps of Digital Citizenship.[6] The Digital Citizenship (DC) framework is an important part of technology curriculum in schools across the world. Students as young as first grade are taught to use digital technologies for safe and effective social engagement. Librarians, professors, and student support professionals play a key role in supporting students' DC content knowledge from school age through college. They use the DC framework to guide instruction while paying particular attention to the nine elements of DC embedded in the three overarching principles. The first principle of DC is "safe." This reminds digital users to always take precautions to protect themselves and others. Three of the nine DC elements are included in the safe principle: digital etiquette, digital access, and digital law. The second principle, savvy, encourages digital users to educate themselves and others. This principle includes digital fluency, digital communication and collaboration, and digital commerce. The third principle, social, reminds digital users to respect themselves and others. The three DC elements included in the social principle are digital rights and responsibilities, digital security and privacy, and digital health and welfare. Digital users who gain the knowledge and skills recommended by the DC framework can successfully cultivate safe, positive, and respectful social participation through a variety of digital platforms.

9 Ps of Digital Citizenship

The DC framework has continuously influenced scholars in the field of educational technology. Some have extended Ribble's work by including additional terms and concepts to support an understanding of what it means to be a digital citizen in today's technology-driven world. One of those scholars, Vicky Davis, is the director of instructional technology at Sherwood Christian Academy in Albany, GA. She created the 9 Ps of Digital Citizenship, which includes a list of nine words connected to digital privacy: passwords, private information, personal information, photographs, property, permission, protection, professionalism, and personal brand. Each of the nine words includes a series of questions that require digital users to think about the choices they make with technology.[7]

The digital technology recommendations from professional organizations complement each other and offer a solid foundation for responsible technology use. These resources can be used to engage stakeholders in conversations related to advocacy, research, and additional funding for resources that can lead to privacy education and protection for all digital users. The standards support content and skills that are valuable for students in all grade levels and throughout adulthood. They provide knowledge and skills that are necessary to safely advance our digital world. See table 16.1 for a table detailing the alignment of the ISTE Standards for Students, the Digital Citizenship framework, and privacy topics.

Whether promoting privacy literacy, adhering to the ISTE standards, or teaching digital citizenship and its 9 Ps, professors across campus are promoting the skills that can help the present generation of college students become more successful. In the following section, a librarian and professors in Professional Studies in Education share why they care about such skills and how they promote them in their classes.

TABLE 16.1

Privacy topics organized by the ISTE Standards for Students and DC.8

ISTE STANDARDS FOR STUDENTS	D.C. ELEMENTS	PRIVACY TOPICS
Empowered Learner		
1a. Set personal learning goals, develop technology strategies	Fluency	Digital learning, safe strategies
1b. Build networks, custom environments, support learning	Communication & Collaboration	Networking, branding, Social Media use
1d. Understand and explore new technologies, troubleshoot	Fluency	Authentic credible digital media & resources
Digital Citizen		
2a. Manage digital identity, reputation, aware of permanence	Etiquette	Digital footprint/identity, permanent trace of digital use, reputation management
2b. Engage in positive, safe, legal, ethical social interactions	Law	Report abuse, terms of use respectful behaviors
2c. Demonstrate sense of rights and duties of using and sharing intellectual property	Rights & Responsibilities	Copyright laws, terms of use
2d. Manage data, privacy, security, awareness of data-collection technology for tracking	Security & Privacy	Personal information privacy settings, digital security, secure online transactions, phishing, trolling
Knowledge Constructor		
3a. Use effective strategies, locate information and resources	Fluency	Secure credible websites
3b. Evaluate resource accuracy, credibility, and relevance	Fluency	Authentic credible resources
3d. Use real-world problems to develop theories, solutions	Fluency	Advocacy for personal branding, positive use of social media
Innovative Designer		
4a. Use design process to generate ideas, test theories, create new artifacts, solve authentic problems	Fluency	Personal branding artifacts & websites
4b. Use digital tools to plan, consider constraints, risks	Fluency & Privacy	Construct user-friendly sites, locked editing settings
Creative Communicator		
6a. Choose platforms, tools, creation & communication skills	Communication & Collaboration	Safe and secure publishing platforms
6b. Create original works, responsible use of resources	Communication & Collaboration	Digital publishing for branding
6c. Communicate clearly and effectively, digital visualizations, models, or simulations	Communication & Collaboration	Proper grammar & spelling

TABLE 16.1
Privacy topics organized by the ISTE Standards for Students and DC.8

ISTE STANDARDS FOR STUDENTS	D.C. ELEMENTS	PRIVACY TOPICS
6d. Publish, present custom content for intended audiences	Communication & Collaboration	Digital publishing, positive content, focus on audience, contribute to digital image
Global Collaborator		
7a. Connect, engage with learners from various backgrounds, cultures, broaden understanding & learning.	Communication & Collaboration	Networking, collaboration, check credentials
7b. Collaborate with peers, experts, community, examine issues from multiple viewpoints	Communication & Collaboration	Networking, perspective taking
7c. Contribute to teams, assume roles, common goals	Communication & Collaboration	Safe collaboration, check credentials, copywrite personal work

PRIVACY LITERACY FOR CAREER READINESS IN ONE-CREDIT LIBRARY/INFORMATION LITERACY COURSES

For many years, Indiana University of Pennsylvania (IUP) Libraries have offered LIBR 151, Introduction to Information Literacy, a one-credit class. Dr. Theresa McDevitt often teaches the class with a focus on information literacy skills related to finding and succeeding in employment, including a privacy literacy module to assist students in developing privacy practices that will enhance their ability to find jobs when they graduate.

Content was developed in collaboration with the university's IT support professionals. These experts deal constantly with the problems resulting from students making poor choices related to sharing information online, from posting inappropriate content on social media to responding to phishing messages for fake job ads. IUP IT support professionals were interested in a partnership to help students become more aware of online privacy best practices and help them avoid mishaps of this nature. They were happy to provide guidance on applicable tips that would help students to be more private and secure. The course objectives developed include the following:

At the conclusion of the module, students should be able to:
- discuss the importance of and methods to practice and maintain good password hygiene;

- discuss the importance of the thoughtful selection of social media security/privacy settings;
- define what phishing is and list some strategies to avoid falling prey to it, particularly in the area of detecting fake job ads and money-making scams;
- define encryption and what encrypted networks are and why they should be used to share sensitive information;
- define VPNs and discuss why they should be used when available;
- discuss the importance of building positive online reputations in job-seeking;
- discuss strategies to evaluate the quality of information before it is shared online (including information on recognizing fake news); and
- list strategies to search online more anonymously (such as the use of DuckDuckGo or using incognito browsers) to remain private but also to find the most relevant information.

Content shared in the class focused on problems resulting from poor privacy practices and simple ways students could avoid such pitfalls. For example, Dr. McDevitt began face-to-face class sessions by discussing an article related to student knowledge of what employers looked for in future employees' online personae and discussed these practices with students. This led to a discussion of other issues commonly encountered by students, and security and privacy tips to avoid them. Students actively participated in class discussions, which invited them to share problems they or their friends had encountered and their positive online engagement strategies. The results were lively and meaningful classes that informed not only the students but the instructor as well.

For the online version of the course, the content was delivered through a reading with embedded videos. Students engaged with the material through short review activities (true/false and multiple-choice quizzes) to reinforce content and through online discussions. Review activities gave students practice in the recall of content. Discussion activities challenged students to reflect on the information presented and relate it to their own lives and respond to other students. (See discussion prompts in appendix A).

PRIVACY LITERACY IN THREE-CREDIT UNDERGRADUATE, GRADUATE, AND POST GRADUATE COURSES

Privacy literacy can be integrated into student experiences within discipline-based instruction, and librarians can support these efforts. Faculty collaborators in the disciplines can refer to disciplinary standards and frameworks to guide privacy literacy instruction.

Privacy Literacy and Professional Engagement on Social Media and Virtual Environments

Drs. Crystal Machado and Melissa Calderon integrate privacy literacy into the student learning experiences in the education degree program. Most of Drs. Machado and Calderon's students are school leaders or pre-service and in-service teachers who have attended schools in rural Western Pennsylvania. These students have reported being cautioned against sharing too much on social media in high school and given little encouragement to or training in how to do so in a positive and professional way. A large majority have made limited use of web-based technology and social media, except to connect with friends and family. Drs. Machado and Calderon believe it is crucial to model how social media is used to create a professional digital persona that shares positive, unbiased, conscientious content.

Drs. Machado and Calderon approach technology and privacy education in similar ways. Both professors agree that privacy education is essential for promoting a society of safe digital users. They feel it is equally as important to experiment with a wide variety of safe technology platforms and urge students to create a professional digital persona, which includes a professional headshot photo, information related to education, employment, career choice, publications, research, extracurricular activities, and evidence of philanthropy. Conversely, they caution students that their professional digital persona should not include any content that may harm a person's online reputation. This includes content that is explicit, biased, or discriminatory toward others. Further, they suggest professionals be cautious about posting content that may cause others to discriminate against them, such as their race, age, disability, marital and family status, religion, or political affiliation.

Establishing Privacy Literacy and Digital Citizenship Norms in Each Course

Drs. Machado and Calderon design assignments that enable students to participate in virtual environments like Flipgrid, VoiceThread, and social media (Facebook, Twitter, and Instagram). In addition to disciplinary knowledge and skills, these experiential, performance-based, reflective activities target positive digital participation, including online reputation management, digital privacy, and digital wellness. The professors take a two-step approach. First, they establish the norms for privacy literacy and digital citizenship at the beginning of the semester. Second, they design assignments and experiential activities that target disciplinary knowledge and develop students' twenty-first-century skills of communication, collaboration, critical thinking, and creativity. These assignments and experiences also provide students with an opportunity to practice the 9 Ps of Digital Citizenship: passwords-info, privacy, personal information, photography, property, permissions, protection, professionalism, and permanence.[9]

Dr. Machado establishes norms for privacy literacy and digital citizenship across undergraduate, master's, and doctoral courses through a welcome letter posted to the course Learning Management System (LMS) two weeks prior to the start of the semester. The letter includes an introductory activity on Flipgrid, a video conferencing platform, which is due before the first session (see appendix B). Recognizing that some students may be inhibited by shyness, social anxiety, and fear of negative evaluation,[10] she includes guidelines that help students figure out just how much they are willing to divulge and ways to alter their digital image. Excerpt 1 (see appendix B) is taken from the welcome letter and posted in the Meet Your Professor section of the Learning Management System. It gives students access to her digital footprint; they can explore the hyperlinked pages to evaluate her online persona, the personal information and photography she chooses to share, and her level of professionalism. Excerpt 2 (see appendix C) is taken from a syllabus. It illustrates how she reinforces the importance of creating a school-friendly teacher Gmail account they can continue to use across platforms after they graduate.

Similarly, Dr. Calderon posts a welcome message on the LMS for her undergraduate education majors before the start of the semester that illustrates the privacy literacy and digital citizenship norms established in the class. She pairs this content with web links to professional technology organizations that are dedicated to practicing appropriate privacy literacy and digital citizenship skills (see appendix D).

Dr. Calderon begins each semester by engaging students in discussions about making conscientious decisions when using digital technology through a presentation, which includes different examples of online content, including social media posts with pictures, comments, shares, likes, hobbies, friends, and other affiliations. She urges her students to participate in anti-biased socio-cultural learning discussions that respect multiple perspectives. The social media examples initiate rich class discussions related to privacy and online reputation management. This collaborative learning method builds critical thinking skills and allows students to construct their own knowledge based on the ideas of all group members. Dr. Calderon continually provides feedback during class discussions to make certain students have a solid foundation of knowledge about privacy, safety, and online content that could support or damage their future. At the end of these discussions, she engages students in a Google name search activity (see appendix E for this activity).

Performance-based Assignments

Guided by ISTE Standards for Educators[11] and Situated Learning Theory,[12] Drs. Machado and Calderon design assignments that require authentic real-life problem-solving, active engagement with technology, and repeated practice to facilitate proficiency in disciplinary knowledge and technology skills. Dr. Machado creates assignments that include a series of authentic learning experiences that culminate in a final project at the end of the semester.

Each assignment includes elements of the 9 Ps and twenty-first-century communication skills. Assignment 1 provides masters students experience in using MS, Zoom, FaceTime, WhatsApp, Google Slides, VoiceThread, and other innovative web-based instructional technologies to communicate, collaborate, think critically, and create a professional development workshop that they facilitate in the cloud.

In her privacy literacy instruction, rather than discouraging students from posting online, Dr. Calderon intentionally trains students to do so safely, positively, and responsibly. One example is the LinkedIn assignment (see appendix F for the LinkedIn assignment). She informs students that LinkedIn is a popular choice for companies who cybervet potential employees and is a beneficial tool for keeping a list of professional contacts. She recommends that students continually update their professional information and add contacts on a regular basis. Students are invited to connect with her and any of the class guest speakers.

Dr. Machado recognizes that social media is rapidly becoming the core way for professionals to reach and communicate with different audiences and customers. She informs students that social media platforms, when used wisely, offer the potential to promote continuous learning as well as professional development and advancement. Recognizing the dangers of social media spaces, which can be formidable, Dr. Machado provides explicit guidelines that students can follow to avoid pitfalls. Some of these are reflected in Assignment 2 (see appendix G), which was designed to provide post-graduate students with an opportunity to interact with professionals on Facebook and Twitter.

Preparing Education Professionals for Ethical and Responsible Practice in Teaching with Technology

As suggested by the Teacher Educator Technology Competencies, which have been endorsed by the Society for Information Technology and Teacher Education

(SITE),[13] Dr. Jacqueline McGinty believes teacher training should include ethical and responsible use of technology in teaching, including instruction on cybersecurity and data privacy. In her ETIT 103: Digital Instructional Technology course for undergraduate students, Dr. McGinty includes information about cybersecurity and the ethical use of technology in learning environments. As part of introducing these competencies for teacher educators, Dr. McGinty provides readings, links, and videos about teacher responsibility for student privacy. For example, she directs students to the US Department of Education website to review the video, *Protecting Student Privacy While Using Online Educational Services*,[14] a short video about privacy protection for students. Students also read about legal, ethical, and socially responsible use from the *K-12 Educational Technology Handbook*, an open-source textbook.[15]

After completing the module, students are given an assignment to research a cybersecurity topic and prepare a presentation for students and colleagues. The assignment challenges students to find peer-reviewed resources and reference them in their presentations, along with professional resources that address teaching cybersecurity skills to their particular audience. Student work is shared in the course discussion forum to promote community learning, resource sharing, and collaboration across teaching disciplines.

In a graduate-level course, ETIT 600: Introduction to Instructional Design, Dr. McGinty presents the concept of data privacy. She argues that instructional design professionals should be well-versed in safe and responsible technology use across different educational environments, and should understand the different educational institutions, stakeholders, and potential security issues in each environment. ETIT 600 students gain skills in evaluating digital tools for safety and privacy. The course readings emphasize the importance of understanding terms of service for digital tools, policies, and procedures for data privacy. In addition, the readings include links to privacy checkup reports for popular apps and additional resources for the responsible use of digital tools in educational environments. A significant assessment for the ETIT 600 course is the evidence-based practice project and presentation where students work in teams to develop cybersecurity training modules. In this activity, students work for a fictional instructional design company contracted to provide cybersecurity fundamentals training modules for different audiences, including K-12 teachers, university professors, and corporate administrators. Students are required to conduct a needs assessment to analyze the audience and context of the educational event. They also create a training outline that includes research-based information on cybersecurity fundamentals and best practices tailored to their selected audience.

For both undergraduate and graduate students, these professors integrate privacy literacy skills into their curriculum to boost student success. Librarians can enhance privacy literacy learning outcomes by sharing information literacy-related content and activities. For example, central to many of the assignments provided is students' ability to find and evaluate relevant and high-quality information sources, whether it is through linking quality professional resources in their LinkedIn accounts or by finding appropriate peer-reviewed professional resources to inform their presentations and projects. Activities that help students identify sources of lesser quality, including fake news, help them build skills that are central to linking their personal brand to quality information.

EXTRA-CURRICULAR PRIVACY LITERACY EDUCATIONAL OUTREACH FOR HEALTH AND WELLNESS

Credit-bearing classes promote the development of students' privacy literacy skills. Co-curricular educational offerings can enhance and reinforce what students learn in courses. The following section will discuss programs offered by two professional employees and peer educators in IUP's Center for Health and Well-Being and a collaborative program that brings together librarians, faculty, and student support professionals in an engaging co-curricular event.

Ms. Jennifer McCroskey and Ms. Ann Sesti are professional employees who work with IUP's Rhonda H. Luckey Center for Health and Well-Being (CHWB). This office offers a range of services that address the components of total well-being, including divisions that address health issues associated with the use of alcohol, tobacco, and other drugs (ATOD) and domestic violence (the Haven Project). Professional employees in CHWB recognize the importance of online sharing and privacy to student well-being and offer a number of programs to address student privacy literacy.

Alcohol, Tobacco, and Other Drugs (ATOD) Programming for Career Success

Ann Sesti, the director of the Alcohol, Tobacco, and Other Drugs Program, employs graduate students who offer educational programs and individual consultation services to assist students in making healthy lifestyle choices regarding alcohol and drug use. In their consultations and programming, participants are presented with information and encouraged to think about the ramifications of their social media posts.

In such sessions, posting images of partying behavior, which may seem harmless but can have a lasting impact on students' lives while they are in college, is discussed. Examples are given of how pictures, comments, and images become a part of one's digital profile and can impact future employability when companies look to hire people who fit their behavioral standards. Participants leave sessions with a clear understanding that posting things online can impact their future success and may be less likely to post questionable photos in the future.

Cyberstalking

IUP's Haven Project offers education and prevention programming on sexual violence, dating/domestic violence, stalking, consent, relationships, and bystander intervention. Ms. Jennifer McCroskey leads its educational programming and outreach efforts. Haven employs peer educators funded through IUP's student wellness fee to assist in outreach efforts. In response to the increase in stalking via online methods, they have begun to include privacy literacy in their stalking prevention educational programming.

In a typical program, they discuss various types of stalking, including cyberstalking. Cyberstalking, or using technology to track or monitor someone, may include the sending of unwanted emails or online messages, the posting of sensitive information, or the spreading of rumors about someone online. It can also involve the use of online public records and searches to learn more about someone or other actions to control, track, or frighten a victim. They discuss how personal information shared online can still be accessed, even with private settings, and the impact of information available through location and tracking. They encourage students to think about what and when they are posting information and consider that certain information can provide online stalkers with schedules and locations. They recognize the student need and desire to participate in the digital world and to educate students in risk-reduction techniques, such as being conscious of information that is posted, keeping passwords and devices protected, being aware of who has access to phone locations via apps, and setting clear boundaries.

To allow students to gain some experience in using the information shared, Ms. McCroskey and peer educators have developed an activity called "Tinder Security Team- IUP." In this activity, participating students review various online profiles to determine if there are any red flags of stalking or not. It is a relatable activity, especially since so many students now use online dating apps to make connections. (See activity in appendix H.)

Such programming, which utilizes peers as educators and engaging activities, reinforces what students learn in coursework. Librarians can assist in these efforts by encouraging programmers to use library spaces as venues for programs or participate in such programming, adding to the discussion with information literacy-based content.

COLLABORATIVE PROGRAMMING FOR PRIVACY LITERACY

Instruction in individual classes and extra-curricular programming has an impact, but instructors and programmers can feel isolated in their efforts to improve privacy literacy outcomes. Collaborative programming that brings together professionals across campus helps build a community where both presenters and participants learn more. The following is a discussion of the evolution of a collaborative panel discussion on privacy literacy on the IUP campus.

Cybersecurity Awareness Month is held every October. College IT security offices use this month as a time to increase awareness of best practices in online sharing with faculty, staff, and students. Librarians on IUP's campus became aware of Cybersecurity Awareness Month through IT support professionals' outreach efforts to promote it through public lectures and tabling outreach in library spaces. A librarian suggested offering a panel made up of the IT support professionals, librarians, popular teaching faculty, and wellness and career development support professionals. Panels have been offered in October for the last few years and have been engaging and well-attended.

Key to the success of these programs has been their collaborative nature. Bringing the diverse expertise and approaches of panelists enhanced the quality of content offered. Co-sponsorship of the event by multiple divisions made advertising and attracting a crowd easier. In face-to-face sessions, food was provided to attract participants. Including an educational game (and prizes) in sessions, both online and in person, made the sessions interactive and engaging. That faculty offered extra credit to their students for attending likely boosted attendance as well. In these panels, each speaker shared privacy concerns they had and how they address the issues in their classes or outreach. In addition to informing students in a fun, engaging way, it was an opportunity for presenters to learn more about what other professors and professionals were doing and to hear from students what they thought about privacy-related topics.

TIPS FOR BUILDING COMMUNITY TO ADDRESS PRIVACY LITERACY

This short review of how faculty, librarians, and student support professionals work alone and together to promote privacy literacy shows what can be done without additional courses, employees, or departments. Here are some tips to find partners and create events based on the authors' experiences:

- **Find partners.** Look for events and courses relating to privacy literacy that are being offered on your campus. Attend sessions or reach out to presenters and offer to help. Assistance can be as simple as offering use of library spaces for tabling, poster sessions, or other outreach activities, paying for refreshments, or providing library resources that help participants to learn more about the topic. Working with others likely enhances the event itself, may be informative for you, and may lead to future collaborations.
- **Faculty committees and development groups.** Participating in faculty committees and faculty development work may lead to partnerships. Dr. McDevitt met a political science professor at an integrating writing across the curriculum workshop. When the professor mentioned a privacy-related poster session activity that her students did, the librarian suggested that the students present their posters in the busy library lobby. It greatly increased the impact of the event and started a continuing partnership for privacy-literacy promotion.[16]
- **Work with student support professionals.** Librarians often partner with student support professionals to provide orientations when students arrive on campus, but the partnership should not end there. The librarian met the wellness support and career development professionals when they did educational outreach in the library lobby. Student support professionals make great partners because they share librarians' concern for promoting student success, know how to attract student audiences, and are often willing to provide refreshments, prizes, and other infrastructure that make events more attractive to students.
- **Work within available standards and guidelines**. Librarians have the ALA Bill of Rights that directs us to value privacy. Other standards and guidelines (such as the ISTE standards for Educators)[17] urge instructors to include privacy literacy-related content. Mentioning such standards and guidelines in presentations, and when approaching potential partners, can guide your integration initiatives and convince them of the significance of your efforts.

CONCLUSION

It is essential for college students to participate in the digital world if they are to succeed in college and find employment after they graduate. Faculty and other professionals can help them to do so in a positive way, make students more likely to land good jobs when they graduate, and prepare them to be positive participants in the online community, which impacts not only their own success but also contributes to the quality of the overall digital community.

In this chapter, we have illustrated how college librarians, professors, and student support professionals can help students build privacy literacy skills by integrating privacy literacy instruction into existing courses and outreach activities. We hope to inspire readers to start or continue similar efforts for promoting privacy literacy that will allow them to help students on their own campuses develop the privacy literacy skills that will help them succeed.

APPENDIX A
LIBR 151 ONLINE PRIVACY AWARENESS ACTIVITIES. ONLINE CLASS DISCUSSION POST PROMPTS

Discussion posts:

After you have finished the background reading for this chapter, please comment on one of the three topics listed below and respond to the comments of two other class participants:

- List one thing in the reading, images, or videos included that you found particularly interesting.
- List one thing in the reading, images, or videos included you didn't know before but you were glad you found out about.
- Offer some advice related to sharing information online that you think others would benefit from knowing.

APPENDIX B
ESTABLISHING PRIVACY LITERACY NORMS WELCOME MATERIALS

Welcome Message Text.
Jan. 14, 2020

My passion...

Welcome to MDL315 Classroom Management and Adolescent Development. This activity will help us to get to know each other before we meet on Tuesday.

1. Introduce yourself (don't mention school or location).
2. Describe your PASSION **outside of work and family.** Better yet, take us there...or show it to us (personal, but school appropriate, please).
3. Interact with each other on the grid.

Let's get this party started. Be yourself and let your personality shine through.

Link: [Flipgrid link] *Password:[password]*

Privacy guidelines: With digital content, your audience could be anyone on the worldwide web; keep this in mind when you post your 90-second (about one-and-a-half minutes) video. Share as little or as much as you feel comfortable sharing with strangers. If you want to conceal your face, you can do so in many creative ways. Like Instagram and Snapchat, Flipgrid provides you with stickies and emojis; use them to hide parts of your face if you desire. Have fun, be creative, and let your personality shine through!

Excerpt 1: Links to Professor's Digital Footprint in Welcome Letter and Meet Your Professor Module in the Learning Management System

Parker Palmer said, "We teach who we are." He is very right. The digital artifacts below will give you a glimpse into my personal and professional life. For many students, I am their first international professor. I created my Timeline and Pinterest board when students said they wanted to know more about the cultural experiences that have shaped the person I have become. My teaching philosophy has stayed constant over the years. The only thing that has changed is that I use many more technological tools to enact my philosophy.

APPENDIX C
TIPS ON CREATING A TEACHER GMAIL ACCOUNT

Excerpt 2: Excerpt from Syllabus

Create a teacher Gmail account. Please ensure that the handle of your Gmail is school-friendly. Some school-friendly examples are teacher123@gmail.com, ilovemath@gmail.com, cmachadolearns@gmail.com. You will use this teacher Gmail to explore a wide range of web-based technologies like Google Docs, Drive, Site, and social media like Twitter, Facebook, Instagram, VoiceThread, Twitter, etc. If you have reservations about using any of these technologies, email me so that I can provide you with accommodations.

APPENDIX D
DIGITAL EXPECTATIONS

Excerpt 2: Excerpt from Syllabus

Digital Citizenship Expectations:

All students must show an in-depth knowledge of the 4 Cs of 21st Century Skills [https://www.aeseducation.com/blog/four-cs-21st-century-skills]. Students are expected to follow essential privacy literacy and digital citizenship content included in the ISTE Standards for Students [https://www.iste.org/standards/iste-standards-for-students], Digital Citizenship Framework, [www.digitalcitizenship.net/contact.html], and the 9 P's of Digital Citizenship [https://iiciis.org/international/2017/11/30/the-9-key-ps-of-digital-citizenship/]. Students will adhere to these expectations through all forms of communication, including assignments, class discussion boards, and published work.

APPENDIX E
GOOGLE NAME SEARCH ACTIVITY

1. Use the Google search engine to conduct multiple searches of your name. Use different combinations of each item.
   - First and last name
   - First, middle, and last
   - Name + (city, employment, high school, college, extracurricular activity, religious affiliation, etc.)
2. Assess the search results of your digital image from the perspective of an employer.
   - Is the majority of the content associated with your digital image positive?
   - Does the content make you look like an honest hardworking employee?
   - Would you hire a person with your digital image? Why or why not?
3. What steps can you take to eliminate undesirable content?
   - Delete the content yourself.
   - Request another user to delete content they posted.
   - Push the negative content down in the search results by significantly increasing the amount of positive content.
4. Review the class assignments that build positive content.

APPENDIX F
LINKED-IN ASSIGNMENT

LinkedIn is one of the top online platforms job recruiters use when cybervetting potential employees. This assignment is a great way to add positive online content. Please review the information below before you create or add to an existing LinkedIn account.

- Profile picture
    - Professional-looking headshot, business attire, approachable facial expression
- Contact Information
    - Full name, professional email, custom URL
- Headline
    - Engaging value statement
    - Consider target audience
    - Important keywords make it easier for job recruiters to find you
- Profile
    - Compile each section (core, recommended, and additional information)
    - Proofread for spelling and grammar errors
- Connections
    - Take a screenshot of your connections
    - Request 25 professional connections
    - Take another screenshot when all 25 have accepted

APPENDIX G
SOCIAL MEDIA AND GLOBAL NETWORK JOURNEY ASSIGNMENT

Are you taking part in macro conversations that are happening on Facebook and Twitter, either passively or actively? Can participation in social media groups help you to shift from "bounded awareness" to "willful awareness"? Will stepping out of your echo chamber help you to notice how the concepts described by Chung, Sensoy, and DiAngelo, and Machado, play out in real life? Begin this journey by:

a. using your teacher Gmail account to join Facebook;
b. joining 10–20 diversity, equity, and social justice groups on Facebook and/or Twitter;
c. networking with different educators by joining 10–15 diversity, equity, and social justice groups on Facebook and/or following 20–30 influential diversity and inclusion advocates on Twitter.
d. curating the valuable resources on Facebook by creating a collection and/or bookmarking/retweeting similar posts on Twitter;
e. periodically using popular hashtags to participate in Twitter chats and gain insight into current trends;
f. keeping track of the questions, concerns, and ethical challenges education professionals voice and others' reaction to these; and
g. enhancing your digital footprint and social media presence as an education professional by contributing meaningful solutions to identified needs (optional: you can choose to be a passive observer too).

Make your learning public by authoring a 10- to 20-page paper, inclusive of screenshots, that documents your journey. Use the guidelines and rubric below to guide you through the process.

a. Begin with a strong introduction that includes a description of your use of social media (purpose for joining, frequency, level of participation) prior to this course (see rubric for additional detail).
b. Describe your use of social media. Who did you follow? Did you observe any of the concepts we explored this semester in action? How did you contribute? What did you learn? This section of the paper should include at least 10 screenshots to help the reader gain insight into the content you

are describing. Please make sure that you blur out the names of people who participated in the discussions you reference.
   c. End with a strong conclusion.

You will be given a numeric score for this assignment based on how well you met the criteria outlined in the rubric.

APPENDIX H
TINDER SECURITY TEAM – HAVEN PROJECT EDUCATIONAL OUTREACH ACTIVITY

After peer educators provide background information related to the dangers of online stalking, they invite participants to review profiles such as the ones below to identify red flags that suggest a student may be the victim of stalking.

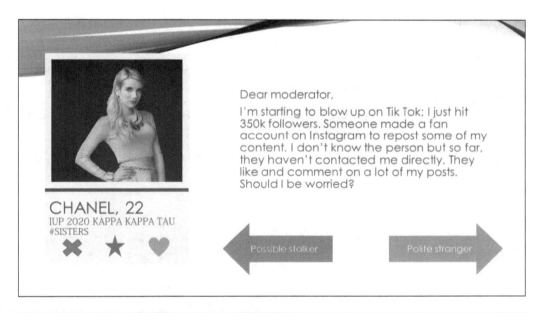

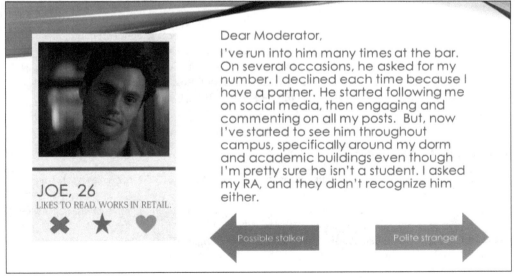

NOTES

1. Jenna Jacobson and Anatoliy Gruzd, "Cybervetting Job Applicants on Social Media: The New Normal?," *Ethics and Information Technology* 22, no. 2 (2020): 175; Aastha Verma and Charu Shri, "Cyber Security: A Review of Cyber Crimes, Security Challenges and Measures to Control," *Vision* (2022): 1.
2. "Library Bill of Rights," American Library Association, accessed August 3, 2022, https://www.ala.org/advocacy/intfreedom/librarybill.
3. Jeff Langenderfer and Anthony D. Miyazaki, "Privacy in the Information Economy," *Journal of Consumer Affairs* 43, no. 3 (2009): 383.
4. Helen Crompton, *ISTE Standards for Educators: A Guide for Teachers and other Professionals* (Eugene, OR.: International Society for Technology in Education, 2017).
5. Mike Ribble, "Digital Citizenship," accessed August 3, 2022, https://www.digitalcitizenship.net/home.html.
6. Vicki Davis, "What Your Students Really Need to Know About Digital Citizenship," accessed August 3, 2022, https://www.edutopia.org/blog/digital-citizenship-need-to-know-vicki-davis.
7. Davis, "What Your Students Really Need to Know."
8. "ISTE Standards: Students," The International Society for Technology in Education (ISTE), accessed September 15, 2022, https://www.iste.org/standards/for-students. The DC content was adapted from Ribble, "Digital Citizenship."
9. "The '9 Key Ps' of Digital Citizenship," IICIIS International, accessed August 3, 2022, https://iiciis.org/international/2017/11/30/the-9-key-ps-of-digital-citizenship/.
10. Robin-Marie Shepherd and Robert J. Edelmann, "Reasons for Internet Use and Social Anxiety," *Personality and Individual Differences* 39, no. 5 (2005): 949–58.
11. Crompton, *ISTE Standards for Educators*.
12. Jean Lave and Etienne Wenger, *Situated Learning: Legitimate Peripheral Participation* (Cambridge: Cambridge University Press, 1991).
13. Teresa S. Foulger, Kevin J. Graziano, Denise Schmidt-Crawford, and David A. Slykhuis, "Teacher Educator Technology Competencies," *Journal of Technology and Teacher Education* 25, no. 4 (2017): 413–48.
14. U.S. Department of Education, *Protecting Student Privacy While Using Online Educational Services*, February 26, 2015, video, https://studentprivacy.ed.gov/training/protecting-student-privacy-while-using-online-educational-services.
15. Anne Ottenbreit-Leftwich and Royce Kimmons, "The K-12 Educational Technology Handbook" (EdTech Books, 2020), https://edtechbooks.org/k12handbook.
16. Aleea Perry, "Privacy, Cybersecurity, and the Constitution: A Poster Session for Undergraduate American Government Students in the Library," in *Library Service and Learning: Empowering Students, Inspiring Social Responsibility, and Building Community Connections*, eds. Theresa McDevitt and Caleb P Finegan (Chicago, IL: Association of College and Research Libraries, 2018), 361–74.
17. "Library Bill of Rights," ALA; *ISTE Standards for Students*, ISTE; Crompton, *ISTE Standards for Educators*.

BIBLIOGRAPHY

American Library Association. "Library Bill of Rights." Accessed August 3, 2022. https://www.ala.org/advocacy/intfreedom/librarybill.

Crompton, Helen. *ISTE Standards for Educators: A Guide for Teachers and other Professionals*. Eugene, OR: International Society for Technology in Education, 2017.

Davis, Vicki. "What Your Students Really Need to Know About Digital Citizenship." Accessed August 3, 2022. https://www.edutopia.org/blog/digital-citizenship-need-to-know-vicki-davis.

Foulger, Teresa S., Kevin J. Graziano, Denise Schmidt-Crawford, and David A. Slykhuis. "Teacher Educator Technology Competencies." *Journal of Technology and Teacher Education* 25, no. 4 (2017): 413–48.

IICIIS International. "The '9 Key Ps' of Digital Citizenship." Accessed August 3, 2022. https://iiciis.org/international/2017/11/30/the-9-key-ps-of-digital-citizenship/.

Jacobson, Jenna, and Anatoliy Gruzd. "Cybervetting Job Applicants on Social Media: The New Normal?" *Ethics and Information Technology* 22, no. 2 (2020): 175–95.

Langenderfer, Jeff, and Anthony D. Miyazaki. "Privacy in the Information Economy." *Journal of Consumer Affairs* 43, no. 3 (2009): 380–88.

Lave, Jean, and Etienne Wenger. *Situated Learning: Legitimate Peripheral Participation*. Cambridge: Cambridge University Press, 1991.

Perry, Aleea. "Privacy, Cybersecurity, and the Constitution: A Poster Session for Undergraduate American Government Students in the Library." In *Library Service and Learning: Empowering Students, Inspiring Social Responsibility, and Building Community Connections*, edited by Theresa McDevitt and Caleb P. Finegan, 361–74. Chicago, IL: Association of College and Research Libraries, 2018.

Ribble, Mike. "Digital Citizenship." Accessed August 3, 2022. https://www.digitalcitizenship.net/home.html.

Shepherd, Robin-Marie, and Robert J. Edelmann. "Reasons for Internet Use and Social Anxiety." *Personality and Individual Differences* 39, no. 5 (2005): 949–58.

Verma, Aastha, and Charu Shri. "Cyber Security: A Review of Cyber Crimes, Security Challenges and Measures to Control." *Vision* (2022): 1–15.

U.S. Department of Education. *Protecting Student Privacy While Using Online Educational Services*. February 26, 2015. Video. https://studentprivacy.ed.gov/training/protecting-student-privacy-while-using-online-educational-services.

CHAPTER 17

LATERAL PRIVACY LITERACY:
Peer-Led Professional Privacy Literacy Learning Experiences

Sarah Hartman-Caverly

Privacy touches on nearly every aspect of library work. ALA's Library Bill of Rights calls on library workers to advocate for privacy,[1] but it is easy for discussions of privacy in the academic library to be relegated to considerations for patron data governance, cybersecurity, and FERPA compliance. While important, these approaches satisfy the requirements of data privacy without recognizing the human need for autonomy privacy: "An individual's ability to conduct activities without concern of or actual observation."[2] Privacy advocacy is most impactful when it advances the benefits of privacy in the human experience.

Before library workers can effectively advocate for privacy, we must understand its function in intellectual activities in particular and in the human condition in general. Exploratory research by Sarah Hartman-Caverly and Alexandria Chisholm points to a theory-practice gap in the privacy literacy (PL) practices of academic instructional librarians.[3] Continuing education in PL can help bridge this gap. This chapter offers content and learning design considerations for PL learning experiences delivered by and for library practitioners. The literature review outlines current practices in continuing education in the library profession, surveys learning design principles from andragogy (or adult learning), and demonstrates their application to PL learning experiences for library workers. The chapter presents four examples of peer-led, practitioner-facing PL learning experiences, detailing

329

their purpose, necessary resources, and results. These cases serve as examples of how andragogy principles can be applied to PL learning design for library workers in order to bridge the theory-practice gap and support library practitioners in more effectively advocating for privacy.

CONTINUING EDUCATION IN THE LIBRARY PROFESSION

The library profession recognizes an ongoing need for regular continuing education and professional development for library workers.[4] In the context of PL, the proliferation and evolution of technologies used in library work, and the considerations they raise for privacy, pose opportunities for continuing education.[5] Library workers also benefit from maintaining familiarity with broader societal privacy issues in order to best "advocate for, educate about, and protect people's privacy."[6] Continuing education, including on privacy-related topics, is a primary function of library professional organizations such as the American Library Association and the Association of College and Research Libraries, along with independent initiatives, including the Library Freedom Project and Library Juice Academy.[7]

Though continuing education is valuable, critics observe that formal continuing education programs can perpetuate structural barriers to advancement within the library profession.[8] Peer-led professional development among library practitioners mitigates many barriers to participation, including cost, travel, and time commitment, as these initiatives are generally offered free of charge, delivered locally, and tailored to the needs of participants.[9] Peer-led professional learning also provides opportunities for in-house subject matter experts to share their knowledge and assume leadership roles on a salient topic of shared interest.[10] These programs are highly impactful when grounded in real-world contexts and designed for collaborative participation.[11]

ANDRAGOGY: CONTINUING EDUCATION DESIGN PRINCIPLES

As an emerging literacy, PL is ripe for peer-led continuing education initiatives in academic libraries.[12] To provide meaningful and transformative learning experiences, facilitators should design peer-led PL programming with sound andragogic principles in mind. Popularized in the United States by Malcolm Knowles, andragogy refers to methods used in adult education and is informed by recognition of adult learner autonomy. Eduard C. Lindeman's 1926 work, *The Meaning of*

Adult Education, is recognized as the foundation of adult learning theory. Lindeman posited that adult learning is

- motivated by learners' *needs and experiences*;
- *life-centered* rather than subject-oriented;
- best accomplished through *experience*;
- often self-directed, with the instructor in a *"facilitator"* role; and
- optimal when learning experiences are *individualized* with respect to learning preferences, time, location, and pace.[13]

Because andragogy is predicated on learner autonomy, it enables self-directed learning by design; interestingly, a study by Karen Bordonaro found that academic librarians expressed a strong preference for autonomy in professional learning experiences.[14]

Meaningful learning is a subdomain of andragogy. In a qualitative study, Ramirose Ilene Attebury characterizes meaningful learning as active, experiential, goal-oriented, and intentional; collaborative, cooperative, informed by multiple perspectives, and emotionally engaging; complex, contextualized, constructive, creative, and critical; and individualized, reflective, and self-directed.[15] Like meaningful learning, Agnes Namaganda situates transformational learning as a subdomain of andragogy that engages the whole participant in an experience that significantly alters their perspective, with a concomitant change in practice.[16] Theorized by Jack Mezirow, transformational learning design requires an opportunity for reflection in order for participants to constructively process the cognitive, affective, social, and practical dimensions of their learning experience.[17] Namaganda's study of professional learning experiences among academic librarians found that discussion, interaction during active and collaborative learning experiences, and practical exercises were most influential to their transformative learning.[18] Intentional andragogy results in learning experiences predicated on a need to know and that are participant-centered, experiential, facilitated, and individualized.

Need to Know

Because adult learners are motivated by their needs and experiences, andragogic learning design should establish a "need to know" early in the learning experience.[19] This "need to know" premise demonstrates how new content knowledge can be applied to real-life situations.[20] The American Library Association's Library Bill of Rights Article VII, which calls library workers to advocate for and educate about privacy, establishes an explicit "need to know" with respect to PL.[21] Article VII can be adapted for individual and institutional contexts through learning design to maximize the relevance of professional PL programming.

Participant-Centered

Continuing education learning experiences are most effective when they are student- or participant-centered rather than instructor- or content-centered. Research in the neuroscience of adult learning suggests that learning design should activate four areas of the neocortex through activities that require "gathering, reflecting, creating, and testing."[22] Additionally, meaningful and transformative learning experiences engage positive emotions to motivate deep learning.[23] Participant-centered learning experiences incorporate opportunities for self-reflection, reflective discussion, and metacognition.[24]

Experiential

Attebury's review of professional development in libraries recommends that continuing education programs "draw on learners' existing experiences, encourage participatory learning, allow for social interactions and relate learning to real-life experiences."[25] Hands-on activities, such as case studies, problem-solving exercises, simulations, group discussions, and opportunities for collaboration, are recommended.[26] Case-based learning is particularly well-suited to developing content knowledge in PL because it allows participants to partake in a "sense-making process" that explores the "possibilities, challenges, and dilemmas" of a real-world privacy scenario.[27]

Research finds that teacher learning is most effective when embedded in practice. Effective continuing education programs for learning and curricular design should engage participants in creating innovative learning experiences as a product of their continuing education.[28] Practical exercises can be complemented by reflection activities that promote metacognition and affective engagement in the learning experience.

Facilitated

Harold Fields wrote of adult education in 1940: "Let the class do the work."[29] The instructor of a peer-led continuing education program should assume the role of facilitator, providing resources, guided explorations, suggestions, feedback, and other support for participants to engage in largely autonomous, self-directed, and collaborative learning.[30] In the teacher learning context, this may include frameworks, templates, exemplar curricula, lesson plans, and learning materials. One study found that digital repositories of teaching and learning materials can support curriculum design by inspiring participants' pedagogical design choices, even when materials cannot be readily adopted into learning activities.[31]

Research reveals that professional learning guided by a facilitator providing exemplar materials positively contributes to participants' development of expertise.[32] Learning design should incorporate multiple learning modalities, including individual work, small group work, and time for reflection.[33] Collaborative learning activities provide forums for social interaction that promotes neuroplasticity, the capacity of the brain to undergo physical changes that are involved in learning,[34] while also creating a venue for peer-to-peer knowledge sharing.

Individualized

Continuing education experiences that individualize teaching and learning most effectively embrace the diversity of participants' experiences, identities, and interests. Andragogic learning design anticipates participants' motivations, preferences, life circumstances, and prior knowledge and experience. Learning design should provide opportunities for self-directed learning, which appeals to library workers' preference for autonomy in continuing education as described by Bordonaro.[35] Practically speaking, it requires flexibility to account for adult learners' life circumstances, including remote and asynchronous participation.[36]

PRIVACY LITERACY FOR LIBRARY PRACTITIONERS

Learning design encompasses the purpose, content, methods, and underlying theoretical basis for a learning experience, articulating the why, what, and how of learning.[37] The following section details the learning design of four peer-led learning activities implemented in PL continuing education for library workers. The Current Awareness Action Plan engages participants in articulating a plan for maintaining and sharing their privacy knowledge. Six Private I's Theoretical Analysis guides participants in the application of privacy theory to identify otherwise hidden privacy harms and considerations, helping participants bridge the privacy theory-practice gap. In Critical Ed Tech Analysis, participants conduct a deep reading of educational technology (ed tech) terms of service and privacy policies in order to advocate for privacy best practices. Finally, participants develop a Privacy Program/Lesson Plan for privacy-related lesson planning or stakeholder communication. Facilitators can implement these activities as standalone learning experiences or scaffold them to deliver a comprehensive practitioner-oriented PL learning experience.

Digital Shred privacy literacy collaborators Alexandria Chisholm and Sarah Hartman-Caverly developed the four featured privacy literacy learning activities for a variety of continuing education contexts. We created the Privacy Program/Lesson Plan for a state library conference workshop,[38] have subsequently used it as a learning activity in an asynchronous online professional development course, and offered it as a takeaway resource for a variety of webinars. We implemented the Current Awareness Action Plan and Six Private I's Theoretical Analysis as scaffolded learning experiences in the online course. We designed the Critical Ed Tech Analysis as a small group activity for an Instruction Community of Practice workshop at our institution.[39] A diverse array of library workers, including administrators, technical and access services specialists, and reference and instruction librarians working in public, school, academic, and special libraries, engaged with these learning activities. The relevance of these learning activities to a wide range of library workers and settings is another benefit of learning design that is intentionally participant-centered, experiential, and facilitated.

Current Awareness Action Plan

Purpose

Many librarians self-report that they either do not know enough about privacy to integrate it into their work, or they are overwhelmed by the pace of change in technology and privacy-related issues.[40] The Privacy Current Awareness Action Plan is designed to build library workers' self-efficacy on privacy and to identify opportunities to share their interests and knowledge with others. **The Privacy Current Awareness Action Plan guides library workers to discover privacy news and analysis sources, incorporate these information sources into their current awareness practices, and commit to integrating current privacy information into a knowledge-sharing or application action plan.**

This activity is divided into three parts. First, participants identify professional (library-related) privacy interests and general privacy interests. Encouraging participants to select their own professional and personal privacy interests is a design choice to make the learning activity participant-centered. Then, participants explore current information sources and select resources that are relevant to their stated privacy interests. To encourage robust information-gathering, participants are prompted to select at least three resources for each privacy interest. Participants also develop an action plan for each resource—for example, following a social media account, subscribing to a podcast, or checking weekly for articles by a columnist on a privacy beat. The activity concludes with participants developing an action plan to apply or share their privacy knowledge, such as by contributing to policy development in their library, authoring a professional blog post, or organizing a reading club or community of practice.

Resources

The Privacy Current Events Action Plan consists of a worksheet (or set of instructions) and a list of curated privacy information sources (see appendix A). Participants are directed to:

- First, articulate your professional and general privacy current awareness interests.
- Then, identify useful professional or general current awareness resources, and develop an action plan for maintaining your privacy knowledge (ex. subscribe, check weekly for updates, listen to the podcast during meal prep, set aside time at work, etc.).
- Finally, commit to some goals for sharing or applying what you know (ex. start a discussion group, contribute to a blog or podcast, develop programming or instructional content, update library policies or practices, etc.)

The Digital Shred Privacy Literacy Toolkit offers a curated repository of information resources for current awareness as well as professional values and policy guidance.[41] Providing a curated repository of relevant resources for the Privacy Current Awareness Action Plan is a learning design choice to deliver a facilitated learning experience. Participants can select resources from the Digital Shred repository or conduct independent research to identify useful sources on their topics of interest. The Privacy Current Awareness Action Plan can be completed in one or two hours.

Results

The Privacy Current Awareness Action Plan helps practitioners inform their privacy efforts by becoming familiar with real-world developments in related industries. Prompting participants to identify their work-related and general privacy interests empowers them to focus on topics that are professionally and personally relevant and satisfies their need to know with respect to privacy topics. This high level of personalization is intended to motivate participants to meaningfully complete the activity and inspire them to commit to the action plan over time. A completed Privacy Current Awareness Action Plan consists of identified topics, information resources selected for maintaining current awareness about each topic, a plan of action for staying up to date with each resource, and a knowledge-sharing plan.

The Privacy Current Awareness Action Plan can be used for personalized continuing education through independent study or incorporated as an activity in a community of practice or discussion group. The action plan supports participants' independent discovery of privacy topics and can be used to scaffold from a guided reading of curated case studies toward a more open-ended exploration of emerging privacy issues in domains of interest. The Privacy Current Awareness Action Plan is a useful tool for professional communities of practice or reading clubs in which participants select readings and lead discussions. It is also a useful tool for documenting and discussing continuing education plans with a supervisor and advocating for time at work to maintain current awareness of professional privacy issues.

Six Private I's Theoretical Analysis

Purpose

Privacy is a complex topic. The benefits and impairments of privacy can impact individuals and groups in myriad ways. The Six Private I's Privacy Conceptual Framework supports privacy analysis that considers multiple dimensions of privacy in order to identify the full range of privacy benefits and to elucidate hidden harms of privacy violations. The privacy dimensions depicted in Six Private I's—*identity*, *intellect*, contextual and bodily *integrity*, *intimacy*, *interaction* and *isolation*—were gleaned from multidisciplinary scholarly discussions of privacy in the human condition.[42] The conceptual framework is a mnemonic diagram that conveys the claim that privacy is about respect for persons, not just protection for data. Six Private I's bridges the theory-practice gap between hypothetical, abstract discussions of privacy and real-world applications of privacy practices.

Six Private I's Theoretical Analysis is an exercise that applies the Six Private I's Conceptual Framework to case study analysis in order to identify privacy-related considerations and actual and potential harms. Participants examine a case study, such as a news article or professional scenario, and use the Six Private I's Conceptual Framework as a theoretical lens to discover privacy dimensions of the case. Through this experiential learning activity, participants consider how individual and group privacy is impacted in the case study, including consideration of individual identities; freedom of thought, belief formation, and expression; ability to regulate personal information flows to preserve contextual integrity; bodily integrity and physical privacy; assurance of confidentiality and participation in intimate relationships; and freedom of association and ability to voluntarily withdraw into solitude. The analytical power of the Six Private I's Privacy Conceptual Framework is most evident in a pre-post-test approach, when participants are asked to identify privacy considerations in a case prior to learning the framework, then reanalyze the same case after learning the framework.

Six Private I's Theoretical Analysis promotes library workers' awareness of multiple dimensions of privacy and supports sound privacy decision-making, policy, operations, and advocacy. Six Private I's is also a communication tool that assists library workers in advocating for privacy considerations with a variety of stakeholders, from patrons to donors, institutional administrators, and public policymakers.

Resources

The Six Private I's Theoretical Analysis requires the Six Private I's Privacy Conceptual Framework (available as a Creative Commons image),[43] a case study or professional scenario for analysis, and guiding reflection questions (see appendix B). An introduction to the Six Private I's framework can be provided via trade literature, scholarly publication, or minilecture.[44] Curated case studies from news articles are available in the Digital Shred Privacy Literacy Toolkit under the Case Studies category and subcategories, such as Education.[45] The Six Private I's Privacy Conceptual Framework reflects the facilitated and participant-centered dimensions of learning design as participants may select a case study from a curated repository or discover one through their own exploration. Guiding questions include:

- What privacy considerations, benefits, or harms can you identify as a result of applying the Six Private I's to your analysis?
- Did you recognize new ways to discuss privacy issues with patrons or other library stakeholders?
- Does your knowledge of privacy theory change how you think about privacy in practice?
- How will your knowledge of privacy theory inform your teaching practice or other library work?

As previously noted, it is particularly impactful to have participants analyze their privacy case prior to learning Six Private I's and revisit the same case analysis after learning the framework. The Six Private I's Theoretical Analysis activity can be completed in one or two hours.

Results

The Six Private I's Theoretical Analysis activity engages library workers in learning privacy theory and applying it to library practice through experiential case analysis. Participants develop PL by learning privacy theory; internalizing key privacy considerations with the mnemonic diagram, the Six Private I's Privacy

Conceptual Framework; and applying privacy theory to analyze a case study or professional scenario. Theoretical analysis using the Six Private I's conceptual framework supports library practitioners in bridging the theory-practice gap by informing their privacy-related policies and operations with relevant theory. The conceptual framework can also guide the practical privacy evaluation of library and ed tech systems, as in the Critical Ed Tech Analysis activity described below. Six Private I's itself serves as a tool for communicating the full spectrum of privacy values and harms to library stakeholders. The model further serves as a framework for communicating privacy benefits and impacts to library stakeholders, including hidden harms and other dimensions of privacy that can be difficult to articulate.[46] The Six Private I's Theoretical Analysis supports library workers in bridging the theory-practice gap between privacy scholarship and real-world applications.

Critical Ed Tech Analysis

Purpose

Academic library workers use a variety of library systems and ed tech in their work. These systems implicate library workers in the data lifecycle. When this data is generated about students, patrons, library stakeholders, or the library worker's own professional activities, it presents privacy considerations. **The Critical Ed Tech Analysis activity engages library workers in analyzing the privacy impacts of library and ed tech systems**.

The Critical Ed Tech Analysis experiential learning activity provides participants the opportunity to apply privacy theory and critical analysis techniques to actual library and ed tech systems that they use for library operations. During the Critical Ed Tech Analysis activity, participants work in groups to review the privacy policies and related terms of service for a library or ed tech system of their choice. They apply integrated privacy considerations—including institutional privacy policies and professional guidelines—to critically consider the privacy impacts of these systems commonly used in academic libraries. Informed by their critique, participants then propose a best practice for data use in academic libraries or higher education. The Critical Ed Tech Analysis activity demonstrates that privacy advocacy is not diametrically opposed to data collection and use in libraries and shows how knowledge of privacy theory can inform ethical data use that is necessary to library operations.

The Critical Ed Tech Analysis activity prepares library workers to actively consider the privacy impacts of library and ed tech systems rather than passively adopt these systems into their work practices. Library workers who are aware of these privacy impacts are better able to advocate for ethical use of these systems or to propose more ethical alternatives. The Critical Ed Tech Analysis activity is an example of an applied privacy theoretical analysis, as in the Six Private I's Theoretical Analysis described above. This activity allows library workers to bridge the privacy theory-practice gap by using theory to inform their critiques of library and education technology systems and data lifecycle practices in librarianship.

Resources

The Critical Ed Tech Analysis activity requires a specific library or ed tech system (or systems) for analysis and access to the privacy policies and related terms of service for the system(s). Additionally, access to relevant institutional policies and related professional guidance enables participants to reference these guidelines in their critical evaluation and proposed best practice. Participants can convene as small break-out groups, either in real-time or asynchronously in a threaded discussion, by self-selecting a specific library or ed tech system to analyze. During the Critical Ed Tech Analysis activity delivered as part of the community of practice workshop, participants chose from a curated list of technologies, including

- enterprise online collaboration platforms (Microsoft Teams and GSuite for Education),
- a learning analytics and student success platform (EAB/Hobson's Starfish),
- library public services platform (Springshare Libapps),
- academic integrity software (TurnItIn),
- a web conference platform (Zoom),
- a learning management system (Canvas), and
- a library services platform (SirsiDynix Symphony / BLUECloud analytics).

Break-out groups were directed to skim the privacy policies and related terms of service for their selected system and to discuss the privacy considerations in light of relevant policies and guidelines. Each group was asked to report out a recommended best practice based on their critical analysis.

In a break-out group setting, it is helpful to have a group facilitator who is familiar with the system privacy policies and terms of service documentation and can guide their fellow group members to the most relevant sections for their review. Having a group facilitator saves time that might otherwise be wasted skimming to identify the most useful sections of the documents for analysis. A worksheet or guiding questions for the critical analysis will assist participants in considering a robust range of system features and uses, and their privacy implications (see appendix C). Guiding questions include:

- What types of data does the system collect? (Consider consciously given, automatically monitored, and modeled data.)

- What is the utility of this data? Is it actually helpful? To whom?
- How does the system impact privacy? Consider the Six Private I's: identity, intellect, integrity (contextual/bodily), intimacy, interaction/isolation.
- Do you think students are aware of how their data is used? Are there PL learning opportunities presented by the system?
- What's surprising about this privacy policy? What concerns do you have after reading the privacy policy?
- What privacy configuration options are available? Consider the control paradox. How useful are they?
- What privacy best practices do you recommend for using this system?

While knowledge of privacy theory, such as is depicted in the Six Private I's Privacy Conceptual Framework, will be useful to participants in completing their critical system analysis, it is not a prerequisite. Twenty-five minutes was allocated to the Critical Ed Tech Analysis activity during the community of practice workshop; this activity could meaningfully be extended to an hour or more.

Results

The Critical Ed Tech Analysis activity supports library workers in critically evaluating library and ed tech systems in light of their privacy impacts. Participants familiarize themselves with the privacy policies and related terms of service of a specific library or ed tech system and critically analyze its data flows and their implications for privacy. Participants conclude their critical analysis by proposing best practices for system configuration and the data lifecycle informed by privacy theory, institutional policies, and professional guidance. The Critical Ed Tech Analysis activity functions both as a participant-centered, experiential learning activity and as a practical method of evaluating and configuring library and ed tech systems to preserve privacy benefits and mitigate privacy harms. This activity supports library workers in bridging the privacy theory-practice gap by incorporating theory-informed critiques into the process of system evaluation and configuration. A completed Critical Ed Tech Analysis not only identifies potential privacy harms but also proposes solutions that enable functional library operations while upholding privacy. Combining theoretical privacy analysis with practical evaluation and problem-solving, the Critical Ed Tech Analysis performs well as a small group activity in professional learning communities. The techniques in the Critical Ed Tech Analysis are also transferable to practical use by library workers in units responsible for the selection, configuration, implementation, and evaluation of library and ed tech systems and any relevant policies or practices.

The Critical Ed Tech Analysis activity positions privacy analysis as intrinsic—rather than adversarial—to the data lifecycle of library and educational technology systems.

Privacy Program/Lesson Plan

Purpose

Educating about and advocating for privacy are responsibilities of privacy-literate library workers.[47] Academic library workers cite lack of time to develop PL programming, and lack of time to implement PL learning activities into their instruction, as critical barriers to their PL efforts.[48] **The Privacy Program/Lesson Plan activity supports library workers in strategically planning and implementing PL programming in their local contexts.** It guides library workers through a needs assessment and program planning process and links to resources at point-of-need to provide ideas, information, and teaching materials for privacy programs.

The Privacy Program/Lesson Plan template outlines key considerations for planning and implementing a PL instruction session, workshop, or other programming. Participants identify their audience, articulate outcome statements, outline activities, develop a promotion and outreach plan, describe the overall program, identify team members or other program partners, itemize needed materials and budgetary costs, and determine how the impact of the program will be assessed. The back of the template links to useful resources for many of these planning considerations. The Privacy Program/Lesson Plan activity encourages backward design thinking so that participants consider the outcomes they want to achieve with their audience and develop a lesson or program plan that is tailored to achieving those outcomes.[49] The Privacy Program/Lesson Plan activity prepares library workers to communicate privacy information to others.

Resources

The Privacy Program/Lesson Plan activity uses a worksheet template that guides participants through the process of applying backward design to strategically plan a PL program (see appendix D). The worksheet includes fill-in-the-blank fields for the following program plan elements:
- Audience
- Outcome Statement(s)
- Activities
- Promotion and Outreach Plan
- Activity/Program/Resource Description

- Team/Community Partners
- Materials and Budget
- Impact/Assessment

The back of the worksheet refers participants to relevant resources for many elements of the program plan, including privacy-related content and learning activities, goal and learning outcome guidelines, promotion and outreach strategies, and program assessment techniques. Finally, participants are encouraged to share their program or lesson plan in a relevant open educational resource repository. The Privacy Program/Lesson Plan takes as little as forty-five minutes to complete as a standalone learning experience and can be extended into the feature activity of a professional development workshop session. Facilitators can also incorporate the Privacy Program/Lesson Plan activity into a series of PL workshops or self-study activities or offer it as a takeaway resource from a relevant professional development session.

Participants in the Privacy Program/Lesson Plan activity benefit from some introduction to PL theory or other learning experiences. Thilo Hagendorff's article, "Privacy Literacy and its Problems," provides a useful critique of common approaches to PL and their limitations. Hagendorff claims that many approaches to PL suffer from inequitable access to PL learning experiences, a false assumption about the rationality of privacy decision-makers, a preoccupation with front-end privacy features, and the transfer of privacy responsibilities from state and corporate actors to end users.[50] These challenges to PL efforts are important to consider as they can exacerbate privacy harms. Such a theoretical grounding best prepares participants to plan a PL lesson or program that increases audience members' awareness of these underlying privacy dynamics, rather than glossing over—or worse, reinforcing them.

Results

A completed Privacy Program/Lesson Plan provides participants with a roadmap for successfully sharing their privacy knowledge. Participants begin by considering their audience, including diverse patron communities, donors and governing boards, public policymakers, and other library stakeholders. Next, they craft outcome statements, which range from instruction session learning outcomes to a privacy-friendly update to library policies or operations. Participants then design activities to achieve the planned outcomes or select relevant activities from among the resources provided. Participants develop a description and promotion and outreach plan for their program. Next, participants consider the practical aspects of implementing their program, including any team members or community partners they should include, material needs, and related budgetary costs. Finally, participants are encouraged to develop an impact assessment plan for their session.

The planning template and associated resources are designed to inspire participants to create an optimal privacy learning experience meaningfully tailored to a specific audience. The activity demystifies backward design and takes the guesswork out of privacy lesson or program planning. Additionally, implementing the impact evaluation or assessment section of the plan enables participants to continually improve their privacy program or lesson plan over time. When developed in the context of guiding theory, such as Hagendorff's critique of PL, the Privacy Program/Lesson Plan presents an opportunity for library workers to close the theory-practice gap. The template is easily adapted to plan PL communications with other stakeholders, including peer professional development or staff training sessions, advocacy with library or institutional administrators, or promoting privacy efforts to donors or sponsors. The Privacy Program/Lesson Plan is designed to support library workers in educating about and advocating for privacy with a wide range of audiences and stakeholders.

Crafting the PL Professional Learning Experience

The four featured PL learning experiences—Current Awareness Action Plan, Six Private I's Theoretical Analysis, Critical Ed Tech Analysis, and Privacy Program/Lesson Plan—can each be implemented independently as standalone learning activities or scaffolded together to develop a sustained learning experience. Participants who are just embarking on their PL learning journey will find the guided self-reflection in the Current Awareness Action Plan useful as a starting point. It can also be adapted as a planning resource for PL reading clubs or communities of practice. In a multi-week continuing education course, facilitators Chisholm and Hartman-Caverly instructed participants to reexamine a news story from their Current Awareness Action Plan using the Six Private I's conceptual framework, scaffolding to the Theoretical Analysis activity and demonstrating the utility of the framework in uncovering hidden privacy harms. In Critical Ed Tech Analysis, participants apply Six Private I's to a real-world scenario involving the adoption or configuration of a library or ed tech system. Critical Ed Tech Analysis scaffolds from the Six Private I's Theoretical Analysis and provides an opportunity for participants to close the theory-practice gap by utilizing PL to ethically inform their professional work. The Privacy Program/Lesson Plan guides participants in designing a PL learning experience for a specific audience. Originally conceived for backward design of PL lesson plans for students, the Privacy Program/Lesson Plan is readily adapted as a communication plan for work with other stakeholders whose connection to the library will be enhanced by their understanding of PL and privacy as a core value of libraries, such as administrators, trustees, donors, and policymakers. Participants in a continuing education course cohort, community of practice, or reading club also benefit from reviewing and discussing each other's completed activities. These four continuing education learning activities are flexible, extensible, and interdependent by design so that they can be used in various combinations to provide rich and relevant PL learning experiences for library professionals.

Evaluations from two PL initiatives in 2021, a conference presentation and the community of practice workshop, demonstrate the value of learning design to professional PL learning experiences. Participant ratings were unanimously positive for the conference presentation on theory-driven PL instruction, where the Privacy Program/Lesson Plan was introduced as a takeaway resource.[51] Citing the curated Digital Shred Toolkit and Privacy Program/Lesson Plan worksheet, multiple participants noted that they left the presentation with ideas and resources for developing their own PL programming. Results from the PL community of practice workshop[52] evaluation indicate that participants highly value the participant-centered, experiential, and individualized design of these learning activities. All consenting respondents rated the learning experience as excellent or good. One respondent commented that the variety of activities provided a "robust" learning experience, leading them to notice nuances of privacy they had not previously considered. Multiple participants observed that providing individualized and asynchronous learning experiences made the program more accessible to a wider range of library workers. Relatedly, another respondent who self-identified as a staff member expressed that the participant-centered and facilitated design of the learning activities empowered them to feel confident about participating fully alongside library faculty. These observations are consistent with positive anecdotal feedback we've received about the inclusive, accessible, and high-impact design of these practitioner-oriented PL learning activities.

IMPLICATIONS FOR PRACTICE

Effective privacy advocacy requires relevant privacy knowledge and sound self-efficacy. PL programming for library professionals should support them in cultivating, applying, and sharing their privacy knowledge through their library work. PL programming is most impactful when it provides strategies and resources for participants to independently build and maintain their PL after the program has concluded. Successful programs will also connect theory and practice to maximize the transferability of privacy concepts across areas of library work. In order to enhance participants' privacy advocacy, PL learning experiences designed for practitioners should incorporate best practices in adult education. Table 17.1 summarizes the andragogy principles that are exhibited in each of the professional PL learning experiences described in this chapter.

TABLE 17.1

Professional learning design principles applied to PL programming

	CURRENT AWARENESS ACTION PLAN	SIX PRIVATE I'S THEORETICAL ANALYSIS	CRITICAL ED TECH ANALYSIS	PRIVACY PROGRAM / LESSON PLAN
Need-to-know	Participants acquire knowledge of privacy current events to build self-efficacy.	Participants apply privacy theory to uncover hidden harms and other privacy considerations.	Participants apply privacy theory to advocate best practices in library systems use.	Participants effectively communicate the importance of privacy to stakeholders.
Participant-centered	Participants self-identify personal and professional privacy interests for current awareness planning.	Participants select case studies for analysis.	Participants select library or ed tech system for evaluation.	Participants determine audience and context of privacy communication.
Experiential	Participants explore curated resources to complete a current awareness plan.	Participants apply privacy theory to identify privacy harms and considerations in a case study.	Participants work in small groups to conduct a close reading of system terms of service, privacy policies, and related institutional and professional guidance to develop a best practice.	Participants use curated resources to develop a PL programming or communications plan.
Facilitated	Participants are provided with curated resources and a worksheet template; feedback from peers and facilitators is provided in a group discussion.	Participants are provided with curated resources and a worksheet template; facilitators provide feedback.	Participants are provided with curated resources and a worksheet template; small group discussion is facilitated by a team "expert" who is familiar with activity materials.	Participants are provided with curated resources and a worksheet template; feedback from peers and facilitators is provided in a group discussion.

TABLE 17.1
Professional learning design principles applied to PL programming

	CURRENT AWARENESS ACTION PLAN	SIX PRIVATE I'S THEORETICAL ANALYSIS	CRITICAL ED TECH ANALYSIS	PRIVACY PROGRAM / LESSON PLAN
Individualized	Activity can be completed asynchronously and a fillable PDF may be printed and completed in hard copy if preferred.	Activity can be completed asynchronously and a fillable PDF may be printed and completed in hard copy if preferred. Accompanying minilecture is captioned and transcribed to enable multiple modes of engagement.	The activity is highly customizable to each participant's professional context (instruction, systems administration, circulation, library administration, etc.).	Activity can be completed asynchronously and a fillable PDF may be printed and completed in hard copy if preferred. The activity is highly customizable to each participant's professional context.

Library workers are called to protect, educate about, and advocate for privacy.[53] To answer this call, library operations should be imbued with privacy best practices, library instruction should include consideration of PL concepts, and library workers should feel able to communicate the value of privacy to library stakeholders. Libraries within and beyond the academy could serve as sites to cultivate local privacy coalitions that effectively advocate for all members' shared individual and collective privacy interests. In order to achieve this, library workers themselves must be privacy literate. Peer-led professional PL programming is one path forward.

ACKNOWLEDGMENTS

Thank you to open reviewers Melissa Mallon and CL for your thoughtful comments on the initial draft of this chapter. Your feedback generated many improvements in the writing and structure that I know readers will appreciate! Any remaining faults are mine alone.

Thank you to the planning committee for the Penn State University Libraries Instruction Community of Practice Spring 2021 Workshop—Alexandria Chisholm, Carmen Cole, Russell Hall, Emily Mross, and Andrea Pritt—for your roles in crafting an inclusive and impactful peer-led professional learning experience.

And extra thanks to Alexandria Chisholm, the *sine qua non* of Digital Shred, without whom none of this work would be possible. You challenge and inspire me to be a better, more intentional teacher every single day.

APPENDIX A
CURRENT AWARENESS ACTION PLAN

PRIVACY
CURRENT AWARENESS ACTION PLAN

First, articulate your privacy current awareness interests. Then, identify useful professional and general current awareness resources (check out the **Current Awareness** and **Professional Values & Policy Guidance** sections of the Digital Shred Privacy Literacy Toolkit at sites.psu.edu/digitalshred), & develop an action plan for maintaining your privacy knowledge (ex. subscribe, check weekly for updates, listen to the podcast during meal prep, set aside time at work, etc.). Finally, commit to some goals for sharing or applying what you know (ex. start a discussion group, contribute to a blog or podcast, develop programming or instructional content, update library policies or practices, etc.).

Name

Professional interests

General interests

Professional resource #1

Action plan

General resource #1

Action plan

Privacy Literacy in Libraries: From Theory to Practice | Week 2   Library Juice Academy

Professional resource #2	General resource #2
Action plan	Action plan

Professional resource #3	General resource #3
Action plan	Action plan

Privacy knowledge-sharing or application plan

Alex Chisholm (aec67@psu.edu) and Sarah Hartman-Caverly (smh767@psu.edu), 2021.

APPENDIX B
SIX PRIVATE I'S THEORETICAL ANALYSIS

Week 3: Exploring & Applying Privacy Theory

Privacy topics & case studies
Revisit the topics you investigated in Week 2. List your topics and link to any relevant case studies.

Topics:

Case studies:

Application of privacy theory
Reflect on what you learned from the Six Private I's micro-lecture. Use this conceptual framework to re-analyze your case studies.

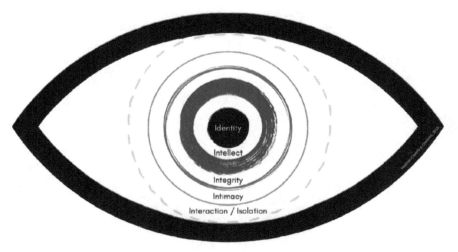

Hartman-Caverly & Chisholm, Six Private I's Conceptual Framework

Privacy Literacy in Libraries: From Theory to Practice — Library Juice Academy

Applying the Six Private I's, did you identify any additional privacy considerations? Did you recognize new ways to discuss this topic with patrons or stakeholders?

Take time to reflect on what you have learned about privacy theory. Will this knowledge change how you think about privacy? Will it inform your teaching practice / library work moving forward?

Alex Chisholm | aec67@psu.edu   Sarah Hartman-Caverly | smh767@psu.edu

APPENDIX C
CRITICAL ED TECH ANALYSIS

Sample worksheet - Privacy and Dx Workshop break-out activity critically examining ed tech

[System Name]
[Link to privacy policy or related terms of service]

The following are reflective, guiding questions for discussion but your group is not required to answer each one! Remember that your takeaway for the large group is to: develop best practices for data use in higher education, such as student-facing disclosures, opt-in/-out mechanisms, privacy-friendly alternate assignments / learning experiences, syllabus statements, and customizing ed tech settings.

1. What types of data does the system collect? (Consider consciously given, automatically monitored, and modeled data.)

2. What is the utility of this data - is it actually helpful? To whom?

3. How does the system impact privacy? Consider the Six Private I's: Identity, Intellect, Integrity (bodily / contextual), Intimacy, Interaction / Isolation

4. Do you think students are aware of how their data is used? Are there privacy literacy learning opportunities presented by the system?

5. What's surprising about this privacy policy? What concerns do you have after reading the privacy policy?

6. What privacy configuration options are available? Consider the control paradox - how useful are they?

7. What privacy best practices do you recommend for using this system?

Alex Chisholm and Sarah Hartman-Caverly, 2021.

Suggested attribution:
CC BY-NC-SA Chisholm, A. & Hartman-Caverly, S. (2021). Sample worksheet for ed tech break-out activity from privacy and Dx workshop (peer / professional). [link]

APPENDIX D
PRIVACY PROGRAM / LESSON PLAN

PRIVACY PROGRAM/LESSON PLAN

- AUDIENCE
- ACTIVITY // PROGRAM // RESOURCE DESCRIPTION
- OUTCOME STATEMENT(S)
- TEAM // COMMUNITY PARTNERS
- ACTIVITIES
- MATERIALS & BUDGET
- IMPACT // ASSESSMENT
- PROMOTION & OUTREACH PLAN

PLANNING RESOURCES

ACTIVITIES & CONTENT IDEAS

Digital Shred Privacy Literacy Toolkit
https://sites.psu.edu/digitalshred/

Use the toolkit to find:
- Teaching materials
- How-tos
- Case studies
- Digging deeper (privacy theory)
- And more!

PROMOTION & OUTREACH RESOURCES

Professional Groups / Guidance:
- ACRL Library Marketing & Outreach Interest Group
    - https://bit.ly/2Om3DRQ
- PLA Marketing Strategies
    - https://bit.ly/2xa86Nt
- Choose Privacy Promotional Materials
    - https://bit.ly/2PVUaUy

Design Tools:
- Canva - https://canva.com
- Smore - https://www.smore.com/

SHARE YOUR MATERIALS!

We encourage you to share your materials in an OER repository!

WRITING LEARNING OUTCOMES

Tips on Writing Learning Outcomes:
- https://bit.ly/2o5Auja

Bloom's Taxonomy:
- https://bit.ly/35ckEnB
- https://bit.ly/30MW492
- https://bit.ly/2EcTOwx

ASSESSMENT RESOURCES

SMART Goals Template
- https://bit.ly/2OlpfgV

Library Assessment Resources - The City University of New York
- https://bit.ly/2lpQ93H

Evidence Based Library & Information Practice journal
- https://bit.ly/2pEzEtR

RUSA Project Assessment & Evaluation
- https://bit.ly/1TKvRyL

PASSIVE PROGRAMMING RESOURCES

Choose Privacy Everyday - Programs
- https://chooseprivacyeveryday.org/programs/

LibGuides Community [search 'privacy']
- https://community.libguides.com/

CONTACT INFO

Alex Chisholm
aec67@psu.edu

Sarah Hartman-Caverly
smh767@psu.edu

Alexandria Chisholm & Sarah Hartman-Caverly, 2021

NOTES

1. "Library Bill of Rights," American Library Association, accessed January 10, 2022, https://www.ala.org/advocacy/intfreedom/librarybill.
2. Lisa Ho, "Privacy vs. Privacy," *EDUCAUSE Review* (February 25, 2015), https://er.educause.edu/blogs/2015/2/privacy-vs-privacy.
3. Sarah Hartman-Caverly and Alexandria Chisholm, "Privacy Literacy Instruction Practices in Academic Libraries: Past, Present, and Possibilities," *IFLA Journal* 46, no. 4 (2020): 314, https://doi.org/10.1177/0340035220956804.
4. Ramirose Ilene Attebury, "Professional Development: A Qualitative Study of High Impact Characteristics Affecting Meaningful and Transformational Learning," *Journal of Academic Librarianship* 43, no. 3 (2017): 232, https://doi.org/10.1016/j.acalib.2017.02.015; Brian E. C. Schottlaender, "Developing Tomorrow's Library Leaders," *portal: Libraries and the Academy* 20, no. 2 (2020): 227, http://dx.doi.org/10.1353/pla.2020.0010.
5. Muhammad Rafiq, Munazza Jabeen, and Muhammad Arif, "Continuing Education (CE) of LIS Professionals: Need Analysis & Role of LIS Schools," *The Journal of Academic Librarianship* 43 (2017): 25, https://doi.org/10.1016/j.acalib.2016.10.004.
6. "Library Bill of Rights," ALA.
7. "Webinar: Privacy Literacy Work at the Frontier of Intellectual Freedom," ALA Office for Intellectual Freedom, last modified April 20, 2020, video, 59:10, https://youtu.be/uDQWpqpF2RU; "ACRL IS Virtual Engagement Committee: Current Issues Panel Discussion – Privacy Literacy," Association of College & Research Libraries, last modified December 4, 2020, video, 58:55, https://youtu.be/IpxKsEgUrqE; "Quick Courses to Sharpen Your Privacy Skills," Library Freedom, accessed January 13, 2020, https://libraryfreedom.org/crashcourse/; "Privacy Literacy in Libraries: From Theory to Practice," Library Juice Academy, accessed January 13, 2022, https://libraryjuiceacademy.com/shop/course/274-privacy-literacy-in-libraries-from-theory-to-practice/.
8. Christina Neigel, "Professional Development for Library Workers: Exposing the Complicated Problems of Equity and Access," *Partnership: The Canadian Journal of Library and Information Practice and Research* 11, no. 2 (2016): 1–7, http://dx.doi.org/10.21083/partnership.v11i2.3795.
9. Beth R. Hendrix and Alyse E. McKeal, "Case Study: Online Continuing Education for New Librarians," *Journal of Library & Information Services in Distance Learning* 11, no. 3-4 (2017): 346, 351.
10. Ramirose Attebury, "The Role of Administrators in Professional Development: Considerations for Facilitating Learning Among Academic Librarians," *Journal of Library Administration* 58, no. (2018): 409, http://doi.org/10.1080/01930826.2018.1468190.
11. Joke Voogt, Jules Pieters, and Natalie Pareja Roblin, "Collaborative Curriculum Design in Teacher Teams: Foundations," in *Collaborative Curriculum Design for Sustainable Innovation and Teacher Learning* (Cham: Springer, 2019), 12–13; Jimmy Jaldemark, Marcia Håkansson Lindqvist, and Peter Mozelius, "Teachers' Beliefs About Professional Development: Supporting Emerging Networked Practices in Higher Education," in *Networked Professional Learning: Emerging and Equitable Discourses for Professional Development*, eds. Allison Littlejohn, Jimmy Jaldemark, Emmy Vrieling-Teunter, and Femke Nijland (Cham: Springer, 2019), 151.
12. "2021 Environmental Scan," Association of College & Research Libraries Research Planning and Review Committee, 17, last modified April 2021, https://www.ala.org/acrl/sites/ala.org.acrl/files/content/publications/whitepapers/EnvironmentalScan2021.pdf.
13. Malcolm S. Knowles, Richard A. Swanson, and Elwood F. Holton, "A Theory of Adult Learning: Andragogy," in *The Adult Learner* (Amsterdam: Routledge, 2005), 39–40 (emphasis added).
14. Karen Bordonaro, "Adult Education and Academic Libraries," *Information and Learning Science* 119, no. 7/8 (2018): 425, http://dx.doi.org/10.1108/ILS-04-2018-0030; see also Attebury, "The Role of Administrators," 415.
15. Attebury, "The Role of Administrators," 233.

16. Agnes Namaganda, "Continuing professional development as transformational learning: A case study," *The Journal of Academic Librarianship* 46, no. 3 (2020), 2, https://doi.org/10.1016/j.acalib.2020.102152; see also Attebury, "The Role of Administrators," 233.
17. Attebury, "The Role of Administrators," 233.
18. Namaganda, "Continuing professional development," 4.
19. Knowles, Swanson, and Holton, "A Theory of Adult Learning," 64–68.
20. Jovita M. Ross-Gordon, Amy D. Rose, and Carol E. Kasworm, "The Adult Learner," in *Foundations of Adult and Continuing Education* (Somerset: John Wiley & Sons, 2016), 230.
21. "Library Bill of Rights," ALA.
22. As cited in Ross-Gordon, Rose, and Kasworm, "The Adult Learner," 229.
23. Ross-Gordon, Rose, and Kasworm, "The Adult Learner," 237.
24. Ramirose Ilene Attebury, "Adult Education Concepts In Library Professional Development Activities," *New Library World* 116, 5/6 (2015): 305, http://dx.doi.org/10.1108/NLW-08-2014-0100; Ross-Gordon, Rose, and Kasworm, "The Adult Learner," 228.
25. Attebury, "Adult Education Concepts," 303.
26. Ibid., 304.
27. Jens Jørgen Hansen and Nina Bonderup Dohn, "Design Principles for Professional Networked Learning in 'Learning Through Practice' Designs," in *Networked Professional Learning: Emerging and Equitable Discourses for Professional Development,* eds. Allison Littlejohn, Jimmy Jaldemark, Emmy Vrieling-Teunter, and Femke Nijland (Cham: Springer, 2019), 133.
28. Voogt, Pieters, and Roblin, "Collaborative Curriculum Design," 10, 14.
29. Harold Fields, *Journal of Adult Education* XII (1940): 44–45, as cited in Knowles, Swanson, and Holton, "A Theory of Adult Learning," 44.
30. Tjark Huizinga, Nienke Nieveen, and Adam Handelzalts, "Identifying Needs for Support to Enhance Teachers' Curriculum Design Expertise," in *Collaborative Curriculum Design for Sustainable Innovation and Teacher Learning*, eds. Joke Voogt, Jules Pieters, and Natalie Pareja Roblin (Cham: Springer, 2019), 123.
31. Huizinga, Nieveen, and Handelzalts, "Identifying Needs for Support," 128.
32. Voogt, Pieters, and Roblin, "Collaborative Curriculum Design," 13.
33. Bordonaro, "Adult Education and Academic Libraries," 428.
34. Ross-Gordon, Rose, and Kasworm, "The Adult Learner," 229.
35. Bordonaro, "Adult Education and Academic Libraries," 425.
36. Ibid., 427–28; Knowles, Swanson, and Holton, "A Theory of Adult Learning," 64–68.
37. Hansen and Dohn, "Design Principles for Professional Networked Learning," 131.
38. Alexandria Chisholm and Sarah Hartman-Caverly, "Overexposure: Shining a Light on Privacy Literacy Programming" (conference workshop, Pennsylvania Library Association Conference, Erie, PA, October 2019), https://doi.org/10.26207/1pfz-w180.
39. Sarah Hartman-Caverly and Alexandria Chisholm, "Privacy and Dx (Digital Transformation) Workshop [Peer/Professional]," ACRL Framework for Information Literacy Sandbox, accessed January 12, 2022, https://sandbox.acrl.org/library-collection/privacy-and-dx-digital-transformation-workshop-peerprofessional.
40. Hartman-Caverly and Chisholm, "Privacy Literacy Instruction Practices," 314.
41. Alexandria Chisholm and Sarah Hartman-Caverly, "Digital Shred Privacy Literacy Toolkit," accessed January 12, 2022, https://sites.psu.edu/digitalshred/.
42. Hartman-Caverly and Chisholm, "Privacy Literacy Instruction Practices," 306–08; for more information, see the chapter, "Privacy As Respect For Persons: Reimagining Privacy Literacy With The Six Private I's Framework."
43. Alexandria Chisholm and Sarah Hartman-Caverly, "Six Private I's Privacy Conceptual Framework," Digital Shred Privacy Literacy Toolkit, accessed January 12, 2022, https://sites.psu.edu/digitalshred/2020/10/01/six-private-is-privacy-conceptual-framework-hartman-caverly-chisholm/.

44. Alexandria Chisholm and Sarah Hartman-Caverly, "Vitamin P: Why Privacy is Good for You (And Good for Society, Too)," Voices of Privacy Blog, accessed January 12, 2022, https://chooseprivacyeveryday.org/vitamin-p-why-privacy-is-good-for-you-and-good-for-society-too/; Hartman-Caverly and Chisholm, "Privacy Literacy Instruction Practices," 306–08; Sarah Hartman-Caverly and Alexandria Chisholm, "Privacy in Theory," filmed June 2, 2021, video, 18:32, https://psu.mediaspace.kaltura.com/media/Privacy+in+Theory/1_2rqdznxc.
45. Chisholm and Hartman-Caverly, Digital Shred Privacy Literacy Toolkit.
46. Julie E. Cohen, "Turning Privacy Inside Out," *Theoretical Inquiries Into Law* 20, no. 1 (2019): 1, accessed January 12, 2022, https://www7.tau.ac.il/ojs/index.php/til/article/view/1607/1709.
47. "Library Bill of Rights," ALA.
48. Hartman-Caverly and Chisholm, "Privacy Literacy Instruction Practices," 314.
49. Donna Harp Ziegenfuss, "Backward Design: A Must-have Library Instructional Design Strategy for Your Pedagogical and Teaching Toolbox," *Reference and User Services Quarterly* 59, no. 2 (2019): 107–12.
50. Thilo Hagendorff, "Privacy Literacy and its Problems," *Journal of Information Ethics* 27, no. 2 (Fall, 2018): 130.
51. Sarah Hartman-Caverly and Alexandria Chisholm, "Transforming Privacy Literacy Instruction: From Surveillance Theory to Teaching Practice" (conference presentation, LOEX 2021, online, May 13, 2021), https://doi.org/10.26207/417p-p335.
52. Hartman-Caverly and Chisholm, "Privacy and Dx (Digital Transformation) Workshop [Peer/Professional]."
53. "Library Bill of Rights," ALA.

BIBLIOGRAPHY

ALA Office for Intellectual Freedom. "Webinar: PL Work at the Frontier of Intellectual Freedom." Last modified April 20, 2020. Video, 59:10. https://youtu.be/uDQWpqpF2RU.

American Library Association [ALA]. "Library Bill of Rights." Accessed January 10, 2022. https://www.ala.org/advocacy/intfreedom/librarybill.

Association of College & Research Libraries [ACRL]. "ACRL IS Virtual Engagement Committee: Current Issues Panel Discussion – Privacy Literacy." Last modified December 4, 2020. Video, 58:55. https://youtu.be/IpxKsEgUrqE.

Association of College & Research Libraries Research Planning and Review Committee. "2021 Environmental Scan." Last modified April 2021. https://www.ala.org/acrl/sites/ala.org.acrl/files/content/publications/whitepapers/EnvironmentalScan2021.pdf.

Attebury, Ramirose. "The Role of Administrators in Professional Development: Considerations for Facilitating Learning Among Academic Librarians." *Journal of Library Administration* 58, no. (2018): 407–33. doi: 10.1080/01930826.2018.1468190.

Attebury, Ramirose Ilene. "Adult Education Concepts In Library Professional Development Activities." *New Library World* 116, 5/6 (2015): 302–15. http://dx.doi.org/10.1108/NLW-08-2014-0100.

———. "Professional Development: A Qualitative Study of High Impact Characteristics Affecting Meaningful and Transformational Learning." *Journal of Academic Librarianship* 43, no. 3 (2017): 232–41. https://doi.org/10.1016/j.acalib.2017.02.015.

Bordonaro, Karen. "Adult Education and Academic Libraries." *Information and Learning Science* 119, no. 7/8 (2018): 422–31. http://dx.doi.org/10.1108/ILS-04-2018-0030.

Chisholm, Alexandria, and Sarah Hartman-Caverly. "Digital Shred Privacy Literacy Toolkit." Accessed January 12, 2022. https://sites.psu.edu/digitalshred/.

———. "Overexposure: Shining a Light on Privacy Literacy Programming." Conference workshop presented at the Pennsylvania Library Association Conference, Erie, PA, October 2019. https://doi.org/10.26207/1pfz-w180.

———. "Six Private I's Privacy Conceptual Framework." Digital Shred Privacy Literacy Toolkit. Accessed January 12, 2022. https://sites.psu.edu/digitalshred/2020/10/01/six-private-is-privacy-conceptual-framework-hartman-caverly-chisholm/.

———. "Vitamin P: Why Privacy is Good for You (And Good for Society, Too)." Voices of Privacy Blog. Accessed January 12, 2022. https://chooseprivacyeveryday.org/vitamin-p-why-privacy-is-good-for-you-and-good-for-society-too/.

Cohen, Julie E. "Turning Privacy Inside Out." *Theoretical Inquiries Into Law* 20, no. 1 (2019): 1–31. Accessed January 12, 2022. https://www7.tau.ac.il/ojs/index.php/til/article/view/1607/1709.

Hagendorff, Thilo. "Privacy Literacy and its Problems." *Journal of Information Ethics* 27, no. 2 (Fall, 2018): 127–45.

Hansen, Jens Jørgen, and Nina Bonderup Dohn. "Design Principles for Professional Networked Learning in 'Learning Through Practice' Designs." In *Networked Professional Learning: Emerging and Equitable Discourses for Professional Development,* edited by Allison Littlejohn, Jimmy Jaldemark, Emmy Vrieling-Teunter, and Femke Nijland, 129–46. Cham: Springer, 2019.

Hartman-Caverly, Sarah, and Alexandria Chisholm. "Privacy and Dx (Digital Transformation) Workshop [Peer/Professional]." ACRL Framework for Information Literacy Sandbox. Accessed January 12, 2022. https://sandbox.acrl.org/library-collection/privacy-and-dx-digital-transformation-workshop-peerprofessional.

———. "Privacy in Theory." Filmed June 2, 2021. Video, 18:32. https://psu.mediaspace.kaltura.com/media/Privacy+in+Theory/1_2rqdznxc.

———. "Privacy Literacy Instruction Practices in Academic Libraries: Past, Present, and Possibilities." *IFLA Journal* 46, no. 4 (2020): 305–27. https://doi.org/10.1177/0340035220956804.

———. "Transforming Privacy Literacy Instruction: From Surveillance Theory to Teaching Practice." Presented at LOEX 2021, online, May 13, 2021. https://doi.org/10.26207/417p-p335.

Hendrix, Beth R., and Alyse E. McKeal. "Case Study: Online Continuing Education for New Librarians." *Journal of Library & Information Services in Distance Learning* 11, no. 3-4 (2017): 346–54.

Ho, Lisa. "Privacy vs. Privacy." *EDUCAUSE Review* (February 25, 2015). https://er.educause.edu/blogs/2015/2/privacy-vs-privacy.

Huizinga, Tjark, Nienke Nieveen, and Adam Handelzalts. "Identifying Needs for Support to Enhance Teachers' Curriculum Design Expertise." In *Collaborative Curriculum Design for Sustainable Innovation and Teacher Learning*, edited by Joke Voogt, Jules Pieters, and Natalie Pareja Roblin, 115–37. Cham: Springer, 2019.

Jaldemark, Jimmy, Marcia Håkansson Lindqvist, and Peter Mozelius. "Teachers' Beliefs About Professional Development: Supporting Emerging Networked Practices in Higher Education." In *Networked Professional Learning: Emerging and Equitable Discourses for Professional Development*, edited by Allison Littlejohn, Jimmy Jaldemark, Emmy Vrieling-Teunter, and Femke Nijland, 147–64. Cham: Springer, 2019.

Knowles, Malcolm S., Richard A. Swanson, and Elwood F. Holton. "A Theory of Adult Learning: Andragogy." In *The Adult Learner*, 35–72. Amsterdam: Routledge, 2005.

Library Freedom. "Quick Courses to Sharpen Your Privacy Skills." Accessed January 13, 2020. https://libraryfreedom.org/crashcourse/.

Library Juice Academy. "Privacy Literacy in Libraries: From Theory to Practice." Accessed January 13, 2022. https://libraryjuiceacademy.com/shop/course/274-privacy-literacy-in-libraries-from-theory-to-practice/.

Namaganda, Agnes. "Continuing Professional Development As Transformational Learning: A Case Study." *The Journal of Academic Librarianship* 46, no. 3 (2020), 1–5. https://doi.org/10.1016/j.acalib.2020.102152.

Neigel, Christina. "Professional Development for Library Workers: Exposing the Complicated Problems of Equity and Access." *Partnership: The Canadian Journal of Library and Information Practice and Research* 11, no. 2 (2016): 1–7. http://dx.doi.org/10.21083/partnership.v11i2.3795.

Rafiq, Muhammad, Munazza Jabeen, and Muhammad Arif. "Continuing Education (CE) of LIS Professionals: Need Analysis & Role of LIS Schools." *The Journal of Academic Librarianship* 43 (2017): 25–33. https://doi.org/10.1016/j.acalib.2016.10.004.

Ross-Gordon, Jovita M., Amy D. Rose, and Carol E. Kasworm. "The Adult Learner." In *Foundations of Adult and Continuing Education*, 215–53. Somerset: John Wiley & Sons, 2016.

Schottlaender, Brian E. C. "Developing Tomorrow's Library Leaders," *portal: Libraries and the Academy* 20, no. 2 (2020): 227–31. http://dx.doi.org/10.1353/pla.2020.0010.

Voogt, Joke, Jules Pieters, and Natalie Pareja Roblin. "Collaborative Curriculum Design in Teacher Teams: Foundations." In *Collaborative Curriculum Design for Sustainable Innovation and Teacher Learning*, edited by Joke Voogt, Jules Pieters, and Natalie Pareja Roblin, 5–18. Cham: Springer, 2019.

Ziegenfuss, Donna Harp. "Backward Design: A Must-have Library Instructional Design Strategy for Your Pedagogical and Teaching Toolbox." *Reference and User Services Quarterly* 59, no. 2 (2019): 107–12.

CHAPTER 18

CONCLUSION:
Privacy Work is Library Work

Sarah Hartman-Caverly

From nineteenth-century debates over the merits of protecting the identities of suspected book thieves[1] to the obligation to maintain patron confidentiality in the original early twentieth-century American Library Association Code of Ethics[2] to the addition of privacy in the Library Bill of Rights and recognition of privacy as an expanding literacy in the twenty-first century,[3] library work has long acknowledged the value of privacy in the library experience.

Where libraries serve as sites of personal exploration, experimentation with ideas, and liberation from orthodox views, we recognize that the potential for our community members' reading and viewing histories to be scrutinized or surveilled has a chilling effect on their pursuit of information and enrichment. We further acknowledge that many of our community members experience social, political, and economic vulnerabilities and may face sanction, ostracism, or further marginalization if their library records are exposed. As stewards of the historical and cultural record, libraries have a shared obligation to preserve and make discoverable primary sources that are authentic to their time, while balancing the needs of those represented in special collections to keep certain aspects of their lives and identities private or reserved to a specified context. Designing library systems, processes, and workflows to ensure the privacy and confidentiality of community members is one facet of privacy work as library work.

Building on this foundational privacy work, libraries are now turning our gaze outward to examine the state of privacy culture beyond our walls. Library workers are finding that the extraction imperative of surveillance capitalism is infiltrating our vendor-supplied systems and subscription services, subjecting users to data capture and analysis while engaging with library resources. We are questioning the privacy implications of educational technologies that authenticate student identities, monitor their course activities, capture and transmit their creative work, evaluate their academic integrity, and assess their academic progress, and we are finding that our teaching colleagues in the disciplines frequently do not have answers to these questions. More fundamentally, we are wondering what role privacy will play in the lives of our students, some of whom had digital footprints before they could walk. In order to pursue an education, access healthcare, begin a career, make purchases, and move through the world, we are all increasingly required to acquiesce to terms of service that permit tracking and funnel us into feedback loops of chutes and nudges. In much of the world beyond libraries, privacy appears obsolete.

As long as people value the ability to explore ideas freely and draw their own conclusions, privacy matters. As long as people desire the ability to discover and shape their own identities, privacy matters. As long as people prefer a state of bodily autonomy and the ability to freely pursue intimate relationships without interference, privacy matters. As long as people wish to participate in a broad range of social roles, relationships, and associations—and to withdraw from social participation into solitude—privacy matters.

Once impaired, privacy can be difficult to repair. Potential threats to privacy in everyday life are now not only ubiquitous but relentless. The current state of privacy culture demands a robust response. But whose job is it?

A 2019 survey of academic instruction librarians found that 20 percent of the respondents who reported engaging in privacy literacy instruction did so because no other unit on campus was offering it. In the same survey, no respondents reported another campus unit delivering privacy literacy instruction as a potential barrier to this work.[4] An exploratory 2022 survey of undergraduate students found that 98 percent of respondents declared that privacy is somewhat or extremely important but that more students learned about privacy issues from news and current events (36 percent) and from friends and family (18 percent) than from class content (17 percent) or academic research (6 percent).[5]

Library workers can meet this need. We have expertise in information flows and ethics to bring to bear on privacy issues. We have relationships within our institutions and communities that offer us seats at the right tables. And we have classrooms full of students who are interested to know more.

PRIVACY WORK IS LIBRARY WORK—BUT THAT DOESN'T MAKE IT EASY WORK

To be effective in our privacy work, we will need to make time, make space, and make resources. We need time to develop and maintain our own privacy knowledge, to craft privacy-literate practices and learning experiences, and to implement these practices in our work and deliver these experiences in the classroom. We need space to achieve privacy outcomes; privacy work must become a valued and recognized sphere of professional responsibility that is concomitant with other dimensions of our roles. And we need resources, from privacy policies, workflows, and audits to lesson plans, learning objects, and talking points, so that privacy work can become a sustainable part of our professional repertoire.

Let every website cookie notice, every clickwrap privacy policy, every surveillance camera, every personalized ad, and every swipe, tap, and keystroke be your invitation to privacy work. The next chapter of privacy work in libraries is yours to write.

NOTES

1. "New York Library Club," *Library Journal* 11, no. 1 (January 1886): 24–25, https://hdl.handle.net/2027/mdp.39015036908674?urlappend=%3Bseq=48%3Bownerid=13510798896760356-54.
2. "Midwinter Council Minutes," *American Library Association Bulletin* 33, no. 2 (1939): 128–29, https://www.ala.org/advocacy/sites/ala.org.advocacy/files/content/proethics/codeofethics/coehistory/1939code.pdf.
3. "Library Bill of Rights," American Library Association, last modified January 29, 2019, https://www.ala.org/advocacy/intfreedom/librarybill; "2021 Environmental Scan," Association of College & Research Libraries Research Planning and Review Committee, last modified April 2021, https://www.ala.org/acrl/sites/ala.org.acrl/files/content/publications/whitepapers/EnvironmentalScan2021.pdf.
4. Sarah Hartman-Caverly and Alexandria Chisholm, "Privacy Literacy Instruction Practices in Academic Libraries: Past, Present, and Possibilities," *IFLA Journal* 46, no. 4 (2020): 313–14, https://journals.sagepub.com/doi/10.1177/0340035220956804.
5. Jordan Clark, unpublished data, Penn State University Institutional Review Board study number 00018906.

BIBLIOGRAPHY

American Library Association. "Library Bill of Rights." Last modified January 29, 2019. https://www.ala.org/advocacy/intfreedom/librarybill.
———. "Midwinter Council Minutes." *American Library Association Bulletin* 33, no. 2 (1939): 128–29. https://www.ala.org/advocacy/sites/ala.org.advocacy/files/content/proethics/codeofethics/coehistory/1939code.pdf.
Association of College & Research Libraries Research Planning and Review Committee. "2021 Environmental Scan." Last modified April 2021. https://www.ala.org/acrl/sites/ala.org.acrl/files/content/publications/whitepapers/EnvironmentalScan2021.pdf.

Hartman-Caverly, Sarah, and Alexandria Chisholm. "Privacy Literacy Instruction Practices in Academic Libraries: Past, Present, and Possibilities." *IFLA Journal* 46, no. 4 (2020): 305–27. https://journals.sagepub.com/doi/10.1177/0340035220956804.

Library Journal. "New York Library Club." *Library Journal* 11, no. 1 (January 1886): 24–27. https://hdl.handle.net/2027/mdp.39015036908674?urlappend=%3Bseq=48%3Bownerid=13510798896760356-54.

ABOUT THE AUTHORS

Jamie Marie Aschenbach has her JD from Seattle University School of Law and her MLIS from the University of Pittsburgh. She currently lives in Connecticut where she is the head of Access Services. She helped develop her library's privacy policy among other policies and procedures currently used throughout the library. In her free time, Jamie likes snuggling with her three cats and two miniature dachshunds, playing video games, knitting, and reading graphic novels. She is also a moderator on a popular subreddit.

Andrew D. Asher is the assessment librarian at Indiana University Bloomington, where he leads the libraries' qualitative and quantitative assessment programs, conducts research on the anthropology of information, and teaches research methods in information science. His most recent work examines search and discovery workflows of students and faculty, information fluency development, and the ethical and privacy dimensions of learning analytics data. Asher holds a PhD in sociocultural anthropology from the University of Illinois at Urbana-Champaign and has written and presented widely on applying ethnography and mixed-methods research in academic libraries, including the co-edited volume, *College Libraries and Student Culture*.

Adam Beauchamp is a humanities librarian at Florida State University Libraries serving as liaison to the departments of History, Philosophy, and Religion. His responsibilities include research support, information literacy instruction, and collection development in these disciplines. Adam specializes in primary source literacy, both in teaching students to critically evaluate primary sources in disciplinary contexts and in supporting instructors to integrate primary sources into their pedagogy.

Joshua Becker is the information literacy and assessment librarian and an associate professor at Southern New Hampshire University. In 2020, Joshua was named the Christos and Mary Papoutsy Distinguished Chair in Leadership Ethics. Joshua holds an MSLIS from the University of Illinois and an MAT in English education from Boston University. A committed advocate of lifelong learning, his research interests include metaliterary instruction, universal design, and information ethics.

Kristin A. Briney is the biology and biological engineering librarian at the California Institute of Technology and the author of the books *Data Management for Researchers* (Pelagic Publishing, 2015) and *Managing Data for Patron Privacy* (ALA Editions, 2022). She has a PhD in chemistry and an MLIS, both from the University of Wisconsin-Madison. Her research focuses on research data management, institutional data policy, and patron privacy vis-a-vis library data handling. Kristin is an advocate for the adoption of the international date standard ISO 8601 and likes to spend her free time making data visualizations out of yarn and fabric.

Dr. Melissa Calderon has been a professor of early childhood education, pre-K through fourth grade for fifteen years. She previously taught at the Indiana University of Pennsylvania and the Community College of Allegheny County. She teaches in the Education departments at Westmoreland County Community College and at the University of Pittsburgh at Greensburg. She conducts privacy education and online reputation management workshops for students, teachers, and administrators. She is passionate about helping all digital users understand the benefits and dangers of their online content, believes that awareness and education are essential for promoting a society of safe digital users and that creating a positive digital image is necessary and possible for everyone. In her instruction, she stresses the importance of both personal privacy and the development of a positive online persona because lack of online content can also negatively impact students. She can be contacted at: calderonm@westmoreland.edu.

Alexandria Chisholm is an associate librarian at Penn State University Libraries and liaison to the Berks campus' first-year experience program and science division. She has over ten years of reference and instruction experience at both private and public baccalaureate- and doctoral-degree granting institutions. Chisholm's research focuses on privacy literacy, with special attention on digital wellness and algorithmic transparency as well as information literacy and student engagement. Together, Alex and Sarah Hartman-Caverly created the Penn State Berks Privacy Workshop Series, collaborate on privacy literacy research and professional development, and maintain the Digital Shred Privacy Literacy Toolkit.

Virginia Dressler is the digital projects librarian at Kent State University. Her specialty areas are project management of digital projects and reformatting of analog collections for digital collections. She holds an MLIS from Kent State University and MA in Art Gallery and Museum Studies from the University of Leeds. She is the author of *Framing Privacy in Digital Collections with Ethical Decision Making* (Morgan & Claypool, 2018).

Liz Dunne is the instruction and reference librarian at Florida State University Libraries. In this role, she coordinates the libraries' college composition instruction program, tutoring program, Research Help Desk service point, and she co-coordinates the libraries' virtual reference services. She also serves as the liaison to the Human Development & Family Science department. Her research interests include critical pedagogy, universal design for instruction, and systematic instructional design.

Mary Francis is a full professor and director of the Karl Mundt Library at Dakota State University. In addition to authoring several peer-reviewed articles and two monographs with ACRL related to librarianship, she has written and contributed to several works focused on privacy including a review of how privacy is considered within professional codes of ethics from library associations around the world, which was published by *Library Quarterly* in 2021.

Abigail Goben, MLS, is an associate professor and data management librarian at the University of Illinois, Chicago, where she additionally serves as the data policy advisor for the Office of the Vice Chancellor for Research. Goben teaches coursework in data management, clinical informatics, information and data literacy, and evidence-based medicine. Recently, she completed participation as a co-investigator for the IMLS-funded DataDoubles project, a US-based study examining undergraduate student perceptions of student privacy and library participation in learning analytics. Her current research projects include the #WomenLaborCOVID project, which examines the impact of the pandemic on women in the workforce, identifying accessibility needs for data set reuse and preservation, and a ten-year retrospective of data librarian job ads. She can be found on Twitter as @hedgielib.

Sarah Hartman-Caverly, MS(LIS), MSIS, is a reference and instruction librarian at Penn State Berks, where she liaises with Engineering, Business and Computing division programs. Sarah delivered her first privacy literacy workshop, "Is Big Data Big Brother?," in 2014. She co-facilitated a faculty learning community examining learning analytics through a privacy lens in 2017 and a professional community of practice workshop on privacy in 2021. Sarah's research examines the compatibility of human and machine autonomy from the perspective of intellectual freedom, and she publishes and presents on privacy literacy and other topics as part of this work. She earned her MS(LIS) and MS in information systems from Drexel University College of Computing & Informatics (then iSchool) and holds a BA in anthropology from Haverford College. Outside of the library, Sarah is an edible gardener, chicken herder, and homemaker. Together, Sarah and Alex Chisholm created the Penn State Berks Privacy Workshop Series, collaborate on privacy literacy research and professional development, and maintain the Digital Shred Privacy Literacy Toolkit.

Margaret Heller is digital services librarian at Loyola University Chicago and the author of *Community Technology Projects: Making Them Work* (ALA Editions, 2019). She has been a longtime participant in DLF privacy-related efforts and is active in library professional organizations. She served as president of Core, a division of the American Library Association from 2022–2023.

Dr. Kyle M. L. Jones is an associate professor in the Department of Library and Information Science within the School of Informatics and Computing at Indiana University-Indianapolis (IUPUI). He earned a PhD from the University of Wisconsin-Madison iSchool in 2015, an MLIS from Dominican University's School of Information Studies in 2009, and a BA from Elmhurst College in 2007. His research focuses on information ethics and policy issues associated with educational data mining and analytic practices, such as learning analytics, within American higher education institutions. His published research is accessible in top journals, like the *Journal of the Association for Information Science and Technology*; *Learning, Media and Technology*; *Communications of the ACM*; the *Journal of Documentation*; *College & Research Libraries*; and other journals. For more on his research, see https://thecorkboard.org/.

Lori Lysiak is a reference and instruction librarian at Penn State Altoona and is the liaison to the Division of Business, Engineering, and Information Sciences and Technology. Over multiple years at the United States Patent and Trademark Office as part of the Patent and Trademark Resource Center program, Lori completed basic and advanced seminar training. She facilitates patent and trademark information literacy to students of entrepreneurship and engineering design courses and co-authored a peer-reviewed journal article on the role of patent research in the start-up life cycle. She provides outreach on the topic of patents at the Altoona

LaunchBox for adult learners and assists inventors and other community members seeking patent information and support.

Dr. Crystal Machado is a professor in the Department of Professional Studies in Education at Indiana University of Pennsylvania (IUP), where she works with pre-service and in-service teachers, faculty, and administrators. Prior to joining IUP, Crystal worked in Pakistan as a K-12 teacher, an administrator, and a middle/high school assistant principal. Crystal's commitment to creating equitable, technology-rich learning environments, and mentoring is reflected in her teaching, research, and service. She uses Freire's problem-posing pedagogy in the classroom to promote high levels of student engagement, critical thinking, cross-cultural competence, and reflective practice. She has shared her expertise at the international level through her service as Technology Leadership SIG chair for the Society of Information Technology and Teacher Education (2016–18), as reviewer for eight peer-reviewed journals, and her scholarship, which has been published in prestigious journals and edited books. She may be contacted at cmachado@iup.edu.

Melissa N. Mallon, MLIS, is associate university librarian for teaching and learning at Vanderbilt University. Mallon has published, presented, and taught professional development courses in the areas of online learning, instructional design, and the impact of information and digital literacies on student learning. Her books include *Partners in Teaching & Learning: Coordinating a Successful Academic Library Instruction Program*; *The Pivotal Role of Academic Librarians in Digital Learning*; and the co-edited volumes, *The Grounded Instruction Librarian: Participating in the Scholarship of Teaching & Learning* and (forthcoming) *Exploring Inclusive & Equitable Pedagogies: Creating Space for All Learners*.

Sara Mannheimer is an associate professor and data librarian at Montana State University, where she helps shape practices and theories for data curation, publication, and preservation. She supports data education and discovery initiatives, including as project lead for the MSU Dataset Search. Her research examines the social, ethical, and technical issues of a data-driven world. She holds an MS in information science from University of North Carolina at Chapel Hill and a PhD in library and information science from Humboldt University of Berlin.

Jennifer McCroskey has been the sexual violence prevention educator in Indiana University of Pennsylvania's Haven Project since 2018. She holds a bachelor's degree in elementary education with an educational psychology minor from Indiana University of Pennsylvania (IUP). She has been involved in prevention education for over ten years. She is fortunate enough to work with graduate assistants, peer educators, volunteer specialists, and volunteers to bring education and awareness to students, faculty, and staff on the topics of sexual violence, domestic/dating violence, bystander intervention (Green Dot), healthy relationships, consent, and stalking. She is the IUP campus coordinator for Green Dot Bystander Intervention Training and is also a certified Green Dot trainer. She can be contacted at: jmccrosk@iup.edu.

Dr. Theresa McDevitt is a government documents/outreach librarian at Indiana University of Pennsylvania and is co-director for Scholarship of Teaching and Learning for IUP's Center for Teaching Excellence's Reflective Practice Project. She teaches a credit-bearing information literacy class which includes a privacy literacy module and she works with faculty and professional employees on campus to increase student awareness of the importance of thoughtful online sharing. She can be contacted at: mcdevitt@iup.edu.

Jacqueline McGinty, PhD, is an associate professor and is the program coordinator for the Education, Training, and Instructional Technology graduate program at Indiana University of Pennsylvania (IUP). Dr. McGinty is the associate director of instructional design with IUP's Center for Teaching Excellence. She coordinates and develops faculty training on instructional design, digital technologies, and effective facilitation methods. Dr. McGinty serves on the board of NeverTechLate, a program focused on digital literacy training for older adults. In addition to her position on the board, she is the lead instructional designer for the organization. Dr. McGinty designed a comprehensive curriculum for NeverTechLate and continues to work on additional programming. Her scholarship includes digital literacy and ethics, accessibility, access, and inclusion, faculty training, and program development. She can be contacted at: jmcginty@iup.edu.

Paul McMonigle is the engineering instruction librarian at Penn State University Park. Besides his role as principal information literacy instructor to the College of Engineering, he is also the liaison to the School of Engineering Design and Innovation (SEDI) and the Departments of Acoustics, Aerospace Engineering, Architectural Engineering, Civil and Environmental Engineering, Engineering Science and Mechanics, Industrial and Manufacturing Engineering, Mechanical Engineering, and Nuclear Engineering. His research interests include engineering literacy instruction, integrating technology into the classroom, outreach and engagement with student organizations, and the experiences of military and veteran students.

Emily Mross is the business librarian and library outreach coordinator at the Madlyn L. Hanes Library, Penn State Harrisburg. Emily's research focuses on skill-building outreach for academic library users, including financial literacy, business intelligence, digital literacy, and spirituality.

Michael R. Perry is the head of Assessment and Planning at Northwestern University Libraries. In this role, he coordinates work around assessment, strategic planning, project management, and organizational analysis. His research interests include data privacy and learning analytics.

Mariana Regalado, MA, MLS, is professor at Brooklyn College, City University of New York. There, as head of reference in the library, she assists students to become smart, curious, and confident information seekers. With her research partner, Maura Smale, she has published on their research into the daily experience of undergraduates as students at the City University of New York in a wide variety of journals and in a monograph, *Digital Technology as Affordance and Barrier in Higher Education* (Palgrave, 2017). In 2018, they published an edited collection, *Academic Libraries for Commuter Students: Research-based Strategies (ALA)*, that brought together research into the experiences of commuter students in libraries at institutions around the country. More recently, she has been a member of the research team on the IMLS-funded DataDoubles project investigating undergraduate student perceptions of privacy and library participation in learning analytics.

Dorothea Salo is Distinguished Teaching Faculty III in the University of Wisconsin-Madison Information School. She has written and presented internationally on scholarly publishing, libraries in the digital humanities, copyright, privacy, institutional repositories, linked data, and data curation. Her "Recover Analog and Digital Data" project rescues audio, video, and digital data from obsolete or decaying carriers. Salo holds an MA in library and information studies and another in Spanish from UW-Madison.

Ms. Ann Sesti has been employed by IUP for the past thirty-one years and has over thirty-five years of experience in the drug and alcohol prevention/treatment profession. She is a licensed counselor in Pennsylvania and is the director of the Alcohol, Tobacco, and Other Drug Program at IUP. She is an active member of the Pennsylvania State System of Higher Education Alcohol and Drug Coalition. In addition to her involvement on campus committees, she is considered a strong ATOD regional consultant. She is a certified Brief Alcohol Screening and Intervention for College Students (BASICS) facilitator conducting training nationwide. She can be contacted at: annsesti@iup.edu.

Maura A. Smale is chief librarian in the Mina Rees Library and professor in Digital Humanities and Interactive Technology & Pedagogy at The Graduate Center of the City University of New York. Her research interests include undergraduate academic culture, critical librarianship, open educational technologies, and game-based learning, and she has served as co-director of the City Tech OpenLab, an open digital platform for teaching, learning, and collaboration. With Mariana Regalado of Brooklyn College, she published *Digital Technology as Affordance and Barrier in Higher Education* (2017), exploring the ways that CUNY students use technology in their academic work. Their edited volume, *Academic Libraries for Commuter Students: Research-based Strategies*, published in 2018, explores commuter students' library use at public colleges and universities around the US.

Dustin Steinhagen is a cyber defense PhD candidate at Dakota State University. His current research centers on protection of the human being in the face of rapidly advancing technology, with a focus on defending the human mind. He developed and taught DSU's social engineering course and is published in several research fields, including neuroprivacy, privacy ontology, and privacy education.

Andrew Weiss is a digital services librarian at California State University, Northridge. He has worked in libraries for fifteen years, focusing on scholarly communication, copyright, open access publishing, and institutional repositories. His most recent research has focused on fake news and misinformation, with several papers published on the topic since 2020. He has also examined the implications of the mass digitization of print culture, including looking at Google Books, HathiTrust, and other massive digital libraries. He has written three books, each focusing on some of the problems and issues related to information science and digital information. In *Big Data Shocks* (2018) and *The Dark Side of Our Digital World* (2020), he touches upon issues related to fake news and misinformation. He also writes about privacy and the proliferation of big data and surveillance capitalism. He lives in Los Angeles with his wife, daughter, and three dogs.

Andrew Wesolek serves as the director of Digital Scholarship and Communications (DiSC) at Vanderbilt University. The DiSC Office supports students and researchers in the areas of scholarly communication, copyright, GIS, research computing, and data analysis and visualization. Wesolek's research and professional interests focus on library support for new forms of open scholarship and infrastructure, with a critical examination of the implications of this emerging scholarly communication environment. His books include *Making Institutional Repositories Work* and *OER: A Field Guide for Academic Librarians*.

Lindsey Wharton is the interim director of Service Strategies at Florida State University Libraries. In that role, she provides oversight of the Teaching, Learning, and Engagement unit, encompassing instruction, reference, outreach, digital media, and online learning services. Lindsey leads library integrations within the learning management system, coordinates the eTextbook program, and serves as the liaison to the College of Social Work, Office of Distance Learning, and International Programs.

Scott W. H. Young is an associate professor and user experience and assessment librarian at Montana State University and serves as editor-in-chief of *Weave: Journal of Library User Experience*. As a researcher-practitioner, he develops theory and practice in the field of library assessment, with a focus on participatory design, service design, and ethics. He holds an MA in archives and public history from New York University, an MS in library and information science from Long Island University, and a PhD in library and information science from Humboldt University of Berlin.